THE COSTU
DESIGNER'S T(

The Costume Designer's Toolkit explores the wide-ranging skills required to design costumes for live performance in theater, dance, opera, and themed entertainment. Arranged in chronological order to create a design, each chapter describes tools, strategies, and techniques costume designers use to create lively and believable characters within a story environment. The book provides a step-by-step outline of the costume design process beginning with developing as an artist and creating an artistic vision for a script. It covers a wide range of topics, including:

- Assessing the scope of a production
- Understanding design thinking and the creative process
- Project management and budget forecasting
- Collaborating with and leading creative teams
- Current practices in costume rendering and communication
- Mixing purchased, rented, stock, and built costumes to form a design
- Designing a garment with impact
- Fitting costumes on performers
- Combining grit and grace for a successful career

Each topic includes case studies and tips from experienced professionals, identifies vital skills, describes techniques, and reveals the essential elements of artistic leadership, collaboration, and cultural acumen.

The Costume Designer's Toolkit is the perfect guidebook for the student, aspiring, or early-career costume designer, to be used alone or in costume design university courses.

Holly Poe Durbin is an award-winning costume designer for theater, opera, independent film, and themed entertainment. She has collaborated with notable actors such as Tom Hanks, Rita Wilson, William Shatner, Martin Short, and Tessa Thompson to create engaging characters. She has worked internationally, on Broadway, Off-Broadway, and in regional theaters around the United States including the South Coast Repertory, the Old Globe Theatres, Mark Taper Forum, St. Louis Repertory, Cincinnati Playhouse, Portland Center Stage, Shakespeare Center LA, and Playmakers Repertory in North Carolina. She was the costume director for the Center Theater Group in Los Angeles and is the head of costume design studies at the University of California Irvine.

THE FOCAL PRESS TOOLKIT SERIES

Regardless of your profession, whether you're a Stage Manager or Stagehand, The Focal Press Toolkit Series has you covered. With all the insider secrets, paperwork, and day-to-day details that you could ever need for your chosen profession or specialty, these books provide you with a one-stop-shop to ensure a smooth production process.

The Properties Director's Toolkit
Managing a Prop Shop for Theatre
Sandra Strawn and Lisa Schlenker

The Costume Supervisor's Toolkit
Supervising Theatre Costume Production from First Meeting to Final Performance
Rebecca Pride

The Stage Manager's Toolkit, 3rd edition
Templates and Communication Techniques to Guide Your Theatre Production from First Meeting to Final Performance
Laurie Kincman

The Lighting Supervisor's Toolkit
Collaboration, Interrogation, and Innovation toward Engineering Brilliant Lighting Designs
Jason E. Weber

The Assistant Lighting Designer's Toolkit, 2nd edition
Anne E. McMills

The Projection Designer's Toolkit
Jeromy Hopgood

The Scenic Charge Artist's Toolkit
Tips, Templates, and Techniques for Planning and Running a Successful Paint Shop in the Theatre and Performing Arts
Jennifer Rose Ivey

The Costume Designer's Toolkit
The Process of Creating Effective Design
Holly Poe Durbin

For more information about this series, please visit: www.routledge.com/The-Focal-Press-Toolkit-Series/book-series/TFPTS

THE COSTUME DESIGNER'S TOOLKIT

The Process of Creating Effective Design

HOLLY POE DURBIN

Routledge
Taylor & Francis Group

NEW YORK AND LONDON

Cover image: Shutterstock

First published 2023
by Routledge
605 Third Avenue, New York, NY 10158

and by Routledge
4 Park Square, Milton Park, Abingdon, Oxon, OX14 4RN

Routledge is an imprint of the Taylor & Francis Group, an informa business

© 2023 Taylor & Francis

The right of Holly Poe Durbin to be identified as author of this work has been asserted in accordance with sections 77 and 78 of the Copyright, Designs and Patents Act 1988.

Library of Congress Cataloging-in-Publication Data
A catalog record for this book has been requested

ISBN: 978-0-367-85827-8 (hbk)
ISBN: 978-0-367-85828-5 (pbk)
ISBN: 978-1-003-01528-4 (ebk)

DOI: 10.4324/9781003015284

Typeset in Amasis MT Std
by Apex CoVantage, LLC

This book is dedicated to those who have done much to professionalize the field of costume design and claim rightful recognition of that professionalism. Many thanks to the foresight and courage of Joy Spanabel Emory and Sarah Nash Gates; Deborah Nadoolman Landis; Elizabeth Wislar, Jeanette Aultz, and Genevieve Beller of Costume Professionals for Wage Equity; and all the costume designers who educate their producers every single day.

CONTENTS

Preface   ix
Special Thanks   xi
Prologue: The Eight Costume Jobs   xii

PART ONE
THE DESIGNER'S TOOLS   1

1. What the Costume Designer Brings to a Production   3

2. Collaborative Creativity   9

3. Design Elements Create a Picture   18

4. Color Creates Emotions   31

5. Design Principles Create Meaning   43

6. Fabrics Create Definition   56

PART TWO
A DESIGNER PREPARES   71

7. Getting Paid: All That Glitters . . .   73

8. Script, Plot, and Story   84

9. The Mechanics of a Script   92

10. Characters Engage the Audience   101

11. The Story Unfolds on a Stage   112

PART THREE
A DESIGNER EXPLORES   121

12. Generating Ideas   123

13. Adding Authenticity with Research   132

PART FOUR
CONCEPT DEVELOPMENT   143

14. The Design Approach   145

15. Designing the Character Costume   155

16. Communicating the Costume Design   165

PART FIVE
FEASIBILITY   175

17. Defining the Scope of a Show   177

18. Budgeting Creative Projects   191

19. Leading Teamwork   207

PART SIX
PRODUCTION   215

20. Pull it Together: Sourcing and Organizing Costumes   217

21. Styling Menswear   228

22. Meet Your Maker: Made-to-Order Costumes   239

23. Accessories and Costume Props   249

24. Hair and Makeup Design   262

PART SEVEN
EVALUATE   279

25. Preparing for Fittings   281

26. Fitting Garments   293

27. The Rehearsal Period   305

PART EIGHT
REFINE THE VISION   315

28. Dress Rehearsals   317

PART NINE
OPENING AND EPILOGUE   331

29. Design Documentation   333

30. Growing Your Art   338

Appendix – Sample Resume   342
Index   343

PREFACE

I landed my first costume design job in a summer stock company as a 19-year-old college student. I was working for the summer at The Troupe Theatre in Colorado Springs. I distinctly recall my shock when the costume designer I was assisting – a fashion designer who decided she did not like doing stage costumes after all – suddenly left in mid-season. I was promoted overnight from a lowly apprentice to fill her shoes. Although I had worked a bit in my high school and university costume shops, I was in *no* way prepared for the enormity of being the artistic and managerial leader of a department. Artistic Director David Thompson must have seen something in me. My fellow staff and actors were very supportive, but the pressure was grueling. I not only survived that summer, but emerged *convinced* I wanted to be a costume designer.

I searched the local university library for a book that would teach me what I needed to know. I found many books, but at that time the books were either ancient tomes more concerned with historical costume, collections of illustrations, or textbooks arranged for classroom delivery: certainly not a practical format for someone in the trenches. There was no single book that functioned as a manual – do this, then that, and voila! you will have produced a show with credibility. Since that time long ago, many books have been published and our profession is much richer for it. But few address what I needed then – how costume designers really spend their days. For instance, we often spend far more time in costume stock and fittings than creating drawings for a show, so I dedicate much more space in this book to these practicalities. I've set myself a large challenge – is it possible to present enough information to lend confidence to those who are new to the job, or those who have been doing the job but have a nagging feeling they are not really an "artist"?

Although there are many costume training programs, and I am the head of one such program, every day I meet working costume designers who had no formal training in design. The entertainment field is much more meritocratic than it is given credit for. It rewards grit and grace. It rewards solid work ethics, good working relationships with producers and directors, and passionate drive. It rewards those who know how to maneuver a project through complex timetables, those who develop good performer and vendor relations, and those who practice solutions-based thinking coupled with flexibility. It rewards those who navigate the dichotomy that the way things "ought" to be are seldom how they really are. After 30 years in the industry, I'm convinced these qualities are just as much a part of design talent as the artistry. Many people actually *cannot* operate in the gray zones of entertainment design, cannot realign to shifting expectations, and cannot negotiate the confusion of competing interests.

I often meet people who discovered their passion for costume *after* their college years; those who came to it from related areas; and many who've worked their way up through costume shops, rental houses, and wardrobe crews who now wish to jump into design. Or they fell into an unexpected break, as I did. I hope it *is* possible to create a book that will reach out, grab early career designers by the shoulders, and point them in the right direction with practical advice and pride in our profession. I wish to aid those who, like my 19-year-old self, have a passion for performance storytelling, possess the drive, and who find the gumption to try. This book introduces the contemporary practice of costume design in roughly a chronological order of the steps that mirror the foundational skills and the creative and operational process of creating costumes. There are many switchbacks in the process and no two productions are alike. Yet an aspiring designer could begin with Chapter 1 and proceed through Chapter 30 to fully realize a staged project. The more experienced reader – or one in a hurry – can skip whole parts of the book or skip ahead for practical techniques.

My approach assumes the reader has *some* exposure to the costume field: working in community theater, a performing arts high school, arts camp, a university or professional costume shop, wardrobe crew, rental house, or creating independent projects. Costume design is a complex field that requires a larger spread of skills than other design areas, especially when direct relationships with the performers are factored into the picture. Another important element not to be overlooked – in American practice, costume designers are often called upon to be more self-sufficient and do more jobs for the same design fee than other designers, who are usually assigned a larger support staff. It was not possible to address everything in one book, so for additional practicalities, I recommend the companion book *The Wardrobe Supervisor's Toolkit*. Each chapter recommends extra resources for specific expertise to build a crucial library of foundations and skills.

Several years ago, I was offered an opportunity to design a delightful production of *Much Ado About Nothing* for Theatreworks in Colorado Springs, the same city where I began my journey. This time I returned as an experienced designer with the confidence to thoroughly enjoy the creative process. Convinced the universe meant me to come full circle, I reflected on how much I'd learned in the intervening years and what a remarkable profession costume design is. This book grew from the collective body of the costume community – generous and supportive colleagues whose expertise helped me grow in my career and produce this book. I hope it helps others make the most of their lucky breaks.

SPECIAL THANKS

To the mentors who came before me: Carolyn Smith Poe, Leanne Mahoney, Alan Armstrong, Dunya Ramicova, Brant Pope

To those who travel beside me: Bonnie Kruger, Marcy Froehlich, Julie Keen

To those who come after me: D. Larsson, Sebastian Rock, and especially Ayrika Johnson who contributed much more than she knows.

PROLOGUE

The Eight Costume Jobs

This book addresses the huge process of designing costumes for live performance. I have combined common terms and processes used in the theater with terms and ways of thinking used in film, themed entertainment, and creativity studies. These fields are newer and had to articulate the process of creativity more recently than theater has. Theater is an older art form handed from generation to generation through an informal or formal apprenticing system. Both film and themed entertainment are well aware they mix visual elements and verbal elements to create a total experience. Theater seems conflicted about this mixture, with periodic claims made that a good design is "invisible" or that actors could just as successfully perform *Hamlet* wearing black shirts and sitting on stools. The idea for this type of performance is an adequate substitute for a fully realized production – even a minimalist one – would be a very foreign concept to the ancient humans who invented visual performance in every culture in the world. Design thinking, history, and theory are just coming into their own as theoretical fields in the early 21st century. This book refers to current research in design thinking and cognitive research underlying the way humans perceive both the physical world and the creative process.

Costume designers are artists who interpret a verbal construct, the script, into a visual one, the staged presentation. This work can be described as five overarching aspects of design. Costume designers use visual tools to define the **world building** rules for both physical and emotional concepts. Like the set designer, the costume designer creates an ongoing **stage picture**, or scene-by-scene composition, of shapes and proportions in individual costumes and together as a group. Like the director, they create appropriate costumes to define **individual characters**, and like lighting and sound designers they illuminate **change arcs** through time or as a result of plot points.

Costume designers **collaborate** with actors as equal partners to create characters using skills such as human psychology, storytelling tropes, and how audiences interpret visual signals in clothing. The costume designer must also understand the many ways actors may create a character. Some actors seek a movement or behavior as the framework. When costume designer Penny Rose worked with Johnny Depp to create the now iconic Jack Sparrow costume, he came to the first fitting with the idea of imitating the Rolling Stones' Keith Richards.

> He arrived with the body language already in his head . . . he knew he was going to be Keith Richards. I didn't know that. . . . We had six hats on the floor, just samples made in Rome. . . . He put on the leather hat, he looked in the mirror and he said, "This is my hat."[1]

Sometimes the costume designer must wholly create a character that has few or no lines, pitching that idea to the actor. One common such situation is classic scripts featuring groups of lords, soldiers, or servants that appear once to advance a single plot point. Actors playing such undefined roles are grateful for a signature item such as glasses, facial hair, or a distinctive garment to distinguish that ill-defined character. Some actors want a task *to do* that will define a character such as fiddling with a knife holder, a cigar, a pocket watch. The successful costume designer does not need to train as an actor to work with actors but must develop a sensitivity to what each actor's process may be.

Eight Aspects of Costumes

The practical act of creating costumes consists of **eight** skill sets that require different areas of expertise. The smaller the budget for an organization, the more these jobs may combine. For instance, a storefront theater or student film may not hire eight people to fully complete these areas of responsibility. Most of the work may fall to the costume designer alone or with one helper. Those jobs require a generalist who can do a bit of everything and who enjoys creative problem solving to deliver higher production values than the budget would ordinarily afford. Higher budget productions or unionized projects will complete the costume team with more specialized personnel, providing a more efficient and proficient workflow and higher quality work. Some organizations may organize the costume designer's job using outdated perceptions because that is the way "it's always been done."

Since the job of costume design is not always correctly understood, every costume designer should first define the scope of the project when working with a new organization. Before accepting a job new to them, many designers will consult friends or colleagues who may have worked there before to assess resources and expectations. I propose that we costume designers educate producers so that none of the eight areas of responsibility vanish just because the budget is low. Someone must still perform these tasks to some level, so it is vital to define them and manage expectations accordingly. Only by quantifying the expectations for each job can we compare expectations, working conditions, pay, and even assess if we can afford to take this particular job. It is our duty to our fellow costume designers to educate producers who may have no idea that the costume design job is so large. While producers or production managers may routinely hire multiple scenic personnel and provide a technical director to lead the scenic construction, that same staffing is not always automatically given to costume designers, unless we work collectively to reinforce the scope of the job.

Table 0.1 Eight Jobs of Costume Design

Area of Expertise	Possible Job Titles	Specific Tasks
Costume Design	**Costume Designer**	Overall vision; collaborate with director, creative team, and actors; make all artistic decisions; conduct fittings; attend meetings with all makers; choose fabrics, garments, and accessories; oversee wigs, hair, and makeup vision
	Associate Costume Designer	Responsibility for specific areas of the design in conjunction with the costume designer, for example chorus costumes, extras, etc.
	Assistant Costume Designer	Employed by producer. Sourcing pulled, rental and purchased costumes, set up fitting room for every fitting, take designer notes, oversee duplicate costumes and other logistics, oversee purchasing and shopping staff

(Continued)

Table 0.1 (Continued)

Area of Expertise	Possible Job Titles	Specific Tasks
Costume Management	**Costume Director**	Employed by the producer to oversee the entire costume department operations. Hire labor and set work hours, departmental and individual project budgeting, future planning, delivering a project on time and under budget, maintain inventory and costume stock, special projects and remounts. May include some design duties.
	Costume Shop Manager	Employed by the producer to oversee the entire costume department operations, setting work hours, departmental and individual project budgeting, future planning, delivering a project on time and under budget, maintain inventory and costume stock.
	Purchasing Agent, Shopper	Source purchased items locally and ordering, shipping and returns, reconcile purchasing accounting, maintain shopping records for repurchase, stock inventory
Costume Construction	**Work Room Supervisor**	Directs the manufacturing floor, often a head draper
	Draper or Tailor	Creates original patterns and fits costumes
	Specialty Makers	Special items such as soft sculpture, animal suits
	First Hand	Assistant to a draper or tailor, directs stitchers
	Stitcher	Machine and hand sewing specialties
Costume Crafts	**Supervisor & Artisan**	Oversees the department and head artisan
	Millinery	Hat maker and hat styling
	Armor – Metal, Plastics	Special manufacture
	Sculptural Elements	Special manufacture
	Leather Work	Special manufacture
Fabric Dye & Modification	**Crafts/Dyer**	Generalist
	Dyer/Painter/Ager	Specialist
Hair and Wigs	**Hair and Wig Stylist**	Generalist
	Wig Maker	Specialist
Makeup	**Makeup Application**	Generalist, backstage crew
	Prosthetics	Specialist
	Special FX	Specialist
Wardrobe	**Crew Head**	Backstage supervisor
	Dresser	Backstage crew

Two large aspects of doing the design job require definition. One is the amount of support staff and expectations for the costume department. *Is* there a costume department, or just the designer? A second concern is the strike of a show after closing night. By that time, most designers are well off contract and on to other pursuits. Theaters may expect the costume designer to return for strike duties to break apart the show and return it to storage. Costume designers do have one rubric of comparison to use when assessing these aspects of a job – parity with the scenic designer. Scenic and costume designers often share the same or similar training. They are both visual designers working with a pre-visualization process, leading a manu-facturing phase and consulting (or doing) the proper installation. Both assess the suitability of their visual components in technical rehearsals and make adjustments. Does the scenic designer have more support, such as a technical director, shop foreman, carpenters and props? Is the scenic designer required to return for load out and strike? Asking each producer to explain their decisions will unearth some long-held biases. While no additional support may appear, perhaps the costume designer can negotiate a larger fee or add-itional weekly compensation for the actual work she performs.

Time Tracking

Start the habit of tracking your hours and mileage in some kind of journal. It is increasingly difficult to account for the on-call nature of many creative jobs when texts, emails, rehearsal reports, and phone calls require timely responses at all hours of the day. It may be most effective to establish a daily median or average time spent in this manner, and automatically add that to your time journal for every single day. Just as tax accountants will designate an allowable meals or per diem amount for their clients who travel, it is reasonable to assume you spend 15–30 minutes per day, or more, on digital communications. Larger tasks, such as uploading sketches to file sharing, would be added onto that. There are several time and expense tracking apps that embed information in a calendar or notebook. This information will result in a unique snapshot of how *you* as an individual designer operate. You can begin to develop strategies about where to streamline your tasks, or if a producer you really want to work with just cannot afford a reasonable fee, you will have data to negotiate a compromise – what steps to leave out? Lessening your workload is the fastest way to give yourself a raise, and how we spend our time is more in our control than we think. One example is reducing the drawing or pre-visualization time for a low-budget project. If the fee is very low, perhaps the designer provides tear sheets for each character, but no sketches. Or if drawing is a vital creative step to make decisions, reduce or delegate another task such as budget tracking or striking the show. As long as these intentions are discussed and mutually agreed to, both parties will know what to expect.

> "When I dare to be powerful – to use my strength in the service of my vision, then it becomes less and less important whether I am afraid." —Audre Lorde

The Artist in the Room

As you negotiate expectations, don't give away your power to be considered a contributing artist. Many producers do not understand what costume designers bring to a production. Remember that rendering substitutions such as character collages can still be artistically arranged. You will be treated as your pre-sent yourself to be. If you resort to sending screenshots of digital shopping carts, you will be regarded and treated like a shopping gofer. The same goes for shows that are entirely pulled from stock or a rental house. Always establish the expectation that you are an artist and a skilled interpreter of scripts. Artistic contributions bring obvious creative satisfaction to designers, who are, after all, visual storytellers. But before a costume designer can concentrate on the artistic elements, there is a larger framework to assess: what

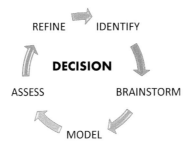

REFINE   IDENTIFY

DECISION

ASSESS   BRAINSTORM

MODEL

Figure 0.1 Each creative decision requires a loop of its own, cycling from identifying a challenge to refining the solution.

is the costume designer expected to bring to *this* production? The freelancer has an automatic prompt to discuss this at the beginning of a new project. The resident designer may struggle more with conversations about expectations once the job is underway, but always look at the start of a new project as the opportunity to plan. Discuss your thoughts for ensuring the best success for any project – after all, that is what everyone wants. Are the designer's expectations the same as the producing organization's expectations? There are few professional guidelines, unless the producer uses a formal union contract, and, even then, each structure reflects the local infrastructure rather than an abstract idea of how things "should" be done. Theaters with a vast stock will expect it to be used. Those without an inventory will expect designers to rent, buy, or build in various incarnations. Most misunderstandings arise from different presumptions that are never accurately verbalized. Then costume designers may find themselves *assuming* they will do more or less than the producer expected. When the misunderstanding comes to light, the designer is harried; it is too late to fix, professional relationships are frayed. Assessing the job is the first step for any artist; this phase is referred to as **defining the scope of work**. There is more information on job assessments and negotiations in Chapter 7, Getting Paid, and Chapter 17, Defining the Scope of a Show.

The Creative Process

I've arranged this book in an order that approximates the steps of the creative process (see Figure 1.0). Each larger box represents the steps of producing a project, such as **concept development** and **opening**. The second row of white boxes translates each producing step to its corresponding creative function, such as **explore** or **refine**. The bottom boxes elaborate the actual tasks designers accomplish in each step. For instance, to **evaluate** a show requires both **critique** and **revision**. Each designer will march through these steps very differently, or even differently for each show. One might require a long period of blue sky exploration. Another time, that same designer may be handed a set approach, such as the revival of a prior show. In that case, it is more appropriate to dive right into feasibility planning. Of course, every creative process *must* include switchbacks and do-overs. Creating a graphic representation of creativity is automatically incomplete, as each step along the way involves its own decision-making loop.

Expecting the Unexpected

Anything can happen during a creative project, especially one with multiple collaborators, a compressed timeline, and a public opening. Every designer might struggle to think of a few shows that went completely as planned. Playwright Oscar Wilde noted that "To expect the unexpected shows a thoroughly modern intellect."[2] The wise costume designer learns to accept that anything can happen and probably will at the least convenient time. This is where experience comes into play. Many designers develop a hunch that something will not work out, avoiding many problems before they occur. Each chapter will conclude with one real example of where things went wrong and some possible solutions.

Figure 0.2 Looking forward.

Credit: Theater figure, Meissen Manufactory, 1750–52. Gift of Irwin Untermyer, 1964. Metropolitan Museum of Art, New York. www.metmuseum.org

Notes

1 Howell, Peter. "Fitting Oversized Egos into Small Packages." *Toronto Star*, May 6, 2011. Accessed November 21, 2019. www.pressreader.com/canada/toronto-star/20110506/284803577672322.
2 Wilde, Oscar. 1899. *An Ideal Husband*. London: Leonard Smithers and Co. Accessed December 1, 2021. Internet Archive archive.org/details.idealhusband00wildrich.

PART ONE

THE DESIGNER'S TOOLS

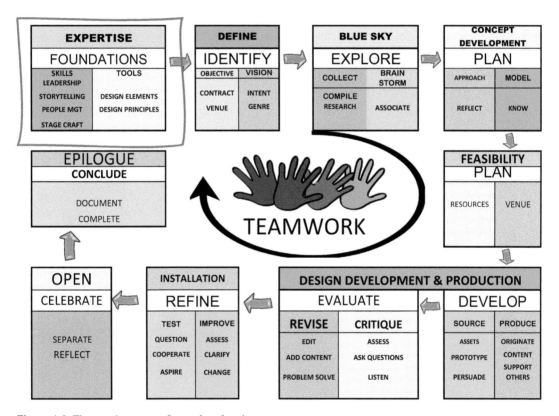

Figure 1.0 The creative process for produced projects.

Credit: Holly Poe Durbin and Ayrika Johnson

1.
WHAT THE COSTUME DESIGNER BRINGS TO A PRODUCTION

Entertainment creators are optimistic people. That does not mean they are relentlessly cheerful, but that they live in the world of *potential*. They envision ideas that did not exist before. They work in new teams for each project, within constricting budgets, and meet uncompromising deadlines. After all that, their efforts are publicly criticized by audiences and reviewers. These complications are enough to discourage most people, yet entertainment creators thrive in this work. Why? When asked, most respond they feel a calling or it's the only place they feel at home. Recent research supports what many theater artists instinctively feel – that they were born to dream.[1] They share the characteristic of **foresight**, or the talent for seeing possibilities. Theater artists score significantly above the general population in **analytical reasoning**, or the ability to arrange ideas and concepts into a system. Designers and technicians specifically score highly in four aptitudes: **structural visualization**, or the ability to imagine objects in three-dimensional space; **design memory**, the ability to remember images and patterns; and **observation**, the ability to remember visual details and their positions. Not surprisingly, designers also excel in **color discrimination**, or the ability to distinguish very fine differences in colors. So it may indeed be true when theater people say they have a calling for this profession.

What Do Costume Designers Bring to a Production?

Costume designers are an essential part of **world building** for every project. Because most people wear clothing every day, it is easy to forget that costume communicates an entire visual language to observers. It affects individual wearers, too. Anyone who has dressed in formal attire for a wedding knows it affects our behavior and our sense of self. Costume designers are the **artistic leaders** of a vital visual element that will profoundly affect both what the audience thinks and how the performers feel.

"Anytime you talk about the look of the film, it's not just the director and the director of photography. You have to include the costume designer and the production designer." —Spike Lee[2]

Costume Designers Visualize an Approach Ahead of Time

The creative team of director and designers defines the story world together. They explore a story for themes, metaphors, and ideas. Designers translate those ideas into visual elements such as color, texture, and shape. They articulate visual rules to guide the hundreds of

DOI: 10.4324/9781003015284-2

decisions on every project. In turn, costume designers envision and communicate that aesthetic to their collaborators: performers, vendors, makers, crew members. One example of an overarching visual rule is assigning unique colors to each group of characters. It might be cliché to use the old Hollywood rule of assigning a dark hat to antagonists and a light hat to protagonists, but those approaches are still used in many current fantasy stories today.

Costume Designers Create Characters

Designers create believable characters in collaboration with the actor and director. They translate human foibles and habits into visual cues the audience can read. This ability requires an understanding of psychology, sociology, fashion theory, story mechanics, people-watching skills, and an appreciation for the stagecraft of acting. One example of a character trait is older people dressing in slightly out-of-date styles. Some elders freeze their looks at a time they felt happiest, others keep clothing longer from a sense of thrift. Or perhaps they no longer care what others think.

Costume designers create the **backstory** for each character. Without this step, a production risks looking like all the characters shopped at the same store minutes before their entrance. Adept backstory research uses keenly tuned research images, avoiding

Figure 1.1 This ca. 1905 wedding party shows that young girls wore age-appropriate fashions different from adult women.

Credit: Augusta Curiel, Wedding in Paramaribo, Rijksmuseum, Amsterdam http://hdl.handle.net/10934/RM0001.COLLECT. 484441

high-fashion images and favoring photographs of real people when appropriate. Very few people today dress in runway-worthy fashions, many mix new pieces with old pieces, creating an individual look. All people create idiosyncratic images: mingling a necklace given to us long ago with earrings purchased today, keeping the same hairstyle or jeans for decades, an aversion to certain colors or patterns. These details create a believable character.

Costume Designers Create Arcs of Change

Characters may change with the passage of time or changes in mindset. The most obvious example is a character who ages in a story or appears more youthful within flashbacks. Other instances include changing the overall color scheme to indicate emotional shifts in the story. For example, characters who begin as companions but end as enemies may shift from compatible colors to opposing colors. Creating arcs draws on the designer's understanding of the script, and how characters react to changes.

Costume Designers Stage Stories for an Audience

Telling effective stories requires seeing the script from the audience point of view to create an intended impact. The costume designer addresses specific requirements written into the script. Common examples of stage requirements that advance the stage presentation are tear-away costumes, fast changes, actors playing two characters, or special effects. Designers measure if their preconceived ideas support the living work as it evolves and they make adjustments along the way.

Costume Designers Are Problem Solvers

Every show reveals challenges along the way and designers work throughout to find solutions. They must be open to change but also never lose sight of the integrity of the design. One common challenge is discovering the timing for a costume change is shortened by the architecture of a particular theater when an actor cannot travel to an entrance as anticipated. Many challenges in our industry have to be solved quickly and with the cooperation of several people. Since challenges are part of every creative job, designers must develop a strategy of **solutions-focused thinking** that removes emotion from the equation.

> "When you concentrate much on the faults, you shall be at fault. When you always focus on the solutions, you shall always be a solution." —Ernest Agyemang Yeboah[3]

Costume Designers Contribute Unique Expertise to the Production

Some directors are accomplished visual artists themselves. But no matter how visually gifted a director may be, most have not dedicated themselves to the many skills a costume designer brings to a production. Costume designers must look at a show through three lenses: the large picture of how everything looks onstage together, the medium view of creating individual characters, and the close up of designing the specifics of each garment and accessory. Mastering these three areas of expertise requires years of practice and artistry.

Costume Designers Are Artistic Leaders

Just as directors must trust the design team to create the world they envision, designers in turn rely on others to bring each costume to life. Designers lead without absolute authority, as they rarely directly employ workers. They are not always in control of who builds their show. Designers work with every kind of shop, every skill level, and every level of willingness. Some shops are so skilled they make work better than the designer could imagine alone. Other colleagues are enthusiastic team members but less skilled, some are distracted by several projects at once, some work for dispiriting bosses or just put in time for the paycheck. Designers also rarely set the budget for a production. They must coax as fine work as possible using advanced people skills. The designer is the one and only person on a project that tracks all aspects of the costume design at once. Actors appreciate their own costume but may not see the entire stage picture. Costume makers

will contribute greatly to the creation of garments but may not read the script. Kent Thompson, former producing artistic director of the Denver Center and Alabama Shakespeare Festival acknowledges that artistic leadership has special attributes: "A strong leader must set the vision, goals and expectations . . . and hold everybody accountable. However, the core job more often is leading by persuading, inspiring, asking and cultivating allies."[4]

Many costume designers begin their careers more oriented to the daily routines of the costume shop: the excitement of fittings; the camaraderie with costume makers; the delicious collections of fabrics, trims, and costume storage. This is especially true if the designer began as a costume maker or manager or if their job combines those roles with costume design. But to be a truly effective storyteller, the costume designer must develop creative allegiance to the **story**: the script, the rehearsal process, and the experience presented onstage. This can sometimes create awkward moments with co-workers and colleagues, but the designer must keep the big picture in mind.

Why Are Costume Designers Leaders?

We have to coax and persuade people every step of the way.

We can't be timid, or the show won't get done.

It's important to include everyone in the project; they have to have stakes too.

We constantly problem solve on our feet because people need answers all day.

We have to keep a goal in sight but be flexible in how we get there.

We have to separate facts from feelings to be effective.

We have to strategize large projects and many small details.

—Jennifer Clark, Cassie Defile, Matthew Martinez, Ashton Montgomery, Lauryn Terceira

What's Missing?

It's worth noting what is missing from the discussion so far. It does *not* contain requirements such as *skilled in every area of knowledge, draws beautiful renderings, went to the right school,* or even *has the most talent.* Certainly none of these attributes will hinder a career, but they are no guarantee of success, either. Costume designers are ultimately not judged by these things. They are judged by the production on stage and the process of getting to the stage. For every successful designer whose original talent or school connections allowed them to waltz right into a job, there is one who advanced using persistence and a good work ethic. For every magnetic outgoing personality who charmed their way into a career, there is an introvert who barely negotiates the days they have to talk to groups. Creating the costumes for a show is very like those adventure tales that thrust an unprepared heroine into a new journey. What you do along the way will define a successful outcome.

Thinking Like a Designer

How do designers envision a new approach for a project? British researcher Nigel Cross coined the term **designerly thinking** as a discipline in itself that could be quantified with its own "things to know, ways of knowing them and ways of finding out about them."[5] He notes that design problems are generally ill-defined, poorly structured, or frustrating. Unlike math equations or physics, there are few rules or correct answers. Defining the problem is actually the first step of designerly thinking. A typical costume design problem might be "How do people dress in the land of Illyria in Shakespeare's *Twelfth Night* or in Westeros for *Game of Thrones*?" Of course, there is no correct answer and no defined structure to find an answer. Cross contrasts designers to scholars and scientists who are encouraged to suspend judgment as long as possible, until more is known.

Instead, designers tackle problems to be solved within a very short time span. Creative thinkers gather what they *do* know about a question and just *begin.* "At its core is the 'language of **modeling**.'"[6] Modeling refers to all the ways we test an idea. In costumes, that includes a research collage or sketch, a muslin mock-up, and a fitting. We begin with one idea and define, refine, and change direction as new ideas or limitations present themselves. In other

words, design is **process oriented**; designers discover more about the problem zig-zagging to new ideas. Cross further notes that designerly thinking includes an appreciation of materials and planning, making, or doing. Master designer Tim Brown, founder of the landmark innovation company IDEO, says, "If we take a different view of design and focus less on the object and more on design thinking as an *approach*, we might see results with bigger impact."[7] Brown also finds the act of framing the design challenge informative in itself, urging deeper discovery. He begins with a first stab at writing the design challenge, keeping it short and simple enough to remember. It can be statements or questions or a mix of the two. Using a system he calls the **Five Whys**, he asks *why?* five times about a situation. He suggests avoiding the pitfall of defining the challenge too narrowly or too broadly. There should be room to explore creative solutions but not too broad as to leave the designer stumped where to begin. Test this version of design thinking by seeing if you can come up with five questions in just a few minutes.

Juliet Capulet and the Five Whys

For the play *Romeo and Juliet*, the designer specified this challenge: design a style of costumes for Juliet that defines her character and comments on her predicament. By asking *why* five times, we dive into her character.

1. **Why** was Juliet so desperate she would risk *faking her own death?* She had no power in her conservative family and society, her family values duty over personal desires.
2. **Why**? She felt trapped in a system that did not consider her an individual.
3. **Why**? A loveless marriage to Paris is a trap or final act that cannot be undone, ever. She fears she will be living a version of death.
4. **Why** did she think the unthinkable – loving *marriage is something she should have or deserve?* Juliet is a rebel in her time. She takes risks and devises plans where many young girls might not.

5. **Why** *did her parents want to marry her off right away?* Her independence of spirit may have been a source of worry for them. Was she a rebellious teenager in her parents' eyes, and they deemed it better to marry her off too young, rather than risking her ruin – a form of social death?

Figure 1.2 Juliette's beach pajamas

This style of thinking led to the costume design for Juliet's character in a production by Shakespeare LA. Set in the 1920s, Juliette was conceived as a youthful rebel with short cropped hair and wearing a scandalous new style of pajama trousers (Figure 1.2). The audience first sees her sneaking a cigarette on her balcony, a stance that was drawn into the costume sketch. This moment established that her gamine, rebellious personality was too upsetting for her family, still grounded in Victorian mores.

Your Unique Artistic Practice

Every costume designer improves by reflecting on their finished work, assessing what was effective and what did not achieve its intent. One effective way to develop a critical eye is to assess other designers' work. Other fields, such as law, business, and medicine, use **case studies**: in-depth analysis of a specific real-world situation. It is an effective way to practice analytical skills and develop an artistic vocabulary. Any performed work is a suitable example for a case study, as long as it can be viewed more than once to analyze the visual mechanics. The subject is a personal choice. Are you looking for examples of a specific kind of design? Think

about films or plays that have won awards. Are you exploring what your unique aesthetic is? Choose a film or recorded live performance you admire. Chances are your aesthetic may be closely aligned. Many artists with a strong visual style studied the work of a hero. Both author Daniel Handler (*Lemony Snicket's Series of Unfortunate Events*) and film director Tim Burton (*Batman*) admired the work of illustrator Edward Gorey, noted for his ink drawings of characters in perilous situations. Although both Handler and Burton modeled their work on Gorey, they each developed their own style. Their work is an homage, not copying. Learning to verbalize what you see in work you admire will hone your awareness of artistic vocabulary and strategies.

The final step is to define your own creative process, working methods, and artistic voice. For many designers this is a long journey. Choreographer Twyla Tharpe articulates the creative process in *The Creative Habit: Learn It and Use It for Life*. She observes that creativity stems from **work habits**, not lightning strikes of genius. "I've learned that being creative is a full-time job with its own daily patterns. That's why writers . . . like to establish routines. . . . Over time, as the daily routines become second nature, discipline morphs into habit."[8] She notes it will be easier to draw on creative ideas with a consistent practice. Her book provides examples and exercises to jump start creative thinking that many artists have found inspiring.

Figure 1.3 Illustrators have long served as inspirations for design styles.

Credit: (Left) Steinlen, Théophile-Alexandre *At the Bar*, Fil Blas Illustré Vol 7–8, n.d. 1899? (Right) Cham, *Paris Fashions Anticipating Bombardment*, Album du Siége 1871. Both images via Old Book Illustrations.com

One habit that benefits a costume designer is **drawing** one thing, no matter how small, every day, or committing to a set number of drawings per week. The real reason for drawing is training your brain to really *see* an object's silhouette, proportions, and details. Some find copying exercises useful – copy a great masters sketch, favorite motifs in a textile print, or one detail in a vintage fashion plate or painting. Another idea is using themes or prompts, such as drawing 100 hands using your own hands or photographs as models. There are many online communities dedicated to supporting a drawing habit, as well as books showing specific methods. In a very short time, you will have gathered a large body work – a record of your potential and artistic practice – and you will feel more like an artist. Do the drawings have to be good? Who cares – this is your practice, like doing yoga. You are exercising your hands and brain; you will gain confidence and sophistication about shapes and details through habitual drawing.

An art teacher tried an experiment in a ceramics class. Dividing the students into two groups, he announced the first group would be graded solely on the *quantity* of work they produced. The second group would be graded solely on the *quality*. Those producing quantity had to create a certain amount for the grading, but those producing quality only had to produce one work. At grading time, a curious result emerged: the highest quality work was actually produced by those in the quantity group. It seemed that while the quantity group was churning out pounds of ceramic pots, they learned from their mistakes. The quality group, however, sat theorizing about perfection, and in the end had little to show for their efforts.[9]

Another vital routine that directly benefits designers is **feeding your image bank**. This could be visiting one cultural event or location each week with new sights, sounds, and ideas. Visit a museum, a gallery, a jewelry store, a new neighborhood, or street festival. Designers foster their precious ability to remain curious about new things. And you never know when you will need to know something.

Expecting the Unexpected

No matter how much a costume designer prepares, no plan is foolproof. Creative projects live in the gray areas; there are many things that will never be fully known at the start of the project. Actors will be recast, blocking will change, the fabric you want will sell out before you can purchase it. Yet the deadlines or opening nights are public and nonnegotiable. Costume designers develop the rare ability to work toward a goal while remaining approachable and adaptable without endangering the integrity of the overall design. Strive to approach all challenges with an open mind and willing heart. If you have a reputation for good will and thoughtful assessment, your collaborators will trust your opinions.

Additional Resources

Aspelund, Karl, *The Design Process*, 3rd ed., Fairchild Books, 2015.

Tharpe, Twyla, *The Creative Habit, Learn It and Use It for Life*, Simon & Schuster, 2006.

Online drawing communities include Doodle Addicts, DeviantArt, Art Station, and Ello.

Notes

1 Barsotti, Scott T. "Are Theater Artists Hardwired?" *Howlround Theater Commons*, October 19, 2015. https:// howlround.com/are-theatre-artists-hardwired.

2 Uncredited Author, "Spike Lee on Do The Right Thing's Legacy." *The Guardian Network*, October 6, 2009. https://youtu.be/6sGKhANz99A.

3 Yeboah, Earnest Agyemang. n.d. Goodreads.com. Accessed July 1, 2021. www.goodreads.com/quotes/ tag/solution-focused

4 Thompson, Kent. 2019. *Directing Professionally*. New York: Methuen Drama, p. 187.

5 Cross, Nigel. 2007. *Designerly Ways of Knowing*. Basel: Birkhäuser Verlag AG, p. 17.

6 Ibid.

7 Brown, Tim. 2009. "Designers-Think Big!" Filmed July, 2009 at TEDGlobal, Oxford, England. Video, 14:45. www.ted.com/talks/tim_brown_designers_think_big? language=en

8 Tharp, Twyla. 2009. *The Creative Habit*. New York: Simon & Schuster, p. 6.

9 Bayles, David and Orland, Ted. 1993. *Art and Fear: Observations on the Perils (and Rewards) of Artmaking*. Santa Cruz, CA: The Image Continuum.

2.
COLLABORATIVE CREATIVITY

The creative process is the act of making connections between ideas. We often think of the story of Sir Isaac Newton's flash of creativity when he witnessed an apple falling to the ground, using that moment to define gravity. While that *was* a moment of pure genius, what is often left out of the story is his 20 years of study leading up to that moment.[1] Designers bring their own years of experiences to each project, but they never have decades to prepare a single project. Preparation times for a specific project can vary greatly, depending on when an organization forms the creative team. Many established theaters contract designers well in advance to ensure the team has adequate time for groundwork. But it is not uncommon for circumstances to dictate a short deadline. Over time, designers develop a strong understanding of their own process to get best results, but they also learn how to accelerate or truncate it when needed. Will the fast prep result in the designer's best work? Sometimes yes, sometimes no. Designers learn how to support their best efforts – how to take shortcuts, negotiating due dates or even forgoing a job that did not allow sufficient preparation.

Every producing organization uses slightly different terms for the steps in creating a production. Deadlines in United Scenic Artist contracts stipulate due dates for things such as *rough designs*, *final designs*, *technical rehearsals*, and *opening night*. Individual theaters may add other deadlines for *research* or a *costume plot*. Due dates are effective benchmarks, but they don't describe the actual *creative process* needed to step from one deadline to the next. The theme park industry invented its process so that people from very different disciplines, such as concept art and electrical engineering, might work toward common goals. Walt Disney Imagineering President Robert Weis suggested a series of terms that have been widely adapted.[2] These terms correspond to the creative process graphic in Figure 1.0.

- **Define**. The process begins with **activation**, or defining the challenge. Understand what you're being asked to do, with whom, for whom, and by when. What elements are an absolute requirement, and can you fulfill them? Are there any contstraints to work around, and can you work with those limitations? Consider the impact of the performance venue on the creative project. Finally, factor in the expectations of the performing organization. The next step is to **energize** the project with a preliminary idea of the director's vision. Assess the needs of specific story genres or story style that may influence rehearsals and performance. For instance, musicals operate within certain parameters and expectations, as do dramatic plays. The USA 829 union designer typically receives one-third of the total design fee on signing a contract to reserve their time and begin the project.
- **Blue sky.** This phase is the most intoxicating, the first rush of ideas with the director and creative team. The designer **explores** possibilities through script and story analysis, consulting experts and **collecting** research. Designers **brainstorm** and consult specialists if there are

DOI: 10.4324/9781003015284-3

unusual requirements. This phase culminates in an initial approach with enough details to explain the design direction to others. The costume designer presents ideas to the director, fellow designers, and perhaps a costume shop manager.

- **Concept development.** Refine the **approach** with feedback from the director. This phase results in a design **plan** and an initial visual representation such as sketches or character collages that serve as early **models** for the design. Typical contract obligations for this phase include creating formal research presentations and/or rough sketches. Progress through this step is usually compensated in a union contract with another one-third of the total design fee, payable when sketches are submitted.
- **Feasibility.** This phase includes assessing **labor**, **materials**, and **budget**, or how the design may be realized using available resources. The designer makes adjustments and compromises in consultation with the director, the production manager, or the costume shop manager. Costume planning may stipulate origin points for some garments, such as use of stock, rentals, purchasing, and custom builds.
- **Design development.** The detail work of designing, including final sketches and sometimes schematics for built items such as working drawings or pattern research. Designers may work with samples or prototypes. Prototyping for costume designers is bringing to life what we imagined on paper: **sourcing** from rental houses, pulling from stock, purchasing, and beginning the process of made-to-order items with mock-ups.
- **Production.** Many creative decisions are made while manufacturing the design. Constructing, fitting, and altering costumes usually runs simultaneously with rehearsals. The costume designer juggles both commitments of tending to the costume shop's schedule and understanding rehearsal progress. **Revising** the design occurs in fittings, which serve as the first **critique**. Some ideas are rejected – what looked good on paper or on the rack doesn't always translate to the actor's body. The designer may return to the research or exploration phase for more ideas. By the time a costume designer completes fittings, each idea has been modeled three or more times: as a research collage or a sketch, when sourcing garments and fabrics, and fitting the actor. At the end of this step, the show is ready to move to stage.
- **Installation.** Loading costumes into the performance venue and dress rehearsals represent the final phase of the creative process: **refining** the design. It is important to reserve the emotional and creative energy for this final, hectic phase. A vital driver of this phase is **testing** the design in place with all the other design elements and the actors. The costume designer takes a step back to assess the effectiveness of their work and **improve** things that do not live up to the intent.
- **Opening and epilogue.** This is the celebration and *letting go* process. Designers finalize their documentation, establish maintenance and show quality standards, and close financial records. The USA union designer receives the final one-third of the design fee, payable on opening night.

Working in Creative Teams

Costume designers do not work alone and it is this collaborative creativity that makes entertainment design unique. Creative teams don't behave predictably and they consist of individuals with their own opinions. As if maneuvering group dynamics is not challenging enough, each producing organization will use its own systems. Add to this mix the unforgiving deadline of opening – and we have the perfect equation for stress. Research of theater workers found that while they overwhelmingly favored collaboration, they did not score as highly in this aptitude as assumed. Theater artists also favor developing individual "artistic expertise" and "actualizing . . . aesthetic point of view."[3] It is this conundrum that is the heart of creative collaboration. Costume designers act as ambassadors, reconciling their creative goals with the greater good of the show. They operate like surfers maneuvering an ever-shifting environment to achieve the final result. The key to reconciling individual aesthetics and collaboration lies in effective communication.

Communicating With a Director

Directors are ultimately responsible for the effectiveness of everything on stage, regardless of which team member originated the idea. Do all the elements contribute to the storytelling and to the artistic goals? Did the show stay on course, on schedule? Was it artistically successful? Directors value clear communication from their design team, using whatever means necessary to describe ideas. In an ideal process, you will have several early meetings with a director to confer over the ideas created through script analysis (see Chapters 8–11). However, the fast pace of contemporary schedules can result in fewer meetings, making the stakes for each conversation higher. The wise costume designer uses each meeting to advance their goals sufficiently.

The director's work style will dictate how rehearsals proceed and that will impact the costume designer's job. Some directors are *methodical*, planning a logical arc for each day's work and striving to hit benchmarks on certain days. Others are *organic* thinkers; they avoid tight plans and they respond to rehearsal discoveries to guide their progress. Many directors fall somewhere in between these two styles, with some aspects of the show highly planned and others allowed to grow in rehearsals. Some directors prefer using a large number of rehearsal costumes to choreograph specific movements into the show. Rehearsal costume expectations have been rising sharply in recent years and may affect the costume designer's labor and budget. It is important to plan this requirement from the beginning instead of negotiating a surprise later on. Some directors will add extra music, pre-show choreography, or create storytelling transitions from one scene to the next that are not obvious in the script. After working with a director on multiple productions, the costume designer will understand what to expect, but it is important in these early discussions to *never assume* the script contains the entire picture of a production. A few questions sharing each other's working style can help build trust.

Directors and designers agree that extended discussions about the script are one of the joys of being in this business. However, as team members travel to different locations or work on several projects simultaneously, the typical number of meetings may look more like this:

Get-to-Know-You Meeting

This may be part of the interview process or it may be the first meeting with the director after you're hired. If the two of you have never worked together, the ideal scenario is a casual meeting, such as a coffee shop, with adequate time to discuss your personal reactions to the script and working methods. The contemporary reality may be a video call. Most directors are interested in getting to know their future collaborators as people, and many want to have a good time working with their team. The director may have ideas for the production well in the works, or may be waiting for input from the designers before finalizing an approach. Try to get a feel for how the director thinks. Many directors and designers have standard questions they like to ask each other. Make a list of things you'd like to know from a director. Even though the first meeting is casual, designers prepare a full understanding of the story. Discuss your immediate reaction to the story and script, the emotional impact, or the format. This meeting is for deep listening, enthusiasm, and brainstorming. The designer learns to surf their way through this meeting, changing direction or following ideas as needed. Take notes during the meeting so you can remember what excited the director and what did not. You want the director to leave this meeting with faith that you will dedicate time and attention to their project.

What Should You Bring to This Meeting?

- A thorough initial reading of the script – two readings are better.
- List of general questions from your readings to aid discussion.
- Inspiration images such as an artist's work relevant to the script; be as nonliteral as possible to spark conversation. Be flexible if the director has other ideas.

- Be prepared to describe ideas or, better yet, make hasty scribbles. The proverbial "sketch on a napkin" is a true aspect of entertainment design and it shows the director you can think quickly.
- Possible "what if" and "why" questions for brainstorming. What if we don't use a strictly realistic approach? Why is the play formatted in such short scenes?

Concepts and Questions to Share With the Director

What is the biggest driver for ideas in this production?

What images strike you as the most arresting in this script?

Why are we doing this script now? What makes it relevant to today's audience?

Are there "givens" in the script that can't be changed without derailing the story or themes?

What level of realism or exaggeration is appropriate for this production?

What should the big take away be for the audience?

Are there tonal shifts important to the story – suddenly funny, sad, bittersweet?

What changes are you making to the script?

What is the casting structure, such as actors playing multiple characters?

Are you considering casting against type, older, younger, gender swap, or nonbinary?

Are there characters on stage not written into the script – extras, stage crew?

What are the turning points, such as time or plot twists, that might trigger costume decisions?

Are there emotional arcs to feature?

Try to determine if that director will have your back if the going gets tough.

First Design Conference

This meeting is the first time the full creative team delves into performance concepts. This is a good time to bring preliminary ideas to the group. Regional theaters with larger budgets fly the entire creative team to visit the performing venue and get the project underway as a group. This is the costume designer's opportunity to sit in different parts of the theater to view people onstage. Are performers close to the audience or far away? Does the angle of seating mean many of the patrons are looking from above or below? Be a visible part of the creative team to establish yourself. Theaters that work with a cadre of local designers may set aside a time all the designers can meet in person with the director. Smaller theaters or independent productions may not have a formal process, preferring the designers set up their own meetings. The director will not know the design deadlines for each area, so each designer must push their process along in a timely manner. If the costume designer has not worked with a specific theater before it is vital to **ask questions** about what type of meeting schedule to expect. Start with the person who presented your contract and ask them to walk through the entire production process and every deadline. If the theater does not initiate meetings, the costume designer must initiate conversations with the director to get the project rolling.

It's important to show significant progress in every meeting. How have you explored or enlarged ideas from the initial meeting? In many ways, this meeting is a pitch – you are proposing ideas for the director's consideration. If the director describes a desired effect, toss around thoughts on how costumes might contribute to their intent. Many designers like to present initial research or color ideas for responses from the director. If the producing organization does not schedule a group meeting, be sure to introduce yourself to the other designers another way and ask to see their inspirations. At the close of this meeting, make sure you have enough information to develop ideas to the rough design stage. Determine what areas need more exploration and research.

What Should You Bring to This Meeting?

- A costume scene chart. Making this chart will spark many questions for this meeting. (See Chapter 8.)
- Initial visual research such as books, collages, mood boards that begin to define the world of the story. Organize it effectively, but don't target the information too tightly. Your mind should not be made up yet.
- Imagery that communicates essential information such as the costume silhouette, textures, or emotional impact.
- Ideas or questions about the broad strokes of color, texture, light, mood, tone, silhouette.
- An understanding of the narrative structure – any turning points or plot points that create dramatic moments to discuss with the director. (See Chapter 9.)
- Understand script costume requirements such as obvious fast changes or specialty items.

Subsequent Meetings

A typical design contract designates some formal due dates for research, rough designs, and final designs. How each designer arrives at these deadlines is at their own discretion. Always schedule check-in meetings with the director, and get their approval before submitting a deliverable to the costume shop or production manager to meet contractual deadlines. The producers will certainly understand if a few items are being revised at the director's request, but their workflow will be compromised if the ideas you've given them do not have approval from the director. The costume designer must take the initiative to present information early enough to give the director time to respond.

What Should You Bring to These Meetings?

Present any deliverables such as sketches to the director about a week before each is due to the theater per contract. Part of the designer's expertise is imagining ways to communicate with each director that will keep them informed but not burden them with minutia. Training programs put an extraordinary emphasis on creating costume sketches, but that may not always be the most effective model, and they are not the only means of communication. Finished painted sketches will show all your collaborators what to expect, but not all directors can interpret sketches or visualize how a small swatch of fabric will fall on the figure or move onstage. They might react better to seeing a yard of fabric in motion, or dress forms with sample costumes on them. Some directors cannot adequately describe what they want, but they know what they *don't* like to see. Do not assume that just because a process "should" be a certain way it must stay that way. Stay tuned to the individual needs of each project.

Questions to Ask Directors About Their Work Style

- Are there ways costume renderings fail to prepare them to understand the final design?
- Do they wish to attend any fittings, and do they want daily fitting photos?
- Do they react best to printed material or shared digital files?
- Do they have time to react to email questions, or is it best for you to visit at the top or end of designated rehearsal days for a quick conference?
- Do they have certain processes or dislikes you should know about?

Start each meeting with a brief verbal summary of your **big ideas** and themes. Then present your ideas **scene-by-scene** to show the director how the characters will look as the play progresses. Represent your ideas visually with research, storyboards, research collages, or sketches. Explain how the costumes contribute to the narrative and their vision. Showcase turning points or arcs of change in the script that affect the costumes (see Chapter 8). Point to specific decisions about each character and what you want to express to an audience. Talking confidently about the script and characters reassures the director you understand storytelling. Ask the director for specific feedback, steering the costumes toward a desired impact, or tone, or **effectiveness**. If you or the director wish to review the arc of a single character, lay your ideas out again **character-by-character** for a closer examination.

Collaborating With Fellow Designers

Ideal communication with other designers begins during the earliest phases of the project. In the worst-case scenario, the costume designer is hired late and has to play catch up with the rest of the team. Be proactive getting the visual information you need from the production manager or fellow designers. Most projects establish an online file-sharing site for designers to access each other's work. Contribute and update costume information to this file: research, sketches, color plots, and swatches. The entire design team must understand the world-building aesthetics of this production.

Scenery intersects with costume for **visual harmony** of colors and textures (see Chapter 5) and during **movement** such as entrances, traffic patterns, and floor textures. Some intersection points include:

- Can the period skirts fit through the doors or fit on scenic elements?
- Does the hoop skirt fit on the furniture?
- Will several actors in large costumes travel up backstage stairs or stand on a backstage platform?
- Is there room for a quick-change booth?
- Will shoe heels catch inside scenic tracks or rain grates?
- Will movement on the floor abrade the knees or seat of trousers?
- Do floors have to be mopped with anti-slip products?

Lighting designers and projections designers intersect with costume **colors**, **textures**, **mood**, and actors' **skin tones**. Some intersection points include:

- Challenging costume colors
- Supporting projections on the body
- Use of hats casting shadows on faces
- The range of skin tones in the cast

Sound designers intersect with costumes on a performer's **body**. Wireless mic packs must be held securely with *the antenna straight up or straight down*. While pre-made mic pack holders are now widely available, the costume design or specific movement may require a custom solution. Packs can be held around the thigh, attached to underwear, held around the waist, built into pockets, or disguised underneath a wig. Some intersection points include:

- Where the mic pack attaches in the costume
- The style, size, and color of mic pack to incorporate into fittings
- The style, size, and color of wand on the face
- Where the wand or lavalier intersects with earrings, hairstyles, or wigs
- Operation of fast changes for the mic and pack

Working With an Assistant or Team

Each project presents unique logistics. Honestly assess the skill set required each time. Will the costumes be built by multiple vendors, requiring a team with strong people skills and the ability to multitask? Will the costumes be rented from multiple sources, requiring team members skilled in paperwork and shipping? Many projects now have multiple digital platforms to manage, so do you need someone with digital skills? Perhaps the team needs several assistants or production assistants who swing in and out for short tasks. Another helpful thing designers can do when forming a team is to honestly articulate their own preferences and avoidances, so they may hire a team with complementary skills. One effective design team formed on the basis of their body clocks; the designer was a morning person, an associate was a night owl. Between them the project had nearly 24-hour coverage. Some theaters employ a resident design assistant the designer may not know. Setting expectations and boundaries up front will be a relief to everyone. Present your foibles with humor and grace, acknowledge your preferences and dislikes. In some cases, an assistant is a graduate student or intern that may not have the type of experience this project requires. If assistants are still learning the intricacies of a period, for instance, educate your team members using ideas like a style guide showing the correct rise of men's trousers, use of cuffs or pleats in trousers. Or better yet, ask the assistant to create that style guide to learn those requirements.

Working With Performers

Every show requires different styles of communication with performers. Always consult the director before beginning communication with their cast. Some costume designers and directors like to share design information early so actors arrive with characters in mind. Some directors wish to present the entire world at once, asking the costume designer to withhold information until a certain date. Working with stars may require costume consultations ahead of time. Many costume designers and costume shops like to email their cast ahead of time to introduce themselves and ask about special concerns or collect sizing information. Establishing an early rapport with the actors can foster trust. Working with performers requires a healthy dash of salesmanship, a lot of deep listening, and the self-confidence to focus on solutions, not feelings. Performers will sometimes offer feedback generated by personal desire or by new discoveries in rehearsal. They must always perceive the costume designer is a part of the solution, not a barrier to overcome. Does that mean you succumb to every request? No. There are times you will defend some decisions on artistic merit, but that is only effective if the director will support your

Figure 2.1 A working sketch communicating construction details.

Credit: Courtesy of Ayrika Johnson

position. In every case, however, it is important to establish a productive line of communication with the best version of the show in mind.

Working With Costume Makers

Costume designers work with a number of shops or makers and each will have their own way of doing things. Just as designers assess the best way to communicate with directors, they must also develop effective conversations with costume makers and vendors. Designers act as ambassadors representing the interests and goals of the director and the storytelling. Presenting the costume design in an exciting way is key to selling it. People will work harder on projects that interest them. Respecting their abilities and suggestions as well as asking for changes in diplomatic ways will help foster a productive work environment. Work rooms also appreciate clear communication about expectations and details, especially for made-to-order garments. While makers will work with anything provided – a sketch or a scribble – they appreciate visuals with specific details such as the research your design is inspired by, line drawings showing dressmaker details, or vintage garments to study. Many shops prefer to use copies of drawings *before* they are painted to see the details; finished sketches communicate the artistic intent of the final costume, but the original drawn lines indicate intent of construction.

Asking how a shop works and their areas of expertise will save a lot of missteps. Ask if each shop features specialty workers that could enhance your designs, such as leather working, embroidery, or hand knitting. The resident designer or a designer in a hyphenated job such as designer-shop manager will be more involved in fostering a work culture than guest designers. A productive work environment that positions your team for success will always encourage people to work their best. Devise a communication system so everyone understands the deadlines, workload, and recent changes. Creative workplaces thrive on transparency and a communal atmosphere that allows experimentation without the stigma of failure. In these cases, designer-managers must take time to study more formal management techniques.

Effective Critique

Working collaboratively does not mean that everyone agrees with the outcome. It *does* mean that every member of the team makes positive progress toward the same goal. It means respecting deadlines so that others can absorb the information and contribute the next round of work. It means really listening to others, discarding preconceived notions. Effective collaboration requires kind but honest feedback. Sometimes this means having to critique someone's work. Learning to have difficult conversations with grace is a large part of a costume designer's toolkit. One technique to steer critique is the **rule of three**. This technique ensures that you are talking *with* a person, not *at* them. Begin with a **declarative** statement that is a compliment:

how that person's work contributes successfully. "Your work shows delightful proportions!" Follow that with a **qualifier** statement: the critique of the element not meeting expectations. Express it as your opinion, ask questions, solicit solutions, and brainstorm. "The patch pockets are not working for me. Is it something about the placement, or maybe the size?" End with another **compliment** or hopeful statement about how well the project will turn out. "This dress is going to be perfect for our character!"[4] Sometimes the designer has to admit the colleague did what was asked, but the result is not going to work. That is the reason we invest time into mock-ups and fittings.

Steering Delicate Conversations With Collaborators

- **Assume good will**. Imagine the situation from that person's point of view. Creating performances requires every person to feel vulnerable and judged. They may say things poorly out of stress or fear, but their ideas may still be valid.
- **Find something to appreciate.** Is it their ideas, their working method, their gentle or funny personality?
- **Listen deeply**. Put feelings aside and commit to thinking about the discussion.
- **Ask questions**. Questions that help each other assess the *effectiveness* of a choice are productive.
- **Understand the role of** *quality*. Assess the craftsmanship used to create an item. Perhaps an idea is effective, but it was made badly. Would adjusting the quality save this costume?
- **Seek feedback**. Ask about items you may be debating to include them in the process. Everyone wants to know their contribution is appreciated.
- **Do not accept toxic or abusive behavior**. No one should tolerate bullying or allow it to continue.

Sizing Up Collaborative Creativity

Costume designers create shows in groups that do not always behave like other work groups. An understanding of the creative process itself can help the designer achieve effective collaboration. Designers use advanced communication skills to effectively work with the director, fellow designers, costume makers, and performers. To effectively communicate, designers assess and critique their own work and the work of others.

Expecting the Unexpected

Occasionally we will work with a nonverbal director who cannot describe what they wish to see for a show. This process effectively asks the creative team to present multiple ideas in what one designer termed "concept shopping." Costume designer Ann Hould-Ward (*Beauty and the Beast*) notes in such a situation

> I have to remind myself I will have to do a large amount of research. Then I'm going to have to really put it out there and see. I have to remember it's incredibly difficult for [the director] too. You just have to fish for it for a while.

Choreographer Lar Lubovich agrees, noting "It's incredibly hard to remain creatively fertile when you only hear rejection."[5] This situation may test a designer's mettle at first but may also result in an incredibly satisfying artistic experience, knowing that your contributions made a direct impact on the entire show.

Extra Resource

Rees, Bronwen. *Effective Communication Strategies for Designers*. Toptal Designers, undated. www.toptal.com/designers/product-design/effective-design-communication-strategies

Notes

1 Clear, James. 2016. "Creativity Is a Process, Not an Event." *Mission.org*, November 4, 2016. https://medium.com/the-mission/creativity-is-a-process-not-an-event-a41b632a83af.

2 Niles, Robert. 2019. "An Insider's Look into Walt Disney Imagineering's Design Process." *Theme Park Insider.com*, August 22, 2019. www.themeparkinsider.com/flume/201908/6962/.

3 Barsotti, Scott T. "Are Theater Artists Hardwired?" *Howlround Theater Commons*, October 19, 2015. https://howlround.com/are-theatre-artists-hardwired.

4 Albrecht, Karl. 2015. "Have Better Conversations with the 'Rule of Three.'" *Psychology Today*, November 12, 2015.

5 Hould-Ward, Ann and Lubovitch, Lar. 2021. "Global Perspectives and Artistic Practice." Live webcast April 9, 2021 at University of California, Irvine Department of Dance, Irvine CA.

3.
DESIGN ELEMENTS CREATE A PICTURE

Verbalizing a Visual Art

It is miraculous that humans gather visual information through two small spheres in our head, then send it to the brain for processing. Understanding how the brain sorts information helps designers arrange visual information with impact. Researchers describe the brain operating as a loop; it first forms a generalized schematic of the environment using categories – is the environment natural, rural, urban, neat, messy? The brain then adds information every few seconds, populating the general layout with objects that catch its attention; this system is called **orientation attention**. The brain pours more energy into later loops only when it encounters interesting features: this is called **discovery attention**.[1] The brain switches rapidly back and forth between orientation and discovery attention to negotiate daily life. Humans evolved an advanced ability to detect repetition or patterns to make this complex looping system more efficient. The brain compares new information to learned patterns, adding memories, assumptions, hopes, or fears to form a meaning about the object. The more emotion associated with the pattern, the more rapidly it will be seen in detail. In other words, the brain tells itself a *story* about the observed item to add context. Visual elements, then, are strongly connected to our memories and emotions.

The brain converts new visual imagery using both pattern recognition and emotions. Artists organize visual information using time-tested visual rules called the *elements* and *principles of design*. The two categories work together like a cooking recipe. The **elements** are basic ingredients, such as protein or vegetables. The **principles** are the method of cooking those ingredients, such as grilling or poaching. How we combine the elements and the method of arranging them produces an intended effect. Eggs, flour, and sugar can create a baked sponge cake or fried churros. The elements and principles are useful tools for designers to **focus** their research, **shape** their designs, and **critique** their own work to make it better. For instance, costume designers often realize a costume "needs something" or a group of rented costumes aren't working together. Verbalizing what we see using the elements and principles is a reliable way to brainstorm solutions. Sharing a common vocabulary allows us to connect with the other designers and makers working on the costumes. The ability to analyze and verbalize what we see puts mastery of our art into our own hands.

When designers discuss visual goals using generally accepted terms and link their visual choices to elements in the script, their designs show more command. Justine Seymour, costume designer for the Netflix miniseries *Unorthodox*, advises "Always ask *why*, so you can support your ideas. . . . That is when you will be taken seriously."[2] Determining the visual priority for each design creates strong definition. Fashion designer Marc Jacobs explains

> For us, sometimes the silhouette is what drives the collection. Sometimes it's a mix of fabrics. Sometimes it's both. Sometimes it's the decorative

DOI: 10.4324/9781003015284-4

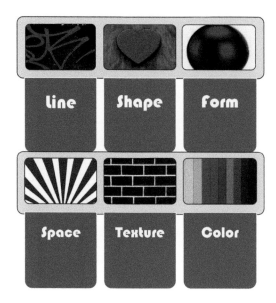

Figure 3.1 The elements of design.

Figure 3.2 This pastel sketch by Edgar Degas uses smooth and hatched line qualities, continuous and broken lines, to evoke light, shadow, and texture.

Credit: The Dancers, The Metropolitan Museum of Art, New York. Gift of George N. and Helen M. Richard, 1964. www.metmuseum.org

aspect . . . there's for us no rule as to what it has to be, but usually there is one or two over-riding approaches.[3]

Designers in every field manipulate the same formal design elements to create projects – graphics, installation art, animation. Costume designers also combine the elements to establish expressive or symbolic qualities that create characters and build a visual world. The six design elements are **line**, **shape**, **form**, **space**, **texture**, and **color**.

Qualities of Line

Costume designers use **line** or **edge** when drawing renderings or when creating garments. Line **quality** refers to the way an artist controls the drawn or painted stroke. We describe the qualities of line using terms of weight: thin and thick areas. Artists further divide lines into several aspects: **smooth** or **continuous** lines can be easily followed, defining a straight or curved direction. **Broken** or **hatched** lines create dashes providing textural effects. **Dynamic** lines change weight or direction; they appear to be more expressive. When these qualities are added together artists refer to lines and edges as **determinate** or **indeterminate**. Determinate edges are easy to comprehend; they are clearly

defined with strong lines. Indeterminate edges are difficult to comprehend; they are diffuse or soft.

Costume designers translate line on the human body three ways:

- The line of a garment
- Repeated lines form patterns
- Garment edges

Designers refer to the **line of a garment** as items that lead the eye in a direction, such as seams or trim lines. Line can also be part of the costume's print or pattern; a pinstripe suit presents a subtler presence than a large chalk stripe suit. Designers use determinate and indeterminate edges through trim or choice of fabric. Garments made of translucent fabrics such as chiffon create indeterminate edges, appearing somewhat ethereal. Another indeterminate line is a broken edge, such as that created by fur. Wild hair surrounding a character's face is composed of dynamic lines that change direction and quality, creating a sense of the unpredictable. Each variation of line carries connotations for character interpretation, as indicated in Table 3.1.

Defining the Body With Line

Garment lines contain **structural lines** – seams, darts, edges, and dressmaker details like pleats or tucks incorporated into the fabric – and **decorative** lines such as trim, scarves, belts, buttons, or other details (see Figure 5.10).

- **Vertical lines** directly lead the eye up and down, dividing the figure into smaller shapes that break up a larger shape. The body in Figure B appears narrower than Figure A.
- **Horizontal lines** stop the eye forming an emphasis. Figure A and Figure C are the same width, but Figure A appears wider.
- **Diagonal lines** provide more interest than vertical or horizontal lines. Figure D leads the eye more actively, making the figure appear taller and narrower.

Figure 3.3 This portrait of Charles 1 shows the cavalier silhouette popular in Europe during the 17th century. The ruff appears to elongate the neck, and the short doublet shape appears to minimize the torso and elongate the legs.

Credit: Daniël Mitjens, 1629. Metropolitan Museum of Art, New York. Gift of George A. Hearn, 1906. www.metmuseum.org

Qualities of Shape and Silhouette

Shape or **silhouette** makes an immediate impact for any design. Remembering that human sight depends on the brain creating a rough schematic before concentrating on details, shape is a key element audiences notice early. Animators use **shape language** as a foundation for characters, knowing that shapes trigger emotional responses.[4] Costume designers use shape to define the historical era, change the silhouette of a performer's body, and make character statements. Humans have been extremely ingenious throughout history in changing the appearance of the body using fashionable silhouettes.

The number of shapes is immense, so designers divide them into the overarching categories of **geometric** and **organic** shapes. Geometric shapes are composed of straight lines or formed with regular rules. We associate these with formality, order, efficiency, predictability; they are scientific and unemotional. Organic shapes appear in nature

and are perceived as creative, irregular, evocative, informal, or emotional.

Costume designers work with shapes in every fitting; all bodies are a delightful collection of shapes that make each actor unique. Every aspect of the human body may be round, square, rectangular, triangular, hourglass, or pear shaped. Part of the challenge for each character is incorporating the given shapes of the performer's body with the desired shapes of a character. Just as designers may add a wig or facial hair to create a character, so might they manipulate the appearance of a specific body part to define a character. A superhero character, for instance, may benefit from the appearance of a top-heavy triangular shape, as if

Table 3.1 Types of Line Quality

Line Style	Path or Direction	Weight or Width	Character Connotation	Effect on Human Figure
SMOOTH CONTINUOUS REGULAR LONG	Straight	Thin	Logical, orderly, mathematical, scientific, precise, elegant, reliable.	Adds interest or direction to figure.
		Thick	Strong, sturdy, reliable, power, forceful, assured, aggressive, traditional, ancient, formal, rigid.	Creates emphasis or focus, calls attention to itself. Modern, graphic, or cartoonish.
	Curved	Thin	Softness, flexibility or fluidity, graceful, sophistication, elegance, relaxation, beauty, less predictable.	More subtle effect, allows repetition for harmonious design, elegant.
		Thick	Deliberate, ornamental, sophisticated.	Creates focus, calls attention to itself, bold, modern.
	Dynamic	Thin	Interest, excitement, tension filled, expressive, informal, crooked.	More subtle effect, allows repetition for emphasis, too many creates confusion.
		Thick		Creates focus, calls attention to itself, bold, modern. Breaks shapes into irregular areas, disguise.
	Horizontal	Thin Thick	Eternal, quiet, restful, harmonious, solid, earthy.	Cuts areas into smaller horizontal proportions, shortens, accentuates width.
	Vertical	Thin Thick	Strength, security, create upward movement, expansive height, majestic.	Cuts areas into smaller vertical proportions, elongates and narrows.
	Diagonal Zig Zag	Thin	Unbalanced, restless, dramatic, active, unstable, exciting, creates tension, unpredictable.	Cuts areas into smaller shapes, jagged, unpredictable.
		Thick		Creates focus, calls attention to itself, bold, modern.
BROKEN HATCHED SHORT	Linear	Parallel short lines	Repetition creates pattern or motifs.	Scientific, mechanical, affects a color surface.
	Cross Hatch	Perpendicular	Repetition creates pattern or motifs.	Scientific or mechanical, used as shading in graphics.
	Irregular	Jagged	Creates unpredictable, tossed motifs or pattern.	Diverts attention from the area used, hides volume.

Figure 3.4 Geometric pattern (left) and organic pattern (right).

Credit: Courtesy of the Public Domain Review. Fruit pattern by William Morris. Image by rawpixel.com

they could bear the burden of extreme responsibility on their shoulders. An innocent character may benefit from rounded shapes to imitate children or puppies, evoking that sense of cuteness. A designer may choose to use straight or long shapes for a character who is rigid or severe.

Defining the Body With Shape

Costume designers use shapes to define characters. Silhouettes carry a strong impact for elongating, shortening, or communicating nonverbal messages (see Figure 3.5).

- **Rectangle.** Eliminates adult gender characteristics such as bust, waist and hips. Focal point neck, face, and legs. Signifies youth, or solidity.
- **T shape.** Accents shoulders, offsets wide hips, eliminates waist emphasis, signifies strength, power.

- **Wedge.** Enlarges shoulders, eliminates waist, hips.
- **Blouson or kimono.** Enlarges top of body, widens or eliminates the waist. Focal point hips or upper torso. Softer shape than T shape or wedge. Signifies maturity.
- **A line.** Enlarges hem of garment, drawing the eye down or up toward the face. Features shoulders, eliminates waist and hips. Focal point face or hem. Signifies freedom, ease. If used as a skirt, features small waist and softens hips.
- **Sheath.** Follows the figure, emphasizes the most dominant feature of the body. Signifies sensuality or allure.
- **X shape.** Features wide shoulders and skirt hem, emphasizes waist. Signifies power of female form.
- **Drop waist.** Eliminates the waist and thighs. Adds volume to the entire figure. Focal point hips.

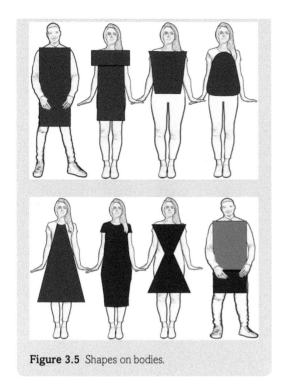

Figure 3.5 Shapes on bodies.

Qualities of Form and Volume

Form and **volume** are three-dimensional, representing the amount of space an object occupies. Like shapes, volumes are categorized with organic and geometric origins; they are regular or irregular, formal or informal. A Greek column is a formal volume; it is regularized and appears to follow mathematical pattern rules. A sculpture made of found objects appears informal, or not adhering to rational rules. Costume designers consider volume when each character turns in space, manipulating how the garment looks from all sides. The audience can rarely compare all sides at once, so managing volume gives the costume designer an element of surprise. Does the back of a costume portray different information than the front, as if the character were putting on a façade or hiding something?

Remembering the brain engages **orientation vision** first, the audience will first judge the **volume** of a character compared to their environment to make sense of everything it sees. An expansive character often has more power or status, while those who appear smaller are less powerful. There are noteworthy exceptions to this rule, such as the mid-19th-century crinoline cage skirt fashionable just as society dictated women's retreat to the domestic sphere only. Even though they and the cult of femininity occupied great space, large skirts and strict manners restricted their ability to perform well in the public sphere, turning women into ornamental objects. The exact location on the body that a large or small volume falls is important; it can add interest, humor, or surprise. A garment made of hard, geometric volumes piques interest by contrasting with the softer human form.

Using Space in Storytelling

The scenic environment may combine abstract two-dimensional elements with three-dimensional elements to create the performance space. Human vision distinguishes between flat objects and dimensional objects easily with the brain focusing on a three-dimensional object first. Performers are automatically part of the three-dimensional space; the brain finds people much more worthy of study than a flat surface next to or behind them. The brain compares a human to the space it occupies for context. The brain tells itself one story about small humans in large spaces: for instance, people may take up an insignificant space within a larger one like a cathedral. We think the opposite about large humans in tiny spaces, wondering if they dominate or if the situation is comical or suffocating. Designers arrange objects in a dimensional environment in another way using **positive** and **negative** space. Positive space is the main focal point of an image (such as an actor) and negative space is everywhere else. Both aspects of space can be manipulated within any composition to create focus. Negative space throws focus on the main figure by retreating into background, but sometimes the negative space is interesting on its own, gaining focus. Positive and negative space in costume design is most often visible when we look at the *garment* as one type of space and the amount

Figure 3.6 This bustle dress displays different qualities on the formal beaded front than on the softly draped back.
Credit: Dress by Mrs. K.B. McComb, Courtesy of the Metropolitan Museum of Art, New York. Gift of Mrs. Francis M. Brennan, 1975.
www.metmuseum.org

Figure 3.7 The figures in this ancient Syrian cylinder seal show clothing abstracted into interesting volumes.
Credit: Artist unknown, Metropolitan Museum of Art New York. Gift of Martin and Sarah Cherkasky, 1988. www.metmuseum.org

of *revealed skin* as its opposite. An evening gown revealing skin through the shape of its neckline or cutouts in the torso will show an interplay of positive and negative space. Which is perceived as positive space will depend on the contrast of colors between gown and skin. (See Figure 3.9)

Don't Touch That! The Qualities of Texture

Have you ever seen something so unpleasant that you were physically repulsed without even touching it? Humans make those snap judgments based on stored memories, pattern recognition, and the primal desire to avoid harm. Texture is the feel or appearance of a surface. People perceive texture in two ways – **tactile**, or that which we can feel if blindfolded, and **implied** or **visual**, that we see with our eyes but cannot feel. We associate these faux textures with something we have felt in the past or we imagine what it *might* feel like. Entertainment designers must master both tactile and implied texture. We combine real textures with faux effects to direct what the audience sees. Costume designers work under stage or film light, which flattens textures and adds different qualities. We use tricks such as over-painting to enhance textures or deepen the contrast between elements. When encountering a new texture, we make rapid distinctions whether it is a **natural** or **manufactured** element. Natural textures always display some slight variations or imperfections, conveying a sense of familiarity. Manufactured textures are static and systematic. They display a rigid uniformity not possible in nature.

The Interplay of Light and Surface

Have you ever noticed at dusk when the light fades, your vision interprets everything as a dull color and surfaces look flatter? Dim light affects our ability to see color and depth perception. The same is true when we use only our peripheral vision – we will clearly catch movement, but colors reduce dramatically, making it difficult to distinguish between similar hues such as red, orange, or yellow. Light is the key ingredient to see texture and color clearly, using three intersections – the **light source**, the

Figure 3.8 The back of this dress uses positive and negative space to create interest.

Credit: Photo by Jake Melara on Unsplash.com

Figure 3.9 The natural texture of drying mud shows natural irregularities (left). The manufactured surface of this building is rigidly uniform (right).

Credit: Photo courtesy of the author (left); Selfridges, Birmingham. Photo by Steve Cadman. Licensed under CC BY-SA 2.0. https://www.flickr.com/photos/98115025@N00/49908616 (right)

surface itself, and the **light receiver** – our eyes or a camera. Light from a source must bounce off the surface and into our eyes for us to see an object fully. If the angle of bounced light misses our light or color receptors (rods and cones) the details blur. Figure 3.10 shows this relationship.

Just as with edges, surfaces and textures may be **determinate**, that is, clear to see and easy to comprehend, or they may be **indeterminate**, indistinct or partly hidden. Figure 3.11 shows a building wrapped in fog that filters light and therefore much of the color or texture information we rely upon for quick assessments. This uncertainty makes us feel unsettled and we may interpret it as spooky, reflecting discomfort with hidden information. Our evolutionary instincts suspect it might be dangerous because anything could hide there. We may also find it mysterious and beautiful. The ballerina in Figure 3.12 wears a tutu that also displays an indeterminate surface. We detect the shape but much of the detail is lost to us. Our brain supplies context from memories, telling itself a story that we might find the ballerina ethereal or sublime, not threatening.

Visual theorists classify textures in categories using reaction to light as the major identifier. The first category is **reflection**: a smooth texture surface such as satin fabric bounces light directly into the eye. The smoother the surface, the more light waves bounce off. The angle of the light source, the surface, and the eye must align, otherwise even the shiniest object – beads or sequins – will be as visible onstage. More than one costume designer has spent countless labor hours attaching sequins to costumes only to lose the effect in dim, ambient lighting. Figure 3.13 demonstrates that only the

Figure 3.11 Building in fog, displaying indeterminate surface.

Credit: Buenos Aires Fog by Matito is licensed under CC BY-SA 2.0. https://www.flickr.com/photos/42348675@N00/544516403

sequins in the correct position bounce light into our eyes. The other sequins vanish in the shadows. Few things in nature are truly reflective, such as water and some minerals that form in crystals.

A slightly rougher surface will bounce light with a scattered array. We call this **diffuse** light. This is more common in nature and can be found where there is oil content such as pearls, fur, human hair, and feathers to name a few examples. We call this effect **luster**. Light scatters off the surface with some light directly hitting the eye, but most will be slightly offset. Humans detect the subtle distinctions in light on the surface. Heavy textures with deeper surface crevices create small shadows identified by our depth perception, which catches our interest.

Light waves pass through some surfaces, bending in a new direction called **refraction**. These semi-clear surfaces are termed **translucent**, and

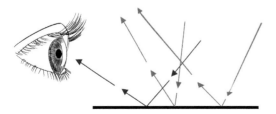

Figure 3.10 Light directly entering the eye will be detected clearly. Light missing the receptors in our retina will be seen less clearly.

Figure 3.12 Ballerina Pavlova, tutu displaying indeterminate surface.

Credit: Anna Pavlova in the Fokine/Aaint-Saens *The Dying Swan*, St. Petersburg, 1905. Wikimedia Commons

Figure 3.13 Light bounces off reflective surfaces such as green sequins. The sequins whose light waves connect directly with our eyes are visible, the others are shadowed.

Credit: Photo by Karolina Grabowska from Pexels

they appear to softly glow when in contact with light. Thin fabrics such as chiffon, lace, or organza display this quality. The clearest surfaces are **transparent**, with light passing through them. This is a refined or manufactured effect, as few things in nature are this transparent. **Matte** surfaces trap light using pigment color to absorb it or texture to redirect light waves. The most absorbent surfaces feature a special surface, such as velvet, with individual yarns standing on end to deflect and trap light. (See Figure 3.15) We see highlights where directional light bounces back to our eyes, but areas with trapped light hide the surface texture.

Designers manipulate color and texture together to affect what an audience sees. A smooth-textured surface will make a color appear brighter, and a rougher texture will soften the color, adding shadow effects. Colors affected by texture this way are sometimes termed ***broken*** colors. (See Figure 3.17) Textures have physical loft or presence and

can be used to sharpen or blur the edges of the human body. Rougher textures soften the body, making those surfaces and edges appear indeterminate. The roughest textures, such as fur, completely obscure or extend the edges of the body, functioning as an artificial silhouette. Smooth, lustrous, or shiny surfaces feature the contours of body parts, as seen in fitness gurus encased in thick spandex. Medium or average surface textures are more neutral, emphasizing the color of the surface and defining edges fairly clearly. Much of menswear wool suiting falls into this category.

The Psychology of Texture

Textures exert a powerful effect on human psychology. Designers manipulate this reaction to create feelings about characters. Josh Ackerman, an evolutionary psychologist at MIT, researched how

Figure 3.14 The smooth surface of pearls creates a soft luster. Light shines from the longest hairs of the fur hats also creating luster. A rougher surface like a wool suit diffuses the light so we detect no shine.

Credit: Pearl photo by Kat Smith from Pexels; *Fur Hats 63619* by Public Domain Photos is licensed under CC BY 2.0; *Club Monaco Wool Suit* by HousingWorksPhotos is licensed under CC BY-SA 2.0

surface qualities affect people's judgments toward objects and even other people. Touching a rough or rigid texture was associated with judging situations or people more harshly. Negotiators sitting in hard chairs were more severe in their opinions and less willing to compromise. Sitting in pliable and warmer chairs softened their stances. Hard surfaces are uncomfortable for humans, but we also rely on their strength and sturdiness for tools and building materials. Hard textures signify an unyielding or resolute nature, but also utilitarian and reliable. Ackerman noted that warmth can raise our empathy level, demonstrating that people

holding warm drinks tended to rate interactions with other people as more friendly. Warmth was also found to alleviate feelings of loneliness. This effect, however, is most powerful when people are not aware of it. "If you pay attention . . . your mind will overrule it," Ackerman says.[5] Designers use this knowledge to craft a level of empathy for characters: one wearing severe, hard clothing will be less liked than one wearing clothing with softer surfaces, such as a cozy sweater. Psychologists have found when people are sad or depressed, they seek warm or fuzzy textures for comfort. Furry or fuzzy textures can also bring relaxation. Psychologists

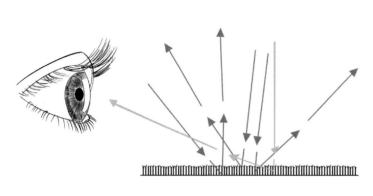 

Figure 3.15 Matte surfaces such as velvet absorb and redirect light waves (left). This velvet waistcoat appears dark where it absorbs the light (right).

Credit: Evening Vest, Courtesy of the Brooklyn Museum Collection at the Metropolitan Museum of Art. Gift of the Brooklyn Museum, 2009. Gift of Mrs. Thomas O. Callender, 1948. www.metmuseum.org

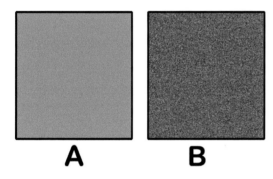

Figure 3.16 Figure A shows a plain color with smooth surface. Figure B shows the same color with added texture. The color in Figure B appears darker. This is termed a *broken* color.

identified one of the most important textures for humans is shiny surfaces, linking this to the importance of finding water as we evolved.[6] We associate feelings of ease, abundance, or wealth with this texture. Too much shine can tip the balance and we find it excessive or showy. A soft sheen is comforting to humans, equating lustrous textures to pleasurable feelings. Plain gold has a luster, not a mirrored shine; we associate this texture with subdued good taste.

Crisp textures such as starched cotton evoke efficiency or excitement or being ready for adventure. Many uniforms are made of starchy fabrics

making us think of discipline and competence. Crunchy textures are associated with frustration, stress, resentment, or anger. Anyone who has ever craved a bag of chips while under stress knows we can derail our anxiety by crunching food. We associate roughness with rustic or unfinished qualities. A rough fabric can feel irritating to wear, constantly pricking the skin. We also associate rough surfaces with animals and primal behaviors. But they can also bring surprise or humor. Michele Clapton, the *Game of Thrones* costume designer, employed a number of rough surfaces to hint at the animalistic nature of the characters. The rougher or wilder the fur, the more we associate that character with animal behaviors. Refined furs make us think of tamer animals whose wilder tendencies are hidden below the surface.

Sizing Up the Design Elements

This chapter examined six of the seven elements of the designer's visual vocabulary: **value, line or edge, shape or silhouette, form or volume, space**, and **texture**. Just as a chef invests time and energy learning everything they can about the ingredients in their recipes, the designer will also gain expertise by observing and reading more about design elements. The final element, **color**, is so powerful the next chapter is devoted to exploring its uses in costume design.

Expecting the Unexpected

Costume designers frequently face the challenge of blending costumes from many sources: custom built, purchased, stock, and rental items. It can be a true dilemma to unpack boxes of rental costumes only to realize they are not as visually compatible with the other costumes as hoped. A command of design elements can assist the designer to verbalize and target the problem areas. For instance, it may be possible to add a common design element to many of the costumes to unify them, such as the focal point of white collars, or the same color trim along key edges. The designer can brainstorm many solutions once the problem is defined in artistic terms.

Extra Resource

Visual Design in Dress, Marian L. Davis, 3rd ed., 1996. Although this book is dated, it has never been surpassed in its complete discussion of applying the elements and principles of design to clothing design. For the designer who would like more practice in this arena, begin here.

Notes

1 Burmester Alex. November 5, 2015. "How Do Our Brains Reconstruct the Visual World?" *The Conversaion.com.* Accessed May 16, 2020. https://theconversation.com/how-do-our-brains-reconstruct-the-visual-world-49276.

2 Seymour, Justine. "Costume Design Salon, Design Showcase West." *Webcast*, June 27, 2021. https://www.facebook.com/uclatft/?epa=SEARCH_BOX.

3 Jacobs, Marc. n.d. "Creating Shapes and Silhouettes." Accessed May 3, 2020. https://www.masterclass.com/classes/marc-jacobs-teaches-fashion-design/chapters/creating-shapes-and-silhouettes#

4 Walt Disney Family Museum. n.d. "Tips & Techniques Shape Language." Accessed June 10, 2021. https://www.waltdisney.org/sites/default/files/2020-04/T%26T_ShapeLang_v9.pdf.

5 Chillot, Rick. Last reviewed June 9, 2016. "Surface Impact." Accessed May 5, 2020. https://www.psychologytoday.com/us/articles/201303/surface-impact.

6 Jaffe, Eric. January 21, 2014. "An Evolutionary Theory for Why you Love Glossy Things." Accessed June 3, 2020. https://www.fastcompany.com/3024766/an-evolutionary-theory-for-why-you-love-glossy-things

4.
COLOR CREATES EMOTIONS

One of the best ways to take design skills to the next level is mastering the art of color. Color is the most complex and evocative of the art elements. Many designers report this is the design element they spend the most time and energy perfecting: choosing a color scheme with the correct impact, shifting dye colors to match that scheme, or adjusting garment colors to the desired effect on stage. The impact of color is so important that sports psychologists discovered wearing the color red will tip the balance among equally skilled athletes: more than 60% of hard-fought matches are won by competitors wearing red.[1]

If It's Purple, Someone's Gonna Die

In her book with this title, colorist Patti Bellantoni documents experiments she created over 25 years with art and film students called *color day*. Each day students wore and brought items to class that evoked a chosen color, such as red, blue, orange, purple. Each color day the same students behaved differently as a group. On red day, the class was emotionally volatile, but blue day was calm. Bellantoni not only documented these reactions, but went on to apply these discoveries to the use of color in popular films. This book is a comprehensive study of the nonverbal information we receive from color. It is a wonderful resource for designers who want to study the use of color.

The human eye can potentially see roughly one million different colors – much more than we have a vocabulary of names to describe them.[2] Today's plethora of color names is the result of 18th- and 19th-century studies into pigments for the textiles industry. Adding to the complexity of color, no two people see colors the same. Our physical ability is dictated by the number of rods and cones in our eyes. Additional social and cultural norms attach meanings to colors. While some people cannot see certain colors or are color blind, others have more than the usual number of receptors. Many artists may have more color sensitivity naturally but have certainly consciously trained to see more colors than average people. And yet, even with advanced training, color is one of the most difficult things to match by memory. With all this confusion surrounding color, the most reliable way to choose, communicate, and remember color is to use color swatches and approach every color discussion as if it were a session at the United Nations – admit everyone uses a different language and carefully define your terminology. Each designer has a personal relationship with color; some get a sense of the color palette for a project first, while others carefully control those choices after much thought. All designers have strong opinions about the use of color. They learn to direct the eye with color and to affect emotional response toward a character.

DOI: 10.4324/9781003015284-5

The Vocabulary of Color

Everyone is familiar with the idea of a **color wheel** – arranging colors in a circle to illustrate how they relate to each other. Color theorists have identified four aspects used to quantify the qualities of every color:

- **Hue** – the technical term for color created by pigment or light
- **Intensity**, or saturation – the purity or density of pigments used to create a color
- **Value** – the lightness or darkness of a color
- **Temperature** – the warmth or coolness of a color

Understanding these four qualities of a color enables the designer to choose and adjust their colors in controlled and sophisticated ways to achieve a result.

What Hue See Is What You Get

We use the term **hue** to denote where each color falls on the light or pigment spectrum. Technically, items do not contain color; they contain chemicals we call pigments. When light hits that object, some of the chemicals absorb certain light waves and others are rejected, bouncing back to our eye. The bounced-back color is what the human eye sees as color. Since pigment absorbs some light waves, pigment color systems are termed **subtractive** color. Many industrialized societies use about 11 basic categories for basic colors: black, white, red, green, yellow, blue, brown, orange, pink, purple, and gray.[3] Those with an interest or training in color apply fanciful names to variants of each hue, such as *rose*, *magenta*, *baby pink*. Although *hue* is the correct term, most of the time designers use the more general term *color* until it is time to have a detailed conversation with a fellow designer, painter, or dyer.

Intensity and Saturation

Intensity, or **saturation**, refers to the purity of a color or how much pigment is present in the mix. More pigment and the purity of that pigment results in more vivid or saturated hues. For example, mixing a large amount of paint with very little water will result in a dense, saturated version of that color. If that color were laid on paper, very little or no paper shows through. The same paint mixed with a lot of water looks more translucent; it is lower saturation. If that color were laid on paper, more of the paper background shows through. (See Figure 4.1.)

Intensity describes the purity of the pigment, or if there are other colors mixed in with a hue. The eye focuses first on objects with high color intensity. Pigments used with high intensity or saturation make an object appear larger and move it forward in our depth of field. (See Figure 4.2.) Designers can use saturation or intensity to create focus or emphasize a leading character, for instance, while background characters wear desaturated colors. This is a common color scheme used in large crowd scenes on stage or screen. The next time you watch an epic film with hundreds of extras, study the designer's use of color saturation and value for background characters.

Figure 4.1 Mixing more water into watercolor paint reduces the intensity, or the amount of the pigment in the wash. The top of this brush stroke is high-saturation magenta and the lower part contains more water, creating a lower saturation magenta.

Value and Color Shifting

We use the terms **tint**, **tone**, and **shade** to describe where colors fall on a spectrum of light to dark: the **value** scale. Mixing a hue with white creates a **tint**, otherwise known as *pastel* variations. Mixing a hue with gray creates a **tone,** and adding black to a hue creates a **shade** (see Figure 4.3).

Designers discuss these alterations to colors often, usually lumping all the ways of making a

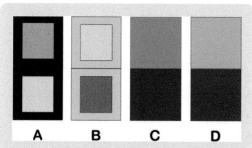

Figure 4.2 Intensity of colors.

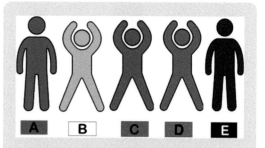

Saturation or Intensity and Human Vision

- Figure A shows that *light* saturated hues placed against a *dark* background advance the most, and pure yellow appears closest of all in our depth of field.
- Figure B shows that light saturated hues placed against a *light* background will recede toward the background or reduce focus. Light violet remains more forward in our depth of field than other hues.
- Figure C shows that low saturation or a tint reduces the apparent size of an object. Both blue squares are same size but the lighter one appears larger.
- Figure D shows that placing two colors of equal intensity next to each other will create the optical illusion of vibration or competing focus.[4]

Color Value and Human Vision

- Figure A shows a blue color or hue.
- Figure B adds white to create a tint or pastel version of blue.
- Figure C adds gray to create a tone of blue.
- Figure D shows another way to create the *tone* of a hue, that is, by adding *the opposite hue* on the color wheel to neutralize it. Many painters and dyers prefer this method, as it prevents a hue from becoming murky.
- Figure E adds black to create a shade of blue.

shade or tone into one term: *toning down*. Many designers will also use the term *desaturate* to mean any of these ways to shift a color. While technically desaturation refers to removing some pigment, it is rarely practical to remove an exact amount of pigment from fabric. Instead, costume designers often substitute shifting color value. One special technique appropriate for mixing colors in costumes is **glazing**, or layering different semi-transparent colors to create the final color. Leonardo Da Vinci was a master of this paint technique, using it to create some of his signature effects.[5] Costume designers use it not only for painting renderings but also in the way they manipulate fabrics. Fabric layering places a translucent fabric such as chiffon over a different colored base fabric. The color the audience sees is the blend of both colors, and the base fabric provides a lively shifting contrast, especially in movement. (See Figure 4.4.)

One last aspect of color value is the distinction between *muddy* and *clear* colors. A designer may want to muddle colors for a particular project, such as a chorus of peasants or background characters. We often use descriptive phrases to communicate this intent: such as wanting the characters' clothing to appear as though they had been washed in a muddy creek. To define that descriptive intent more precisely, the desired muddy colors could be *desaturated tones* and *shades*. In contrast, clear colors show more purity or *intensity*. Controlling the *value* of hues gives designers a sophisticated way to control the color palette onstage. Characters may wear different colors, but if they all share the same *value* they will still be perceived as a group. Designers may elect to emphasize one character, for instance, by using a lighter or darker value than

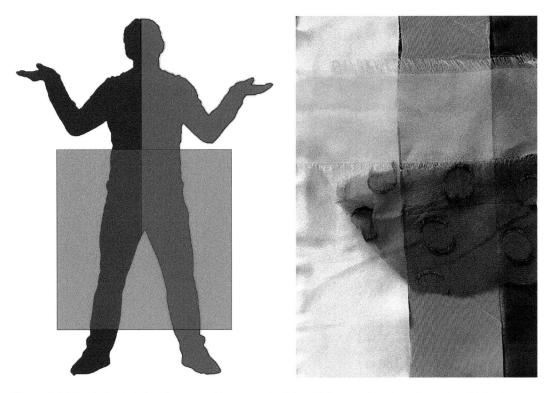

Figure 4.4 The glazing technique layers semi-transparent paint or fabric over a base layer to create a third color. Note that opposite colors such as green and orange neutralize each other.

the others. Some hues are naturally lighter than others, for example yellow is lighter than blue. Each hue, therefore, has an equivalent on the gray scale on its own. Understanding this relationship is informative for balancing pigments in a stage picture. For further information on color equivalencies on the gray scale, see the Extra Resources section.

Color Temperature

Color **temperature** refers to the relative coolness or warmth of a specific hue. Colors roughly divide into the **warm** category (yellow, red, orange, rust) or the **cool** category (blue, green). Some color theorists distinguish a **neutral** category – an equal mix of cool and warm colors that is useful for analyzing skin tones or custom dye mixtures (see Figure 4.5). An **undertone** is the secondary hue any mixed color displays, changing the character of that color. Seeing these slight variations in color takes practice by comparing colors to each other and verbalizing what we see. Cognitive

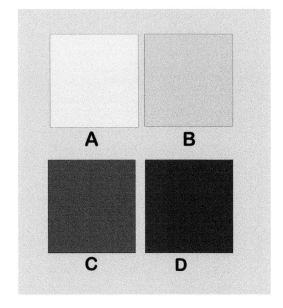

Figure 4.5 Figure A is a cooler yellow, with an undertone of blue. Figure B is a warmer yellow, with an orange undertone. Figure C is full intensity red, and Figure D is a neutralized brown with a red undertone.

scientists have noted a universal human tendency to communicate more efficiently about warmer colors than cool colors. They theorize language developed most about topics people wish to discuss and the things we want to talk about most are warm-colored, such as people, animals, and food. Backgrounds like grass, sky, and water tend to be cool colors.[6] Marketers and retailers research colors carefully to pinpoint consumer buying habits. Their research establishes that warm colors do indeed stimulate our metabolisms and slightly raise our body temperature. This data led many fast food restaurants to decorate primarily in yellow and orange tones, encouraging patrons to eat faster and leave sooner, creating a quick turnover of tables.

Undertones

Every color has an undertone or a secondary hue used to mix that color. When we step away from color theory to investigate how actual dyes and pigments are manufactured, we see that colors are complex mixes of pigment with dramatic undertones. This is particularly true for *black*, *gray*, *red*, *brown*, and *purple*. Take the example of black: color theory defines black as the absence of all light. Light waves are absorbed into a surface leaving little to bounce back to the human eye. Black pigment, therefore, is a mixture of *all* pigments to absorb all colors so that nothing bounces back to our eyes. Each dye and pigment formula for black, gray, brown, and purple is made differently; when used onstage, each will display very distinct undertones of the blue, yellow, green, or red used to mix it. Because of this, many artists think custom-mixed blacks are livelier and darker than the usual commercially available paints in tubes. Any costume designer who has tried to match tuxedo trousers and jackets from rental stock will see one garment, such as the jacket, displays reddish undertones under stage light while the trousers may glow with a greenish undertone. The resulting undertones make the outfit appear mis-matched, but in daylight they looked passable. An awareness of these undertones is a lively and subtle way to manage colors onstage. Two characters dressed in brown will evoke different emotional responses if one wears a cooler olive brown and one wears a warmer rust brown. It takes some practice to see undertones. The fastest way to practice this skill is sorting through brown fabric swatches. Sort them into groups with different undertones such as yellow-brown, red-brown, or green-brown.

Figure 4.6 These brown fabric swatches sort into subgroupings by undertone: neutral, red, green, orange, and yellow.

Defining Color Schemes

Designers take great pains to adjust single colors for costumes. But colors are rarely seen by themselves – they take on new meanings when juxtaposed with other colors to form a color scheme. Costume designers use the **pigment** or **subtractive** color wheel to quantify terminology for the ways paint or dye colors relate to each other. Figure 4.7 illustrates the traditional flat wheel used to name color relationships. All color schemes rely on some degree of contrast to define their relationship. Some color schemes are so fundamental we have given them specific names based on their relationships to each other. Three of the most common color schemes use hues opposite each other on the wheel, or **complementary** color schemes. These schemes use the highest amount of contrast between colors.

Each color scheme provides its own connotations and emotional impact. A primary color scheme can look vibrant, optimistic or childlike, or filled with energy. It can also lend quick identification, for example the color schemes used in athletic uniforms. There are many more color schemes that designers choose. (See the Extra Resources section.)

- **Monochromatic**. One major hue and its tints, tones, and shades; a low-contrast color scheme that evokes peaceful feelings or dull, unchallenging.
- **Analogous**. One major hue and the colors next to it on the color wheel in any or both directions; a low-contrast color scheme that adds interest to a tight color scheme.
- **Split complementary**. One major hue and the two colors across the wheel; a high-contrast color scheme that evokes excitement.
- **Triadic.** Any color scheme that uses three colors evenly spaced around the wheel; a high-contrast color scheme that evokes excitement.
- **Quadratic or tetradic**. Any color scheme that uses four colors as two complementary pairs; a high-contrast color scheme that evokes interest or excitement.

We rarely use color schemes in their simplest forms as seen on the color wheel. Many costume designers combine any complement-based color scheme with a monochromatic or analogous one to expand the allowable colors onstage. In other words, not using

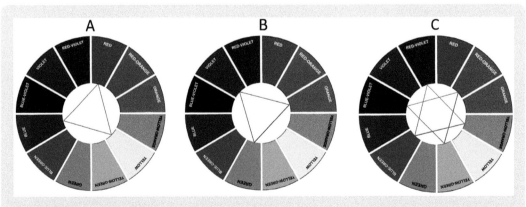

Figure 4.7 Color wheels combined

Complementary Colors on the Pigment Color Wheel

- Wheel A designates three pigments as **primary** colors: red, yellow, and blue. Using these colors is called a primary color scheme.
- Wheel B names three **secondary** colors, located at the midway point between two primaries: green, orange, and violet. Using these colors is a secondary color scheme.
- Wheel C shows six **tertiary** colors: a blend of the hues on either side of it. A typical tertiary color scheme uses red-orange, red-violet, blue-violet, blue-green, yellow-green, and yellow-orange.

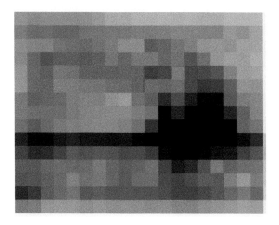

Figure 4.8 *Most* of the hues in this composition are low value or grayed versions of blue and violet. This unifies the color scheme. *Some* colors are complementary – orange, yellow, and green. This adds interest. The *least* amount of high value colors adds focal points or accents: orange, magenta, and black.

just blue, but adding all its monochromatic tints and shades for variety. Artist Marc Chagall summed up this practice as "All colors are the friends of their neighbors and the lovers of their opposites."[7] There are a number of websites that allow a designer to experiment, mix, and share color schemes before deciding on a final approach (see the Extra Resources section). Some designers use a rule of thumb to control a color scheme using the rule of **most**, **some**, **least**. For example, unify *most* of the colors with the same value, intensity, and temperature, most of the colors are warm or cool or bright or desaturated. Add s*ome* colors that contrast in some way to the first rule so the composition isn't flat. Last and also *least*, add small amounts of high contrast color to scatter around as an accent. (See Figure 4.8)

The Truth About Color Wheels

Everyone is familiar with the pigment or subtractive color wheel learned as children, seen in Figure 4.7. But that color system is not as useful of a guide for professional color users. As everyone soon discovers, it does not hold true when mixing pigment colors, other than operating as a vague roadmap. It also does not illustrate how designers really use color. The more complete color wheel

– the **partitive** wheel – is worth closer examination for designers. It was developed by Albert Munsell in the early 1900s using scientific testing of vision. He noted when people stared at a saturated color and then glanced away, the eye filled in another color, an **afterimage** caused by fatigue in the retina. Using this method, he did away with the idea of primary colors, instead identifying five colors as **principle colors**: **red**, **green**, **yellow**, **blue**, and **violet**. (See Figure 4.9.) He designated the afterimage color obtained from each principle color as it's opposite on the color wheel. These **secondary** colors are **magenta**, **orange**, **blue-violet**, **blue-green**, and **yellow-green**. In other words, the five primaries don't pair with each other across the color wheel. Each pairs with its own afterimage across the color wheel. This system is much more accurate in predicting color mixes, resulting in a notation system that is easy to communicate to others. It also creates a more expansive use of colors that work with human vision. Munsell further extended the two-dimensional color wheel into a three-dimensional form to correlate how designers vary color using neutrals, tints, tones, and shades. His work resulted in a three-dimensional color graphic and a large system called a Munsell tree (Figure 4.10, left). For more information on the Munsell Color System, visit Munsell.com.

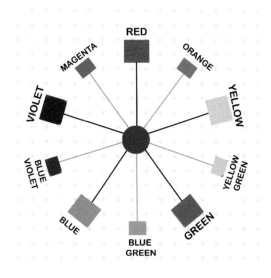

Figure 4.9 The Munsell or partitive color wheel.

 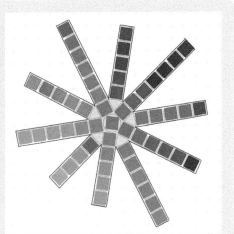

Figure 4.10 Munsell tree (left); Munsell shades (right).
Credit: © Science Museum Group, London (left)

The Munsell tree uses a 3-D representation of how artists use color. It uses an X–Y axis graph to record a pure hue in three dimensions or attributes: **hue**, **value**, and **intensity** or saturation.

- The vertical Y axis or inner trunk of the "tree" represents the **value** of the hue, recording each hue on the inside center, or point 0.
- Moving **up** the Y axis from point 0 shifts the value up on the gray scale, creating tints, or adding steps of white to that hue.
- Moving **down** the Y axis from point 0 shifts the value down on the gray scale, creating shades or adding steps of black to that hue.
- The horizontal X axis, or rows radiating from the center, records the **intensity** or saturation of each hue. The most saturated hues are on the farthest edge from the trunk on any line, called a branch. Each branch of the tree is a different length, as each hue has slightly different properties.
- Moving outward from the trunk to the end of the branch saturates the hue. Moving toward the center trunk neutralizes the hue or desaturates it.
- The figure at right shows a bird's-eye view of hues radiating from the trunk to the edge, gaining more saturation or intensity.

The Munsell tree became the basis for a universal color notation system, making it possible to pinpoint a specific hue and its intensity anywhere on the tree by assigning numerical symbols. This categorization makes it possible to communicate color information and color matching. The Pantone® Color System, a company that publishes numerous color books and offers color services, uses this type of color system. These color books are a staple for designers to choose color schemes with the same value or intensity or to communicate colors to others. Pantone® colors, along with other similar color-numbering systems, are embedded as a color library in Photoshop and Illustrator. Pantone® is a standardized way to communicate color to collaborators who may be located in a different city, country, or across town. For example, if each person owns a Pantone® book, a designer can use the color number to tell a dyer the fabric should be dyed to that specific color. Even if the collaborator is in the same room, this system gives two people an excellent way to communicate more expertly.

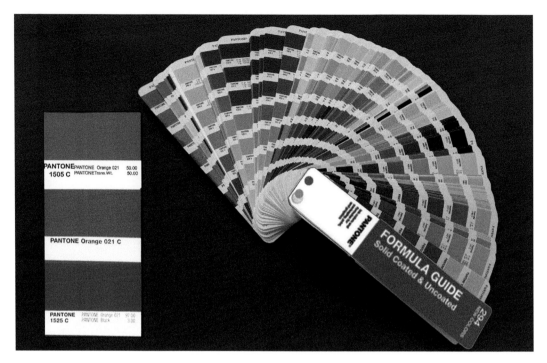

Figure 4.11 Pantone® products are organized into one collection for print products and another for fabric and general product design. The color chips are available in matte and glossy finishes. Use matte colors for textiles, except shiny fabrics. The inset shows a series of color formulas.

Defining the Body With Color

Designers are professional colorists, understanding not only how to manipulate color for impact in the stage picture but also to create effects for characters.

- **Monochromatic colors** present few obstacles to the eye, allowing it to move up and down the body uninterrupted, adding height, a sense of calm, and elegance (Figure A).
- **Analogous or tonal colors** achieve many of the same goals as the monochromatic, but may add more interest (Figure B).
- **Polychromatic colors** use more contrast, breaking up the body into smaller areas and presenting a number of focal points or obstacles to the eye. Creates a cheerful or trendy tone; may cause confusion for the eye and may disguise parts of the body (Figure C).

- **Intensity** creates a focal point leading the eye directly to the area of placement to flatter a feature or add height, such as the bright collarr (Figure D).
- **Simultaneous contrast** colors are opposite each other on the color wheel, forming a high contrast that exaggerates their differences. If one is warm and the other cool, the warmer color will create focus (Figure E).

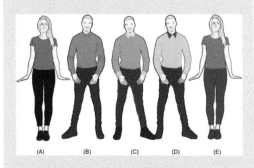

Figure 4.12 Silhouettes color scheme.

A Blaze of Glory: Costume Colors and Stage Light

Everything that costume designers create will be seen under some kind of light: stage light, film light, architectural light, ambient light, day light. Designers learn to anticipate or collaborate early and often with the lighting designer to create the final result. Four physical properties of light affect the way costumes appear on stage.

- **Intensity** or overall strength of the light source determines many other aspects of light. The mid-day sun is at full intensity, emitting the most light. Intense light flattens what we see, and low-intensity light dims the sense of color and texture.
- **Direction** is one of the most evocative features. Light shining on an object casts a shadow. The human brain needs shadows for depth perception, separating flat from dimensional objects. Bright light that eliminates shadows renders an object flat-looking and diminishes interesting textures. Shadows are an artistic tool, too, that define space and mood. A large space may be diminished by casting shadows. An important aspect of shadows is the angle of the light source; lower angles cast longer shadows. A too low angle may flatten the object it is illuminating or create specialty effects such as the footlight effect used in old horror films, lighting the figure from below. Much of the time, lighting designers employ multiple light angles from many sources to provide depth and to round out the appearance of the actor.
- **Quality** refers to the way the light itself appears.
  - *Soft light* is *diffused* or spread over a wide area, such as the way a sheer window curtain breaks up the direct light of the sun, spreading it in all directions. Shadows created by diffused light are soft and can be formless.
  - *Hard* light is sharp, creating distinct edges in the shadows of objects it illuminates.
  - *Textured* light is a combination of soft and hard, such as alternating with small shadows under a leafy tree. Lighting designers use a number of *gobos*, or a partial screen in front of the lens, to create many special light textures.
- **Color** of light is the most obvious property, and one that costume designers tend to notice first. Light color can be described using many of the same terms as pigment: *hue*, *saturation*, and *value* on the gray scale. However, light is **additive** color: mixing all colors of light results in the color white, not black like pigment. The light primaries of red, green, and blue when mixed will produce secondaries just like the visual or pigment color wheel. The light secondaries are cyan, magenta, and yellow.

It's not necessary for the costume designer to be able to mix colored light, but both lighting designers and costume designers must communicate with confidence about the final stage picture. Pigment and light colors will combine to create some very unexpected results. It is wise for both lighting and costume designers to understand the combination of colors that will *neutralize* each other, changing the color of the costume to gray or brown. This can be used intentionally to create a surprise reveal of color, but should be avoided other times (see Figure 4.13). If in doubt, conduct a rough test by shining a small flashlight through a sample gel book onto a fabric swatch (see Figure 4.14).

Sizing Up the Element of Color

This chapter explored the way designers think and communicate about color using universal terms to describe the qualities of color: hue, intensity or saturation, value on the gray scale, temperature, and undertones. Color wheels are a traditional method for choosing and understanding the relationship of colors used together in a stage picture or a costume.

Expecting the Unexpected

Dress rehearsals present a common color dilemma when the costume colors look very different under the stage lights. The combination of stage and surface color is tricky, and it is a normal and expected task to make adjustments in dress rehearsals. If it is early in the technical rehearsals stage, don't panic! Lighting designers often work in real time, lighting

| | LIGHT COLOR | | | | | | |
	BLUE	BLUE-GREEN	GREEN	YELLOW	ORANGE	RED	RED VIOLET
BLUE	BLUE	LIGHT BLUE-GREY	LIGHT BLUE	DARK BLUE-GRAY	BLACK	GRAY	BLUE
BLUE-GREEN	DARK BLUE	DK BLUE-GRAY	DARK GREEN	GREEN-BLUE	DK GREEN BROWN	BLACK	DARK BLUE
GREEN	OLIVE GREEN	LT GREEN GRAY	GREEN	BRIGHT GREEN	DARK GREEN	DARK GRAY	DK GREEN BROWN
YELLOW	GREEN-YELLOW	GREEN-YELLOW	GREEN-YELLOW	YELLOW	YELLOW-ORANGE	RED	DARK ORANGE
ORANGE	LT BROWN	LT BROWN	LT BROWN	ORANGE	ORANGE	ORANGE-RED	SCARLET
RED	PURPLE BLACK	DK MAROON	MAROON	RED	ORANGE-RED	RED	RED
RED VIOLET	DARK VIOLET	MAROON	VIOLET	LT BROWN	MAROON	RED-BROWN	VIOLET

(Left axis label: **PIGMENT COLOR**)

Figure 4.13 The effect of blending of light color and pigment color.[8]

Figure 4.14 Testing a fabric swatch by shining a small flashlight through a gel sample. Combining a cerulean blue light gel with a magenta fabric swatch produces a blue-violet result.

Figure 4.15 Saturated stage light affects the color of costumes. This orange dress neutralizes on one side under blue light, but yellow light on the other side creates interest.

Credit: Photo by cottonbro from Pexels

over the rehearsal and sometimes several steps behind the stage action. Save your early comments until the end of the rehearsal, unless the lighting designer asks your opinion while in the scene. At the end of rehearsal confer privately with the lighting designer. Don't make the decision to re-dye everything in the show based on the first rehearsal – once the lights are fully set, the costumes might once again appear incorrect. If you plan to re-dye or add to the aging, consult with the lighting designer first about what changes they will make. The most productive information you can tell a lighting designer is to note in which scene the costumes looked best or correct.

Extra Resources

Color Inspirations, Jeanette deJong, Routledge, 2021.

Color Studies, Edith Anderson Feisner, Fairchild Publications. There is no more comprehensive study of color theory than this guide.

If Its Purple, Someone's Gonna Die, Patti Bellantoni, Focal Press. A fascinating study of how color affects human emotions using examples in film.

Color Values in Grayscale Equivalents. Download a comparison chart from VectorStock www.vectorstock. com/royalty-free-vector/color-values-in-grayscale-equivalents-vector-1544368

Digital Color Scheme Finders

Adobe CC Color, a free color-scheme site, also available as a phone app to derive a color scheme from a photo

Print Magazine.com 51 Best Color Sites for Designers www.printmag.com/post/50-best-color-sites-graphic-designers

Stage Lighting and Pigments Roscoe Laboratories "How to Color Stage Lighting to Enhance the Color in Scenery, Costumes and MakeUp." https://hosting.iar.unicamp.br/lab/luz/ld/Diversos/maquiagem/Lights28.pdf

Notes

1 Williams, Cassidy. 2017. "Wear Red and You'll Win Gold." *Samford University Center for Sports Analytics*, October 23, 2017. https://www.samford.edu/sports-analytics/fans/2017/Wear-Red-and-Youll-Win-Gold.

2 Leong, Jennifer. 2006. "Waves and Optics." *The Physics Factbook and Encyclopedia of Scientific Essays*. Accessed June 30, 2020. https://hypertextbook.com/facts/2006/JenniferLeong.shtml.

3 Gibson, Ted and Conway, Bevil R. 2017. "The World Has Millions of Colors. Why Do We Only Name a Few?" *Smithsonian Magazine.com*, September 19, 2017. Accessed January 10, 2018. smithsonianmag.com/science-nature/why-different-languages-name-different-colors-180964945.

4 Feisner, Edith Anderson. 2001. *Color Studies*. New York: Fairchild Books, p. 52

5 Ibid., p. 54.

6 Gibson and Conway. "The World Has Millions of Colors."

7 Coelho, Paulo. 2021. "Chagall's Wisdom." *Paulo Coelho Stories & Reflections*. https://paulocoelhoblog.com/2014/05/07/character-of-the-week-marc-chagall/

8 Inspired by Fuchs, Theodore. 1963. *Stage Lighting*. Trenton, FL: Ayer Company Publishers and Feisner. Color Studies.

5.
DESIGN PRINCIPLES CREATE MEANING

What is a "good" or "bad" design composition? Are good designs beautiful, or at least satisfying to the eye? Costume designers use both pleasing and unsightly compositions to create characters that look appealing or unsettling. For designers, the better assessment is whether a composition is *effective* – does it create the intended outcome? An ineffective composition does not convey the intended message, although it may be beautiful. The last two chapters discussed the design *elements* and some of the ways costume designers use them to create compositions. As essential as the design elements are, designers do not apply them alone. All of the elements gain meaning through association with each other. The ways we combine design elements to create meaning are the **principles of design**.

Every source names slightly differing principles, even using different quantities such as seven, nine, or even 12 principles of design. This confusion reveals the power and importance of design principles. The nine principles costume designers use consistently are

- **Balance**
- **Contrast**
- **Emphasis**
- **Unity** or **Harmony**
- **Variation**
- **Movement** or **Direction**
- **Proportion**
- **Scale**
- **Repetition, Sequence,** and **Rhythm**

Costume designers use these principles to create compositions on the actor's body and also within the entire stage picture. They are a vital way to share a nonverbal language with an audience.

The Principle of Contrast

The human eye is very sensitive to contrast; it notices contrast before other qualities, and it is key to all the other principles. Every child who has played games of "what doesn't belong in the picture" is exercising that powerful connection between the eye and the brain. Every design element and principle may be contrasted with an opposing idea to create an effect, making this the most versatile of the visual tools. **High contrast** is stark, and it attracts our notice first: light vs dark, large vs small, smooth vs textured, straight vs round. Contrast creates interest

DOI: 10.4324/9781003015284-6

and **focal points** that command attention at the place where the highest contrast occurs. The traditional business suit is built on the principle of high contrast: the dark jacket and trousers contrasting with a white shirt focus our attention toward the face. High contrast lends authority to the wearer. **Low contrast** combinations do not capture our attention as easily and the eye glazes over details. They appear compliant or pleasant. Costume designers use degrees of contrast within a garment to create focus on a part of the body. They also do the opposite: use low or high contrast to disguise areas. Contrast is one of the most potent tools costume designers use to distinguish characters from each other. Wealthy characters may wear clothing that contrasts in every way with the poor characters; clean, well-fitted clothes made of delicate fabrics contrast with grubby, ill-fitting clothes made of sturdy, highly textured fabrics.

Figure 5.1 This portrait demonstrates the use of a high contrast focal point – the white collar juxtaposed with black coat and hair creates emphasis near the face.

Credit: Aman-Jean, Georges Seurat. Courtesy of the Metropolitan Museum, New York. Bequest of Stephen C. Clark, 1960. www.metmuseum.org

The Principle of Emphasis

The principle of **emphasis** uses any visual element to draw attention to a specific area of the composition. Designers steer the eye toward areas of the body to make a character statement, and they can use any element to achieve that goal.

- The brain will notice *positive* space before *negative* space.
- An item may be a focal point if placed in *isolation*.
- *Detailed* or more complete objects take priority over *indeterminate* or unfinished objects that appear to recede.
- *Saturated* colors create emphasis over *desaturated* colors.
- *Center placement* draws attention before the edges of a given space.
- *Convergence* is another type of placement that creates emphasis when lines or shapes lead the eye to a focal point. The converging lines of the farthingale skirt (Figure 5.9) lead our eyes to the waist.
- Humans naturally place priority on *faces* as the main locus of communication.
- Unusual or *unexpected* objects will create emphasis over a range of other similar objects.
- A strong *line* within a costume emphasizes the area of the body near it, for example trim on a neckline will bring focus to the skin beneath it. A diagonal line such as a military sash or baldric will call attention to the chest and shoulder.
- Adding *light* with beads and sequins creates focus.

Contrast and emphasis work hand-in-hand. The costume designer uses contrast and emphasis to create a hierarchy among characters, steering the audience eye to look within the stage picture. Emphasis is a vital part of visual storytelling, as the costume designer matches the intent and tone of a scene or script to the type of focus they provide. It might be useful for the designer to ask "If this were a film, would this scene be in close up, medium shot or long shot?" That answer provides an idea of what kind of focal placement serves the scene or story best.

Defining the Body With Emphasis

- **Top** emphasis places strong focus on the shoulders or near the face. Shoulders appear wider, balances hips, features the face (Figure A).
- **Middle** emphasis cuts the figure in half. Widens the waist and hips as well as adds focus there (Figure B).
- **Bottom** emphasis draws the eye downward, away from the face (Figure C).
- **Top and bottom** emphasis stops movement of the eyes, shortens the figure, draws attention away from the waist (Figure D).
- **Corsage** is unbalanced emphasis at either the top, middle, or bottom, adding interest and slightly elongating the figure. It emphasizes any feature near it (Figure E).

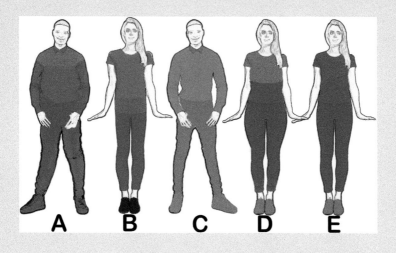

The Principle of Balance

Balance describes the **stability** between elements in a composition. Each element has visual weight: a vitality or force only evident when compared to other elements. In other words, some elements appear heavier, such as dark colors, while pastel colors appear lighter in weight. There are five common styles of balance that costume designers use frequently.

- **Symmetrical** or **formal** balance is found everywhere in nature. The sides of a formally balanced composition mirror each other across an imaginary centerline. Formal balance can be described as a ***rule of twos***: two halves create the whole balance. This balance is the most stable, evoking connotations of reliability,

durability; it is stationary and enduring. The human brain can process a symmetrically balanced composition quickly.

- **Asymmetrical** or **informal** balance requires more effort to determine its behavior or qualities. It can be lyrical and satisfying or abnormal and upsetting. Informal balance can be described as using the ***rule of three***: two objects in asymmetrical balance require a third visual element to achieve some kind of equanimity.
- **Unresolved** or **off-balance.** If a composition displays tension, it is **off-balance**. It can be intriguing or unsteady. Costume designers use the actor's body as a canvas and although everyone has some asymmetry to their features, our brains smooth out most inconsistencies. Extreme asymmetry in faces or

bodies garners our attention and can be used to create humor, empathy, or fear.

- **Radial** balance arranges elements in a circle, creating a strong focal point in the center. The Elizabethan ruff created radial balance around the head putting emphasis on the individual's ability to think, as befitted the Renaissance mindset of emerging humanism.
- **Color** or **tonal** balance. Individual colors appear to have visual weight; blue appears heavier than yellow. Costume designers balance color and tone within a garment and across the entire stage picture.

Figure 5.3 The top of this dress uses symmetrical balance: both sides are the same. The skirt uses asymmetrical balance: the hip drape balances the vertical embroidery on the right side of the skirt.

Credit: Wedding Ensemble, Herman Rossberg. Courtesy of Metropolitan Museum of Art, New York. Gift of Mrs. James G. Flockhart, 1968. www.metmuseum.org

The Principles of Scale and Proportion

Proportion and scale are closely related ideas. **Scale** compares the size of objects, ranking them by mass or importance; this is also called the **hierarchy principle**.

- A **larger** element will appear more important than a smaller one.
- A **bolder** element will appear more important than a delicate one, even if it is the smaller of the two.
- A **geometric** object may appear more important than an **organic** one because it is more easily assessed by the brain.

We judge the scale of an object in performance by comparing it to the size of the actor's body and by how much space it occupies on the stage. Scale affects our perception of depth or *perspective*. Larger

Figure 5.4 This painting demonstrates a tonal balance between blue and yellow. The dark blue work sleeves are small areas within the composition, but possess more visual weight or emphasis than the larger areas of yellow.

Credit: Jean-Francois Millet, *Woman with a Rake.* Gift of Stephen C. Clark, 1938, Metropolitan Museum of New York, www.metmuseum.org

Figure 5.5 Panier dress.

Credit: Dress, ca. 1750. Metropolitan Museum of Art, New York. Rogers Fund, 1936. www.metmuseum.org

Figure 5.6 The royal panier dress demonstrates larger scale than the ordinary dress of these peasants, who appear less imposing.

Credit: Peasants, Willem van de Velde. Courtesy of the Metropolitan Museum of Art, New York. Gift of Roys N. Brown, 1929. www.metmuseum.org

objects appear to be closer, while smaller objects appear to be farther away in the picture plane.

The principle of **proportion** compares the total size of an object to the size of its inner parts. We traditionally break the human body into proportions using head size as a measuring device. A realistic human is about seven and a half heads tall, while an exaggerated fashion figure is nine heads tall with severely elongated proportions. Even two people the same height may have very different proportions. One may have longer legs and a short torso, the other may have a long waist and short thighs. Generally speaking, legs make up about half of the body and hips, torso, and head comprise the other half. (See Figure 5.7.)

Western art uses an ideal proportion developed by the ancient Greeks called the **golden mean**. Contemporary mathematicians discovered that this set of proportions also explains many formations found in nature; they call it the **Fibonacci sequence**. These are powerful tools worth further study (see the Extra Resources section). The golden mean is any shape with the proportions of 1 to 1.618. For fashion and the human body, it translates to dividing the body into one section two-fifths of the whole and a second section of three-fifths. In other words, the most pleasing proportions divide a shape just **off** center. This was used to great effect in the 1930s to create a **glamour line** that appeared to elongate the legs and shorten the waist.

Ideas of pleasing proportions are subject to personal preference, passing fashion, and cultural ideals. Many fashions shifted ideal body proportions through either optical illusion or actually pushing and padding the body. Korean hanbok is an excellent example of ideal proportions created through layering many garments; the skirts form a wide bell shape and the visual waistline is raised to shorten the torso. An Elizabethan gown used padding and understructures to create a large skirt. But Elizabethans found the most pleasing proportion was an elongated torso accentuated by an exaggerated bodice that dips low in the front. Understanding the proportions of historical and cultural costume is a key factor in reproducing them for the stage.

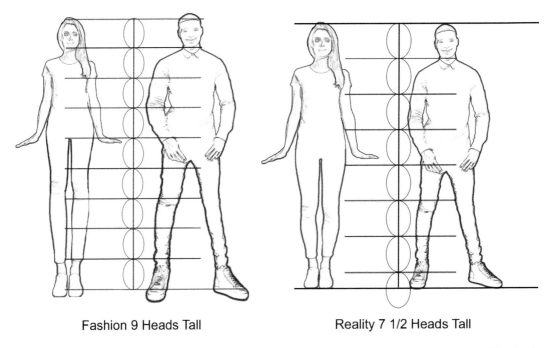

Fashion 9 Heads Tall   Reality 7 1/2 Heads Tall

Figure 5.7 An exaggerated fashion figure may be nine heads tall, whereas average person is seven and a half heads tall.

Figure 5.8 The golden mean divides the body just off center. This proportion was used to great effect in the 1930s to create glamourous proportions.

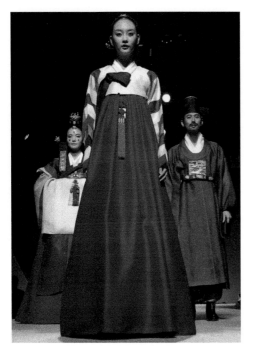 

Figure 5.9 The ideal proportions of a Korean hanbok feature an elongated leg and shortened torso (left). The Elizabethan gown features an elongated torso and padded hips (right).

Credit: Hanbok Fashion Show by Korea.net. Official page of the Republic of Korea is licensed under CC BY-SA 2.0 (left); *Princess Elizabeth*, Robert Peake the Elder. Courtesy of Metropolitan Museum of Art, New York. Gift of Kate T. Davison, in memory of her husband Henry Pomeroy Davison, 1951. www.metmuseum.org (right)

Defining the Body With Proportion

Costume designers alter an actor's appearance using proportions. Subdividing a shape in any direction reduces the impact of that shape. Additional lines shorten, widen, lengthen, or narrow an area.

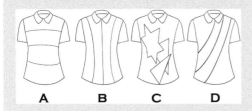

Bodice Divisions

Figure 5.10 (A) Horizontal lines divide this top into wider rectangles, appearing to shorten the torso. (B) Strong vertical lines divide the top into taller areas, thinning the torso. (C) Complex divisions break up usual proportions to disguise the original shape. (D) Diagonal divisions appear to elongate the original shape.

Costume designers do more than shift proportions to glamourize a body. They manipulate proportions and shapes to create attributes such as stronger or weaker, immature, funny or serious, or even adding the element of surprise. A performer's body can be transformed into an immature character by cutting the body into smaller proportions. This strategy was used to great effect in 1960s mod fashions to make young women appear more childlike. A strong character might wear clothing to emphasize the shoulders or make the torso appear larger. Fashions in the 1940s used this effect for women's suits, which lent a heroic appeal.

The designer also evokes a feeling about a character by using **exaggeration**. Any adjective preceded by the modifier "too" is an exaggeration: too big, too small, too short, too long. Designers create an element of surprise through exaggerated items such as too short trousers or a tiny top hat. Extreme exaggeration creates a message because it defies normal expectations.

Figure 5.11 These nurses from the 1940s wear uniforms with wide shoulders, making the torso look larger and more adult; they shouldered great responsibilities in wartime (left). That look is a large contrast to the Mary Quant 1960s minidress that divides the body into childlike, carefree proportions (right).

Credit: Image courtesy of the LCDR Julia Anna Muraresku (Bricker) Collection, USN Nurse Corps. (left); Mary Quant and model Diabolo, 24 March 1969. Jac.de Nijs, National Archives of the Netherlands, Fotcollectie Anefo (right)

The Principle of Movement or Direction

Movement adds excitement to a composition. Designers use it to direct the eye from the main **focal point** to an **endpoint**. After registering a focal point, the brain will naturally try to exit the composition, looking for the next thing. When the eye travels in a specific direction, it is called the **trajectory**. There are several kinds of spatial arrangements that lead the eye this way.

- The eye travels fastest along a **vertical** trajectory. Gothic cathedrals are excellent examples of tall vertical lines pushing the eye upwards toward the heavens.
- The eye travels quickly along a **diagonal** trajectory as it implies movement. This trajectory is evident all around us, for example in double-breasted suits forming a diagonal line of overlapping lapels and an off-center closure.
- **Circular** or curved trajectories create gentle movement.
- The eye is distracted by a **meander** trajectory, one that wanders or follows switchbacks.
- The brain follows items arranged by **visual weight** such as lightest to heaviest.

It is not necessary to create a trajectory or direction in every costume. The lack of obvious direction lends an appearance of stability. If the eye rests primarily on a single focal point, the remainder of the composition recedes. This singular focus is effective for a quiet play that depends on conversation; the costume designer may provide focus near the

Figure 5.12 This hat is very large compared to the wearer's face. This exaggerated proportion creates emphasis.

Credit: The Duchess of Marlborough, Paul Helleu, 1915. Courtesy of Old Book Illustrations

Figure 5.13 The single-breasted suit is more predictable and stable, while the angles of a double-breasted suit appear slightly more daring or even rakish.

Credit: Photo by The Lazy Artist Gallery from Pexels

face and avoid other visual distractions. Direction is an essential tool to distract from body areas or to create optical illusions that appear to alter the figure. The costume designer may wish to change the performer's body to appear rounder, youthful or elderly, taller or shorter, more or less gender specific.

The Principles of Repetition, Sequence, and Rhythm

We associate rhythm with singing, speaking, or dancing. These actions use repeated sounds or motions to express an idea. Visual rhythm also uses repeated elements. A **sequence** is a series of repeated motifs that leads the eye. Familiar shapes appeal to the brain's love of pattern and the eye will connect the dots. Items arranged in a sequence create **regular** or **irregular** patterns. Identical motifs placed with the same spacing create a **regular** rhythm or pattern, like a heartbeat. Some examples are identical ruffles stacked on a skirt forming **regular** repetition, as do the buttons on a shirt. Regular patterns are easy for the brain to quickly assess. Motifs that vary in size or placement create an **irregular** rhythm, much like a bird's song or the sound of tap dancing. Mismatched and missing buttons on a shirt front interrupt the expected rhythm and are irregular. Costume designers use sequences wherever there is a repeated motif such as ruffles, layers, trim, or buttons There are several specialty repetitions with identifying names.

- **Gradation** is a sequence that alters in a continually predictable way, such as a small ruffle on top of a medium ruffle on top of a deeper ruffle. Those predictable size changes form a gradation.
- **Alternation** is repeated motifs that break the pattern of repetition at regular intervals, or alternate. For example, alternating motifs

include using both circles and squares in a sequence.

- **Anomaly** is one item strikingly different from the rest of the composition. The brain will focus on the item that does not fit a sequence or pattern.

Pattern Repetition

Patterns are a special category of repetition with great significance in costume design. A pattern is a visual sequencing of motifs. Designers use patterns

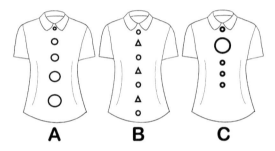

Figure 5.14 These buttons are placed in different kinds of sequences. A is a gradation, B alternates round and triangular buttons, and C illustrates an anomaly that creates focus.

Figure 5.15 These dresses feature regular and irregular rhythm and gradation. The dress at left shows three different proportions on the skirt that form an irregular sequence. The dress at right features a regular sequence of bows placed on the skirt.

Credit: Illustration for *Le Mannequin*, 1900. Frédérick Front. Wikimedia Commons

Figure 5.16 These 1874 bustle dresses show alternating ruffles. The dress at left features green ruffles alternating with pink ones. The dress at right shows small ruffles alternating with rows of puffed fabric.

Credit: La Gazette Rose 1874. Wikimedia Commons

to focus attention, to make a statement about a character, and to affect audience emotions. The human brain evolved to seek a **pattern rule**, so we comprehend them quickly. Designers arrange patterns into distinctive categories.

- **Structural** patterns are three-dimensional and can be felt with the fingers. A series of knife pleats in a skirt form a pattern that is constructed into the garment itself, and can be felt.
- **Visual** patterns are two-dimensional; they are woven, printed, or painted into the fabric and are detected only through the eyes. The pattern in a plaid fabric normally cannot be felt.
- **Symmetrical** patterns and **asymmetrical** patterns use the principle of balance as distinguishing features. Symmetrical patterns are stable and orderly. Asymmetry is surprising and dynamic.
- **Organic** patterns imitate forms found in nature, often utilizing curvilinear features. We associate them with reassuring emotions, free-thinking, or creativity. Organic forms can evoke

feelings of traditional, historical taste in fashion, or mature characters.

- **Geometric** patterns are shape based, orderly, and strive for a predictable pattern rule. They are considered strong, bold, vigorous, or modern.
- **Realistic** patterns use recognizable objects depicted with detailed representation. The brain processes realistic objects before abstracted objects. Realism in patterns may cause a sense of the uncanny, or an unsettled feeling. Viewers attach meaning to the motif.
- **Stylized** patterns require a simplification of line, form, space, and color, reducing the motif to a deliberate composition. Abstraction is the logical extreme of stylization. Flat, abstract motifs suggest youth, informality, simplicity, or a lack of sophistication or subtlety.
- **Natural** patterns incorporating plants or animals are *biomorphic*. Patterns using motifs from nature produce a feeling of calm, improve our moods, and enhance attention. Recognizable objects evoke psychological responses to the subject itself, such as a pattern based on lion heads. The audience may associate the character with lion-like qualities.
- **Manufactured** patterns are completely regularized; no matter how scientific nature may be, there are few mathematically straight lines visible to the eye. When combined with hard or futuristic materials, they communicate a mechanical intent.
- **Regular** patterns are orderly or logical. Regular patterns may communicate varying moods

– such as happy, busy, or royal. But at its heart, we perceive it as the result of orderly effort.
- **Irregular** patterns appear to be random. We associate irregularity with spontaneity, creativity, or disorder.

Order and disorder in design elements or principles are powerful contrasts designers employ frequently to define characters. We can see this quality in the stereotypical "mad scientist" hair. Someone like Einstein is so focused on higher thoughts, he has no regard for the rules of everyday life such as styling his hair. Pattern is a powerful subliminal tool for revealing the psychological make up of a character. For instance, two staid characters may wear similar business suits. One might wear a formal pattern such as pin stripes on her shirt. The other wears an informal pattern, revealing a rebellious streak in his personality.

The Principles of Harmony, Unity, and Variation

Harmony or **unity** creates cohesiveness among the elements and the other principles. Items appear harmonious if they share **visual** similarities such as color, line, shape, or texture. For example, a costume made with rounded seam lines is more harmonious than one using both straight and curved lines. Objects may also share **conceptual** harmony with similar intent or theme; for instance people wearing street fashions influenced by military uniforms are conceptually harmonious. Costume

Figure 5.17 Three styles of floral pattern – realistic flowers (left), stylized flowers (center), and abstract motifs inspired by flowers (right).

Credit: Courtesy of PxHere.com (left and center); *Snowden Theatre Art Deco Flower* by Sandra Cohen-Rose and Colin Rose. Courtesy of the photographers (right)

designers manipulate harmony and disharmony to make distinct character statements. A character who does not appear to be visually or conceptually harmonious may signal the audience to pay more attention, or to be suspicious. Harmonious design should not mean boring design. Overwhelming agreement in a design ultimately results in a loss of meaning; if every shape is round, the eye will glaze over them and the audience will no longer attach a specific message to those shapes.

Harmony must be accompanied by variety to add interest and emphasis. **Variation** can be added visually or conceptually, and every element or principle of design may be varied to create meaning. *Contrast* and *anomaly* are key to variety; if all characters dress in the same color, interest can be added through varying the textures. Costume designers frequently face a challenge of too much unity for characters that must dress in similar garments, such as military uniforms. Some examples of variety to establish character include one soldier wearing a bright new version of the uniform color with crisper textured fabric and shiny buttons, while another wears a dingy desaturated color, limp-textured uniform with dull buttons. The

Figure 5.18 This memorial to American soldiers who fought in Vietnam demonstrates three different ways to wear the same uniform.

Credit: Courtesy of goodfreephotos.com

soldiers may also vary the type of accessories and the way they are worn. A nervous soldier may carry an excessive amount of equipment attached to her belt or in a pack, whereas a laconic one may barely manage to button his shirt.

Unity is closely related to harmony. It is the feeling of completeness or wholeness of all the parts. A unified costume or garment design contains elements that do not compete for attention. Unity is also the hallmark of a successful overall show design: the result of all the design choices working together to give the audience a clearly understood experience. A unified design may contain many un-harmonious elements, if they are used correctly to make a desired statement. In this sense, unity creates a sense of order within the story world.

Sizing Up the Design Elements

This chapter explored the way designers use design principles to create meaning between the design elements. The principles rely on contrast or comparison between the design elements to make value judgments. Principles order the arrangement of a composition to create an overall message and evoke the desired audience reaction.

Expecting the Unexpected

Occasionally a costume designer will be called upon to hide an actor's pregnancy for their role in a performance. In one such case, an actor arrived several months pregnant for a production of *Twelfth Night* as Viola, a character disguised as a man for much of the play. Kollin Carter, long-time stylist for Cardi B, took on the same challenge of successfully disguising her pregnancy for several months until she was ready to announce it. One particularly successful outfit was a corset-trench dress with exaggerated wide shoulders to balance her figure and a boned center section that provided vertical emphasis around the torso and a smooth fit. He notes "A lot of people can't . . . grasp the concept" of a pregnant rapper, because it goes against "what rap women look like visually."[1] Using the tools of focal point and trajectory, visual weight, and proportion, the audience's eye can be misdirected to advantage.

psychological implications of the design elements and principles.

Extra Resources

A Guide to the Golden Ratio for Designers, InVision.com Emily Esposito, October 19, 2018.

The Magic Garment, Rebecca Cunningham, Waveland Press, Inc., 3rd ed., 2019. Chapter 4: The Designer's Tools contains useful charts that document the

Note

1 Hahn, Rachel. 2018. "How Cardi B and Stylist Kollin Carter Hid that Baby Bump." *Vogue Magazine.com*, April 12, 2018. https://www.vogue.com/article/cardi-b-pregnant-kollin-carter-stylist-baby-bump-reveal-conceal

6.
FABRICS CREATE DEFINITION

A young design assistant in New York was terrorized by a crusty old fabric supplier who would not show her fabrics until she could ask for them by name. There were piles and bins and tall shelves of every kind of fabric, including a basement filled with vintage remnants. The store was not set up for easy browsing, although that is exactly what many designers did, finding the perfect fabrics in a forgotten pile. But to get those browsing privileges, she first had to gain his trust. He really put that assistant through her paces – was she looking for *woolen* or *worsted*? *Chiffon* or *marquisette*? The assistant sharpened her vocabulary. Whenever she shopped in other stores where the fabrics were well marked, she kept swatches for her own library and memorized the names, and soon she was browsing undisturbed in that store. Fabric is the costume designers' artistic medium and they know their materials as well as painters or sculptors know theirs.

A contestant on *Project Runway* once observed the producers gave them small fabric budgets because an expensive fabric can make a boring garment look much better, and the judges wished to focus on the design itself. The power of fabric to define a garment is magical, and designers know that fabric has a voice of its own. "The textiles do a lot of the work," says Ruben Toledo of his wife Isobel's fashion design process. "She lets the fabric speak, so sometimes she starts with an idea, but the fabric wants to say something else, so she's ready to go there. You have to be very open and very brave."[1]

Isobel Toledo's process reveals one kind of designing: let the fabric inform the final design. Another way to approach design is to allow the cut or construction to direct the fabric choice. Certainly, many garments combine the two approaches, such as a structured bodice with a draped skirt. Understanding how to choose fabric is key to the design process itself.

Fabric Anatomy

Fabric is such an important extension of our sensory bodies that we talk about fabric using anatomy terms. The ***face*** of fabric is what the manufacturer would consider the "right" side, and the ***back*** of the fabric is the "wrong" side, although designers choose either side at times. We define the ***hand*** of a fabric, or qualities evaluated by the sense of touch such as stiffness or crispness. We also describe fabric in terms of its overall ***body***, or how a fabric drapes or holds air. A fabric such as taffeta will have a crisp hand and possess enough body to stand away from the wearer, trapping air below it. Heavy satin displays enough body to stand away from the wearer, but it's hand may be described as soft or spongy.

The Grain of Fabric

Fabric behaves very differently depending on the direction a designer uses it in a garment. Designers are generally familiar with the three possible directions to use fabric and how that decision affects its behavior: up/down, across, and at an angle. We

DOI: 10.4324/9781003015284-7

Figure 6.1 Toledo dress.

Credit: Hermaphrodite dress. Isabel Toledo (1961–2019), spring 1998 Shot Silk Taffeta. Courtesy of The Museum at FIT, New York

Figure 6.2 Fabric swatches stored on rings aligned with sketches for easy reference.

Credit: Photo by Bonnie Kruger

use the term **grain** to note direction, using the way fabric is made on a machine as the starting point. The term **selvedge** marks the edges of fabric, where the yarns turn around in weaving. They are finished edges that will not ravel, resembling ribbons.

- **Straight grain.** The up/down yarns running parallel to the selvedge. Many fabrics have a thinner yarn in the lengthwise direction. As a result, fabric held up to drape on the straight grain will fall with a more supple hand. The vast majority of garments are cut on the straight grain.
- **Cross grain.** The horizontal yarns running from selvedge to selvedge. Many styles of weave use a thicker yarn in this direction. Fabric held up to drape on the cross grain may be stiffer or show a more buoyant hand than the same fabric draped on the straight-of-grain. This characteristic can be especially useful for full skirts or petticoats that benefit from more body.
- **Bias grain.** Half-way between the straight and the cross. We find the *true bias* by marking a 45-degree diagonal line between the straight grain and the cross grain (see Figure 6.3). Bias fabric is somewhat stretchy, resulting in a close fit to the wearer. This cut was widely favored in the 1930s to create slinky, form-fitting dresses. Using any other angle than a 45-degree diagonal is known as *garment bias*.

A concept closely related to grain is the **nap**, a texture on the surface of the fabric itself. Fabrics such as velvet with a fuzzy or hairy surface lay predominantly in one direction, like petting a cat. If you rub your hand the wrong way, it will feel rough. It is important to cut pattern pieces facing the same direction with napped fabric so the final result is consistent. Other fabrics with woven or printed patterns will display a **direction**. The motifs of a pattern must all face the same direction.

The Fabric Formula

As the young design assistant shopping in New York discovered, there is a seemingly endless number of fabric names to learn. Many names originate in other languages, such as *charmeuse*, a fine grade crepe-back satin. The same fabric name can have different meanings in different countries, for example *muslin* in the United States is called *calico* in Britain. Some names develop from a place of manufacture, such as *dotted swiss* or *denim* (from Nimes, France). Fabric names shift over time, and

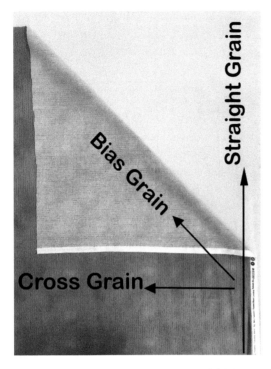

Figure 6.3 Straight, cross, and bias grains of fabric.

Figure 6.4 The same fabric draped three ways behaves differently. Figure A shows the straight-of-grain. The fabric falls in smooth folds. Figure B is the cross grain, which is stiffer. The fabric falls in a straight manner. Figure C is bias grain; the fabric falls in multiple supple folds.

contemporary textile makers use proprietary trademark names such as *Lycra®*, a trademarked name for spandex or elastane fabric. There *is* a way to sort through this morass of terminology using a simple fabric formula. Fabrics may be named after any single step in the formula. The following sections will discuss each element of the formula: the source material, the style of making sources into yarns, the methods of making yarns into fabrics, the ways color or pattern can be added, and finally the many methods of finishing fabric or adding decoration.

In everyday usage, costume designers separate fabrics into two overarching categories:**natural** or **synthetic sources**. Naturals are easy to wear, dye, age, and distress, but those same qualities also make them more susceptible to damage and more labor intensive to maintain and store. Some synthetics may be difficult to dye but they are sturdy and more easily washed. Although recent advances in synthetic fabrics have made some almost indistinguishable from natural fabrics, they may display a slightly different hand than their natural counterparts. Costume designers find they often have to identify the fiber source of an unmarked fabric; they must know if that fabric will take a dye, shrink if laundered, or melt if treated with heat or solvent-based products. Designers use **burn tests** to form an educated guess about the fiber content of fabric. A burn test consists of quantifying four basic behaviors:

- How does a sample of the fabric behave when approaching a flame?
- How does it burn or melt?
- How does it extinguish?
- What type of ash does it leave?

Results may be significantly altered by flame retardants, chemical finishes, or other hidden treatments. But many designers find a burn test adequate to identify a few major characteristics and rule out others. There is a burn test chart readily available online through many sources; see the Extra Resources section.

Figure 6.5 Fabric formula #1: Source.

Sourcing Fibers and Filaments

The most basic component of any fabric is its source structure: fibers and filaments. **Fibers** come from sources in short fluffs called *staples*. The most common staple fabrics are cotton, linen, and wool. We derive a different kind of strand sourced from mulberry silkworms who spin long continuous strands called **filaments**. These silk filaments are lustrous and smooth. Synthetics are manufactured to imitate both fibers and filaments. Understanding that a fiber is not the same as the method of fabric construction will clear up many misunderstandings. For instance, *silk* is not a fabric name. It is a source, and it can be made into any number of fabrics such as *satin* or *shantung*.

Yarn Styles: Two Are Better Than One

Fiber staples are too short to make directly into most fabrics. They must be twisted or **plied** together to create a yarn so it can be woven or knitted. A single-ply yarn is just one twisted yarn, it is subject to stretching and breakage. Two or more

Sample Fabrics Named After Their Yarn Styles

Crepe is the French word for wrinkled or frizzy. Yarns are hard-twisted in opposite directions resulting in a distinctive bumpy and matte fabric.

Bouclé (boo-clay) yarns are heavily curled to create visible loops. They are so distinctive any fabric made from them is named after it.

Elastic yarns are heavily crimped to create a stretch-and-return quality to the fabric.

Figure 6.8 This boucle fabric shows a looped surface created by the yarn style.

Credit: Photo by Skylar Kang from Pexels.com

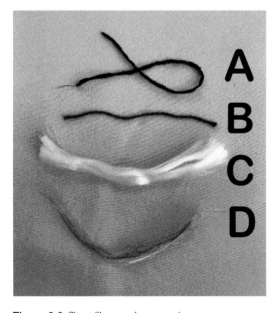

Figure 6.6 Short fibers and are spun into yarns to increase their length and strength, Figures A and B. Silk is a filament, long continuous strands, Figure C. Flax is a fiber made into linen, Figure D. It is made of shorter staples that must be wound together to create a usable yarn.

Figure 6.7 Fabric formula #2: Yarn.

yarns twisted together create strength or introduce color or texture variations.

Woolens and Worsted Yarn Styles

Wool fabrics divide into two major categories based on their yarn constructions: **woolens** and **worsteds**. When sheep are sheared, their coat forms large matted clumps that must be cleaned and untangled before twisting into a yarn. That untangling process is called *carding*. Woolens have been carded so the staples align enough to twist into yarns. Just as with human hair, we could braid our hair after combing, but ends may stick out here or there depending on our natural texture. Worsteds undergo an additional process, called *combing*. Combing pulls away the shorter fibers, leaving only longer, straightened fibers. This produces yarns with a smooth finish that drapes more gracefully. The discarded short fibers are saved to make inferior grades of woolen fabrics called *recycled* or *remanufactured* wool. Other fabric names originate with different textures added to yarns when they are twisted.

Filaments Have Feelings, Too

We tend to think of filaments having a naturally smooth texture. In fact, there are many textures of filaments visible in silk fabrics. There are small, naturally occurring variations called *slubs* that add surface interest and a bit of body to the fabric. Some fabric names use these distinctions.

Figure 6.9 Wool fabric (left) is rougher and thicker than worsted (right.)

Sample Silk Fabrics

- ***Habotai*** or ***China Silk*** – a fine fabric made of smooth filaments (Figure A).
- ***Shantung*** – a dressy fabric used in evening gowns and bridal wear. The surface is lustrous with small visible slubs running horizontally across the fabric (Figure B).
- ***Dupioni*** – silk with double strands that occur when two silkworms tangle their cocoons together (Figure C).
- ***Noil*** – like wool, silk filaments are refined before twisting into yarns. The noils are short fibers leftover from silk processing. Silk noil fabric resembles linen; it is rough to the touch and may fray or pill easily (Figure D).

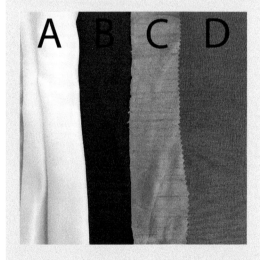

Figure 6.10 Silk fabrics.

Fabric Construction

Of all the elements in the fabric formula, the method of construction produces the most style names. On a daily basis, costume designers distinguish between **massed**, **knitted**, and **woven** fabrics.

Massed or Felted Fabrics

Anthropologists surmise the most ancient method of creating fabric is subjecting massed, overlapping woolen fibers to heat and pressure through a

Figure 6.11 Fabric formula #3, construct.

process called ***felting***. Felt is most apparent now in crafts and armor making.

Knitted Fabrics

This large category includes the familiar **knitted** fabrics we wear every day that stretch when we move.

It also includes two historical techniques that costume designers encounter: **knotting** and **braiding**. Both are ancient techniques; knotting forms the basis for luxurious hand-made laces. Braiding is still used in the making of straw hats. Most knitted garments stretch when pulled, and before the invention of spandex or elastic, knitting allowed comfort and movement for sports garments. Contemporary knits are made on large machines making it an affordable way to manufacture fabrics. Even some fabrics that appear to be woven are technically knits. The secret to working with knits is to match the *direction of stretch* in the fabric with the desired fit on the body. Knits are an important category for performance clothing because of their ability to accommodate movement. Some knits such as thick **ponte** styles can create a semblance of tailoring, allowing even suits or trousers to stretch. But it is vital never to confuse a knit with a woven fabric or to combine knits and wovens unintentionally. Knits fall into four construction categories:

Two-way knit stretches only in one direction, usually horizontally side-to-side.

Four-way knit stretches both vertically and horizontally, making it ideal for extreme motion. Used for leotards, unitards, and athletic wear.

Single knit is made on a circular machine with a single set of needles repeating the same loop stitch. It displays a smooth face and a rougher back. This fabric is named **jersey** and it is commonly used as basic t-shirt fabric. It is soft and lightweight, making it a good option for clingy or drapey garments. One distinctive characteristic is when it is cut, the edges curl, making it a somewhat tricky fabric to sew or store as swatches.

Double knit is made on a machine with two sets of needles and yarns that *interlock* as they go. The fabric appears the same on both sides. The resulting fabric is thicker, more stable, and does not roll when cut. Double knits are less stretchy, and serve well for structured garments that skim the body.

Knits Divide Into Major Style Groups

Rib knit – shows obvious columns or ribs, used for turtleneck sweaters or the cuffs on jackets. Rib construction provides an extreme amount of horizontal stretch (Figure A).

Terry knit – or *French terry* features loops of a soft velvet-like pile on the face, resembling a bath towel. The soft plush texture is used for sweatshirts and plush hoodies. If the fabric is sent through a machine to brush-loosen the fibers, we call it **fleece** (Figure B).

Raschel knit – takes its name from the machine used. They do not stretch well, but they feature decorative pattern effects of lace-like, open textures. Costume designers choose these knits for their surface effects, not their stretch qualities (Figure C).

Sweater knit – a catchall category to describe larger-gauge knitting with discernible textures or patterns (Figure D).

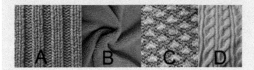

Figure 6.13 Knits.

Woven Fabrics

Woven fabrics account for the largest variety of fabric styles. Many fabrics are named after the distinctive weaving pattern used to create them. Weaving is created on a frame or loom that fastens long yarns in a vertical direction (called *warp yarns*) so that horizontal yarns (*weft or filling yarns*) may be passed over and under each warp to form patterns. There are eight weaving styles that help the designer categorize hundreds of fabrics easily.

Plain or straight weaves. This basic weave passes one weft yarn *over* one and *under* one warp yarn. This over/under pattern can be woven very tightly for fabrics such as cotton shirting, or loosely for fabrics such as gauze.

The combination of yarns and the density of the weave creates thousands of variations, each with a different hand.

Rib weave. A visible rib effect appears on the surface, on the cross grain or the straight-of-grain. It's easy to check if a fabric is a rib; running a fingernail across the fabric will result in a zipper-like sound.

Twill weave. Woven with visible diagonals that run at angles to each other. The diagonal courses are called *wales*. The face and back typically look different, although they may be opposite colors.

Typical Rib Weave Fabric Styles

Bengaline – a dressy silk and cotton fabric used in the 19th century. The ribs may be so small they are difficult to see without a magnifier (Figure A).

Grosgrain – once a common fabric but now seen mostly in ribbons, the ribs are large and easily visible (Figure B).

Ottoman – large ribs created for special effects, creates a rounder effect when sewn or draped (Figure C).

Faille and *taffeta* – fabrics with crisp hand, the ribs are so fine they are difficult to see without a magnifying glass (Figure D).

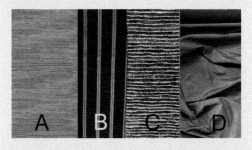

Figure 6.14 Rib weave fabric styles.

Typical Twill Weave Fabric Styles

Denim – before the invention of stretch fibers, twill provided more stretch on the bias than plain weaving. So even though a pair of work pants such as denim jeans are cut on the straight-of-grain, the twill stretches a little in motion, aiding movement and preventing tearing.

Herringbone – a traditional woolen with a V-shaped pattern.

Cavalry – traditionally made of wool with large visible diagonal wales, used in riding pants and some period military uniforms.

Figure 6.15 The stretch of a twill weave allows denim jeans to move more easily than a straight weave.

Satin weave. A shiny fabric named for the floating yarns that bounce light. Satin is **warp-faced**, with the floats formed by the vertical yarns. Satin has been used since the early medieval era, but not all of them were shiny, especially if made from cotton or wool. Most satins have an obvious face and back that differ from each other.

Sample Satin Styles

Duchess or ***Bridal*** – heavy weight with a high luster.

Charmeuse – very light weight shiny fabric with a liquid drapey hand.

Antique – or satin-back shantung uses a slubbed yarn so the face displays a luster and the back a nubby surface, reversible.

Sateen – in contemporary usage, sateen describes a satin weave fabric made from

staple yarns such as cotton. Sateen in **weft-faced** with the floats formed by horizontal yarns.

Figure 6.16 Bridal satin has a high luster (left). Antique satin shows a nubby surface on the back side (right).

Dobby weave. A term now familiar due to Harry Potter books and movies. Dobby the house-elf wore only a kitchen towel or pillowcase, which in traditional weaving was made on a dobby loom. Dobby fabrics use very small geometric patterns that increase water absorption. A contemporary use is ***piqué*** (pee-kay) the fabric seen on the fronts of men's formal shirts. A close look reveals tiny birds eye oval or honeycomb patterns. This fabric is stiffer than straight weaves and holds its shape well.

Brocade weave. Fabric with distinctive multi-color patterns. Brocade has been the principle luxury fabric for the very wealthy since late antiquity. Brocades are made from many fibers and filament sources, making identifying the fiber content with a burn test frustrating. It is more successful to draw out different threads to test them separately. Brocade uses multiple colors in its patterns.

Jacquard (jack-ard) or **damask**. Two-color reversible patterned fabric with the design motifs appearing reversed on the back. The term *jacquard* derives from the special loom to make it. The name *damask* derives from its medieval origins in Damascus, Syria. Damask uses two colors or tone-on-tone coloring.

Figure 6.17 Brocade and damask fabrics display reversible patterns. Brocade displays very different colors on the front and back. The pattern is more detailed on the face of the fabric (left). Damask displays the same color scheme in opposition; the motif and back ground alternate colors from side to side (right).

Pile weaves. Yarns woven over long thin rods to form standing loops on the surface. If the rod has a knife edge, it cuts the loops when retracted, creating standing hairs.

Typical Pile Weave Styles

Terrycloth – fabric with many loops on the surface, used for towels and bathrobes (Figure A).

Velvet – cut hairs standing up from the surface. In contemporary use velvet is made of shiny filaments such as silk and synthetics. Technically, the hairs stand on the length of grain (Figure C).

Panné Velvet – velvet flattened with rollers to appear slick and shiny (Figure B).

Crushed Velvet – velvet with a mottled surface to appear duller (Figure D).

Velveteen – in contemporary use, velvet made of staple fibers such as cotton, linen, or wool with a matte finish. Technically, velveteen is made with its hairs on the cross grain, and the pile is cut shorter and more densely (Figure F).

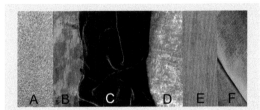

Figure 6.18 Examples of pile weaves.

Corduroy – standing hairs woven in visible channels and rows called cords (Figure E).

Methods of Coloring Fabric

Adding color to fabric occurs at any phase during its construction. Understanding where each colorization step occurs may help a designer choose a fabric for special effects or understand the results of some dye tests. **Colorfastness** refers to how permanent a coloring method is over time. Colorfast cloth will not fade or lose color through normal wear and washing. Poorly fixed or penetrated dye may rub off when worn, known as **crocking**. Colorizing information is sometimes available when purchasing a fabric.

Figure 6.19 Fabric formula #4: Color.

Solution dying colors yarns as part of the chemical process mixing the ingredients before extruding. This color can be nearly impossible to remove.

Stock dyed or **top dyed** fibers are dyed before being made into yarn. Early colorization ensures more penetration of the color into the materials, so the color can be difficult to fully remove. Good colorfastness.

Yarn dyed fabrics include the many textiles that use different color warp and filling yarns such as denim or patterns that rely on color changing to create stripes, plaids, checks, brocades, or damasks. Good colorfastness.

Piece dyed cloth is colored after it is woven or knitted. This is the most common method of adding color. Dying after fabric construction may result in poorer color penetration, making this style of fabric a little easier to remove and recolor.

Garment dying adds color to completed sewn garments, as seen in *tie-dye* effects. The least color-fast of the methods, cheaply dyed garments crock or bleed.

Printing decorates the face of fabrics using methods available since ancient eras. The back of the fabric remains plain.

Costume designer Mark Bridges had the opportunity to work mostly with texture for the 2011 film *The Artist*, shot in black and white and set in 1920s Hollywood. "Without the color to communicate the language of telling the story, I was trying to tell the story through textures, whether it be lamé, sequins and beads for Hollywood, or very flat rough textured wools to communicate down-on-your-heels, or the elegance of satin lapels for evening wear, or the shimmer of a beautiful nightgown. It became a story of textures telling the story."[2]

Sample Printing Methods to Decorate Fabrics

Direct printing uses colored pastes, inks, or dyes to add patterns to the surface of a fabric. This method includes hand stamping, silk screens, and the mechanized rollers used for industrial-scale printing. The latest technology to join direct printing is digital printing.

Discharge printing uses a bleaching paste to remove color from a background. This method leaves light motifs that can be left that way or dyed another color.

Resist process uses a physical or chemical barrier to prevent certain areas of a fabric from absorbing color.

Sublimation printing transfers a design painted or printed on special paper to fabric using high heat and pressure. It is generally only available for synthetic fabrics.

Ombré – colors that fade into each other using special dye techniques.

Burnout velvet or ***devoré*** (duh-vor-ay) uses an acid paste printed onto the fabric that removes part of the pile to create a pattern.

Finishing Methods

Cloth does not look very appealing after is it made or colorized; it may be stained, wrinkled, or off-grain from running through machinery. Fabrics undergo cleaning and chemical or mechanical finishing to improve the appearance, hand, or performance. Chemical finishes include preventing wrinkling or

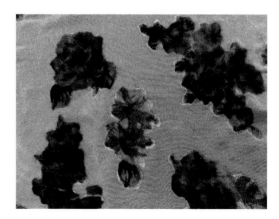

Figure 6.20 Devoré is named after way the pattern is manufactured: chemicals devour or burn only the natural fibers in the velvet weave. The synthetic chiffon base remains, leaving a scattered velvet pattern.

Figure 6.21 Fabric formula #5: Finish.

shrinking, adding sizing to increase the bulk or feel of the fabric, or flameproofing.

- Specialty chemicals change the appearance of the fabric, such as acid washing denim.
- A method called ***plissé*** uses a caustic chemical to shrink or pucker fabric in designated areas. One example is ***seer sucker***, a crinkle applied in stripes.
- Mechanical finishes use heated rollers called **calenders** to smooth a fabric or even add a high shine such as a glaze for ***polished cotton*** or ***chintz***.
- Calenders may add roughness to a fabric, such as brushing up fibers from the surface for ***flannel*** that feels soft or slightly fuzzy.
- Calenders add textures to pile fabrics: ***crushed*** and ***panné*** (pan-ay) velvets derive their names from the finishing process of flattening the piles in multiple directions or one direction, respectively.

The appearance, hand, and body of every fabric is a result of all five components of the fabric formula. Fabric qualities cannot always be predicted exactly, and even very experienced designers have discoveries as they work with a new material. Fabric that behaves perfectly on a dress form may not behave the same on an actor in motion or may not dye in the expected manner. Every designer spends a lifetime learning new things about fabrics and gambling on its final outcome in a garment.

Suit Yourself: Fabric for Tailoring

Fine tailoring was best defined by the bespoke tailors of Savile Row. Bespoke suits concentrated on fine craftsmanship, refined fabrics, and the caché of being a customer of exclusive establishments. Due to the exacting technical methods of construction, purchasing fabrics for tailoring is a collaborative decision.

The designer will work with a tailor with strong opinions. Tailors working in cities without an entertainment industry may be less interested in trying new things that can cut into their already razor-thin margin of profit. Entertainment tailors are, however, used to making suits from fabrics that would stun traditional tailors. Brocade, satin, sequin cloth, and velvet are all regular tailoring textiles for theatrical performance. These choices require careful consultation with the tailor who must compensate for the way the fashion fabric behaves with clever interfacings. The wise costume designer will take the specific personality of a tailor and their labor situation into account before purchasing fabrics for menswear.

Tailoring wools are categorized by weight. Suiting has been getting thinner with each passing decade in the 20th century as we developed more central heating. Many designers are surprised when studying menswear from the early 1900s through 1930s to see how thick the wool was in everyday suits. Wool manufacturers gauge their wools by using a **grams per meter** (g/m) weight classification.

- ***Woolens*** A typical medium-weight suiting wool has a density around 240 to 290 g/m. Heavy weights are typically around 300 g/m.
- ***Worsteds*** are made from staples carded and combed to straighten the fibers. They weave into a smooth finish, creating a harder finish and thinner weight. They are more wrinkle resistant and will recover their hang after wear more quickly than wool. They may have a slight luster and are considered dressier than wool. Worsted ***gabardine*** is a lightweight but tough fabric used to make functional items like overcoats and trousers. It is a twill weave, and at times the diagonal twills can be very apparent. Very lightweight versions are used to make trousers.
- ***Tropical*** or summer weight wools generally have a density of 210 to 250 g/m. These fabrics also

feature a more open weave, allowing air to flow and increasing the comfort level of the wearer. These are less durable than heavier wools.

- **Tweed** is a particularly thick wool, originating in Scotland and Ireland for cold-weather sports attire like hunting. The wool has been carded, but not combed. Tweed is a heavy, durable wool with a thickness of 300 to 600 g/m. It also lends its name to the flecked pattern from this traditional weave, so it is possible to purchase thinner tweed fabrics in contemporary menswear.

- **Superfines** are the finest gauge suiting fabrics. These luxury fabrics include the g/m notation in their retail name, such as Super 200, 180, 150, 120. They are made from fine wool fibers with a smaller diameter, and the most exclusive are made from cashmere, vicuna, or chinchilla sometimes blended or mixed with silk.

- **Wool blends.** Blends bring other characteristics to the fabric. One fine blend intended to make tuxedos incorporates silk. Affordable or budget garments use wool and synthetic blends. Each compromise in wool content affects the way that suit behaves on the body. Inferior blends will not fall gracefully or wear as long.

- **Fashion fabrics**. Cotton, linen, velvet, brocade, and lamé have all been tailored for specialty suits. There may be compromises such as rumpled shoulder seams, curling lapels, and wrinkled trousers. Consider using poly blends to prevent wrinkling.

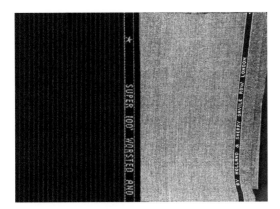

Figure 6.22 The worsted at left is marked as a Super 100 on the selvedge. The worsted at right is a Superfine 150.

Wool weaving has a long history, developing a huge range of woven patterns names such as houndstooth and chalk stripe. The number of named plaids and checks particularly swelled in the 19th century. The costume designer creating suits must be aware of the narrow distinctions made in both current and historical tailoring fabrics.

Putting It All Together: Matching Fabrics to a Design

It's a large task to match the proper textile to a garment design. Many designers naturally gravitate toward color as the starting place, but there may be cases where texture or reaction to light may be priorities. Use the following guide to establish priorities to create criteria for choosing fabric. It can be helpful to articulate the *must haves* or nonnegotiable aspects of each specific design before deciding on the fabric.

- **Intent, mood,** or **feel** of the design. Fabrics have their own feel or mood. Ethereal characters may call for light weight fabrics. Sturdy or structural fabrics do not respond to movement.

- **Construction** parameters. Evaluate the silhouette to eliminate fabrics without the proper structural integrity. A soft fabric won't create a structured silhouette. Stiffly boned garments require a firm but light weight weave. Garments for extreme movement require a either a two-way or four-way stretch. Long skirts that brush the stage floor may shred if the weave is too loose.

- **Weight** or **hand** of the fabric. Some fabrics have a heavy hang or swing. Roman togas require fabric with a certain drapey quality. Fabric that is too light or too easily wrinkled will make those Senators look like bags of laundry.

- **Texture** evokes psychological responses. It is difficult to change the texture of a finished garment, so this quality takes priority over other considerations.

- **Response to texturizing, dye, or paint.** If the surface of a costume will be changed, aged, distressed, or painted, fabrics must be chosen with this in mind. Whenever possible, buy enough fabric to do samples first.

- **Reaction to light.** A sequined gown and a matte jersey gown cannot be easily substituted for each other. Serious or realistic characters may be expressed using fabrics that partially absorb light, such as suiting fabrics.
- **Durability.** Every costume designer has used delicate vintage garments onstage only to have them disintegrate. Costume designers walk a fine line between fragility and durability when creating costumes that imitate realism or historical garments.
- **Color and pattern** are the most powerful of the design elements. If working in conditions with limited dying, then color may vault to top priority.

Swatching for a Production

Brick-and-mortar fabric stores have been vanishing from the American landscape, unless you are lucky enough to be able to shop in a major city with a garment district. With fewer retail stores, it is more important than ever for designers to collect their own swatch libraries for inspiration. Many online suppliers sell samples or entire booklets of their wares. It is well worth the time to create a swatch library in your studio. Always cut swatches from a bolt in the least damaging way – horizontally along the cut end. Remember which direction is the straight-of-grain. If that is not obvious on the swatch, take a photo of the bolt or draw a tiny arrow directly on the swatch to jog your memory. Swatching for a show is more productive if you think in terms *possibilities*. Gather *any* swatch that may fit into the story you are creating. Designers call this collecting a **swatch world**. Eventually you will sort through the fabrics, removing items that don't fit the parameters and assigning them to characters. Having extra swatches allows you to present alternatives if the director or draper votes against a specific fabric. A fabric may also be out of stock when you return to purchase it. You can return to your swatch world for more options, instead of starting over.

Sizing Up Fabrics

The power of fabric to define a garment is magical, and designers know that fabric has a voice of its

Defining the Body With Fabric

Choosing fabrics combines many of the elements and principles of design. Choose fabric not only with the correct hand but to also emphasize the character such as textures that advance or recede in group settings compared to each other and individually.

The Figure Appears Larger or Advances	The Figure Appears Smaller or Recedes
Large, bumpy textures	Smooth textures
Diffused edges enlarging the body	Figure smoothing edges
Sharp angles and lines	Soft curves
Light, saturated or warm colors	Dark, unsaturated, toned or cool colors
High-contrast colors or values	Low-contrast colors or values
Straight or thick lines	Curvilinear or thin lines
Horizontal lines also add emphasis	Vertical lines also add emphasis
Stiff shapes	Soft, drapey shapes
Shiny fabric surface	Matte or absorbent surfaces
Large patterns or prints	Small patterns or prints
Monochromatic colors	Polychromatic colors
Large geometric motifs	Small or soft motifs of any type
Large, bold focal points and details	Delicate focal points and details
Large-scale additions adding volume	Small-scale additions adding little volume

own. Some designs call for the fabric to inform the structure of the garment, and others require the cut or construction to direct the fabric choice. There is a seemingly endless number of fabric names to learn, but there *is* a way to understand how fabrics

Figure 6.23 The ring of swatches at left represents all possible fabrics that could fit into the story world of a production. This designer prints swatch cards on stiff cardstock to staple swatches and record information. The swatch on the right was cut with no selvedge to indicate the straight-of-grain. The designer marked it with a small arrow while still in the store.

behave using the fabric formula of *source, yarn, construct, color,* and *finish.* Choosing fabrics for costumes requires consultation with the maker or tailor, particularly in the case of menswear.

Expecting the Unexpected

Costume designers never stop learning about fabrics because we often create items the textile manufacturer never anticipated. We use the wrong side of the fabric, we turn it to the cross grain, we tear it in strips to weave into our own concoctions. Ruth Carter, costume designer for *The Black Panther,* had to solve a unique fabric problem.

> We wanted to create something special for the Panther suit. I asked what is the *one thing* I can do that hasn't been done to a superhero suit? We stretched a thin skin of fabric over the vibranium muscle suit, and we layered it with the triangle on the front. We were so proud of this suit! You could see the vibranium radiating through the fabric, and we loved it! Then we

put it on a stunt guy, and he blew right through the pants. This fabric was way too thin, so we made a tougher suit. We also brought someone in from the Boston Ballet, and she knew all the gussets and curves. It was a real lesson for me.[3]

Extra Resources

Bespoke Tailoring Basics, The Gentleman's Gazette.com. www.gentlemansgazette.com/bespoke-tailoring-basics/

Dressing the Man: Mastering the Art of Permanent Fashion by Alan Flusser.

Fabric Burn Chart. www.threadsmagazine.com/app/uploads/2013/06/T168_Burn_Test_Chart.pdf

The Fashion Designer's Textile Directory, A guide to fabrics' properties, characteristics and garment design potential, by Gail Baugh. The ultimate guide to the characteristics of fabrics with many photo swatches.

The Ultimate Guide to Suit Fabric Types, Bespoke Unit. https://bespokeunit.com/suits/fabrics/

Wool Gauge Information. https://blog.knotstandard.com/your-guide-to-suit-material-types/

Grabie Wool Company, Queens NY. www.grabiewool.com/

Notes

1 Embassy of Switzerland in the United States. 2010. "Let the Fabric Speak: A Swiss Afternoon with Isabel and Ruben Toledo." *YouTube*, October 3, 2010. Accessed July 31, 2020.

2 Leopold, Todd. 2012. "The Costume Designer: Adding Texture to Storytelling." *CNN*, February 25, 2012. https://www.cnn.com/2012/02/24/showbiz/movies/qa-mark-bridges-oscar/index.html

3 Costume Designers Guild. Comic Con Panel. 2020. "Costumes of the Marvel Cinematic Universe," July 24, 2020.

PART TWO

A DESIGNER PREPARES

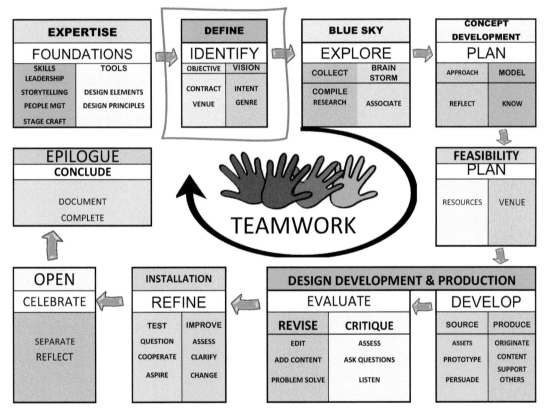

Figure 7.0 The creative process for produced projects.

Credit: Holly Poe Durbin and Ayrika Johnson

7.
GETTING PAID
All That Glitters . . .

A costume designer was working on a large project that would transfer from Los Angeles to the Kennedy Center in Washington, DC. She had spent a long day shopping for shoes and had over 30 pairs of specialized men's shoes in her car. Suddenly, another car darted out of a parking space without looking and ran right into her. Everyone was fine, but the other driver was uninsured. Her insurance company refused to cover the repairs to her vehicle because she was using her personal car to conduct business. Much sadder and wiser, she learned one of the hidden costs of being a costume designer is insuring her car at a higher rate for business coverage if she uses it to shop for shows. There is no agreement among theatrical costume designers about how early in the creative process to start planning these practicalities. Some designers say they cannot concentrate too early on boundaries as it will censor their creativity. Others note that parameters inspire their most creative solutions. Even though designers may approach their process differently there is one thing they all have in common: they must be compensated in some manner. In order to be compensated, the designer must understand the *true* parameters surrounding a job.

The failure to put a show onstage by the delivery date is an expensive and chaotic event that everyone wants to avoid. Most theaters provide a technical director or production manager who will manage the scenic operations, but not all theaters provide that same support to a costume designer, expecting them to perform that task on their own. Costume designers may have to make a lot of practical decisions before or during design development. Larger theaters employ two heads of department: the costume designer and a costume director, costume supervisor, or costume shop manager. In other cases, the producers may assume the costume designer will perform both artistic and operational jobs for one fee. Therefore, many costume designers must proceed artistically and practically at the same time. Learning to quickly assess any job will empower the designer to negotiate more effectively on her own behalf and alert the producers to challenges early.

Are You Working Alone?

Smaller theaters may use the independent-project model, hiring everyone as an independent contractor and keeping few full-time employees. In this case, the designer may be expected to function as their own crew or hire their own additional personnel on behalf of the theater. There is current pushback in the industry against this model. Doing multiple jobs for a project drastically increases the time commitment for the designer and is often not reflected with multiple fees. This practice is much more common with costume designers because technical directors hire and oversee personnel for scenery, lighting, and sound. This is an unfair practice. Not only does it discriminate against costume

DOI: 10.4324/9781003015284-9

designers specifically, but it also severely limits the profession to privileged designers with other means of support. Nonetheless, it is a widespread practice for small theaters, and this book includes many ways the costume designer may approach a variety of projects. For more information consult *Costume Professionals for Wage Equity* cpfwe.org.

Does the Tail WAG the Dog?

Creative projects are not simple to define, yet every show, no matter how large or small, has only five assets: **people**, **time**, **money**, opportunities for **collegiality**, and artistic **opportunity**. When there is not enough of one, that deficit can be made up with the others. For instance, a lack of time can be offset with money to hire more people. A lack of people or labor may be balanced by a longer lead time. A lack of collegiality – or a theater that is very difficult to work with – may be offset by a stellar artistic opportunity or a high fee. In order to assess what each project offers, designers create early **guestimates**, or informed guess estimates of the assets for a show. Other terms used in business circles are *high-level* or *back-of-the-envelope* estimate. A more colorful term for this process captures the limitations: a WAG (*wild-assed guess*) provides a rough guide to the designer – such as, are alarm bells going off? The tail wags the dog when the assets are so out of alignment they paralyze the ability to make all other decisions or adversely affect the costume designer's health or ability to perform the work.

Ten Questions for a New Job

The designer can draw some conclusions from basic information. For instance, a quick review of the script reveals the likely scope of the project, and knowing the collaborators reveals the quality of collaboration.

1. What is the timetable and design due dates?
2. May I read a script?
3. Who are the collaborators, director, and other designers?
4. Is the show cast yet, or is there likely casting to anticipate?
5. What kind of team will I be working with – costume staff?
6. What are the available facilities for design, fittings, stitching, crafts?
7. Is there a workable costume stock for this show?
8. What are the designer's responsibilities in your theater?
9. What sort of budget will I be working with?
10. What is the compensation and how do you pay designers?

The Stages of Labor

There is nothing so clarifying as the time frame allotted to produce a project. Opening night is a public event with extreme pressure to avoid failure. This crucial parameter informs a great many decisions. If a show *could* take six weeks of labor, but you have been contacted with just four weeks' notice and haven't yet designed it, what would make this project doable within the given timeline? What steps can be compressed or abbreviated? Negotiating these ideas at the beginning ensures more top-level cooperation than complaining through the process or running ragged to achieve the impossible. A quick assessment of a project considers two types of time. The first is the **designer's time**; the second is other **labor** assigned to the project. There are really only three ways to approach a lack of time: work longer hours, add personnel to the team so the work progresses faster, or adjust expectations for the outcome. If the designer has been contacted late for a low-budget show, it could make sense to accept the job on the condition that additional labor must be hired, such as a shopper or alterations personnel.

The estimation method in Table 7.1 lists a range of designer labor hours for each type of

Table 7.1 Sample Range of Design Labor Time Frame

Design Phase	Type of Tasks	Smaller or Contemporary 10–25 Costumes	Medium Show 15–30 Costumes	Large or Complex Show 40–90 Costumes	Range of Hours
Explore	Script Analysis & Consultations	8	12	25	51–90–149
Explore	Creative Research	15	30	40	
Define	Costume Lists, Meetings, Communication	12	18	24	
Plan/Render	Rendering or collages	16	30	60	
Feasibility	Meetings: theater, vendors, labor, shops	8	12	30	8–12–30
Develop	Sourcing and transportation	40	65	120	136–243–465
Develop	Overseeing alters or builds, shop time	10	40	80	
Develop	Crafts, Accessories, Wigs, Dying, FX	15	35	60	
Develop	Returns and exchanges	10	15	30	
Develop	Daily emails, scheduling	10	12	20	
Develop	Adjusted paperwork – plots, dressing lists, receipts, accounting	16	24	30	
Develop Evaluate	Attending rehearsals actor talks	10	12	25	
Develop Evaluate	Fittings	25	40	100	
Refine Open	Tech/Dress/Previews	40	60	96	40–60–96
Totals		**235 hours**	**405 hours**	**740 hours**	
Work Weeks *if* 40-hour week		5.8 work weeks	10 weeks	18.5 weeks	
Small Stage/Experimental Theater Hourly Wage If Fee Is		$1,000 fee = $4.25 per hour	$3,000 fee = $7.40 per hour	$4,000 fee = $5.40 per hour	
Larger Stage/Mainstream Theater Hourly wage If Fee Is		$4,000 fee= $17.00 per hour	$5,000 fee = $12.34 per hour	$6,000 fee = $8.10 per hour	

(Continued)

Table 7.1 (Continued)

National Average Wages 2019	U.S Bureau of Labor Statistics
Fast Food and Counter Workers	$ 10.93
Bartender	$ 13.22 (+ $150/day tips)
Emergency Medical Technician	$ 13.70
Meat Packers	$ 14.05
Retail Display & Window Trimmer	$ 14.16
House Cleaner	$ 15.15
Bus Driver	$ 17.13
Elementary Teacher	$ 24.87
Piano Teacher	$ 27.76

Note: This chart outlines possible ways costume designers might allocate their time. This chart assumes little support personnel; adding team members diminishes design hours.

task. Of course, every show and every designer are different, with access to different support systems. One designer may be slow at rendering but fast at pulling costumes from stock. Another may speed through the drawing step but require longer to envision the potential of stock costumes. Tracking *your* individual tasks over several projects provides a general idea of your time use. The first step is to quickly guestimate how much design time this show may require, using your experience as a guide. If you are unsure, consult another designer who has worked for that theater for tips.

The next step is to guestimate how much labor the designer will have access to. This topic is covered in greater detail in Chapter 17, Defining the Scope of a Show. Although the designer may wish to consider the scope of a project in more detail here, most projects require a general calculation whether the theater's proposed timetable reasonably accommodates likely costume production time. Some elements to consider in the estimate:

- **Fittings**. Fittings add up quickly, especially with large casts. Each actor will require at least 20–30 minutes per costume fitting time. Period shows or complex projects may require 1 hour per costume. Will a second fitting be needed if the first costumes don't work out? A safe estimate is to assume 25% of the actors will require a second fitting. Built costumes may require two fittings.
- **Typical labor.** See Chapter 17 for estimates on building and altering costumes.
- **Availability.** Is anyone working full time on this show, or are they juggling several jobs or a full-time day job? How many hours per day will be dedicated to this show?
- **Specialty labor.** Does this project call for a specialization such as working with leather, tailoring, or complex surface modification? Is that labor available at the time needed?
- **Age/dye/paint.** Costumes that must be treated require both treatment time and wash/dry time. A few costumes such as men's shirts could be one afternoon of work. Treating many costumes or using specialty techniques could add three days or more.

- **Trim.** Adding embellishment to costumes is extremely expensive and time-consuming. A detailed show may require extra time. How can this be managed?
- **Rehearsal costumes.** There is a trend to provide more and more costumes for rehearsals as extreme movement becomes more popular. Is the costume area expected to spend time fitting, altering, and repairing rehearsal items? Negotiate this ahead of time.
- **Photo calls.** Does the theater use an early marketing strategy, and is the costume designer expected to have those costumes done first, or provide substitutes?
- **Rentals package.** Has a package been identified and rented, or is the designer expected to source and arrange that? How long of a lead time will there be after the rentals arrive?
- **Matching rental package.** What contingency plan is in place if a cast member does not fit a rental package costume. Must that costume be duplicated to match the set? How will this be handled?
- **Rentals restoration.** Some rental outlets require new alterations be taken out and all trim restored before returning after strike. How will this be handled?

Advice From Costume Designer Genevieve V. Beller

"I start at the '100 hour' principle and multiply by my hourly rate, which varies based on several factors but I always know my minimum. Then I look at what I will reasonably be able to accomplish in those 100 hours. Do I have those hours available? Do I need to bring in assistants or additional labor? How much will that cost? Then I ask what the market will bear. I go to my costume colleagues for this as opposed to job boards or producers. What is the average rate in my area for this work? Where do those rates intersect given my location and desirability? Are my labor estimates reasonable? Next, I look at materials. Will I be needing more expensive fashion fabrics?

Is durability a factor? Am I buying twice the zippers I need and additional fabric for repairs because acrobats put more strain on their garments? I estimate what I think I will need per costume (this can be a ballpark) then add 15%.

I add it together and subject it to the *PITA* test: is this amount of money worth the emotional labor to complete the job, given my other obligations? How much do I need to be paid to justify the *Pain In The Ass*? You could also call this supply and demand: the products are my time, attention and literal physical needs. What's left is 1) determining if the labor/materials budget is adequate. ALWAYS separate these from your fee in a contract and insist on separate checks lest your budget be taxed as income and 2) negotiating a higher fee based on the above considerations. If there is no wiggle room in the fee, then I can choose to negotiate expectations: only 1 sketch adjustment, less time on site and a **change of scope** clause into my contract. If/when I take the job, I use a time tracker app to log my hours. This helps me to keep on top of my personal labor budget and aids me in estimates the next time a project comes along."[1]

For Love or Money?

The costume designer must make a quick WAG calculation about how adequate a budget is before accepting the job. In most circumstances, it is not productive to do a detailed budget breakdown so early. Rather, the designer wants to develop some sense of what this show offers and how the budget advances or impedes their ability to design. In fact, that may be one of the early interview questions a producer asks the designer – can you do this show for our budget? Detailed budgeting is covered in Chapter 18, Budgeting Creative Projects. This discussion focuses on how to develop a back-of-the-envelope estimate while assessing a job.

You will need three important numbers for a guesstimate: the **budget**, a hunch about typical **hidden costs**, and a rough number of **costumes**.

Budget Number	$1,500.00
MINUS **Hidden Costs** * 10%	− 150.00
EQUAL **Total for Costumes**	**$1,350.00**
Total for Costumes	$1,350.00
DIVIDED **Number of Costumes**	÷10.00
EQUAL **Cost per Costume**	**$135.00**

Hidden costs are often overlooked, sometimes accidentally borne by the designers themselves or accomplished by seat-of-the-pants solutions. These costs are items that make the job possible: sewing supplies, gas and parking, printing costs. The designer may discover the theater's sewing supplies must be completely replenished on their watch, or the low budget necessity to shop in thrift stores uses much more gas and parking than one-stop shopping in a more expensive store. Each designer develops a sense of their own needs. Starting with a standard percentage that works in your circumstances is all that is required at this phase. The preceding sample shows a quick calculation of $135 head-to-toe for each costume. Is that a workable number for this project?

When Is the Sacrifice Worth Making?

Creative people do not measure success with just one ruler. Everything about a project may look lamentable, but when a project beckons sometimes we cannot resist. One of the most intoxicating callings is **artistic** opportunity. Does this project offer the chance to create something you've been wanting to do, or will it stretch your creative skills? Another hook is **collegiality** or the opportunity to create with interesting or like-minded people. This category includes not just friendship and collaboration, but **values** as well. Does a project align with goals you find important, such as community education or social justice? Every designer who has worked for a long period of time has taken some jobs that were artistically mediocre but paid very well. There is no shame in paying the bills. Every designer has also accepted a project that pays little or nothing but offers personal opportunity. There is also no shame in feeding the soul.

Define your own version of success for *this* project. But double check your motives. Just like the dangers of gambling, designers must recognize they may not always make decisions in their best interest. Limit the number of no/low-pay projects you do in the year. Or resolve the project will not *cost* you money. Perhaps agree on a mileage reimbursement in lieu of pay. Or arrange to keep the costumes in exchange for your labor. Then once you decide to take on that project, enter it with an open heart.

Costume Designer Kristin Sauter has worked with big and small companies as wardrobe with the national tours of *Rent, Mama Mia*, and *August Osage County*. But she also designs for community theater when she's home. She explained, "On the community or local theater level, everyone is really doing it for love." She does not look to those projects for her actual income. "Get everything in writing" she advises. She negotiated a situation where the director added 12 tango dresses to a show, insisting the extra expense had been approved. The theater, however, did not approve spending more money and she was caught in the middle. Asking for proof of approval caused some tensions at the time but proved to be the very thing that protected her. "Sometimes very little of what we do comes down to the actual design. It's all the hoops you jump through – sometimes the design comes second."[2]

> "Money won't create success. The freedom to make it will." —Nelson Mandela[3]

Working With a Costume Supervisor

The designers' job will be considerably different when the theater employs a head of department with the responsibility of delivering the product to the stage on time and under budget. Typical job titles include costume or wardrobe supervisor, costume director, and costume shop manager. Much of the labor of financial record keeping and overseeing labor will be their responsibility. They may also divide sourcing duties with the designer and oversee costume building. This position coordinates the operational aspects of the project:

- Hiring and supervising labor
- Tracking spending and creating financial reports
- Maintaining stock and inventory

- Making fitting requests
- Monitoring and ensuring progress on the project
- Liaison to other departments such as wigs/ makeup and wardrobe crew
- Creating or collecting fabric estimates for builds
- Maintaining the show bible
- Managing long-term vendor relationships

The designer/supervisor team is based on clear communication and trust. The costume designer creates the story for each character and stays attuned to the story as it develops in rehearsals. It is vital to share these artistic goals with the supervisor so both work toward the same goals. Costume supervisors have worked with a number of designers and their styles; they are skilled at adapting to each designers' vision. Supervisor Rebecca Pride notes "exceptional levels of emotional intelligence are required by the costume supervisor in order to get the best out of the workroom team and in their interactions with the costume designer and the actors."[4]

Paper Trail or Vapor Trail?

Research the theater or producer you will be working with if they are new to you. Have others in your circle worked there? Determine the aesthetic point-of-view and, if possible, see a current production. Check for online interviews and see a current show or view recorded clips. Evaluate prior production photos online to determine how well they support production values. Indicate in your interview that you appreciate some of their work. Remember that you are interviewing them as much as they are interviewing you, and come prepared with a few questions so you will set an engaged tone. When you are offered the job, ask about their expectations for the next step to formally start the process. Remember though, that no matter how well the interview goes you don't have the job until you sign a piece of paper proving that. If you are working on a handshake agreement, both the theater and designer are taking a great risk. What if the show is canceled suddenly, and the designer has un-reimbursed expenses? If a contract is not available the designer has every right to submit a simple

Letter of Agreement (LOA) for signature. An LOA sets the terms of any working relationship between two parties. For more information on sample LOAs, see the Extra Resources section. Some elements to include:

- Project or show title
- Credit as costume designer
- Bilateral agreement: designer agrees to deliver costumes, theater agrees to pay
- Starting and ending dates
- Amount of payment, manner and dates of payment
- Show budget
- Design delivery steps and due dates
- Method of design approval – who signs off?
- Dates the designer is required to be in residence
- Any extra terms negotiated by the parties such as mileage reimbursement, allowable expenses
- Known allowances or impediments, such as the designer is out of town on certain days
- Financial methods available for sourcing – petty cash, gift cards, company credit card
- Signatures of designer and theater representative

Design work can take many weeks or months to complete. It is reasonable and traditional to receive several payment steps as work is partially delivered. The typical steps used by United Scenic Artists contracts include one-third payment upon **signing** the contract, one-third upon delivering the design or pre-visualization **package**, and one-third on **opening** night. Each theater defines what the design package entails: research, sketches, costume lists, and anything else that would allow the design to be realized. This may also be broken into smaller deadlines. Theater has long been an uncertain business and shows have been cancelled before opening. The three-step method ensures the designer will be paid for at least some portion of their work, if not all.

Politely but firmly decline if the producer expects to combine the design fee and budget in one payment. That is a dangerous practice that *could* be interpreted that you were paid "under the table," an illegal practice for them and for you. If the

producers can write one check, they can write two. Otherwise, the IRS may expect you to pay taxes on the budget – the entire amount of the check issued to you. Or, you, as a conscientious tax payer must take time at the end of the year to document the show receipts and purchases to deduct from that amount, leaving only your fee. Either way, the theater is ignorantly asking you to accept outsized risks and undertake additional accounting on *their* behalf. Every state governs differently, especially when it comes to classifying gig workers and independent contractors, so don't be afraid to consult professional sources such as a tax preparer or an attorney. See the Extra Resources section for more information.

Many theaters pay nonunion designers as independent contractors. If that is their policy, then make sure both parties uphold that practice correctly. In general, the theater must ask you to file a W-9 with them when more than $600 is paid for either goods or services within **a calendar year**. The theater must then issue a 1099 for your tax returns. Inspect this 1099 carefully when it arrives to ensure they have not accidentally included any petty cash advances or reimbursements as part of your income, or you may be liable to pay taxes on the whole amount. If there is an error, ask them to reissue the 1099. Theaters often outsource this task and the outside accountants don't always understand this distinction.

As an independent contractor, uphold your end of the bargain by running a responsible business and invoicing the theater in a timely manner for payment. Consider declaring yourself a sole proprietor, and set up a small business so you can deduct your expenses. Just because the producers are nice people doesn't mean they are knowledgeable financial experts. Even if someone hands you a check with no paperwork, submit an invoice after the fact marked **paid**, showing the pay date, their check number, and the goods or services you rendered. Keep a scan of their check. As a precaution, copy all receipts and financial reports before handing them into the theater. They will serve as a legal record of the transactions. As an independent contractor, you may legally own any costume you've created using your own materials and labor and you can sell it to the theater or retain ownership afterwards. One designer of a national tour used her own stock for the leading lady's dress. She kept it, and was hired several times after that for remounts – hopefully because of her talent, but perhaps also because she owned the dress.

> "The price of anything is the amount of life you exchange for it." —Henry David Thoreau[5]

Overcoming Fear of Negotiation

It is scary to negotiate and to stand up for yourself, especially if you are new in the business working with personal friends. Many designers fear they will earn a difficult or demanding reputation. Often the designer is eager for exposure and artistic opportunities; some producers are willing to take advantage of that or they operate with old obsolete ideas about costume design. This imbalance of power can be particularly acute in locations where there are few theaters. Some producers may act insulted

S Sample Design Company

INVOICE

Street Address	**Date**
City, State, Zip code	**Invoice #**
Phone	
Email	

Bill To:

Company Name
Street Address
City, State, Zip code
Phone Number
Company Contact

Item Description	Unit Price	Discount	Amount
Costume Design for *Into the Woods* Final 1/3 Payment, Opening Night 11.16.20	$800.00	N/A	$800.00
Rental 1 Red Cape with decorative patches 2 week run 10 performances	$35.00	0%	$35.00
Subtotal			
Invoice Total			**$835.00**
			DUE ON RECEIPT

Make all checks payable to:

Designer Name or Company Name
Tax Payer ID or SSN

Figure 7.1 Sample invoice. Most financial software generates invoices, or the designer may create their own template.

if a designer questions the job offer. But stop to consider what is really being offered: they are asking to benefit from the value the costume *designer* brings to their show. They may be asking you to beg and borrow on their behalf, calling in professional and personal favors. At the same time, the costume designer may be excited to work with this group of collaborators and this exciting script. It is easy to be snared by our own artistic desires.

The key to negotiation is to separate artistic concerns from practical concerns, unwinding the emotion of your artistry from the business side. Are you a much better advocate for others than for yourself? Then become an enthusiastic advocate for the *project* itself. The project will be its best if it has certain things. Also consider the health of the costume community. Agreeing to work in absurd or impossible conditions drags every costume person down, too. Ultimately, you appear more experienced and more of an asset if you know how to deliver a good project. Start negotiating any way you can manage; declare yourself the sole proprietor of your design company and use your company name. More than one early career designer has used their tax accountant as an excuse, noting they insist on certain kinds of conditions, paperwork or payment methods. (Never mind the tax accountant may be their cousin giving advice once a year.) If you absolutely cannot manage it, form a collective with colleagues for mutual support – agree on working conditions and do role-playing negotiation exercises. Compare contracts with your designer community and the other designers on the show to check not only the fee but the number of weeks residency for that pay.

Weak Words, Throwaway Phrases, and Self-Sabotage

Check to see if you are unwittingly using conciliatory language. These verbal ticks broadcast mixed messages and undermine our authority or self-worth when presenting ideas. Here are some of the biggest offenders to wipe from your vocabulary.

Just. This word reduces your expertise, contribution, or work to insignificance. Many people use this word much more than they realize. "It's just a skirt." A skirt that someone must use their time and talent to think about the correct look, source, fill out financial paperwork, discuss, fit, alter, label, and take to a dressing room.

Apologies. You don't actually have to utter the words "I'm sorry" to issue an apology. Leading an idea with excuses about why it isn't good is a *big* apology for taking people's time to listen to you. "These don't quite say what I want, but here are the sketches." Own your work, present it, and don't tell people to discount it. Not everyone can do what you do.

Feel. Phrasing your opinions as feelings reduces their impact. Own your ideas. "I feel this is right" is weak compared to "This is right."

Think. It is stronger to *think* than to *feel*. But watch how you use this word. Make sure it is not a qualifier. "This looks good, I think" reduces your authority. "This looks good" is a strong statement.

Sizing Up Getting Paid

Costume designers frequently oversee operational and administrative tasks along with the job of designing their part of a staged production. It is vital to quickly estimate the actual job and its likelihood for success. Every creative project has five assets: **people**, **time**, **money**, **collegiality**, and **artistry**. Designers decide for themselves if a show's combination of assets are workable and attractive opportunities. They use guestimates or back-of-the-envelope appraisals to predict the likely experience. Every show requires an understanding in writing with the producer or a paper trail of detailed invoices.

Expecting the Unexpected

The tax benefits to being a sole proprietor can be very advantageous. You may deduct art and business supplies, local mileage, subscriptions, conference fees, travel, and all professional growth. It's helpful to understand what it actually costs you per year to be a designer: the cost of doing business. If you've never done this, start with last year's records. Resolve yourself to one awful afternoon of sorting through your files. Access your spending history on credit cards, debit cards, and digital transfer apps. You spent money on books, museums, and going to shows. You bought printer ink, you went to copy places. Divide those un-reimbursed expenses into two kinds of expenses: *professional growth* includes the money you spent keeping relevant in your field such as buying books or attending conferences. *Overhead* includes transportation, office supplies, and the actual space you work in if it is separate from your family space, portions of your phone bill and internet service, software fees. Use Google Map instructions to recreate the kind of shopping trips you make routinely to add up likely mileage you were not reimbursed for.

When you have an estimated overhead amount, divide it by the number of days you interviewed for and worked on design jobs. That total is the daily overhead cost for you to be a costume designer. With this knowledge, you can begin to negotiate with potential producers how you might transfer some of these costs to their budgets. If it costs you more to be a designer than the market will bear, that is important information. Perhaps you need other sources of income that could be related to your design business, such as selling a product online. Or you take a different job that pays the bills. Begin your accounting system right away – it can be as casual as throwing your physical receipts in one manila envelope within easy reach. Or you may wish to use digital tracking apps. Ask your auto insurance carrier if you can add business insurance only as needed by the month. If you use digital financial software, begin tracking expenses. Add a mileage app to your phone.

Extra Resources

TCG Salary Survey. *Theater Communications Group*, 2020. https://circle.tcg.org/resources/research/salary-survey

Moody, James L., *The Business of Theatrical Design*. Allworth Press, 2002.

Carey, Kirstin, *Starving Artist No More, Hearty Business Strategies of Creative Folks*. Small Talk Marketing & Communications, INC, 2005.

Bethke, Kelly, "A Creative's Guide to Starting a new Business." *Fast Company*, November 9, 2018. www.fastcompany.com/90264055/a-creatives-guide-to-starting-a-new-business

Warnes, Bryce, "The 5 Best Mileage Tracker Apps in 2021," *Bench*, April 7, 2021. https://bench.co/blog/operations/mileage-trackers/

United Scenic Artists Project Agreements www.usa829.org/Contracts/Union-Project-Agreements-UPAs/Union-Project-Agreements-UPAs

Letter of Agreement Sample Rocketlayer.com www.rocketlawyer.com/business-and-contracts/business-operations/business-partnerships/document/letter-of-agreement]

Volunteer Lawyers and Accountants for the Arts – includes a national list of resources https://vlaa.org/get-help/other-vlas/]

Notes

1 Beller, Genevieve V., Excerpt from Facebook post and as told to the author, December 7, 2021.

2 Sauter, Kristin 2021. Personal interview with the author, September 8, 2021.

3 McKenna, Amy. n.d. "15 Nelson Mandela Quotes." *Britannica*. https://www.britannica.com/list/nelson-mandela-quotes.

4 Pride, Rebecca. 2019. *The Costume Supervisor's Toolkit*. New York: Routledge, p. 8.

5 Martin, Kristi. 2017. "The Price of Anything Is the Amount of Life You Exchange for It." *Thoreau Farm.com*, February 28, 2017. https://thoreaufarm.org/2017/02/the-price-of-anything-is-the-amount-of-life-you-exchange-for-it/

8.
SCRIPT, PLOT, AND STORY

The term **script analysis** is a shorthand term that means studying three separate components of a production: the script, the plot, and the story. **Story** is the reason we stay in our seats – to discover what happens to engaging characters inhabiting a compelling world. The **plot** arranges the events of the story in dramatic fashion. Some plots follow chronological order while others manipulate time using flashbacks or foreshadowing. The **script** is a document that converts the story and its plot into a performable format. Each of these manifestations of the project contributes to the dramatic intent of the production. The costume designer must be adept at understanding the ***impact*** of story, the ***flow*** of plot, and the ***mechanics*** of script.

Designers read scripts systematically to prepare for the design process. The designer stands in for the audience during the first reading, experiencing the story the way the audience is intended to do. Note what makes an immediate impression, and where you lost track of "reading a script" and followed the story just to see what happens. This reading provokes the experience the playwright intends. Did the story evoke a specific mood? Was it calm? Chaotic? Funny? If the chosen language is complex, it may be necessary to read parts again before you completely comprehend the story. The second full reading focuses on the world, characters, and events. Many designers take notes in the margins to highlight requirements, ideas, and questions. These notes will prompt questions for discussion with the director. Subsequent readings are technical, focusing on the plot structure, literary devices, and events that pertain to costumes.

The combination of script, plot, and story leads the creative team to sources of inspiration and suggests larger themes to interpret in their designs. It is too daunting and counterproductive to begin any script exploration directly searching for themes and concepts. There are many lists of questions available to help designers begin their discovery, such as one created by dramaturg Elinor Fuchs. Her article "Visit to a Small Planet" is one list created for critics and theorists that has been passed among designers as a guide to story analysis. (See the Extra Resources section.) The article asks questions such as *How does the story open? What is the first image or event? What is the element of chaos, and how is it righted?*[1] Dr. Fuchs is quick to point out where many go astray is to dive too quickly into the characters without first exploring the world of the story. The important goal is to lift yourself out of assumptions, to start a fresh look at each project. Every character is a product of their society and its rules: understand the world of the story, first. After a time, designers develop their own lists of questions or signals.

DOI: 10.4324/9781003015284-10

"Don't go into a play looking for theme and meaning first: those will show up naturally when you have a grasp of the plot." —Eric Appleton[2]

Questions to Ask Yourself About Stories

Just the Facts

Who, What, When, Where, Why, How

Opinions and Arguments

What is the conflict in this story?

How is it revealed? Resolved?

Are there opposing forces? Two people, two views of life, two courses of action?

What makes the story "good"?

What appeals most?

Inanimate Characters

What is noteworthy about the setting?

Does it have power, exert influence?

Doe the setting or an event operate like a character?

Fatal Attractions

Do the characters have flaws?

What is appealing about each character?

What does each character want?

Pictures and Words

What images come alive in this story?

How does the passage of time affect the story?

Do actions or words speak louder?

Is realism important to this play?

Whispers and Roars

What opinion might the playwright have about the events?

Is there anything distinctive about the playwright's style?

How does the playwright establish tone?

Figure 8.1 Story – Plot – Script

The Script Is a Blueprint

The script breaks the story events into *acts* or *scenes* that can be performed on a stage. Some actors may play more than one role to lend significance to the story or to ease the theater's salary burden. The characters come and go in carefully timed exits and entrances. Scenes follow one another instantly or incorporate black outs to separate them. Two scenes may be staged simultaneously, or may be happening at the same time with characters stopping and starting dialogue so the audience can follow both conversations. The playwright matches theatrical formatting with the story to create a meaningful framework, and this is part of their artistry. The script format also conveys a rhythmic structure. Many short scenes placed together lend a staccato quality, perhaps promoting confusion or a cinematic quality as if we were watching a film of the story. The mechanics of the script reveal so much important information for the costume designer that it is discussed in the next chapter.

The Plot – Analyzing Turning Points

The plot of a story describes what events take place and the order they occur. We often use a five-step formula to describe the typical structure of a plot: the **introduction**, **rising action** where the story builds in tension and excitement, the **climax** is the peak of conflict. The **falling action** is when problems are solved, and the **resolution** is where we discover the final outcomes. These plot phases can be too large for the designer, as much of the play constitutes rising action. **Turning points** are smaller junctures that bring a fresh perspective to the plot, revealing motivations for costume decisions. For instance, a character plunged into despair by events may appear distracted and disheveled. This kind of costume change reflects the *dramatic intent*, and if done correctly will appear so natural the audience may assume it was written into the script.

The play *Romeo and Juliet* breaks into five major **turning points** within the plot. The **beginning** or setup is where we establish the locale and time period, meet the characters, and establish the normal world before any conflict occurs. We meet Romeo and Juliet in their respective environments, establishing they are part of wealthy feuding families.

- The *first* turning point is an **opportunity** leading to a new direction in someone's life. Romeo crashes a party and meets Juliet.
- The *second* turning point is a **new plan** or new ideas leading to action. Romeo woos Juliet and they marry in secret.
- The *third* turning point is the **point of no return**, raising the emotional stakes to the highest point. Romeo kills Tybalt and is banished. When Juliet's father forces her to marry Paris, she devises the plan to fake her death. Once Juliet takes the sleeping potion,

the plan is set in motion and there is no turning back.

- The *fourth* turning point is a major **setback**, leading to the final effort to resolve the problem. The setback for Romeo and Juliet is miscommunication: The Friar's letter to Romeo describing her plan does not arrive in time and he believes her to be dead.
- The *final* turning point is the **climax** – or the point with the most tension or emotion. Romeo rushes to Juliet's mausoleum and drinks poison, dying right next to her. Juliet wakes up mere moments later expecting to see Romeo, but instead finds him dead. She kills herself with his dagger.

A costume designer for this play could use turning points to motivate changes in a character's outward appearance. Romeo's costumes may start the story fashionable and dashing when he is a young man with serial love interests. The first turning point is the party scene where he wears a disguise. The second turning point could motivate altering his appearance as his mindset or circumstances change. Wooing Juliet under her balcony may be the first time he presents his true self to anyone – perhaps he removes much of the disguise, appearing in simple shirt and trousers. The third turning point leads to Romeo's banishment. Perhaps his color palette turns darker to reflect his state of mind after killing Tybalt and losing Juliet. The final turning point, at Juliet's grave, presents the opportunity for Romeo's costumes to appear disheveled or torn after a frantic ride to Juliet's grave. These costume changes inform the narrative, bringing to life a character's emotional arc. It may be helpful to incorporate turning points in the costume scene chart to track emotionally charged events. Figure 9.6 in the next chapter applies different colors in the appropriate Act/Scene columns to mark each as a turning point.

"A film requires a beginning, middle and an end. But not necessarily in that order." —Jean Luc Godard[3]

Plot Gags and Gimmicks

A script may contain performer-driven events added by the playwright, by performers themselves during rehearsals, or as a result of design inspiration. A **gag** is an old-fashioned show business term originating from vaudeville for one such event. It is a short funny story, joke, trick, or physical action meant to entertain on its own. The term *sight gag* specifically refers to visual humor without words. The difference between actors' physiques can form a sight gag, such as an extremely short person and an extremely tall person trying to dance. There are costume gags, too, such as a comic character wearing ridiculous clothing. One example of a costume gag is the opening of Act Two in *Peter and the Starcatcher*. After the intermission, back lighting reveals dark silhouettes that appear to be voluptuous female forms. But when the front lights are brought up, the audience discovers they are really men dressed as drag mermaids, which provokes a round of laughter and applause.

Gimmicks are events meant to attract attention either as a single spectacular event or as a repeated event. They may or may not be humorous but must be eye-catching. One gimmick seen frequently on the streets is a sidewalk sign twirler advertising a nearby store. The unique appearance and acrobatic skill attracts attention. Gimmicks are also derived from vaudeville, and there is even a song in the musical *Gypsy* advising "*You Gotta Get a Gimmick!*" sung by three strippers who demonstrate their identifying elements; Electra wears a light up costume, Tessie Tura imitates a ballet dancer, and Mazeppa plays a trumpet. The Pixar movie *The Incredibles* makes fun of gimmicky superheroes. Gimmicks may be subtler than strippers and superheroes. Some characters develop a signature look meant to distinguish themselves from the crowd, such as a handlebar moustache or wearing only track suits.

The Story: Manner of Presentation

At the start of every show, directors and designers ask themselves "What is the *story* we want to tell, here?" They are not wondering about who does what to whom. They are thinking about why this production is interesting *now*. A large aspect of story is the **manner** in which it presents itself to an audience. Does it describe details realistically and the characters interact with a realistic environment? One example may be an extended meal requiring the correct furniture and props. A television show such as *Jane the Virgin* relies on realistic depictions of homes or neighborhoods. This manner is ***descriptive***, and it fits any story that would lose its meaning if the actors were to act without a detailed world. Another manner of presentation is ***evocative***, using environments or interactions that are suggested, with details left to the imagination. Could the characters behave believably in a suggested or abstract environment? Shakespeare wrote his plays with suggested environments: a forest, an island, a rampart. It was not necessary to see Verona to believe Romeo and his friends roam the streets in search of entertainment. The dialogue contains much of the information an audience needs to comprehend the story, and the situations and emotions are universal enough to relate to. A third manner is ***presentationalism***, or ***theatricality***. These stories may combine both descriptive and evocative elements. Consider a stage musical where brightly clothed characters interact before stylized scenery. The characters don't acknowledge the environment much, but they do interact with selected set pieces that magically appear when needed. They might sit on a lone piece of furniture to suggest a cafe, or carry a suitcase to suggest a train station. The audience's imagination fills in the rest. Audiences can either listen deeply or look deeply, but rarely both at the same time. Effective storytelling separates complex verbal information from physical action.

> "The more effectively rendered the illusion, the more passive the role of the viewer. Does the viewer lean forward, or lean backwards?" — Tony Caputo[4]

Another consideration for the manner of presentation is the use of language. Is the language contemporary or from another era? Heightened language may create a *formal* tone that informs the design. Television favors the more *informal* use of contemporary spoken English, even if the story may be set in a past era. One example is the HBO series *Gentleman Jack* that used more recognizable contemporary ways of speaking, although it is set in the 1830s. Contemporary theatrical productions of historical plays written in another era may update the era of the story, but most preserve the original language. A final consideration is how the actors appear within the story. Are they perceived first as actors who are portraying characters, do they ever step out of character to comment on the play itself? Or do the actors inhabit a character so completely we lose track they are not the real people?

It is useful to consider the manner of presentation as a sliding scale. A specific work may fall somewhat more toward a suggestive style or lean heavily toward abstraction. The costume designer must consider how characters will inhabit each manner of story. The scale in Figure 8.2 shows some possibilities from hyperrealism or naturalism to abstraction. There can be many stops along this scale; deciding where the visual elements fall is an exciting part of articulating an approach to the show.

Hyperrealism or naturalism presents a complete illusion of reality. The National Theater in London presented a play titled *The Kitchen* in 2011 that featured a fully functional restaurant kitchen with gas stoves that really worked. All the actions that go into making an omelet were correctly performed by the actors.

Realism lends the illusion of reality onstage, but there may be a fake fire in the fireplace and painted wood grain suggesting paneling. The characters use natural sounding dialogue and imitate human behavior with psychological motivations. The audience agrees that the "fourth wall" of an environment is missing so they can witness real situations.

Presentationism is a large category in performance, encompassing a wide range of styles that are self-aware. A production can be stylistically real, but actors break that fourth wall to address the audience directly. Or a production may use any number of theatrical conventions, such as a chorus of dancers suddenly entering behind a character.

Stylized productions emphasize artistic approach over realism. There are many visual styles derived from the work of painters, sculptors, or illustrators such as expressionism, impressionism, art nouveau, minimalism, or Afro-futurism.

Exaggeration distorts specific attributes to create a message. Superhero films employ visual exaggeration in the physiques of their characters, separating them from the common person. Exaggeration can be taken to an extreme, called **caricature**, to magnify characteristics or create humor.

Abstraction no longer adheres to the rules of representation. The guiding principle is a concept or principle, such as depicting the body with geometric shapes. One famous use of fully abstract costume design is the Bauhaus school in Germany during the early part of the 20th century.

It is also important to acknowledge that bending or breaking stylistic expectations is exactly how notable productions are made. Always ask if

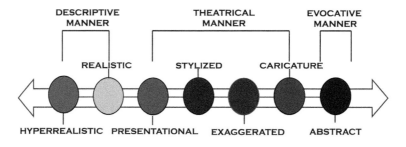

Figure 8.2 Abstraction scale and manner.

Credit: Courtesy of Ayrika Johnson

Figure 8.3 This 1931 Broadway production of *The Bandwagon* starring Fred and Adele Astaire successfully combines stylized scenery and more realistic costumes. Costume Designers Kiviett and Thomas Dennis Williams.

Credit: Florence Vandamm, *The Bandwagon*. Courtesy of Broadway Photographs, David Shields Collection

this production would benefit from breaking the "rules." Contemporary productions mix modes of presentation very successfully, often pairing evocative scenery with realistically detailed costumes. The costume designer then considers how to bridge that gap with an evocative gesture such as using only solid colors or a minimalist approach.

Story Genres and Categories

Some stories are based on conventions that developed over time, called genres. Genres signal some audience expectations such as the tropes and visual requirements of a western or film noir. There are a large number of categories of stories. For instance, *Harry Potter* is an example of a story type using *group protagonists*, or a category known as a "buddy story." The adventures require the combined talents from Harry, Hermione, and Ron for success. An understanding of typical story structures and plot devices is particularly helpful to the designer. (See the Extra Resources section.)

Story Tone or Mood

Tone describes how the audience experiences a story emotionally. It is an attitude or general atmosphere conveyed through word choices, style of dialogue, situations, or categories of character. Tone provides an emotional framework such as solemnity or humor. Each production uses an overall tone or mood, but the momentary tone will shift within the story to incorporate humor, sadness, or tension. One excellent example of shifting tone is the Disney+ series *WandaVision*, which shifted from broad sitcom cheer to personal crisis.

Story Givens and Moments

Every story rests on assumptions that make the world and its action ring true. There are some pieces of the puzzle that must fit together to make the story believable. Elements than cannot change without altering the premise or outcome of the story are called **givens**.[5] Some examples of nonnegotiable givens can be found in Margaret Atwood's play *The Penelopiad*, a reworking of Penelope's story as she waited for Odysseus to return after the Trojan War. Atwood sets the action in Hades. One **given** then, is that the audience must believe everyone they see is dead and trapped in the afterlife. Scripts also feature important events that require attention or evoke audience response. We can call these **moments**; they are an opportunity to reinforce ideas with design elements. It's easy to determine major moments in a musical. The regular action pauses as the musical interlude amplifies a character's emotions. The lights will shift, the quality of the sound changes, dancers appear – all these elements define that moment as special. A subtler moment is Romeo spotting Juliet at a masked ball; he falls in love with her at first sight. How might this moment be staged to create dramatic focus on two characters in a crowded room? How might costumes contribute to this important moment? Moments such as these are of paramount interest to the costume designer and will lead to lively discussions with the director.

Story Time: Fixed or Interpreted

Most stories use a definite time period incorporating the manners, morals, or mindset of that era. Costumes are the best indicator of time period. Using historical costumes presents some trade-offs. They present the embodied environment for the characters, but often restrict movement. Each historical garment is a balancing act: enhancing one goal but also impeding another. Discuss this balance with the director; plan where to locate the line of compromise. Does the director wish the actors to move with some reasonable historical bearing? Or, will the characters use active movement more favored in contemporary staging? If so, where should the costumes adjust to this expectation? Some contemporary stage practice mixes historical eras in an eclectic manner. One such trend is to set scripts in a "period-ish" or "timeless" manner. This approach can be wildly creative, but that does not mean there are no aesthetic rules. It is even more important for the costume designer to define the rules of such a world.

Story Location

Where a story takes place is an integral part of the story itself. Costume designers are dress detectives, deeply researching the people and locations of stories to understand each in detail. They must know the weather in each season and local habits or trends. They obtain obscure photos, scour people's family memories, photograph people on street corners, conduct interviews with every kind of profession, visit similar locations, use Google Earth, study the backgrounds of paintings for details of everyday life, and read historical material. They determine where each character must have gotten their clothing in that world – are they sewn at home or store bought? Designers especially seek qualities of the environment that will lend a unique approach to the clothing. For instance Katori Hall's play *Hoodoo Love* takes place in Memphis, Tennessee, during a hot summer in 1933, before air conditioning. The costume designer may enhance that aspect of the story by using limp, wrinkled cotton shirts that show perspiration.

Finding Themes or Design Concepts

Once you have recorded your thoughts about the story and the plot, it is time to reflect on overarching meanings or "big ideas" that may help the designer create a visual approach. We call these ideas **themes**, and they enliven the work by focusing the message of the play. Playwrights have something to say when they approach a story – what is the audience supposed to take away from this experience? You can begin to discover themes by asking what the play is *about*. Answer without referring to the events in the plot. What does the author think about the world of the story, or the nature of humanity? Characters often directly state a message as part of their dialogue. What lesson did the protagonist learn or how did key characters change? Does this story remind you of other famous stories, and in what ways? The theme can be elusive, and always requires reflection. There are two important tools that can hold a clue for theme hunting.

Motifs and Parallels

Many stories make use of two powerful narrative devices to construct themes. Most audience members are not aware of them at the time, but once you've detected them they are hard to overlook again. The first device is **motifs**: items such as an idea, word, sound, or image that takes on a significance through *repetition*. It is easy to see a motif in the musical *Hands on a Hardbody*, where a big red truck dominates the stage. Contestants who hope to win that truck must stand with a gloved hand fixed to it for as long as it takes to be the last one standing. The truck is a huge motif that stands in for the hopes and dreams of every contestant. The musical *Hamilton* uses the word "shot" repeatedly as a motif with great significance. It is first used when Hamilton and his friends drink shots in a pub musing how they will not throw away their shot, or opportunities in life. At the end of the musical, Hamilton does throw away his shot in a duel with Aaron Burr, who did not.

The second narrative device is **parallels**, or story elements that resemble each other, inviting comparison between characters, items, locations, or situations. The audience pieces together information themselves, and it is a powerful form of communication. The movie *Parasite*, directed by Bon Joon Ho, features two families on opposite ends of the economic scale. Both their houses feature large picture windows. The poor family's window is patched together from many panes of dirty glass. It's partially sunken below the ground, revealing garbage-laden streets and drunkards. The wealthy family's window is one perfect pane of expensive glass that looks out onto a calm patch of lawn protected from the ugly city. The audience cannot help but compare the two windows, elegant metaphors for each family's view of the world. Try to detect any use of motifs and parallels in the story or consider adding visual motifs for a poetic dimension.

Designers often use **metaphors**, or equating two unlike things, to brainstorm about themes and messages. Do the characters resemble other people or objects in their behavior or their situation? Perhaps the characters resemble beautiful birds trapped in a fancy cage that peck each other from frustration. A character may resemble an emotional battleship or tank. A character's dialogue might resemble an archeologist or detective, always digging deeper into ordinary issues. A character may remind a designer of a squeaky wheel or a meandering river. Capture those ideas to consider how they might translate to costume choices, and to direct your research for ideas.

Sizing Up Plot and Story

The costume designer must be adept at understanding all three aspects of script analysis: the *impact* of story, the *flow* of plot, and the *mechanics* of script. Important elements of the plot are *turning points* that cause motivations to change the appearance of characters. Plots also incorporate acting or visual *gags* and *gimmicks*. Important elements of the story include the *manner* of presentation, *genres*, *tone*, *time*, *location*, and *givens*, or *moments*. Designers read the script multiple times to detect themes to serve as a foundation for the design approach. Two important literary devices that may lead to ideas about them are *motifs* and *parallels*.

Expecting the Unexpected

Devised shows or new works undergoing rewrites during rehearsals pose a special challenge to the costume designer. It requires an ability to think deeply and plan, but still remain agile enough to change in mid-stream. For instance, analysis and costume scene charts for devised shows may be a continual work in progress. The best strategy is real time, in-person collaboration during rehearsals and rapid idea generation. Those who like working in this manner find it exhilarating and rewarding. Rewrites to historic scripts are common; we feel great liberty to juggle the work of long-dead playwrights such as Shakespeare to make them more relatable. New plays will receive regular rewrites as rehearsals reveal a need for adjustments. A thorough understanding of the story will help the costume designer stay flexible, understand what the story gains with additions, and how costumes may contribute to the new goal.

Extra Resources

Art and style movements Artcyclopedia.com

Illustration style history, Normal Rockwell Museum www.illustrationhistory.org

American illustration styles, AmericanIllustrators.com

Story genres 144 Genres and Subgenres for Fiction Writing. www.servicescape.com/blog/144-genres-and-sub genres-for-fiction-writingwww.servicescape.com/blog/144-genres-and-subgenres-for-fiction-writing

Backwards and Forwards: A Technical Manual for Reading Plays, David Ball, 1983.

Visit to a Small Planet: Some Questions to Ask a Play. Elinor Fuchs https://web.mit.edu/jscheib/Public/foundations_06/ef_smallplanet.pdf

Notes

1 Fuchs, Elinor. 2004. "Visit to a Small Planet: Some Questions to Ask a Play." *Theater*, 34(2): pp. 4–9.

2 Appleton, Eric. 2014. "Mechanics and Meaning: Script Analysis Lessons from Design History." *TD&T*, 50(2).

3 Sterritt, David. 1999. *The Films of Jean-Luc Godard: Seeing the Invisible*. Cambridge and New York: Cambridge University Press, p. 20.

4 Caputo, Anthony C. 2003. *Visual Storytelling: The Art and Technique*. New York: Watson-Guptill Publications, p. 31.

5 DeKoven, Lenore. 2006. *Changing Direction A Practical Approach to Directing Actors in Film and Theatre*. New York: Elsevier Focal Press, p. 63.

9.
THE MECHANICS OF A SCRIPT

The script provides the structure for the entire production. Playwright Sam Shepard described his view of writing scripts: "For me, playwriting is and always has been like making a chair. Your concerns are balance, form, timing, light, space, music. If you don't have these essentials, you might as well be writing a theoretical essay, not a play."[1] The script is a machine and to unlock the formal information within it, the designer must extract complex, specialized information. Playwrights have made a number of decisions they consider important to the manner of presentation. One of these is the way they designate scenes. Traditional *theatrical* formats use longer acts or scenes to divide key events. Contemporary formats can be *cinematic* in approach: short scenes that leap around in location or time with little opportunity for performers to leave the stage.

The scene format may prescribe what kind of costume design is desirable. Designing incorrectly for the intended scene structure may cause havoc once the production gets to the stage. The designer tracks the structure using a **scene breakdown chart** that provides a snapshot of the entire show. The script provides several fundamental pieces of information for the costume designer:

- The order of scenes and events
- The characters of the play
- The number of actors cast to play those characters
- Which actors play what characters
- When each character appears onstage

These elements seem very straightforward, but a closer inspection of many scripts reveals the designer must do some detective work to see the whole picture.

Breaking Down the Script

Put aside what you know about story and plot, except for those scenes you've determined to be *turning points*. Read the script again for technical information. You will need pencil or pen, highlighter, optional adhesive page flags, and an optional straight edge.

- Flip through the script to mark the **beginning** of every scene. Fold down the corner or attach a page flag. Consulting the script in future will be much easier if it is divided into sections. Highlight the Act/Sc number on each page or label the page flag (Figure 9.1).

- Draw a line at the **end** of each scene. Many scenes end in the middle of a page so this serves as a visible reminder. If you are planning to do a French scene breakdown (see the next section) draw a different type of line (new color

DOI: 10.4324/9781003015284-11

or dashes) when major characters *enter* a scene part way through.

- At the start of each scene, list the **characters** in the scene.
- Note the **location** and the passage of **time**.
- Read the script again to detect **embedded actions** or events that may affect costumes. These can be part of stage directions or implied in dialogue. For instance, a character referring to their pocket watch must carry one. Characters who enter from a rain storm might be wet. Any violence may be marked with stage blood, later bruises, or bandages.
- Note the central **action** and **intent** of each scene – just five to ten words. Why is this scene in the play? This forces us to think about the essence of each scene.

The script will look like a well-thumbed shopping list after a thorough breakdown. There is a special type of expertise we gain only by digging deep into the nuts-and-bolts structure of a script. Over time, this

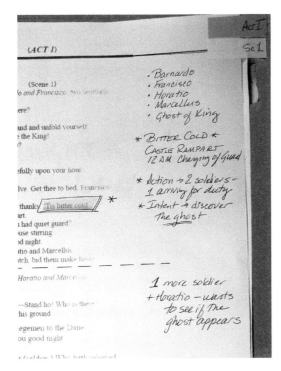

Figure 9.1 Script breakdown notes for the first scene of *Hamlet* with notes on the side that summarize who is in each scene, the location, action, and intent.

knowledge becomes ingrained as part of our theatrical knowledge, and we develop a sense of how scenes on the page will play out on the stage. The act of taking notes forces our brains to verbalize the format of a performed art. Scripts for film follow a specific format that can be automatically broken down using script software. (See the Extra Resources section.)

The Casting Plan and Cast Size

The costume designer must know the casting plan to break down the script thoroughly. Prior to auditions the director and producer decide how many performers they can afford to pay and what kind of contract or pay scale pertains to each performer. Casting plans directly impact the costume designer's workload. For instance, a straightforward design may increase in scope if the producers cast two performers in some roles as swing performers. Or, will there be an ensemble added, understudies, or other extras? The first order of business for the costume designer is understanding the actual number of performers to expect. In some cases, there will be fewer actors than characters, and some performers will play more than one character in the story.

Some smaller roles may be combined, eliminated, or assigned to other cast members. Does the script include unnamed roles as a crowd, servants, lords, reporters? Will the cast double as those roles, or will there be extras? Will stagehands wear costumes for some scene transitions?

The second casting consideration is the decision to use traditional or alternative casting. Will **inclusive** casting or nonbinary casting affect the way a particular character would dress? Does inclusive casting present the opportunity to feature performers' cultural heritage in their costumes? Lastly, are characters or extras **visible** onstage in ways not apparent in the script, for instance do servants appear in the background of scenes when they have no lines? Consult the director for their plans, and how they will assign roles to actors.

The Costume Scene Chart

Planning the design begins with transferring the script information to a **costume scene chart**. It is a timesaver to use a template to gather information. Creating a digital chart facilitates adding or moving rows and columns of information should there be rewrites or casting changes. The designer will continue to use this chart throughout planning and fittings. Post it in the fitting room so everyone understands the costume changes. Backstage staff and crew will use the costume scene chart to plot backstage routines. Stage managers will use the costume chart in rehearsals to track costume changes and blocking. Choose which format of scene chart best fits the way scenes progress in that script. The standard style for traditional plays is the **act/ scene** breakdown using divisions written into the script. The alternative format is the **French scene** breakdown using actor entrances as divisions. A final choice is the **musical** or opera scene breakdown that adds songs and dance breaks into the chart.

Act/Scene Breakdown

The act/scene breakdown works best for plays with a traditional structure of longer scenes grouped together into acts. Scene breaks indicate a change in tone, time, or location. Scene breaks conclude a major segment of the story, providing a pause. These breaks and pauses are **non-diegetic** elements that are not part of the story world. The audience does not believe the characters see the stage lights dim, or a change of scenery. These are theatrical conventions outside of the characters' awareness. Figure 9.2 shows an example of the play *Angel Street*, using the act/scene format.

French Scene Breakdown

This format received its name in 17th-century France when early dramatic productions were performed

Angel Street			
	Act I	**Act II**	**Act III**
Scene Information / Character	*Late afternoon- 5 p.m.* *Chilly London weather* *Pimlico district, 1880*	*Past 6 p.m.* *Chilly London weather* *Pimlico district, 1880*	*11 p.m.* *Chilly London weather* *Pimlico district, 1880*
Mrs. Manningham	-Onstage	-Onstage -Exits on "Heaven's name" (60) -Enters after Elizabeth leaves (67) -Exits on "Good-bye" (77)	-Enters on "ta-ta" (90) -Exits on "you yet, Madam" (99) -Enters on "take him away" (103)
Mr. Manningham	-Onstage -Exits on "believe me" (26)	-Enters after Rough gets his hat (60) -Exits & Enters on "yes, sir" (63) -Exits & Enters on "yes" (64) -Exits on "good night, Elizabeth" (66)	-Enters on front door shutting (81) -Exit with policemen after they return to the room (l07)
Nancy	-Enters on "come in" (6) -Exits on "directly, sir" (8) -Enters on "to the play!" (13) w tea set -Exits on "muffins directly" (13) -Enters & Exits during recitation w muffins (15) -Enters on "Come in" (19) -Exits on "you may go" (20)		-Enters on bell ring (81) -Exits & Enters on "Certainly, sir" (82) -Exits after bringing tray to Mr. Man & Enters after going upstairs (82) -Exits on "Good night" (87) -Enters on drawers closing (87). -Exits on "pleasure, sir" (87) & Enters when Manningham moves to fireplace (88) -Exits on "go on, Nancy" (89), Enters after Manningham returns to the fireplace (89) -Exits after Mrs. Manningham appears (90)
Elizabeth	-Enters on bell ring (4) -Exits after being given money (4) -Enters on "Come in" (18) -Exits on "Yes sir" (19) -Enters after knocking (26) -Exits on "call him in" (28) -Enters w Rough (28) -Exits on "isn't it?" (28)	-Enters on "please, please go" (57) -Exits on "Heaven's name" (60) -Enters after bell ring (60) -Exits on "him go" (67) w tray	-Enters after Mrs. Manningham is slapped (I 07)

Figure 9.2 An excerpt from a scene chart for *Angel Street*. The script uses three longer acts. The designer chose to note the exits and entrances by page number in the main body of the chart.

Credit: Courtesy of Ayrika Johnson

in aristocratic homes using existing rooms as the scenery. There were few options for special lights or a curtain, so dramatists such as Racine and Corneille wrote their scripts to be performed without physical or technological shifts. Scenes began and ended when a new character appeared, shifting the tone or direction of events. These signals are **diegetic**, or native to the world of the story. This scene chart works well for plays written with very long acts. The costume designer who wishes to closely track any play may adapt this French scene breakdown to any script, as seen in Figure 9.3. This format results in extremely detailed charts.

Musical or Opera Breakdown

Musical scripts cycle between dialogue-only scenes that advance the plot and musical numbers that explore the accompanying emotions. Additional performers such as chorus may enter for a dance break, and melt away when dialogue resumes. Tracking dialogue, singing, and dance creates another layer of logistics for the costume designer. Figure 9.4 documents one style of scene breakdown for a musical.

Creating the Costume Scene Chart

Many designers use table-formatting software to create scene charts, such as Google Sheets, Excel, or Word. Three parts of a scene chart hold crucial information:

- **Information banner** at top divided into acts and scenes
- **Actor/character columns** at left
- **Plot area** displaying scene data at the pertinent horizontal and vertical intersections

The **information banner** includes horizontal lines that tag specific information to each appropriate scene. Every designer will include slightly different information, depending on their own personal style and the needs of each production. The information banner for the *Parade* scene chart (Figure 9.4) consists of the top eight horizontal lines. Information banners may include:

- **Story day, time of day, passage of time**. This notation provides the passage of time at a glance. Every story begins on *Day 1* or *Night 1*. From that starting spot, track the passage of time and time of day. Scenes that share a common time are labeled *continuous (cont)*. A story that takes place over four months uses a different tone and pace than one that takes place over one day. This information may not be as obvious in a script as you would think, requiring deduction and consulting the director. Is passage of time important in this show? If so, changing clothes to indicate time jumps or seasons may be an important visual element that costumes contribute to the audience experience.

- **Location of each scene.** Understanding where each scene takes place is essential to what characters wear. Costumes may be the only indication of shifting locale, such as adding coats and hats to communicate the characters are now outdoors. Ask where each character was before arrival and the mode of transportation they might have used. Consider details such as a coat, backpack, or purse to create that backstory.

- **Scene pages.** There are two important pieces of information we learn from knowing the length of a scene. The first is how long actors are on stage, also indicating how long *offstage* actors have to perform costume changes. The second advantage to recording page numbers is that rehearsal notes or notes from actors are often communicated by page number, not act and scene. The chart will be a quick guide for reading rehearsal notes.

- **Brief summary of action or dramatic intent.** Brief notes to highlight what happens in each scene. Unlike actors and stage managers, costume designers generally don't work through the script every day. But they make many decisions in the course of a fitting requiring an understanding of each scene's intent. The scene note also forces the designer to articulate what is *most important* about that scene, or why that scene is in the play in the first place. This knowledge can be powerful information for design choices.

PETER AND THE STARCATCHER	P 1	Prologue P 2-3	Prologue P 3	P 4-6	7-9	sc 1 10-14	sc 1 15-17
Locale/Scene Name	Bare Stage **BEGIN ENSEMBLE MODERN** Dreaming	**Transform Costumes & Docks**		**Two Docks of Porstmouth**	**Ragtag Neverland Sailors VS Sharp Seamen Wasp**	**Docks Dodo Talk Amulets Evil Cat**	**Molly's Cabin**
Story Points	Ensemble costumes	Pre-Stache Starts the Story	Grempkin is cruel	Slank Marks a Trunk	Sailors & Seamen Song, Peter out of Crate	Amulets	Alf flirts with Bumbrake Molly runs
ARIELLE CHIN **Molly Aster** — *no other roles*	X	X		X	X	*Molly + amulet under her dress*	*Molly*
JAKE NATHAN **Boy/ Peter** — *no other roles*	X		X	X	X		
JOE DANIEL **Prentiss** — (Leader issues) Sailor/Pirate, Seaman, Mermaid	X		X	X	*Sailor/Pirate and/or Seaman* (Uniform hat)	*Sailor & Seaman* (Uniformed)	
JORGE NUÑOZ **Ted** — (Food Issues) Sailor/Pirate, Seaman, Mermaid	X		X	X	*Sailor/Pirate and/or Seaman* (Uniform Hat)	*Sailor & Seaman* (Uniformed)	

Figure 9.3 An excerpt from a costume scene chart for *Peter and the Starcatcher* using the French scene breakdown format. Each act is divided into page columns using actor entrances as the key.

			ACT ONE					
PARADE ATLANTA GA 1913			SC 1			SC 2	SC 3	
			Green Field & Tree	[REVEAL]	Atlanta Street	Frank's Bedroom	Atlanta Street- Parade	
		M u s i c a l / N u m b e r	#1 *Prologue: Old Red Hills of Home*	Parade passing, Peachtree St Atlanta	#1A *Old Red Hills Pt 2*	Confederate Memorial Day	#2 *Anthem: Dream of Atlanta*	#2A *How Can I Call this Home?*
			PAST 1862	DAY 1 1913 Morning	April 26,	DAY 1 Cont	DAY 1 CONT	
			Outside	Outside	Outside	Inside	Outside	
			martial, sentimental, slow		martial, sentimental, slow		upbeat, martial, 30 secs	sentimental
			p 1 -4			p 4- 6	p 6-12	
Young Confed Soldier	Crisp new uniform, newly enlisted, full pack		X					
Fiddlin' John	country fiddler							x
Old Confed Soldier	same soldier many years later?				X		X on float	
Judge Roan	Old fashioned							
Aide	City Aid				X			
Lucille Frank	Jewish, mid 20s, quintiessential southern wife, deferential, well mannered					X doing her hair		
Leo Frank	Jewish, older than Lucille, 30s? Reserved, stiff, thick glasses, works for Lucille's Uncle pencil factory, as					X 3 pc suit, tie, watch chain	X moving thru crowd	

Figure 9.4 Excerpt from scene chart for *Parade* noting musical numbers in separate columns for focus. Columns with green headers are musical numbers. Columns of dialogue scenes use gray headers.

The **actor/character columns** may look different before casting and after casting is complete. Designers usually work well ahead of casting and may not know which actors will play multiple roles. Start with a *character* column listing all the roles in the script, each on their own line, as shown in Figure 9.2. After casting, insert the actor's name to match their roles, as in Figure 9.3. Align the roles to each actor making sure to copy and paste the *entire* horizontal line of their data. This method creates an actor grouping of roles that instantly reveals when that actor changes costumes to a different role, and when that results in fast changes. For instance, in Figure 9.3, actor Clive Jacks plays three different roles. Casting decisions are sometimes made without thinking about the time to change costumes between scenes or between roles. If the costume designer catches a conflict early enough, he may negotiate solutions with the director before blocking begins.

Plotting the Costume Looks

The **plot area** documents information about each actor in each scene. Begin with an X in each intersection of actor and scene indicating that character appears onstage. (See Figure 9.4.) This first pass tells the designer where each actor is at all times. Check to see if there is anything unusual,

such as two characters played by the same actor appearing in the same scene. As planning progresses to the second phase, add a general **costume number** to each actor in each scene. (See Figure 9.5) The costume an actor wears at top of show (TOS) is their #1 look. The next time they appear onstage, determine if a new costume

Romeo & Juliet	Act	ACT ONE							
	Scene	*SC 1*		*SC 2*		*SC 3*	*SC 4*		
	Day & Time of day	Sunday Day 1 Mid July 9 AM		Day 1 Sunday Afternoon, cont		Day 1 Sunday Eve, Dusk	Night 1 Sunday		
	Location of this scene	Street		Capulet House	Street	Capulet House	Before the house	Capulet House- PARTY	
	Script Page	p2- 3	p3-6	p6	p6-8	p8-11	p11-14	p14-17	
	Brief Summary, intent of scene or action	Prince Enters, threatens death, Romeo is missing	Romeo loves Rosalind	Paris asks for Juliet, she is too young.	Capulets prepare feast, Romeo sees guest list	Paris to woo Juliet, Dinner bustle begins!	Sneak into Party, Queen Mab speech	Romeo, sees Juliet, Tybalt sees Romeo	Fated lovers meet
Tom Page — ROMEO MONTAGUE			1 day wear		1 day wear		2 Party look	2 party look	2 Party look
Sissy Smith — JULIET CAPULET						1 day wear- pants?		2 party look	2 party look
Pedro Juarez — CAPULET		1 day wear- suit		1				1	
Moneesha Chatterjee — NURSE						1 day wear		2 Party look	2

(A)

	LORD MONTAGUE	1 daywear- suit							
Daniel Pak	PETER Capulet Servant, comic part			2 vest look	2 vest look	2 vest look		2 vest look	
	FRIAR JOHN								
Carla Amira	PRINCE ESCALUS of Verona	1 day wear, regal						2 party look regal	
	APOTHECARY drug dealer								

(B)

Figure 9.5 Detail of *Romeo and Juliet* costume scene chart after casting is complete. Note the multiple roles assigned to Daniel Pak. The red arrow notes when an actor changes roles quickly.

is required. Label that #2, and so on. It's not necessary yet to know exactly what the character will wear to complete this step. This is an exercise in logic and possibilities. Begin with basic looks: would the character appear in day wear, evening wear, pajamas, outerwear such as coat and hat, work or party wear? Noting the passage of time or time of day for each scene alerts the designer to judge if costume changes are necessary. When characters appear later in the day or the next day, have they changed clothing? Note any cause for change such as a jump in the timeline, a change in weather or season, or the impact of a plot point such as a party or violence.

The designer may reach beyond pure logistics when plotting the looks for each character. They may wish to change costumes differently than indicated in the script to support narrative goals. One example is changing the color palette to match seasons or an emotional arc. The scene chart is so crucial that some designers use the breakdown process to start their creative juices. In cases where the designer considers *turning points*, *motifs*, and *parallels* as reasons for changing

clothing it is informative to add these to the scene chart, as in Figure 9.6. Charts for complex shows may be very elaborate with color coding and extra information, while others remain spartan. The possible costume changes documented on the chart forms the basis for detailed conversations with the director.

The Costume Count and Costume Lists

The costume scene breakdown provides a way to gauge the scope of the show. Add the looks for each actor and for the show as a whole, to create an initial **costume count**. Use partial numbers to indicate smaller changes: adding a jacket *or* hat is one-quarter of a costume. Adding a jacket *and* hat is one-half of a costume, while changing a shirt, tie, and jacket is three-quarters of a costume. Early knowledge of the number of costumes is critical to every aspect of planning. A discovery that a relatively small cast show might actually require 25 costumes will have ramifications for the budget and the designer's time. Compromises or changes should be discussed with the director before the designer heads too far down

Romeo & Juliet	Act	ACT ONE								ACT TWO		
	Scene	SC 1		SC 2		SC 3	SC 4			SC 1	SC 2	SC 3
	Day & Time of day	Sunday Day 1 Mid July 9 AM		Day 1 Sunday Afternoon, cont		Day 1 Sunday Eve, Dusk	Night 1 Sunday			Night 1 Late Night/Early AM	Night 1 Late Night/Early AM	Day 2 Early Monday AM
	Location of this scene	Street		Capulet House	Street	Capulet House	Before the house?	Capulet House- PARTY		Capulet Window exterior	Capulet Window exterior	Friar Laurence cell- Mon
	Script Page	p2- 3	p3-6	p6	p6-8	p8-11	p11-14	p14-17		p 17-18	p 19-24	p 24- 27
	Brief Summary, intent of scene or action	Prince Enters, threatens death, Romeo is missing	Romeo loves Rosalind	Paris asks for Juliet, she is too young.	Capulets prepare feast, Romeo sees guest list	Paris to woo Juliet, Dinner bustle begins!	Sneak into Party, Queen Mab speech	Romeo, sees Juliet, Tybalt sees Romeo	Fated lovers meet	The window/balcony scene	the window/balcony scene	Romeo asks Friar Laurence to marry them
Tom Page	ROMEO MONTAGUE		1 blue linen suit		1 blue linen suit		2 Party	2 party	2 Party	2A removes part of costume	2A pirate shirt, trousers	FC IN 1 blue linen
Sissy Smith	JULIET CAPULET					1 play suit	2 party dress	2 party dress			3 robe, pjs	
Pedro Juarez	CAPULET	1 lt grey suit		1 lt grey suit				1 lt grey suit				
Cesar Galleo	FRIAR LAWRENCE											1 garden apron, shirt sleeves
Moneesha Chatterjee	NURSE					1 rust/white dress + apron	2 Party Dress	2			3 nightgown, robe	

Figure 9.6 Excerpt of a final costume scene chart for Romeo and Juliet. Columns filled with color are plot turning points.

the path of creating the design. A higher-than-expected costume count encourages the designer to think early of ways to streamline their design. For instance, a character may keep the same trousers and shirt for multiple scenes, changing just their sweater and tie for variety.

The next step is to consolidate all this information onto the **costume list**. Begin with each character and transpose the number of looks from the chart to the list. Again, the designer does not have to know great detail about each costume. Listing the type of costume is enough to start the next steps of the design process. Using the scene chart in Figure 9.5 the initial costume list for Romeo might look something like this:

Romeo Montague

#1 Day wear, better/wealthy, bright color
#2 Party wear, rented that day, face mask or hat
#2A Balcony look – sheds part of party look to reveal, or adds cloak to hide?
#3 Day wear #2, midway color, more adult
#3A Undress look, shirtless?
#4 Day wear #3, dark color
#4A Day wear #3, disheveled, remove jacket, vulnerable?

Four Costumes, Seven Looks or Variations

The designation of a letter after a number, such as 2A, indicates a *variation* of the prior costume. A variation may be an item removed or added, or a different manner of wearing the same costume. This list captures four costumes for Romeo: three day wear and one party regalia, and also reminds the designer there are three variations of Romeo's costumes to plan to reveal his emotional arc. This list will serve as a handy budget calculator as well as a list of research or renderings to track.

Sizing Up Script Mechanics

The script provides the structure for the entire production, and it is the bedrock the entire team consults over and over to stay on track. The playwright's desires are not only contained in the narrative dialogue, imagery, and themes but also in the format chosen to present the narrative. Designers break down the script to focus on the structure and its contribution to the performance. A **script breakdown** translates into the **costume scene chart** that gives the costume designer an important tool for both artistic and logistical decisions. The designer documents the scope of the project through making a **costume count** and **costume lists**.

Expecting the Unexpected

A costume director was charged with managing the upcoming premiere of a new play, *Angels in America*. It had received a smaller workshop production and this would be the first major premiere in a regional theater. The set had been designed and was well under construction. But no costume designer had been hired. With just a few weeks to go before first rehearsals, the costume director went to see the in-house producer. "We need to hire a costume designer so I can start pre-production planning" she explained. "What's the hurry?" he asked. "It's just a modern dress show." The costume director learned there were never two more terrifying words than "*It's just . . . .*"

Extra Resource

Film Script Breakdown Software Video Collective. www. freelancevideocollective.com/how-to-complete-a-script-breakdown-free-template/

Note

1 Shephard, Sam. n.d. "Playwright Quotes and Aphorisms About Play." *Quotespopular.com.* https://quotespopular. com/playwright/about/play.

10.
CHARACTERS ENGAGE THE AUDIENCE

Audiences want to watch compelling stories; they want to ride the emotional or intellectual roller coaster offered. Compelling stories are about specific characters who have come alive with vivid details. The costume designer's contribution to those details is integral to audience immersion. Creating engaging characters resembles the circular ripples that form around a rock thrown into a pond. The smaller inner circles expand from the center, growing larger as they move. The script is the center; actors and designers accumulate information through deduction and exploration to create fascinating characters. This detective work is called **dramaturgy**: asking questions and providing context for the characters. Costume dramaturgy collects three types of information: ***script clues*** reveal observable and implied information. Costume designers then add deductions using ***group dynamics*** and ***clothing psychology***.

Figure 10.1 Observable character traits.

Part One: Clue Hunting in the Script

Costume dramaturgy is a comprehensive probe of the context within a play. This step is sometimes called "reading between the lines." We will augment this script exploration with research in Chapter 13. Designers search for three kinds of information within a script: observable traits, implied qualities, and descriptive information. **Descriptive** information may originate with the playwright or may be information characters tell about each other. One character may describe another as witty or slow, large or small, or dark or light. **Observable** information is factual information provided by the playwright, revealed in dialogue or that comes to light during the plot. Observable traits include:

- **Age.** In many societies elders receive a measure of respect, and some forms of clothing are considered appropriate only for older or younger people.
- **Social status or wealth.** Characters show status when they display symbols of wealth or valued symbols. It is informative to rank characters in order of status, power, or wealth to inform costume choices.

DOI: 10.4324/9781003015284-12

- **Occupation.** Many people wear signals of their occupations even when dressing casually. For instance, some professional men prefer khaki trousers as casual wear instead of jeans, or their casual shirts still include a collar, such as a polo shirt.
- **Geography**. People are very influenced by what others around them are wearing. Those who work in rural areas dress very differently from those in the city.
- **Situation.** People dress very differently for different *situations* such as social occasions, sporting activities, working at the office, staying at home.
- **Historical era.** Audiences are not expert in accurate period dress; yet they have a keen sense of authenticity and consistency. Historical costumes affect the way actors move and the mannerisms they use.
- **Gender spectrum.** Many classic productions use socially imposed constructs of gender. Contemporary productions are rethinking these old dictates, and some new plays are written to challenge this, such as *Men in Boats* by Jaclyn Backhaus.
- **Props** or accessories the character handles during action.

Implied information isn't explicitly stated or created by the playwright. This information comes from hearing the dialogue and thinking about the situations or actions in the script and possible backstory for each character. Using your own life experience, think about each character walking through their days in the story. In some cases the designer gleans information from the script mechanics itself.

- **Top of show.** When the story begins, where are the characters in the first scene? Indoors in their own home, or are they outsiders arriving in someone else's space? How did they get to that location, what mode of transportation? How would that affect their dress?
- **Emotional arc**. Do characters grow increasingly upset or disheveled, lose or add items of clothing?

- **Language** or manner of speaking, correct grammar, formal speech, street slang. Do they speak the language in the play with an accent?
- **Actions** that affect the character such as a fight or duplicity. What do these actions say about a character?
- **Mechanics** of the script or literary devices that group characters.

"No other training but theater taught me to organize the character arc and how to divide that into sections" —Ruth Carter, costume designer for *The Black Panther*[1]

Types of Roles in the Script

Important aspects of casting and script mechanics can define the roles in the script. This information ranks the importance of each role to the outcome of the plot and story.

- **Leads** carry the bulk of the plot. The designer may wish to create focus for these characters in the design. However these characters often experience a great deal more character development than others and their costumes may not have to transmit as much immediate information as other roles.
- **Ensemble** casts work together equally as a group. The designer in that case may wish to equalize the design, ensuring no one single character pulls too much focus.
- **Featured** roles appear throughout the story operating as a foil or driver of action. They may be the leading character's best friends, parents, or enemies.
- **Supporting** roles appear during specific scenes or plot lines to provide information or challenges.
- **Dependent or minor** roles appear once or a limited number of times with few lines. They populate a location or situation, such as servants, waiters, delivery people, neighbors. They may vanish from the story after their scene.
- **Group** roles include the chorus in operas, and an ensemble of extra players in dramatic plays. *Extras*, *atmosphere*, or *supernumeraries* are silent roles tied to a specific location. They are

part of the stage picture as villagers, peasants, soldiers, street vendors.

It is common to divide limited budget and time between rankings of characters. It makes sense that more money and labor would be spent on the leading roles to incorporate more detail or better-quality materials. However, there are cases where costumes for smaller roles can be inversely important: silent roles have no other way of imparting information except their appearance, so the costume must be complete and communicative. A leading character who is onstage most of the time will have more character development in their dialogue and action, making overt signals in the costumes less necessary.

Types of Characters in the Plot

We rank *script* roles by the amount of time they appear onstage, whether they have lines or how much they impact the plot. There is another aspect to characters – a closer look at the reason they are in the story. Dividing characters by their plot function provides a wealth of information for the costume designer.

- **Dynamic characters**. Most often the protagonist and immediate companions who change or learn something in the course of the story. They create a noticeable story arc. Costumes may reflect the change or the physical effects of this arc.
- **Complex characters** undergo some changes and exhibit some subtleties, but their story is not the subject of this tale. One example is Lucius Best or Frozone in *The Incredibles*. Costumes may undergo changes in the story to reflect some changes.
- **Symbolic characters** represent something larger than themselves, often tied into the theme of the story. One example is Gabriel, the older brother in August Wilson's *Fences*. He represents salvation and blows a trumpet for Troy's funeral, evoking the angel Gabriel.
- **Static/stock characters** do not change although they participate in the plot. The Dursleys, Harry Potter's aunt and uncle never change through the years of opportunity to learn from their mistakes. Costumes may

remain similar through the passage of time, establishing variations on a single look.
- **Trope characters** are defined mostly by a single trait or quality. They could almost be in any story. For instance, the cop with no personality who arrives to arrest someone, a bag lady, and comic relief characters. They serve as living illustrations of a type.

"I definitely consider myself a character-based designer. It's very important that each character has their own story to tell. I like to think of where they came from, I like to think of where they are right now and I like to think of where they're going. That's my job as part of the storytelling team to help tell that story with the way the costumes look, feel, move and how they help the actor." —Jill Ohanneson, costume designer *For All Mankind, Dexter, Six Feet Under*[2]

Figure 10.2 It's easy to identify a character wearing a trope or iconic costume such as this cowboy's ensemble.
Credit: Courtesy of the Smithsonian National Museum of African American History and Culture

Grounding Character With Backstory

Characters are not born on the day the story begins; they have led a life that brought them to this point. Many people wear clothing they've owned for some time, changing their wardrobes less often than the fashion industry makes us think. A character's jewelry may be entirely inherited from family members and therefore be more old-fashioned than the rest of their outfit. A character may never iron or hang up clothing, so everything has visible wrinkles. And we all know people who own a favorite pair of jeans that is well over a decade old. These kinds of details lend authenticity to a character. By contrast, some stories feature characters with little backstory evident in their clothing. One such show is the Netflix series *#blackAF*, created by Kenya Barris who stars as a fictionalized version of himself, a very successful television producer. Themes for this show revolve around the difficulty of being a "new money" Black family in today's world. Kenya's character *did* acquire his $2,000 track suits and expensive collectible sneakers recently, and he goes to great pains to hide any vestige of his backstory. Costume designer Michelle Cole costumes the members of this affluent family in actual designer clothing. "I'm not afraid of color and texture. Each person wears a different pattern," she notes. "Kenya is a large personality, and in this culture, when we make it, we like to shine."[3]

Part Two: A Group Is the Sum of Its Parts

There is a lot we can discover by thinking about the way characters interact or arrange themselves in the story: what is true for all the characters, and where do they differ? Dividing the characters into *subgroupings* presents organizational information for the costume designer. For instance, there may be a generation gap evident in a story, so clothing differences between parents and children enhance their characters. Costume designers sometimes create characters with little information about them. Stories with many minor characters MAY provide few clues. Shakespeare's scripts, for instance, use lords, dukes, judges, or soldiers that appear in only one or two scenes. In this case, the costume designer often wholly creates the character, providing a base from which the actor will blossom. How will the audience tell these characters apart, and place them in context? This can be even more demanding in film or video where many minor characters appear with few or no lines. What are some strategies to distinguish these and other poorly defined characters?

> "I think we can all read each other like a cheap airport novel just by looking at each other's outfits, if we know what we're looking at. Our clothes overshare our circumstances far more than we realize." —Cintra Wilson[4]

One approach is to provide an identity to each based on group dynamics, or how each character contributes to a group goal. The human brain seeks the certainty of structure or patterns to quickly make sense of the world. The brain supplies a reason why items or people may be in a group. By appearing in a group, the brain will associate them automatically. We see this principle at work whenever a restaurant greeter assumes all those standing near the podium is one seating party. German psychologists developed theories about this human perception they called **Gestalt principles**. European literature provides many examples of characters forming a Gestalt-style whole. Harry Potter, Hermione Grainger, and Ron Weasley together supply all the qualities necessary to defeat Voldemort: courage, knowledge, and loyalty. The original *Star Trek* series joined Captain Kirk (courage), Spock (knowledge), McCoy (empathy), and Scotty (ingenuity) to provide all the characteristics needed to travel where no one had gone before.

The costume designer can create individual characters using Gestalt devices by first determining the group's goal, then assign interlocking roles to each individual using their lines as clues to each personality. For instance, three unnamed Lords may create a scene in a Shakespeare play. Their group function is to tell the audience what was said or decided offstage, providing context for upcoming actions. By carefully reading their lines, the designer can deduce an individual personality trait that contrasts or complements the others. Perhaps one Lord's dialogue shows he has all the information. Perhaps he is well-connected at court, or is a gossip. Another Lord's dialogue may communicate worry for others. A third Lord may have lines that urge the others to tell someone. This is enough information to construct three characters that work as a group: a knower, a feeler, and a doer, or mind, heart, and body.

Character Archetypes: From Jung to *Star Wars*

Archetypal characters are those based on universal patterns of human behavior, recognizable through the ages and around the world. Writers have combined the work of psychologist Carl Jung and literature professor Joseph Campbell to identify characters identified as archetypes. Each archetype fulfills certain roles within a story to engage the audience. Luke, Darth Vader, and Obi Wan are archetypal characters, and Campbell enjoyed a moment of fame in 1977 when George Lucas credited his work with the inspiration for *Star Wars* characters. Hollywood script writer Christopher Vogler, in turn, adapted Campbell's theories into *The Writer's Journey*. That book distills theories into easily identified character groups that apply to many scripted stories. Many adventure, superhero, and epic films follow these characterizations. But these character types can also be used to understand smaller scale dramas. This categorizing of characters by function in the story is a powerful tool used by writers, and costume designers will gain a great deal of character information from using it as well. (See the Extra Resources section.)

Character Archetypes

Identifying the characters of any story using group dynamics, subgroupings, or character typing provides a considerable amount of information that may not be at first apparent in a story. Categorizing character types uses the way our brains work detecting patterns and easily identifiable groups. Archetypes use ancient storytelling tropes to communicate a great deal of nonverbal understanding about a character. Both form the basis for brainstorming about possible character traits. Table 10.1 summarizes some typical characters in literature – many could be the protagonist or antagonists of a story.

Part Three: Clothing Psychology

Costume designers are consummate observers of people in real life, observing the world and storing that knowledge away for the future. Our clothing is an extension of our personality and all the forces that form it. Alison Lurie, a Pulitzer-winning writer published a comprehensive exploration of clothing psychology titled *The Language of Clothes*. She notes

> Long before I am near enough to talk to you on the street . . . you announce your sex, age and class to me through what you are wearing. I may not be able to put what I observe into words, but I register the information unconsciously, and you simultaneously do the same for me. By the time we meet and converse we have already spoken to each other in an older and more universal tongue.[5]

Dressing With Uniformity

Dressing with uniformity declares the individual belongs to a group, a tribe, a profession. Formal uniforms such as military, police, medical workers, communicate authority or expertise in some field. Unofficial uniforms are dictated by what that group considers signs of success or authority. Lawyers, professors – even designers – adopt identifying features in common.

Uniformity is part of a social contract of what is "proper" to wear. Dressing in agreement shows an appreciation for that group's rules, and those who are unaware of these social rules are marked as outsiders. Uniformity is a powerful vocabulary for costume designers working within a story that divides characters into different groups. The greater the difference between character groups, the less they empathize with each other. Or, the costume designer may decide to essentially dress the enemies alike to make a statement about their common humanity.

Table 10.1 Character Archetypes

Characters Who Seek Change	Characters Who Create Challenges	Characters Who Advise or Unlock Answers	Characters Who Unite Forces
Leader	**Shadow**	**Creator**	**Innocent**
Drives the story, takes a physical, emotional, or symbolic journey to right a wrong	Evil character or the dark side of a complex character	Builds new structures, invents new methods, solves problems with skills or knowledge	A pure character whose cause rallies others
Strength: courage, perseverance, moral leadership	**Strength:** intelligent, unrelenting, skilled	**Strength:** creativity, passion	**Strength:** kindness, sincerity, purity
Weakness: overconfidence, hubris, ignorance of rules	**Weakness:** power hungry, greedy, vengeance	**Weakness:** single-mindedness	**Weakness:** vulnerable, helpless, unskilled
Example: Dorothy, *Wizard of Oz*; Chihiro, *Spirited Away*	**Example:** Walter White, *Breaking Bad*	**Example:** Scotty, *Star Trek*	**Example:** Forest Gump; Dory, *Finding Nemo*
Lover	**Rebel or Outsider**	**Guide or Sage**	**Caregiver**
Guided by the heart or romantic love	One who breaks the rules, operates as an outsider or outlaw	A wise figure with extraordinary knowledge	Supports others, sacrifices for the cause
Strength: empathy, passion, conviction	**Strength:** independent, unhindered	**Strength:** wisdom, experience	**Strength:** selfless, loyal
Weakness: irrational behavior	**Weakness:** arrogant, selfish	**Weakness:** cautious, bound to traditions	**Weakness:** lacks ambition or leadership qualities
Example: Juliet, *Romeo and Juliet*	**Example:** Katniss Everdeen, *Hunger Games*	**Example:** Yoda, *Star Wars*	**Example:** Mrs. Weasley, *Harry Potter* books
Explorer	**Trickster or Seducer**	**Warrior**	**Everyman**
Traveler in search of new knowledge	Employs humor or illusion to get what they want	Characters with physical strength and plan of action	A genial character recognizable from life
Strength: curious, driven, open-minded	**Strength:** funny, skilled, shrewd, charismatic	**Strength:** calm under pressure, unwavering, courage	**Strength:** relatable, unpretentious, truth-teller
Weakness: restless, unsatisfied, unreliable	**Weakness:** annoying, one-dimensional, disappointing	**Weakness:** can misjudge enemy, a secret physical flaw	**Weakness:** unsophisticated, can be fooled
Example: Nancy Drew; Marge Gunderson, *Fargo*	**Example:** C-3PO, *Star Wars*; the Weasley twins in *Harry Potter*, Jessica Rabbit, *Who Framed Roger Rabbit*	**Example:** Diana, *Wonder Woman*	**Example:** Mr. Weasley, *Harry Potter* books

Characters Who Seek Change	Characters Who Create Challenges	Characters Who Advise or Unlock Answers	Characters Who Unite Forces
Herald	**Bully**	**Guardian**	**Orphan**
Creates situation that initiates the plot or the sign of new things to come (sometimes an action, not a character)	Abuses others in physical or emotional ways, belittles others	Helps others achieve goals, blocks unwanted characters, helps and serves	Obscure or irrelevant character, powerless, victim of bad fortune or malicious intent
Strength: good or bad qualities, encouraging or vicious	**Strength:** confidence, often well connected	**Strength:** loyalty, confident	**Strength:** perseverance, relatability, independence
Weakness: serves forces of good or evil	**Weakness:** a secret wound	**Weakness:** can be misled or take on too much	**Weakness:** lacks self-esteem
Example: R2D2, *Star Wars*; Mrs. Gulch, *The Wizard of Oz*	**Example:** Draco Malfoy in *Harry Potter*	**Example:** Hagrid in *Harry Potter*, R2D2 in *Star Wars*	**Example:** Harry Potter

"The universal dilemma can be specified succinctly: everyone must wear a uniform, but everyone must deny wearing one lest one's invaluable personal and unique identity be compromised."—Paul Fussell[6]

Rebellious Dressing

Characters who disagree with society may make very conscious choices to advertise those opinions.

Figure 10.3 Groups of peers tend to dress with some uniformity.

Credit: College Students in a University Campus by RODNAE Productions from Pexels.com

Aggressive rebellion wears what is ugly or threatening to mainstream society. Philosophical rebels may quietly proclaim their ideals, such as wearing vegan leather shoes. Rebel groups may create their own uniformity announcing the ideas are part of a larger movement. Subversive personalities may appear to be in step with current dress but choose one item that calls attention to itself or upsets social norms.

Anachronism and Dissension

Anachronistic garments are not usual for a time and place. One common anachronism is the current practice of wearing sports shoes with formal wear or a t-shirt with a business suit. These gestures fly in the face of traditional definitions of what people "ought" to wear. The anachronistic dresser advertises they are still part of a group and benefit from those advantages, but they have a quirky or creative point of view. A person taken out of their natural environment can themselves be anachronistic. A tourist, for example, looks entirely out of place. Another common example is people who do not live in the American West who nonetheless wear cowboy boots or hat.

Artistic, Dramatic, or Exotic

People who think of themselves as artistic or dramatic may wear an eclectic mixture of gender norms, time periods, cultures, or social event clothing to create an original look. One example is mixing dance clothing with street wear. Dramatic personalities may also wear items that broadcast a bigger or more expressive statement: extreme hair colors and styles, a large necklace from an African market, a top resembling a kimono, boots from Tibet. Those who admire the theatricality of costume may wear garments considered over-the-top for the occasion.

Nostalgia

Nostalgic characters admire some ideal notion of a time or place, evoking a fantasy version of that lost mindset. The more ardent the nostalgia, the more literal or complete this symbolic transformation may be. Some of the original hippie fashions were overtly nostalgic, such as "granny dresses" harking back

to an imagined time of their pioneer grandparents before the stresses of modern living. Individuals may develop nostalgia for a time in their own lives, hanging onto a leather jacket, a team jacket, a college t-shirt.

Complexity and Aesthetics

Dressing in complex garments that hide the body or using many colors and patterns treats the body like an art canvas. Complex dressers may be hiding their bodies in favor of constructed statements or exploring the beauty of the art elements. Surface embellishments such as embroidery, crochet, patches, and jewelry add complexity.

Elegance and Gentility

Elegance is rooted in understatement embracing limited color palettes and sleek textures and surfaces. Classic styles always look appropriate without embracing trends. An emphasis on correct fit and flow for the fabric lends elegance, as does

Figure 10.4 This woman wears combat boots in an urban environment. This fashion trend may suggest that modern urban living is a type of battle, and she is prepared.

Credit: Anete Lusina from Pexels.com

Figure 10.5 This 1970s prairie dress style evokes nostalgia for the pioneer era.

Figure 10.6 This cape treats the body as an art canvas.
Credit: Aubrey Beardsley, *The Black Cape*. Courtesy of Old Book Illustrations and Project Gutenberg

avoiding fashions with intentional rips. Genteel clothing does not call attention to itself, enhancing the wearer. Clothing is considered an investment, so a great deal of money is spent to acquire the best, but then it is worn for many years.

Symbolic Attributes

All through time humans decorated themselves using feathers, bones, or fur with special meaning. Wearing part of a wolf transmitted its characteristics to that person and perhaps brought inspiration how to behave. Not much has changed in contemporary society when we wear logo shirts; observers immediately associate characteristics of the logo with the wearer. Costume designer Arianne Phillips chose special accessories for the characters in *Once Upon a Time in . . . Hollywood* that symbolized an attribute. She saw them as good luck charms that revealed the inner world of each character. Leonardo DiCaprio's character Rick

Dalton wore a medallion and belt buckle with the letter "R" prominently featured. Phillips notes that people who wear monograms are arrogant and love to boast. Brad Pitt's Cliff Butt wore a belt buckle that was the logo of the Stuntmen's Association, showing his pride in that work.[7]

Split Personalities

People may be of two minds about social or personal issues. They may mix classic and progressive clothing, or dress the torso differently than the legs. One example is wearing heavy combat trousers and a delicate lacy top. Lurie cites an example of those who have emigrated to another culture; they may keep parts of their native dress to mix with their adopted country.[8]

Generational Divides

It is a common human trait for families or workplaces to wear fashions from different eras that may be as much as ten or even 15 years apart. Some personalities dress youthfully long after an age when society may expect more adult sobriety. Although Lurie notes even the most dignified adults often revert to dressing like kids again while on vacation, perhaps symbolizing their temporary freedom from adult responsibility.[9]

Regional Differences

Stark differences in dressing still exist in the world of connectivity. In spite of our love of the phrase "All American" there is no single way of dressing. In *Fear and Clothing, Unbuckling American Style*, Cintra Wilson breaks the United States into belts such as the Bible Belt, the Gun Belt, the Bourbon Belt, the Garter Belt. She notes that people working in government and related jobs in Washington, DC – the Beltway – have an air-tight dress code that reflects their locked down security mindsets.[10]

Arrested Development

Some people stop their fashion clock at a time when they were happiest or when the new fashions became so objectionable, they stepped out of the fashion parade. *Downton Abbey's* Violet Crawley, the Dowager Duchess, dresses in fashions decades behind her granddaughters, Mary and Edith. She does not agree with encroaching modernity. Karen Patch, the costume designer for the Wes Anderson film *The Royal Tenenbaums* used such an approach, winning a Costume Designers Guild award for the adult characters continuing to dress as they did when children, expressing their arrested maturity.

The Manner of Wearing Clothing

It can be very upsetting to arrive at a social event in the wrong outfit. We fear showing how inept we are about social cues. The opposite sensibility is to show disinterest or disrespect for others by wearing the proper clothing badly. A person may agree to wear the prescribed outfit in a disheveled manner, wrinkled and untucked. Or the wearer may add one outrageous accessory or remove one vital piece. Sometimes a

Figure 10.7 This young woman working in a shoe factory wears a high neck blouse with cameo pin. The photo is probably staged; the formal blouse shows a desire to publicize the fashionable respectability of the factory.

Credit: Frances Benjamin Johnston, Shoe factory, Lynn, Mass. Retrieved from the Library of Congress www.loc.gov/item/2015 647066/.

person is declared a "disgrace to the uniform" focusing on high expectations inherent in some clothing. A careless or disorganized character may wear their shirt untucked or the trousers or skirt rumpled. A reserved person may wear clothing that shows little skin, buttoning a normal shirt high up on the neck. A neurotic character may wear many layers almost as armor or to protect against imagined or feared threats.

Sizing Up Engaging Characters

The costume designer's contribution to creating engaging stories is providing vivid details about each character. Costume designers dissect the script and story for script clues that reveal observable and implied information. They gather ideas from group dynamics, character groups, archetypes, and the psychology of clothing. This in-depth investigation comes from an understanding of script mechanics, story devices, and careful observations from life. The final important step in this process is to collect all this information in one place.

Expecting the Unexpected

A flying director for a well-known flying company traveled the world participating in dozens of productions of *Peter Pan*. He would normally arrive just before dress rehearsals to install the flying tracks. He was often faced with costumes that could not fit over the flying harness or did not allow the rigging points to protrude from the costumes. He learned the company's advanced paperwork, which explained how to prepare the costume, rarely made it to the costume person, but sat on someone's desk. He carried a special pair of scissors just for these occasions and he could see the distress on the costumer's face as he sliced holes through all the layers. He learned that important paperwork might sit in someone's office too long, and he recommends every costumer must be proactive asking about special character requirements.

Extra Resources

The Hero of a Thousand Faces, Joseph Campbell
The Archetypes and the Collective Unconscious, Carl Jung

The Writer's Journey, Christopher Vogler

Uniforms, Why We Are What We Wear, Paul Fussell

Class, A Guide Through the American Status System, Paul Fussell

The Language of Clothes, Alison Lurie

Fear and Clothing, Unbuckling American Style, Cintra Wilson

Writing 101: The 12 Literary Archetypes, MasterClass. www.masterclass.com/articles/writing-101-the-12-literary-archetypes#joseph-campbell-and-character-archetypes

Notes

1 Carter, Ruth. 2020. Interview with Marcy Froehlich, University of California Irvine, October 19, 2020.

2 Cole, Michelle. 2020. "Design Showcase West/Apple TV Costume Design Panel," June 20, 2020. https://www.facebook.com/watch/?v=595895751057194.

3 *Fear and Clothing Unbuckling American Style*. Cintra Wilson, p. 3.

4 Cole. "Design Showcase West/Apple TV Costume Design Panel."

5 Lurie, Alison. 1981. *The Language of Clothes*. New York: Random House, p. 3.

6 Fussell, Paul. 2002. *Uniforms: Why We Are What We Wear*. New York: Houghton Mifflin, p. 5.

7 Bright Side. n.d. "11 Times When the Costumes Were Just as Important as the Actors in Movies." Accessed August 10, 2021. https://brightside.me/wonder-films/11-times-when-the-costumes-were-just-as-important-as-the-actors-in-movies-796984/.

8 Lurie. *The Language of Clothes*, p. 7.

9 Ibid., p. 58.

10 Wilson, Cintra. 2015. *Fear and Clothing Unbuckling American Style*. New York: Houghton Miflin, p. 45.

11.
THE STORY UNFOLDS ON A STAGE

This chapter is the final step in Part Two: A Designer Prepares. After studying the script, story, plot, and characters it's time to confer with the director about translating the production to the stage itself. There are two elements that directly affect staging: the **performance format** and the **architecture** of the performance space. This step pulls all the prior preparation together to align with the director's staging priorities for the show.

> "One of the director's biggest jobs . . . is that of creating a world for the characters to live in – the costumes, the physical setting, the historical details." —Ang Lee, director, *Brokeback Mountain*[1]

Taking Shape on Stage

The director and actors require the entire rehearsal period to create full blocking for a show. Yet there are some priorities the director and designers must discuss well before rehearsals begin. Directors usually think early about how the show will fit into the performance venue, scene **transitions**, and the effect of **architecture** on their priorities. They will have discussed this with the set designer to create a playing space that supports staging.

Transitions and Fluidity

The costume designer creates their own paperwork to document the staging of costumes. The **costume scene chart** is a powerful tool to anticipate how actors will move from one scene to the next. Classic scripts with long scenes might use short black outs between scenes. This style values "theater magic," with one scene ending and the

next beginning revealing no clue how the scenery shifted or actors changed costumes. Cinematic style productions blur the scenes together, so the audience spends little or no time in the dark. Fewer pauses indicate the playwright or director values **fluidity**, or uninterrupted audience attention. The audience will watch the scene transitions and that action may contribute more meaning to the story. When fluidity is the priority, it frustrates everyone if the costume designer plans too many complete changes during scene changes. Conversely, if the script values a complete break between scenes, the show may look unfinished if a character adds only a sweater to jump ahead months or years in the story timeline. Many contemporary scripts are a combination of both approaches, as some characters barely leave the stage while others are offstage for lengthy periods.

Consult the director early about fluidity and costume changes. While the director may not be ready to fully articulate transition blocking, they

DOI: 10.4324/9781003015284-13

OPUS SC	lud e	1	2	3	4	5	6	7	8	9	10
PAGES	1	1-4	4-18	18-20	20-30	30-35	35-44	44-45	46-53	53-56	56-65
Day/Night		DOC	DAY 1 SUN	DOC	DAY 2 MON	FLASH BACK	DAY 2 MON CONT	DOC	FLASH BACK Last Month	DOC	DAY 3 TUES
Time / FALL			Eve		8:30 AM	8:30 PM	Ltr Morning		12:30 AM		
Location			Elliots Apt		Alan's Apt	Elliot & Dorians Apt	Alan's Apt		London Record Studio		Carl's House
TIME PASS		2 YRS AGO	6 Days to WH	2 YRS AGO	5 Days to WH		5 Days to WH	2 YRS AGO	"A few yrs ago"	2 YRS AGO	3 Days to WH
PLOT POINT		Inter view	Grace Auditions	Inter view	Grace is early, Dorian	Dorian gets Lazaras	Decide to play Opus 131	Interview	Elliot leaves recording	Interview	Carl has a DR Appt
MUSIC	Opus 130	Mics on shirts	2nd String Qurt Bartok	Largo, Concerto D Minor Bach	Concerto Two Violins Back 3rd Mvt	Str Qut A Minor Kreisler	Pachel bel Canon D Major		Opus 131	Alla Danza Tadesca O130 Betho	Adagio ma non troppo Opus 131
Notes		B&W Ideal Quartet	Grace Adds New Color	"Ideal Quartet"		When they were Happy		"Ideal Quartet"		"Ideal Quartet"	
CARL Cello		Look #1 Suit #1 Charcoal Shirt #1 off White Knit tie with clip Ecco shoes #1	Look #1B Repeat Suit Trouser #1 Remove jacket Add Sweater Vest #1	Look #1C Remove tie Repeat Sweater Vest	Off stage to change	Off stage to change	Look #2 Olive Corduroy Trousers #2 Shirt #2 Windowpane Shoes #1 Rpt	Look #2B Add Sweater vest #1	Look #2C Add sportcoat #1 Brown	Look #2D Remove Sportcoat #2 FAST CHANGE OUT	Look #3 Remove shirt & Sweater vest Add Pull over sweater #3 Jacket with Pacifyer in pocket

Figure 11.1 An excerpt from the scene chart for *Opus* tracks changes like a storyboard so the director and designer could choreograph costume changes. This scene chart hung in the rehearsal hall to aid blocking.

will have a feeling or tone they would like to achieve. Strive to be a collaborator so that tight costume changes may be aided through blocking. One example of this approach is the play *Opus*, directed by Brendon Fox for the Portland Playhouse and St. Louis Repertory Theater. The action skips in time using a cinematic scene structure. The costume designer and director targeted when full costume changes could safely occur and when to use choreographed partial changes using costume pieces hidden onstage. The actors learned their change actions during staging rehearsals along with all their other blocking to create smooth transitions. This method was truer to the director's intent than trying to apply changes during dress rehearsals, late in the process. These solutions are a good opportunity for the costume designer to influence the way a story translates to the stage.

Questions About Script Fluidity and Rhythm

- Is the director thinking of adding a **pre-show** at the top? Pre-shows set the stage, add a backstory, or explain a relationship between characters before the play begins.
- Is the director planning **entr'acte** intervals not written into the script? Many contemporary scene shifts occur in plain sight of the audience, and some directors will add gags or moments such as waiters setting up a restaurant or witness a character hide before the other characters arrive. These can affect the number of costumes and when actors change backstage.
- Will the director be **cutting the script** or **rearranging scenes**? Classic scripts are often revised, eliminating some characters and turning regular costume changes into fast ones.
- Does the script or director's interpretation require other **costumed scene transitions**? How does this affect when actors change?

The Architecture of Performance

Each venue is unique, and the architecture of both building and scenic design determines some parameters for the costume designer. The most important elements are as follows:

- The **distance** of the audience from the poetic space where the actors perform. Costumes seen from farther away require more graphic emphasis, more texture or higher contrast to be seen. Costumes viewed at an intimate distance may be subtler or even understated.
- Actor **travel patterns** dictate how actors exit and reenter the stage. The stage architecture and the shape of the scenery affect how actors might exit and reenter. Can they travel behind the scenery, or must they walk around the building? These logistics profoundly affect the amount of time available for fast changes.
- **Angle** of vision for the audience, called **sight lines**. The angle of vision may affect the way patrons see the costumes, or even the length of dress hems. Is the audience looking up at the performers, down on them or at eye level? Sight lines may also require actors to travel further backstage before changing to stay out of sight.

The Royal Family at Covent Garden Theatre.

Figure 11.2 A proscenium theater frames a stage, creating a formal, removed tone for the audience.

Credit: Richard Phillips, *Modern London, 1804.* Courtesy of the British Library

- **Backstage** footprint dictates the likely location of fast changes. Is there adequate space behind the scenery or in the wings for a quick-change booth?

Theaters are not just a space to house a performance. Successfully matched plays and places enhance the emotional exchange between the actors and the audience. There is no such thing as a perfect theater, and so it is essential to understand how the spatial layout will affect this play. Walk through every venue before designing it, preferably with the director.

- The **proscenium** provides a physical space between the stage and the audience, such as a large frame and apron or an orchestra pit. This space usually requires heightened contrast, color, or texture to read across the physical separation and extensive seating.
- The **end stage** or **open proscenium** sits at one end of an open space shared with the audience. The poetic space may be defined by architectural elements such as a frame, columns, a free-standing lighting grid or scenic elements. Like the full proscenium, visual elements may require heightened contrast or texture to read.
- **Thrust** stages extend into the audience area so that seating banks around in a semi-circular pattern. This shape places more of the audience closer to the performers, but there can be a reduced visibility in the back seats.
- **Flexible** or **black box** theaters expose the plain walls and stage equipment so the action can be oriented in any direction for each show. The audience seating can move into various configurations. The audience is usually seated within a close range of the performers.
- **Arena** or **island** stages feature a central acting area surrounded by the audience with aisles for exits and entrances. Scenic elements must be severely reduced so the audience can see across the stage, placing more emphasis on the floor, lighting, and costumes.
- **Profile** stages place the audience on risers on two sides of the playing space, often used in found spaces not intended as theater spaces. Usually offers very close views.

Figure 11.3 Counterbalance Theater Company production of *Reading Frankenstein*, a devised collaborative work performed in a small flexible theater with projection screens.

Credit: Photo by Jesús López Vargas (jelopez-stage.com). Starring Abel Garcia, Kaden Kearney. Directed by Annie Loui. Lighting and Scenic Design, Lonnie Alcaraz. Costume Design, Holly Poe Durbin. Sound Design, Vincent Olivieri. Projection Design, Antoinette LaFarge and Morgan Embry.

"Collaboration means building on the capability to find new solutions, combine components, and continuously adapt. In this sense, communication demands the same creative attitude as designing a costume or composing a song – since there is no one solution for every situation, a broad repertoire of experiences supports flexibility and exploring the unknown."[2]

Designing for Fast Changes

A detailed costume scene breakdown reveals another aspect of staging stories unique to live theater: fast changes. Anticipating and planning quick changes is a vital element of any costume design. During the latter half of the 20th century fast changes became much more frequent as playwrights wrote for ensembles of actors or adopted the cinematic approach of writing. What constitutes the timing of a fast change differs with each crew's capabilities and the architecture of the performing venue. For instance, any stage that forces the actor to add travel time between exit and reentrance reduces standard change times to brisk or fast timing. The actual mechanics of a quick change will be addressed in fittings and choreographed in preparation for dress rehearsals.

But there are a number of decisions a designer can make early that will facilitate fast changes. To stay ahead of the process, consider the types of fast changes at our disposal.

- **Skin-out change.** The most extensive costume change requires the actor to change underpinnings or other understructures. In such cases it is advantageous to build as much of the underpinning into the costume as possible, such as boned bodices and petticoats. Plan for the performer to wear a modesty layer such as a chemise to facilitate backstage changes.

- **Full change.** The performer may keep the underpinnings, changing the major garments only. Special closures are often used and many times individual parts of garments are sewn together to create one unit. For instance, a formal tail suit may be sewn into a jumpsuit with hidden zipper to facilitate very fast changes.

- **Partial change.** The performer retains essential parts of clothing, adding relatively easy parts to switch over. Examples include changing a sport coat to a sweater; changing skirts or blouses; adding a shapeless cardigan sweater, walker, and eyeglasses for an elderly character.

- **Module changes.** Costumes are built in special hidden pieces or tear away to create the illusion of a full costume change. Costumes may be underdressed or include special tricks. Some productions of *Into the Woods* use this method for the onstage Witch's transformation from an old hag to a beautiful young woman.

- **Base costume and pieces.** The performer wears essential body garments through a longer segment of the play, adding other garments to indicate passage of time or to play a new character. Ensembles may wear similar base costumes to establish a unified starting point.

- **Onstage or a-vista change.** The performer does not leave the stage, adding or subtracting items visibly during the action or as part of a scene shift. New items are hidden on stage, or laying in plain sight as part of the set dressing.

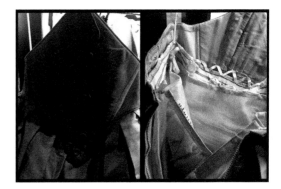

Figure 11.4 A bodice constructed for an ensemble member in *Hamilton*. The diamond shaped bodice fits over another corset to create a finished look. The interior view at right shows the petticoat and skirt sewn together with a back zipper to create a modular fast-change unit.

Credit: Photo by the author, Costume Designer Paul Tazewell

The designer assesses the intent of the script to create a change method that best serves the story. Understanding the sliding scale of realism (Chapter 8) can spark ideas of how changes may enhance or detract from the show. A play such as Moisés Kaufman's *The Laramie Project* lends itself well to a specific base costume assigned to each actor that facilitates all the roles they will play. Costume designer Paul Tazewell used the module system for some ensemble costumes in *Hamilton*. Women in the ensemble wore a foundation of boned bodice and breeches to play male characters, adding a full skirt sewn to a boned bodice to enable a fast change into female characters at times. (See Figure 11.4.) There will always be surprises when blocking changes in rehearsals or rewrites shuffle the timing or order of events; however, advanced planning will free the designer and crew to focus on new information.

In On the Act: Performance Format

Each format of performed stories grew up with its own traditions and expectations. One example is late 19th-century American vaudeville, which combined different acts into one evening of performance. That format influenced much of American entertainment, evident in late night talk shows and *Saturday Night Live*. Understanding performance format expectations affects staging and costume planning.

Musical Theater

The musical theater canon is well-known and performed frequently. Many theaters make extra income renting their musical costumes to others. One of the biggest issues for the costume designer is to ascertain if producers wish to originate a new design, or use an existing one. It can be a real surprise to a designer who anticipates creating an unique a show to discover the theater wants to reprise an existing production. Other factors to consider in the early planning stages include:

- **Using tropes** set by a landmark original production. One example is the 2014 Broadway production of *Cabaret*. William Ivey Long's costume for Alan Cumming as the cabaret MC featured crisscrossed suspenders that have become a trope for that character. Does this production anticipate changing that iconic moment or will it maintain that look?
- **Large companies** of dancers or ensemble performers. The cast may also include doubles, swings, understudies, or specialty performers. It is essential to define the true scope of the production before settling on employment parameters.
- **Body image** expectations. Traditionally, musicals have been rigid in their desired body types, favoring slender, youthful figures for many roles. Will that tradition be an important part of this production, making figure flattery and heavy-duty underpinnings an important part of the costume designer's job? Or will all body types be embraced?
- **Visual stylization**. Musicals are presentational by their very nature; how might the costume design incorporate the required amount of style for this production?

Opera, Light Opera, and Operetta

Like musical theater, there is a well-known repertoire for opera and operetta. Opera companies treasure production values and they invest extraordinary resources in the costumes. Due to that large investment, a company may reuse their costumes for decades or rent entire packages from other companies. Considerations for early planning include:

- **Original design**. What portion – if any – of this production will be an original design? Must new costumes blend with a rental or stock set of chorus costumes?
- **Casting** for vocal ability can override other factors such as age or physical type. It is possible to work with middle aged opera singers cast as young characters, so figure flattery and adjusting proportions may be important requirements.
- **Designing for music**. Opera presents both music and words, but the music will trump the words if the two compete for attention. Songs expressing deep emotions rely on repetitive words so the audience can concentrate on the artistry of the music. Therefore, the costume designer must be proficient in designing for music – the mood or intent may be more evident in music than the libretto.
- **Pageantry**. Musical interludes provide opportunities for processions, fancy balls, or other large design requirements. Ask the director to identify those needs as they may not be obvious when reading the libretto.
- **Large companies.** Opera productions are usually large and may include principles, a double cast of principles, a singing chorus, dancers, and supernumeraries to perform silent roles that augment specific scenes. Does the chorus or corps represent one voice or character, such as a group that will perform in unison? If that is the case, do the costumes closely resemble each other? Or is the chorus a group of individual characters, such as all the town folk in a village or guests at a party?

Smaller or experimental opera companies approach shows differently, deliberately trying to change the need for overblown productions. They may ask a chorus to sing offstage, or create a reduced ensemble. A costume designer may be asked to create new solutions as part of reconceiving an opera.

Devised Work

Ensembles may create a performance together using the rehearsal period to write the show as well as stage it. These works may be based on a particular physical movement style or a mission to include members of a specific community and their stories. This work can be extremely satisfying for the costume designer who enjoys creating on their feet, problem solving, and using found objects or bending materials to new uses. The costume designer will be most successful if they are part of the rehearsal process as much as possible. Designers can offer suggestions or get a new idea from watching the work as it develops. Such works often evolve until the last minute requiring an easy-going temperament. Before working on this kind of project, ask many questions about the group's work style and their expectations.

Dance and Movement

Dancers relate to their bodies on a deep level and their costumes are an extension of not only themselves but their art. The ability to move in every direction is the paramount concern for dance costumes. Design for dance can be a very pure form of expression, treating costumes as parts of a moving composition or a painting in motion. It is essential to attend rehearsals to see key gestures that will feature a part of the body or specific movement requiring focus.

Theater for Young Audiences

Many early career designers secure work with theaters that perform with or for children. Education grants are a lifeline for many performing organizations, and some productions feature a large number of performers to create more acting opportunities. Professional companies performing for children often create shows with very small casts to contain the costs of touring those productions to schools or other outside venues. Ask about limits for packing and transporting costumes before designing them.

Producers Expectations

Another early consideration for costumes is the expectations of the producer or organization presenting the project. Everyone wants to create a show that is both an artistic and box office success, but sometimes compromises must be made. Once you understand the director's ideas for this production, do they match the producer's expectations and their resources? The costume designer will most often communicate with a production manager to exchange operational information. Share the preliminary costume count and expectations from your costume scene chart and early director discussions. Gather information that aids future planning:

- The budget and what it must cover.
- Time allotted for preparation and rehearsals.
- The labor plan for this show: is there a resident costume staff or must the costume designer hire his own crew?
- Are wigs and makeup included in the budget?
- Are there hidden charges that will be deducted from your budget?
- Are there early press photos the designer styles before the costumes are ready?
- Who will track expenses and maintain the systems that theater prefers?

These planning aspects are covered in detail in Part Five: Feasibility. If the designer finds they must plan much of the logistics for a production, it is wise to read that section early.

Sizing Up Staged Stories

Understanding how a script translates to the performance stage provides the final piece of the planning puzzle. The costume scene chart is a powerful tool to anticipate types of **transitions** and **fluidity** with the director early in the process. The director may plan a dumbshow or entr'actes that affect costume changes. Directors will often cut or rearrange classic scripts for new effects, affecting costume changes and timings. The architecture of a space determines distance to the audience, travel patterns, sight lines, and the use of backstage space.

Expecting the Unexpected: Backstage Space

A young design assistant was once pulled into a wardrobe crew call when a dresser fell ill. She took her post backstage next to her rack of costumes for the musical *Gypsy*. One number called for a live lamb onstage, but this production substituted a baby goat. The kid waited for its entrance in a small pen nearby. Unbeknownst to the design assistant, the dresser she was subbing for also performed as the rear-end of a dancing cow. A stage manager frantically stuffed her into the rear legs and pushed the cow onstage. When she returned from her professional stage debut, the goat had munched its way through the costume rack, eating the brims of several straw hats and part of a linen jacket sleeve. There wasn't time to find substitutes, so the show had to go on with a new costume interpretation – thanks to the use of backstage space.

Extra Resources

What Are the Types of Theater Stages and Auditoria? Theaters Trust.org www.theatrestrust.org.uk/discover-theatres/theatre-faqs/170-what-are-the-types-of-theatre-stages-and-auditoria

Types of Performance Glossary: Beginner's Guide. Theater. London www.theatre.london/news/types-of-performance-glossary-beginners-guide

Notes

1 De Koven, Lenore. 2006. *Changing Direction: A Practical Approach to Directing Actors in Film and Theater.* New York: Focal Press, p. xiii.
2 Niermann, Timo. 2019. *Collaboration Backstage, Breaking Barriers for the Creative Network.* New York: Methuen, p. 19.

PART THREE

A DESIGNER EXPLORES

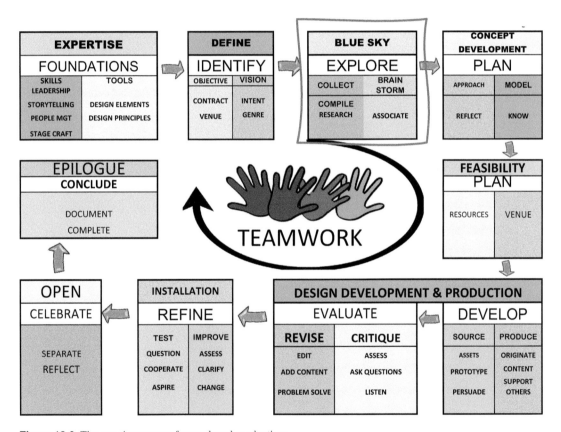

Figure 12.0 The creative process for produced productions.

Credit: Holly Poe Durbin and Ayrika Johnson

12.
GENERATING IDEAS

There are many myths regarding how artists find inspiration to create a design. Some make us think others have great ideas all at once, draw a fully realized rendering effortlessly, or that *real* designers use only certain methods. The truth is designers perform a lot of work to kindle ideas. Inspiration is a continual process through the entire project – not just one grand flash. Remaining open to serendipity provides a great deal of inspiration: an unexpected color combination, a garment in a vintage store, a postcard viewed online, blocking seen in rehearsal. These can seem like *aha!* moments appearing in an instant, but they are the result of much thought ahead of time. The most important job for any designer is to **generate ideas** – as many as possible for as long as possible. The more possibilities a designer starts with, the easier it will be to discern which are mature ideas. It is those second and third ideas, the result of deeper reflection, that are often more interesting and complete. We generate *initial* ideas with little effort when we are actively trying to solve a problem. But sadly, the chances are large everyone else will generate those same ideas. If given more time, our brains continue mulling in the background, even when we are thinking of something else entirely. We can even perform incredibly complex tasks using a kind of autopilot – have you ever driven a car or bicycle while deep in thought about something else? You might arrive at the destination with little memory of actually driving there. Your eyes and brain managed constantly shifting assessments while your conscious thoughts were busy with something else.

"I can't tell you how many times I've started over from scratch. But the bad ideas lead to the best ones."
—Amanda Gorman, poet and activist[1]

What feels like a sudden inspiration may actually be the result of our brains working subconsciously. Understanding how the brain works helps us capture ideas and better recognize them when they occur. Most people have experienced one type of phenomenon when our brains subconsciously work on an idea: **frequency illusion**. Arnold Zwicky, a linguist at Stanford University, coined that term to describe when a new thing you just discovered suddenly pops up everywhere. The method behind this phenomenon is **selective attention**, which activates once you are interested in a new thing or word.[2]

DOI: 10.4324/9781003015284-15

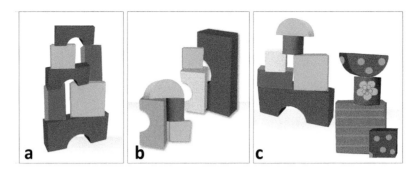

Figure 12.1 Three ways humans approach thinking. Cumulative thinking (A) builds on what we already know. Tangential thinking (B) develops ideas loosely related to our initial approach. Lateral thinking (C) combines ideas from other sources with our current process to think "outside the box."

The brain forms new ideas using several types of thinking.

- **Cumulative**, methodical, or focused thinking is first-wave thinking. It is tactical and targeted. It expands on initial ideas by looking for logical patterns. These first ideas start with solutions used successfully before, or that make logical sense to try.
- **Tangential thinking** is the second wave, producing interesting ideas. These ideas diverge from the original topic, adding *loosely* related thoughts. For example, standing in line for a trendy nightclub may stir the related experience of an airport line. The thinker considers the ways airport security might resemble club bouncers – or what if the TSA used the same selection system as a bouncer, or vice versa?
- **Lateral thinking** uses indirect approaches that we can't always identify. It ignores the implied rules in the problem. These ideas are often described as "outside the box." Media theorist Steven Johnson defines this way humans incubate new ideas as the ***slow hunch***, or collaging them together from different sources.[3]
- **Sensory thinking** is fundamental to many people in the arts. The interaction with the world is ordered through embodied or physical reactions such as smell, sound, and touch. Artists of every type can be more attuned to this way of processing the world.

Sensory thinking plays a large role in creative brainstorming, and may be one reason why we have difficulty explaining what prompts ideas. One example of sensory thinking is learning to ride a bicycle. No one learned it from memorizing a theoretical description. We must experience real-time balance correction for ourselves. Sewing fabric requires a constant adjustment of the fabric under a presser foot, using our sense of touch. Designers may start ideas through hearing music or sounds, touching objects with significance in the script, or imagining dance movements for each character. Some costume designers respond best or first to texture or color, both sensory reactions. They may visit places to gather experiences, such as a museum, junk yard, salvage yard, hardware store, or a costume storage.

"The lawyer and the doctor *practice* their callings. The plumber and carpenter *know* what they will be called upon to do. They do not have to spin the work out of themselves, discover its laws, and then present themselves turned inside out to the public gaze."[4]

Brainstorming for Design Ideas

When ideas do not appear on their own or through experiences, designers must jump start the creative process. What strategies do designers use to launch the process of thinking creatively about a script? How do we encourage the brain to jump from the literal to the imaginative? Many projects begin with a director's excitement. Costume designer Ann Hould-Ward (*Beauty and the Beast*) explains how she starts ideas with a director. "I need to know their passion for the piece. . . . Hearing them express their energy – it's almost like catching fire. I want to know what part of the script instigated doing the piece?" However, not all directors are comfortable or able to describe their vision. In that case "I tell myself it will be three steps forward and one step back. I will have to do a large amount of research and color work for them." But if a director does not know what they want, Hould-Ward knows "it will be up to me to really put the ideas out there and see."[5] When designers must jump start their creative juices, there are some tried-and-true methods that may get the process going, or at least generate ideas for further research.

Ten Ways to Nurture Creative Thinking

- Take a walk – find inspiration from graffiti, nature, people on the street
- Antique stores, estate sales, or Etsy
- Talk to people – find out what they know or remember about situations or places
- Old movies – the older the better, try silent films to visit a golden age of visual design
- Play – games, sports, collecting, and hobbies
- Online sharing sites – Deviant Art, Pinterest, Instagram
- Travel – even a day trip will change your perspective
- Galleries and museums
- Study other illustrators and artists
- Fashion Week – fashion shows are elaborate stage productions

Image Collection

An effective first step is the indiscriminate gathering of images or experiences, collecting anything that catches the eye, even if the designer does not yet know why. Creativity researcher Nigel Cross notes designers have a wide appreciation of material culture. They seek experiences in galleries, entertainment, museums, music, nature, and travel – anything at all.[6] Think of this as feeding your **image** or **experience bank**, gathering items when you see them. Do not wait until you need them, they may be impossible to find then. Reviewing the collection becomes an enjoyable first step starting new projects. Claire Parkinson, the costume designer for the Netflix series *The Politician*, advises "Thinking back on what I wish I knew – to seek inspiration everywhere. And to keep curious – seek out art, travel, food to fill your own cup."[7]

"I am not an inventor, I'm a scavenger." —Ann Bogart, director[8]

Collecting Keywords

Many designers verbalize impressions from a script with short words or phrases. We are familiar with keywords used to navigate search engines; think of design keywords that quantify your impression of a scenario or character. Aim to include at least one word describing each character's emotions. A designer might generate keywords for the character of Esther in the play *Intimate Apparel* this way: she is a *Black seamstress* who *sews corsets* for women from all levels of society. She is *unmarried* at age 35 in the socially *restrictive* era of 1905. Some character keywords might include *kindness, humility, ambition, vulnerable, lonely*. These words might evoke ideas of Esther as a *sitting duck, innocent lamb*, or *babe in the woods*. All of these words and ideas would fuel more avenues of exploration.

Word Banking

This approach takes keywords to the next level. Beginning with an initial list of words, use word association to generate more words. Try to match images to some of the words, allowing the mind to wander as much as possible (see Figure 12.2).

Comparisons

We all speak in **similes**, **analogies**, and **metaphors** in everyday speech, finding similarities between two things. Overused phrases include "it's raining cats and dogs" or "cry me a river." Designers can use these figures of speech to build evocative images and connect an item to an emotional response. For instance, a spirited musical number could be "like" a Bollywood film. A formulaic crime plot may be "like" film noir. Situations may be "like" children's books, characters may make us think of insects or animals. A family's dialogue may sound like chickens fussing at each other. There may be a strong motif in the story, such as Penelope weaving Odysseus a burial shroud every day and secretly unpicking the work at night. Could the image of weaving serve as an analogy for Penelope herself, whose mental and physical state is also unraveling?[9]

The Five Senses

People relate to the world using their senses, and each sense is a powerful tool. Smells can transport us back to childhood, such as smelling favorite foods. Hearing certain music can change our mood or help us focus. Consider the world of the play using all five senses. Are there strong moments in the play that are best described with a sensory reaction?

- **Sight.** Focus on a central person or place and describe that sample with different emotions in mind. Is the world an angry one, paranoid, or relaxed? What might that emotion look like?
- **Sounds** are strongly associated with our mood. Are there distinctive sounds provided by locations in the script? What would the inner emotions of a character sound like if everyone could hear them? A whine, a sigh, or broken glass?
- **Smells** are strongly associated with memory. They also warn us about healthy or unhealthy conditions in the environment. What would the characters or locations smell? Do the characters have signature scents?
- **Touch** is one of the most commonly used senses, although we block out that information a lot of the time. Do you really take time to feel the steering wheel of your car during your drives? Touch is strongly associated with our feelings about the environment. We can detect texture with our eyes, making this a powerful tool. What texture would you associate with each character – if we could hug them would they feel scratchy, fluffy, comforting, sharp?
- **Taste** is strongly associated with consuming, such as food. Thinking about tastes will trigger desires or avoidance. What kind of tastes are offered in the story world, or with each

Figure 12.2 Word banking sample.

character? Would one character taste like dirt, another like cotton candy?

Isolation

Some designers use visual **isolation** to start their creative juices flowing, closely observing and copying images such as small details found in paintings, furniture, costumes, or other objects important to a script or historical era. We isolate parts of an image to look at them in new ways. Create a frame of cut paper to block out the rest of an image, putting focus on the detail. Those details may be the very element the designer wishes to feature in the finished design.

Mind Mapping

This tool combines words and images to encourage **tangential thinking**. It removes traditional notions of ordering or structure, building an intuitive framework around a central theme or concept. A map starts with one main idea placed in the center of a

Figure 12.3 Isolating smaller parts of an image using paper cut with a window. This exercise encourages the brain to see items in new ways.

page or screen, adding branches with related ideas. Any branch can sprout more divisions, and any idea can be linked back to another. Changing colors for different words or images excites the brain to make more connections. Although some devoted mappers have a strict system of shapes and colors, there is no requirement to follow any rules at all. The final result is a treasure trove of keywords and approaches. (See Figure 12.4)

SCAMPER

This word SCAMPER is an acronym prompting seven ways to look at an idea. It was first introduced by Bob Eberle in the book *SCAMPER: Games for Imagination Development*. It begins with an existing idea or work, adding modifications in any order. The thinker subjects the central idea to seven maneuvers: *S*ubstitute the idea with something else, *C*ombine it with something else, *A*dapt it to fit some adjectives or adverbs, *M*odify it to enlarge or minimize or turn it upside down, *P*ut to another use entirely, *E*liminate it or something from the idea, and *R*everse the idea. For instance, if the challenge is to design a monk's robe in a new way, it's possible to think about the original purposes of those robes from these seven points of view.

Starbursting

This technique generates questions about a central idea, rather than leaping directly to answers. It encourages a look beyond assumptions, or what we think we know about a topic. This tool is so powerful it was used by the CIA to locate Osama bin Laden in 2011.[10] This tool uses a six-pointed diagram that resembles a star. Each arm of the star represents *Who, What, Where, When, Why,* and *How*. The brainstormer writes several questions about the central idea, beginning with each word. Some of those questions will lead to new information or new ways of looking at the design issue. (See Figure 12.5)

What-If or Alter-Ego

This exercise was first developed for writers, as a tool to loosen assumptions about characters or

Figure 12.4 This designer used a simple mind map to articulate the elements of Joan Miro's painting to use in costumes (left). The map sparked early ideas for research (right).

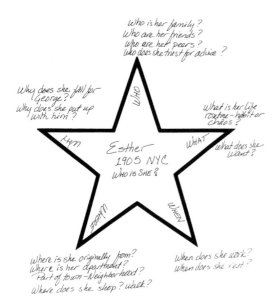

Figure 12.5 A starburst for the character of Esther in *Intimate Apparel*.

situations. It imagines new scenarios or identities for characters in a script. Ask the *What if* question to imagine a character in an alter-ego that matches their behavior or outlook. What if this story happened in a space ship, what crew member would

each be? What if everyone were a species of mushroom or penguin? This exercise can be particularly fun if the brainstormer enlists help from friends or family with different ages or points of view.

> "If I had only one hour to save the world, I would spend fifty-five minutes defining the problem, and only five minutes finding the solution." —Albert Einstein

Capturing and Organizing Ideas

Brainstorming ideas will generate new words, images, and sources. Stop to consider how you will store all these wonderful ideas for future use. We live in the age of information overload. Not only is there more information available than we can possibly process, but it is scattered across multiple platforms. It is easy to lose track of important items that may spark ideas causing us to waste valuable time searching for something we've misplaced. Or worse: we may experience the feeling of being overwhelmed, making it difficult to focus our thoughts. All that creative clutter can

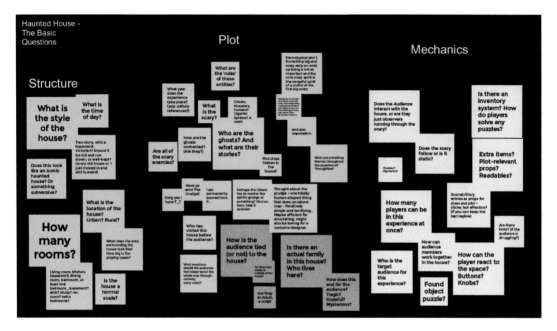

Figure 12.6 Using a Google Jamboard to organize questions and ideas for a haunted house design.

Credit: Courtesy of Jacob Daniel Margolis and Sebastian Rock

substantially raise feelings of stress. Counteract this anxiety by establishing a system you will use consistently. Perhaps something as simple as colored folders or labeled baskets or file boxes. Establish one – no more than two – digital storage locations and divide images into categories. One afternoon spent organizing a show will pay invaluable dividends in speeding your ability to process ideas creatively.

Capturing thoughts is a powerful tool. It allows designers to make correlations between unrelated elements or ask questions leading to more exploration. Two different people will make very different correlations, and this is an important part of developing your unique voice. With our brains working overtime on a design challenge, the next idea may occur at odd times. This can be maddening, so many designers carry a tablet, notebook, or notes app to capture thoughts and scribbles as they occur in daily life.

"Before you can think out of the box, you have to start with a box." —Twyla Tharp[11]

Choreographer Twyla Tharpe describes her system of storing ideas in her landmark book *The Creative Habit*. She starts every dance with a file box. As the piece progresses, she fills it with everything that makes her feel connected to a project: notebooks, news clippings, CDs, tapes, books, photographs, and pieces of art that inspire her. She thinks of it as

a commitment – the simple act of writing a project name on the box means I've started work. . . . Most important, though, the box means I never have to worry about forgetting. One of the biggest fears for a creative person is that some brilliant idea will get lost because you didn't write it down. . . . I don't worry about that because I know where to find it. It's all in the box.[12]

Whatever system a designer chooses, consider that it is

- ***Portable.*** The system is not right for you if you can't access it when you need it.

- ***Sortable.*** To be most effective, ideas must be moved to groups with other ideas. If you can't move the images around to categories or other locations it will be too difficult to wade through.
- ***Restorable.*** A new project may kindle memories that you already researched a topic in the past. You must be able to access the items again.

Many designers use a **design journal** to explore and record the steps of their creative process for each show. Even in these days of digital files, there is no substitute for the eye-to-hand connections made while writing or sketching. Architect Juhani Pallasmaa studied the connection between creativity and the hand in his essay "The Thinking Hand."

> In normal human interaction alone, 80% of communication is estimated to take place outside the verbal and conceptual channel. . . . In the arduous process of designing, the hand often takes the lead in probing for a vision, or a vague inkling which it eventually turns into a sketch, materializing thus the idea.[13]

Sizing Up Ideas

Designers perform a lot of work to create ideas. Inspiration is a continual process through an entire project – not just one grand flash. Eventually, a designer learns to trust that their brain is working behind the scenes mulling over a problem. If the creative process needs a jump start, there are several well-tested techniques that excite tangential, lateral, and sensory thinking.

Expecting the Unexpected

Sometimes our worst fear comes true. A script has not excited the creative juices, but we must give that project just as much creativity and effort as one that *does* interest us. Creative blocks occur most often at the start, stemming from the pressure to do something new that has never been done before. It is possible to circumvent these anxieties by focusing on

Figure 12.7 Pages from a design journal playing with ideas about how 1980s fashions might correlate to Shakespeare's characters in *Measure for Measure.*

the design process *itself* rather than the end result. Step through each phase without preconceived ideas for the results, allowing time for incubation. Increase the chances for breakthroughs by tackling small challenges first. One example is designing the costumes for the least consequential characters first instead of tackling the main characters. The steps to design a servant or peasant are exactly the same as the lead. Once the brain starts working on the smallest challenge, it will automatically gear up for the larger ones.

Extra Resources

Mindmapping, Techniques
Mindmapping.com
For information about other idea mapping apps, visit
    Tallyfy.com or
Design Thinking
Designorate.com explores areas of design thinking and
    innovation.
What If, Writing Exercises for Fiction Writers, 3rd Edition
    Anne Bernays, Pamela Painter. Longman Publishing.
    Writing exercises for creative writing.

Notes

1 Staff. 2021. "7 Questions, 75 Artists, 1 Very Bad Year." *New York Times*, March 10, 2021. Accessed March 14, 2021. https://www.nytimes.com/interactive/2021/03/10/arts/artists-coronavirus-lockdown.html.

2 Staff. 2017. "There's a Name for That: The Baader-Meinhof Phenomenon." *Pacific Standard Magazine*, June 14, 2017. Accessed February 8, 2020. https://psmag.com/social-justice/theres-a-name-for-that-the-baader-meinhof-phenomenon-59670.

3 Bayles, David and Orland, Ted. 1993. *Art and Fear: Observations on the Perils (and Rewards) of Artmaking.* Santa Cruz CA: Image Continuum, p. 95.

4 Johnson, Steven. 2010. "Where do Good Ideas Come From?" *Filmed 2010 at TEDGlobal.* Oxford. Video, Time. https://www.ted.com/talks/steven_johnson_where_good_ideas_come_from?language=en#t-258056.

5 Hould-Ward, Ann. 2021. "Interview with Lar Lubovitch." Streamed April 9, 2021. University of California Irvine. Irvine, CA. Streaming Webinar.

6 Cross, Nigel. 2006. *Designerly Ways of Knowing.* London: Springer-Verlag.

7 Parkinson, Claire. 2021. "Costume Design Salon Panel." Streamed June 12, 2021 via Facebook from UCLA Showcase West/Netflix. Los Angeles, CA. Video. https://www.youtube.com/watch?v=4WuB5WKUisg.

8 Bogart, Ann. 2004. "Interview by Linda Winer." *Women in Theatre*, CUNY TV, November 19, 2004. https://youtu.be/xbdtvYMXsaI.

9 Design concept created by costume designer Sarah Monaghan F. for *The Penelopiad*, Director Sara Rodriquez, University of California, Irvine, June 2021.

10 Intelligence Analysis Exhibit, Permanent Exhibition, International Spy Museum, Washington DC. Accessed July, 2021.

11 Tharp, Twyla and Reiter, Mark. 2003. *The Creative Habit, Learn It and Use It for Life.* New York: Simon & Schuster, p. 78.

12 Ibid., pp. 80–81.

13 Pallasmaa, Juhani. 2009. *The Thinking Hand: Existential and Embodied Wisdom in Architecture.* Hoboken, NJ: Wiley Publishing Co.

13.
ADDING AUTHENTICITY WITH RESEARCH

Ruth Carter's costume design for the Marvel movie *The Black Panther* was widely celebrated for introducing a whole new genre of costumes to the world. She, along with the entire design team, introduced the philosophical and aesthetic of Afrofuturism to mainstream culture. Carter attributes much of her success to her deep research and how working in theater first taught her this skill.

> It doesn't matter who you *are*. If I do the research, I can do a great job on any project. . . . I designed the pilot for *Seinfeld*, and I am not a white Jewish man on the Upper West side of New York. . . . Theater taught me how to do research on what people wore.[1]

Even with a superhero budget, Carter noted there was not enough time to do all that she wanted. She began researching in June 2016 and filming started in January 2017, allowing just seven months to go from first ideas to delivering the first costumes to the set.[2]

What Is Creative Research?

Every designer *wants* to do inspiring research. But it is not always evident where to start or how to organize the process. Use generalized initial research as a spring board to discover more focused information. Initial images inspire free association or give a designer their first bearings within an era, time, and place. But generalized research can be fairly generic or even derivative. The key to *excellent* research is subsequently narrowing the focus. For instance, a vintage fashion magazine will show how merchandizers *wanted* Americans to dress in the 1950s. But, just like today, not everyone dressed in the latest fashions. It is more authentic to find focused sources such as photographs of real people in regional locations similar to your story. Authenticity also demands using research that includes our entire community in each story, and all its racial or cultural forms of dress. This authenticity will establish the designer's authority as an expert on the people in the story.

> "If we knew what it was we were doing, it would not be called research, would it?" — Albert Einstein[3]

Gathering research is an important first step in designerly thinking. It is one way creative thinkers experiment, using *modeling*, or testing what each idea *might* look like. Research is often a favorite step for many designers – the pure joy of diving into new discoveries before having to consider reality. During this phase many designers collect images based on gut instinct; it's not necessary to know why an image has appeal. At first, let the images speak, there will be time to figure out why your brain thought

DOI: 10.4324/9781003015284-16

Figure 13.1 This portrait of musician Dizzy Gillespie from 1947 illustrates that real people dress with more individuality than fashion advertising reveals.

Credit: William P. Gottlieb/Ira and Leonore S. Gershwin Fund Collection, Music Division, Library of Congress.

them right for this project. Some research will not be visual material. Many designers incorporate written sources. They are enthusiastic consumers of books, magazine articles, diaries and letters, etiquette books, and historical studies explaining the story world. Some stories are based on real events or inspired by actual incidents. Researching similar events and actual places, people, or situations opens up new avenues of discovery, and a script based on a prior novel will benefit from the atmosphere and details of the original story. Look for historical or factual information in old newspapers, books, and magazines, enlisting the help of a research librarian. Most will be thrilled to work with a creative topic as a break from their usual routine. Many university librarians help alumni or community members

as they have time and large public libraries advise patrons.

A Cut Above: Authority and Authenticity

The most authentic research addresses both the **factual** and the **emotional** aspects. Scripts present a situation and evoke emotional and intellectual responses to that. Your research must do the same. Comprehensive research will include aspects of the following seven areas.

Factual Information	Emotional Aspects
Location, Events, and Context	Emotional Response to Story
Time, Season, and Era	Mood and Atmosphere
Garments and Accessories	Characterization
Prior Iterations	

Factual Information Research

Researching the era and season will collapse assumptions made about different places and times. It is useful to confirm the average temperature during a season in specific locations. Those who live in one climate often cannot guess the real effect of weather in another climate. Imagine what it could be like to live where the wind blows sand in your eyes all day. What does it feel like to have to put on layers of warm clothing to step outside? If you live in a place that rains frequently, do your clothes always feel somewhat moist? How does fabric behave under all these conditions? Global weather information can be found in an atlas at the library or online.

Researching the garments for a character must be tempered through the location and time of the story. Researching European fashion for a specific era will not address what people really wore outside of those few fashion capitals. The single most telling aspect of placing a costume in a time period is the silhouette, and nothing defines the silhouette as effectively as the underpinnings originally intended to support that fashion. What kind of underwear did each character wear to create their body shape? Research images from historical mail order catalogs or fashion magazines to find examples of those styles and how they altered the human body.

> "Our library caters to anything related to dress," says Leighton Bowers, Western Costume Company's director of research and archive. "There are 30,000 books, catalogues, clippings, notes and periodicals that cover clothing, uniforms, film, sewing, fashion, military, photography, culture, travel. They also include swatch books dating as far back as the turn of the [20th] century. The most popular sources are back issues of Sears and JCPenney catalogues, because unlike fashion magazines, their clothes were available throughout the country to people of various means."[4]

Stories revolve around many types of dramatic political, geological, or personal events. Research the events or those similar to them. What does a shipwreck really look like? What happens to the people onboard – is there a rescue operation? Unless you are working on the premiere of a new work, someone has done your production before and solved the same problems. Reading reviews may lead to some insights. The playwright may have given interviews in magazines or online. Scholars may have published articles or books about any aspect of the project. Many costume designers stop short of actually viewing the costume designs of prior productions, avoiding the chance their own imagination may be hampered by knowing another's decisions.

Emotional Aspects Research

Researching the emotional responses in a story is more intuitive. Emotions may be part of an overall feeling in a play, such as foreboding or optimism. Emotions may come from some tension in the story between characters or the situation or the environment.

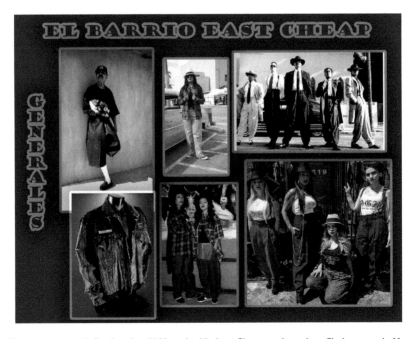

Figure 13.2 Character research for the play *El Henry* by Herbert Siguenza, based on Shakespeare's *Henry IV, Part 1*. Costume designer Cassie Defile used authentic location-based research to augment general research.
Credit: Courtesy of Cassie Defile

"Designers must learn most of all to keep their eyes open, to develop their skills of observation to absorb visual ideas, blend them and translate them. . . . Exposure to beautiful things helps a designer distinguish genuine beauty and quality from fads and mediocrity." — Fatma Mete[5]

Many designers need time to percolate during this research phase. They process a large amount of imagery and possibilities. Well-timed breaks encourage the creative process, allowing that important slow hunch to work in the background. The official term for this process is **creative procrastination**, or allowing ideas to incubate. It is common in physical training to alternate vigorous activity with restful activity, and the same benefits are true for the mind. Allow the unconscious mind to whir in the background.

Curating Research to Tell a Story

Gathering research is fun and many designers could spend weeks or months just doing this creative work. But at some point, the joy ride must develop a destination. The next step is sorting that large bank of images or ideas into categories that best describe the project. This further refines the *modeling* phase of design thinking. As creativity researcher Nigel Cross notes, sorting, assessing, and eliminating ideas correlates to *defining visual rules* for that world. Some designers consider this step as the one where the design comes together – they will make most of their important decisions in this process. Some designers first create a **mood** or **idea board** that symbolizes the entire production and its intentions, tone, colors, and textures. Not every designer uses this process, but it can be a good way to define ideas. Choosing an approach to arrange the mood board is a significant step: by deciding how to best arrange the images, you have also distilled what is most important about the story to you. Many designers can make this leap with images more easily than the written word, and that is part of the power of a mood board. Even if you never show it

to anyone else, it has served a powerful purpose. There are several ways to organize information to create mood boards.

- **Factual.** A collection of items that inform a design about the actual appearances of items, drawing references, idea references.
- **Chronological.** Illustrating a physical or emotional arc from a starting point, through highs and lows. Mood boards for Lynn Nottage's play *Intimate Apparel* could include seamstress Esther's state of mind at the start, emotions during her wedding, her husband's betrayal and finally her resolve at the end.
- **Geographical.** Arranging visual information to create contrasts between different worlds or experiences defined in the story. Mood boards for Qui Nguyen's play *She Kills Monsters* could compare Agnes's everyday world with the imaginary game world she enters.
- **Thematic.** Using metaphorical or actual categories important to the story. One example might be Lucy Prebble's play *Enron*, where characters could divide into predators, enablers, and prey.
- **Tone.** Is the story aspirational or a slice of real life? The average television show is aspirational. Characters wear clothing that is much more put together or costs much more than their real-life counterparts. Aspiration creates prestige or glamour. Matching the tone of the research to the tone of the story can be a good starting point. The Netflix series *#blackAF* features a newly wealthy family and their glamourous lifestyle.
- **Scale.** Is the story ambitious, epic, or grand? Or is it rooted in small everyday situations? Sweeping tragedies and fantasies lend themselves to large-scale designs featuring either conceptual minimalism or overstated grandeur. Matching the research to the "size" of the story explores how costumes relate to the human form. Suzanne Collins' book *The Hunger Games* translated very successfully to epic films.

It can be an enormous challenge to distill the many images collected during research for

Figure 13.3 This mood board communicates thematic ideas for a character based on a blue mushroom.

inclusion in a mood board. This is hard work, and an important step in defining the design approach and choosing images clarifies the mind. If one board cannot hold all the best ideas, make as many as are practical. Creating an effective mood board is a multistep endeavor and like most artistic pursuits, the process is a valuable design phase in itself.

- Use any system that allows you to compare many images at once on a screen or on a table.
- To use your time wisely, do a preliminary cull of items that clearly no longer belong. The act of research has already tuned your brain to the story. Form an image "purgatory" to hold culled images, but don't discard them.
- Consider an overarching approach that appears to mirror this story. Use one of the five preceding categories, or create new ones.
- Sort the images into categories evident from the images themselves. Test what messages they build together. Form new categories to keep the meanings of relevant images alive as long as possible.
- Step back to assess what you've constructed. What are the images trying to tell you? This is an important moment – can you see correlations or repeated motifs you weren't aware of before?
- Arrange the images on each mood board in the way you wish the eye to travel across a mood board. What ideas and images should take focus?
- Add notes on the board to keep track of ideas as needed, or record them in your design journal.

"Nothing is original. Steal from anywhere that resonates with inspiration or fuels your imagination. . . . Select only things to steal from that speak directly to your soul. If you do this, your work (and theft) will be authentic. Authenticity

Figure 13.4 This mood board contains the same information as Figure 13.3. It is arranged in a factual manner, serving as references for ideas or drawing.

is invaluable; originality is nonexistent. And don't bother concealing your thievery – celebrate it if you feel like it." —Film director Jim Jarmusch[6]

Character Collage Boards

Costume designers use another process to sort and correlate images: **character collages**, also called **tear sheets** or **look boards**. Many industries use tear sheets to summarize key information about a product on one page. The single sheet limitation forces designers to choose only relevant information. A character sheet serves the same purpose; the costume designer sorts through many images to assign them directly to each character in a story.

It may be helpful to revisit or include keywords and information collected during script analysis. The designer assesses each image for relevance, keeping those that engage with each character. Images of general interest remain in the image bank for possible future use. This initial sorting reveals holes in the research. *Every* designer discovers they were not researching as thoroughly as they thought. Some of the most common discoveries include:

- Did you get carried away with a few favorite characters, collecting dozens of images for them and few or none for the others?
- Is the research too general, so it does not feature your character's qualities?
- Is the research inclusive, does it feature members of our community inaccurately?

- Do you need more information on specific categories, such as menswear?
- Do you lack information about professional or occupational clothing, particularly in a period setting?

All designers find they must generate more images after this initial sorting. This new wave of research is then more targeted and efficient. It may also be a golden opportunity to use brainstorming techniques to initiate new directions of thought. Just as with mood boards, the designer must give some thought to the arrangement of a character board. Use enough images to communicate the idea, but do not use so many images it is difficult to focus. The human eye and brain gloss over many small images, deciding not to expend energy on each image unless something triggers the imagination. Tell an observer where to look by enlarging some images, and layer others toward the back. Successful character boards evoke a snapshot of that character, forming a bridge from inspirational and emotional images to specific items worn on the human body.

Figure 13.5 This character collage for a show titled *Top Secret* used collages in place of costume renderings. The story takes place at a newspaper office, so the collages were created in black, white, and red. Compositional placement and a limited use of dark red creates visual focus.

Finished collages may take any form the designer finds most useful to communicate information to others. Many designers keep these collages throughout the project to show actors and shop personnel, posting them in the fitting room or using them as a means to verbalize their ideas. Drapers, shoppers, and assistant designers like to work with the original source material to gather intention or specific details. Actors love to see research behind the design decisions; it can form areas for their own exploration. Ellen Mirojnick, the costume designer for *Bridgerton*, was the first designer hired on that project. She created character books that described her aspirational interpretation of Regency fashions using saturated colors and large patterns. Her research

was a great tool because we felt the interpretation that was being asked of us . . . was really important for everyone to be on the same page. It was hugely important they saw exactly what we saw. And so the time we put into the look book was so that if you looked at it, you would understand immediately. We were all able to hit it on the nose from the get go.[7]

Consulting With the Director

Show your mood board and character collages to your director. Use a casual approach for any early research meeting to encourage personal and immediate feedback from the director. Mentally rehearse how you will present information to tell a story. Explain your thought process, the system you used to sort images, and what made the biggest impact on you. Tell the story of your ideas and images using that framework. This session is partly a pitch meeting as you lay out your ideas. This is a tricky line to walk as you do have ideas that you are emotionally invested in, yet nothing should be set in stone yet. Leave room for feedback and brainstorming. It is wise to recall the designer's job is to generate ideas – lots of them. Designers cannot live or die on the reception of a single approach. However, many a passionate, well-constructed presentation has persuaded a director to use the designer's approach.

We learn a great deal from these brainstorming conversations that wander, express tangential ideas, or gather momentum from thinking together. Keep your unused stored images on a phone, tablet, or laptop computer. If the director suggests something you thought about but rejected, retrieve those images from your image bank. If a personal or video meeting is not possible to review research together, the next best option is to post the research collages on a file-sharing site for the director to peruse at her leisure. If this is the case, there is an extra step to add: incorporating verbal or written notes to explain your thought process. Some designers create a scene-by-scene storyboard or walk-through for absentee meetings. Ultimately, effective research serves as talking points for brainstorming. Do not allow the director to flounder through imagery wondering about the glue that holds them together. Some directors prefer very few images; they can only process so much in one sitting or have extremely limited time. If this is the case, schedule more than one meeting or combine both personal and digital communication.

Using Extant Garments for Research

There is no better source of information than studying actual garments from an era or a geographical location. Contemporary clothing is relatively plain so it is hard to envision the delightful details incorporated into even very affordable clothing in the past. These details add enormously to character development, and add authenticity to vintage or period garments. Museums and historical societies often allow those with purpose to study their collections using proper handling. Vintage stores and rental stocks are excellent opportunities to study garments inside and out. The yellow dress in Figure 13.7 features a bias-cut inset that greatly enlivens the typical shift dress. The designer captured a close up of a tab and button detail to decorate a neckline, also in Figure 13.7.

Sizing Up Research

Researching creative projects energizes and inspires the designer to make connections between the words in a script and visual imagery.

Figure 13.6 Excerpts from a costume research storyboard sent to a director with comments to guide him through design choices. It is arranged by scene, showing how groups of characters would look together.

Gathering research is an important first step in the creative process, using *modeling*, or testing possible approaches. Excellent research begins with broader ideas and slowly focuses toward specific ideas. Designers use factual and emotional research, and curate that imagery to tell a story using mood boards or character collages. It is important to schedule some creative procrastination, or a break in the work, to allow the brain to incubate ideas.

Expecting the Unexpected: Research, Design, GO!

On occasion, a designer is hired too late to conduct in-depth research. Producers don't always understand how the artistic process works, and sometimes there are extenuating circumstances. These circumstances are often big breaks, if we can answer that call. Designer Marcy Froehlich recalls one incident in her career.

The call came in around 4:00 on a Wednesday afternoon. My brother, who was working on a documentary, overheard the people in the next cubicle say they had lost their Costume Designer for reenactment scenes, and they were shooting on Friday. "My sister's a costume designer!" It was a documentary for the History Channel on the Ottoman Empire in the 1500's, so that night I did research in my own home library and on the internet. The next morning, I pulled costumes at Western Costume in Hollywood, and did fittings with the actors in the afternoon. That night I did alterations and made a few hats. By the next morning I was shooting on location.[8]

Extra Resources

The Perks of Procrastination, Harvard Division of Continuing Education, October 19, 2016. https://professional.dce.harvard.edu/blog/the-perks-of-procrastination/

The Need for Gender Fluidity in Fashion Beyond Pride, Edited.com, June 16, 2021. https://blog.edited.com/

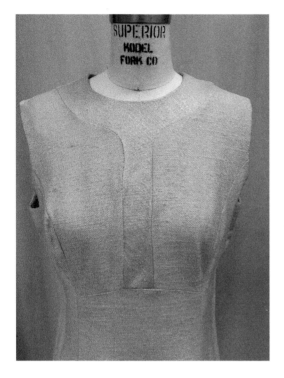 

Figure 13.7 A yellow shift (left) and detail of a pink dress (right).

blog/resources/the-need-for-gender-fluidity-in-fashion-beyond-pride

Fashion, Costume and Culture: Clothing Headwear, Body Decoration and Footwear through the Ages. Sara Pendergast and Tom Pendergast. 2004, UXL. This remarkable book looks at costume history around the world. It is currently out of print, available through libraries. A digital copy may be downloaded from Siam Costumes www.siamcostumes.com/cutters_guides/pdf/fashion_costume_and_culture_-_vol_1_the_ancient_world.pdf

Notes

1 Ruth Carter, Interview with Marcy Froehlich, University of California Irvine, October 19, 2020.
2 Newbold, Alice. 2018. "The Making of the Black Panther Costumes." *Vogue (French Edition)*, February 13, 2018. https://www.vogue.fr/fashion-culture/fashion-exhibitions/story/the-making-of-the-black-panther-costumes-explained-by-their-designer/1130.
3 Pelzer, Kelsey. 2021 "The Man Behind the Theories and Equations." *Parade*, August 9, 2021. https://parade.com/1240718/kelseypelzer/albert-einstein-quotes/.
4 Whitney Friedlander, 107 Years, 2.5 Million Outfits, Countless Characters: Inside Hollywood's "Magical" Mecca of Costumes February 18, 2019. The Hollywood Reporter. https://www.hollywoodreporter.com/tv/tv-features/western-costume-inside-hollywoods-magical-mecca-costumes-1187057/.
5 Mete, Fatma. 2006. "The Creative Role of Sources of Inspiration in Clothing Design." *International Journal of Clothing Science and Technology*, 18(4): pp. 278–293. https://www.proquest.com/docview/228297781
6 Jarmusch, Jim. n.d. "Jim Jarmush's 5 Golden Rules (or Non-rules) of Moviemaking." *Moviemaker.com*. Accessed July 6, 2019. http://www.moviemaker.com/articles-directing/jimmarmusch-5-golden-rules-of-moviemaking/
7 Mirojnick, Ellen. "Costume Design Salon Panel." Streamed June 12, 2021, via Facebook from UCLA Showcase West/Netflix. Los Angeles, CA. Video https://www.youtube.com/watch?v=4WuB5WKUisg
8 Froehlich, Marcy. Interview with the author, August 16, 2021.

PART FOUR

CONCEPT DEVELOPMENT

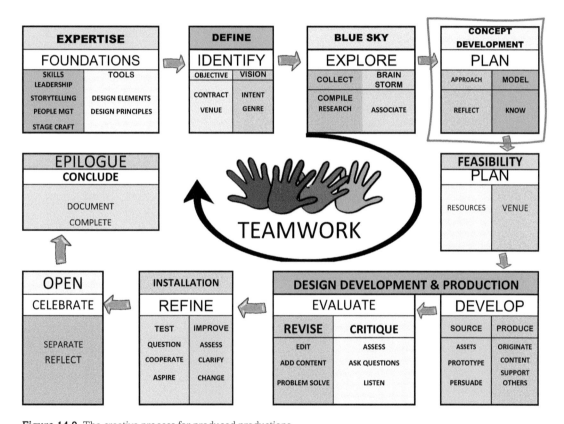

Figure 14.0 The creative process for produced productions.

Credit: Holly Poe Durbin and Ayrika Johnson

14.
THE DESIGN APPROACH

Many designers find they could spend forever in the research and exploration phase; it is delightful to discover new things. However, they must eventually tear themselves away from research and brainstorming to apply their ideas to actual costumes. After gathering so much visual imagery and written notes, how do designers refine their ideas to create the design **approach**? This step is the mysterious part of the journey and designers often cannot verbalize how they do it. What is a design approach, and how can designers bring their unique points of view to the story?

The approach can be illustrated by a single garment: a pair of overalls. For example, during the preparation phase the designer found excellent visual research of overalls; this is the pure documentary evidence of fabric, color, stitching details, style, and fit on one person's overalls. Let's consider how those overalls might appear in different stories. A realistic biographical story might use the overalls exactly as they appear in the research, going to great lengths to duplicate the rips and stains. A story about social disparity may exaggerate those overalls as a metaphor for the struggle of its wearer: extra torn, dirty, sagged, and bleached from years of overwork. A story for young audiences may use clean overalls colored a bright blue that appeals to children. A musical or a broad comedy might interpret those overalls in shiny fabrics or vibrant patterns or focus on the graphic qualities by enhancing the contrast stitching or add edgings. Each of these overalls represents a design approach. The approach is partly choosing what characters wear and partly deciding how to interpret those garments stylistically. If a designer is stuck for ideas, it can be useful to step away from the larger question of *How do I design this show?* to substitute a silly or low-pressure question such as *If there were overalls in this show, what would they look like?* Verbalizing the approach prepares the designer to move forward with more confidence. The design approach formalizes four main ideas about each design:

- Define the **tone**
- Create the **visual style**
- Choose a **color scheme** and **arc**
- Define **focus** and **clarity**

Defining the Tone

Stories use a *manner* of storytelling to confer an attitude – or tone – about the story itself. Just as with vocal tone, it is not what a person says, but how they say it. We explored the term **tone** in Chapter 4 as part of the qualities of color; it means adding gray to a color to produce a subtle variation of any hue. Storytellers also use the term *tone* to mean the manner of presentation or nuanced interpretations of a work. Like color tonality, interpretive tone is a sliding scale of options.

DOI: 10.4324/9781003015284-18

Some examples of tone are comic, joyous, ironic, nostalgic, pessimistic. Designers adjust interpretive tone using visual vocabulary to create a style. The show overall has a tone, but specific scenes will vary within that. One example of tonal shift is the Netflix series *A Series of Unfortunate Events* following the tragi-comic lives of the Baudelaire siblings. Although the overall tone is dismal foreboding, it effectively mixes comedy, hope, and melancholy.

Another possibility to vary tone is creating a hierarchy of exaggeration for individuals or groups. Such was the case for the Netflix series *Bridgerton*. Queen Charlotte, who exerted the most power over the other characters, wore large structured fashions with opulent wigs that commanded attention, just as her royal power would have commanded everyone's attention. The Bridgerton family, a prominent family with long-standing social capital, dressed in a refined, understated manner. Portia Featherington represented social-climbing new money. She dressed herself and her three daughters in exaggerated gowns, acidic colors with gaudy prints or trim. "They're bolder, brighter and more brazen than everyone else, and everything is overly embellished. They just don't know any better," says costume designer Ellen Mirojnick.[1] These three separate tones, or attitudes toward clothing, defined character groups in *Bridgerton*.

Defining Visual Style

The second element used to create a design approach is visual style. We use the word *style* routinely, but what does it really mean? We speak of someone having a personal style, and art historians use the term to group art works into categories of similar appearance, aesthetics, or intentions such as Art Nouveau or Bauhaus style. Style is a dynamic concept that describes how a work arranges visual elements:

- Rules of **composition**
- Methods of **construction**
- Resources of **inspiration**
- Use of **materials**

Returning to the earlier example of overalls, one stylistic interpretation could be adjusting the rules of **composition**: treating the garment as a collection of rectangles. One method of adjusting the **construction** could be to substitute carpentry staples for sewing, or explore deconstruction, wearing the overalls inside out to show the seams and linings. Alternate **materials** might be assembling overalls from paper, plastic, or fine fabrics normally associated with evening wear. **Inspiration** describes the source of ideas. *Bridgerton* designer Ellen Mirojnick explains her inspiration as a combination of historical Regency garments with the 1950s. "We knew that we had to shift the color palette and the fabrications, so from the 19th century, I immediately went to the 1950s and 1960s." She found inspiration in the legendary couture designer Christian Dior's work. She blended the Regency silhouette with Dior's aesthetic by "layering on other fabrics and embellishment. Using either organza, organdy or tulle, we could create another layer on top of the dresses that gives it a new sense." Mirojnick also altered the square Regency necklines to the deeper rounded necklines. "When you go into a close-up there's so much skin. It exudes beauty."[2] This inspiration was successful, because Mirojnick used strict rules to define a consistent style. (To see Mirojnick's mood boards for *Bridgerton*, consult Extra Resources at the end of this chapter.) Adjusting the inspiration, composition, construction, or materials of any object evokes an **intent** that will create an attitude and a response from the audience response, whether emotional or intellectual. Table 14.1 provides sample styles and possible emotional impacts associated with each.

"Style never speaks, but somehow is always saying something." —Mircea Popister[3]

Choosing a Color Scheme and Arc

Color is a powerful component of visual style. It directs the eye and strongly affects tone or attitude by agreeing with or opposing the **context** of the scene or story. The animated feature *The Incredibles* uses color to comment on Bob Incredible's state of mind. When the former superhero works in an insurance office, the color palette is desaturated

Table 14.1 Sample Style Terms

Style Term	Attributes	Intent or Effect
Organic	Natural shapes, broken lines and curves, avoiding straight lines, lack of conformity	Associated with nature and living organisms, old-fashioned, peaceful
Geometric	Straight lines, consistent shapes formed with straight sides, often symmetrical	Machinelike, mathematical, manufactured, ordered, scientific
Abstract	Uses the art elements and principles on their own as subject matter, rather than illusion of reality	Ambiguous, individual interpretation by observer, playful, modern, artistic, expressionistic
Modern	Synthetic materials and plastics, glass or transparency, little surface decoration, bright chemical colors	Forward looking, progressive, cold, intellectual, innovative
Minimalist	Spare color palette, stripped of detail; emphasis on harmony of elements or fine quality of those elements, use of glass	Deliberate, disciplined, modern, sophisticated, cold, austere
Luxurious	Metal tones, shiny surfaces, indulgent materials such as leather, fur, silk, jewelry	Expensive, discerning, rarified
Decorative	Features fine details and patterns, often derived from a style of the past	Eclectic, traditional, eccentric, joyous
Ornate	Layers of details and patterns	Traditional, opulent, fancy
Delicate	Small or thin shapes and surfaces, translucent, detailed	Fragile, elegant, gentle, graceful
Graphic	Flat shapes, pure colors, outlined edges, poster qualities	Bold, striking, dramatic, artistic, expressive
Rustic	Associated with the country Natural materials, dark and rich colors, wood, Americana	Simple, traditional, homey, natural, provincial
Industrial	Features synthetic and metal materials, visible engineering, or structural forms	Technical, mechanical, modern, manufactured
Gothic	Dark color schemes, subject matter emphasizes madness, death, social outcasts, dreams	Eerie, grotesque, mysterious, fear, distress
Nostalgic	Evokes an idealized better time in the past, cozy, familiar, soothing	Sentimental, wistful, backward looking
Glamour	Emphasis on superficial beauty, idealized, less detailed, deliberately posed	Alluring, prestigious, enchanting
Eclectic	Mixes imagery or items from various time periods and cultures	Diverse, liberal, dilettante, nondiscerning, individualistic
Formal	Follows rules of composition or thought, establishment sensibility	Tasteful, academic, official, precise, proper
Vulgar	Lacks sophistication, surprising materials or composition, exaggerated	Ostentatious, crude, indecent, breaking rules of good taste

blues and greens that mirror Bob's feeling of being trapped in a drab existence. When the family visits designer Edna Mode, she gives them new super suits in vibrant red and black. Their new costumes communicate the sense of excitement and accomplishment returning to their lives. Choreographer Lar Lubovitch (*Into the Woods*) notes that costume designer Ann Hould-Ward is an exceptional colorist. She approaches color using two different aspects; the first uses colors that are a direct response from the emotional impulses of a piece, particularly dance. She creates color boards for important moments in the show to show the director. But she also creates a secondary library of other related colors to have on hand

> in case the director wants to subtract or add a color, we can do that. That way they can be part of the process. By the time we get to the painted sketch, they've been on that color journey with me. . . . I find these color boards useful not only at the directorial stage, but also at the shop level for painting and dying. Lighting designers also find them really valuable.[4]

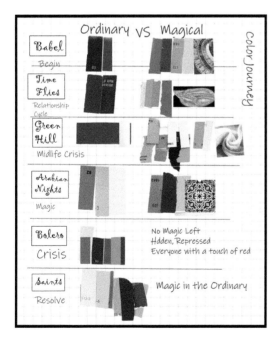

Figure 14.1 A color plot for a production of *Time Flies* by David Ives for the Old Globe Theaters in San Diego.

The color **scheme** specifies the use of color throughout the entire project. Planning how the colors may change in the course of a story results in a color **arc**. Designers may choose colors at any point in their preparation; for some designers it is the first reaction, and for others color ideas develop after due consideration. Most often the designer discusses the colors with the director at the same time they discuss rough design sketches, to frame color within context of the garments. Where do designers find color inspiration? There may be "**givens**" that define the starting points for any scheme:

- **Script requirement.** The story or script may designate specific colors in the dialogue or action. Ask the director if colors noted in stage directions are relevant, as they may be an artifact or open to interpretation now.
- **Director requests.** Directors may have strong color thoughts or aversions. Ask early in the planning process about these ideas.
- **Scenic design colors.** The scenic timetable may be well ahead of costumes, with environment colors already chosen. Study the scenic model or renderings carefully. It can be advantageous to include some of the scenic colors in the costume palette or to ensure contrasting colors.
- **History or custom.** Tradition may predetermine some colors, such as military or sports uniforms, traditional formal wear in black and white, or wedding and funeral attire.
- **Character psychology and relationships.** Audiences read color similarity and contrast easily. This may translate into opposing characters wearing colors that contrast each other. Those sympathetic to each other may wear analogous colors.
- **Performance tradition.** We associate pure hues with comedy, shades or tones for dramatic stories, jewel tones are often used for fantasy, tints and light color palettes for innocence or optimism – although designers do break these rules successfully.
- **Staging challenges.** Some scripts present obvious challenges, such as large rosters of characters the audience may confuse; design solutions can provide identifying markers.

Once the "givens" are taken into consideration, how might a designer expand these ideas? Some sources of color inspiration include:

- **Imagery in the script.** The story may feature strong metaphors or images that suggest color schemes. One example might be strategic conflicts that resemble a chess board.
- **Fashion and decor history**. Historical fashions featured certain colors or trends, as well as marking the onset of synthetic dyes.
- **Art works** or graphic illustrations. Many designers make correlations between the story and works by visual artists that provide a meaningful visual vocabulary.
- **Environmental color.** Everyday life presents a color palette, such as the differences between urban, suburban, and rural color palettes or natural and human-made colors.
- **Color temperature.** Many designers have strong feelings about the relationship between warm colors and cool colors before settling on specific hues.
- **Symbolism.** Colors are associated with different meanings in each culture, and some present universal significance.
- **Color wheel.** Designers may create a custom color scheme using color theory to express a mood or other effect. Review Chapter 4 for traditional color relationships.

Figure 14.2 This mural's bright colors could serve as the inspiration for a color scheme.

Credit: Photo by Toa Heftiba Şinca from Pexels

Costume designer Paul Tazewell described some of his color decisions for *Hamilton*. One early decision was the array of off-whites and beiges at the top of the show.

> It became clear from our workshop that the prologue required a neutral look so that we would see the full ensemble, principles and all (except for Burr) as a seamless group. They present themselves as the creators of story that we are getting ready to see.

The color for Hamilton himself was a "request of Lin: Hamilton being dressed in green, the color of money." The other symbolic color was "The purple of Jefferson emphasized his rock star status. I was channeling Jimmi Hendrix and Prince, which seemed appropriate for Daveed's own performance style and dramatic hair."[5]

There are many books and websites available providing popular color schemes for historical eras, color ideas from nature, and other inspirations. There are excellent digital tools available to aid experimenting with color schemes (see Chapter 4). For instance, Adobe CC Color provides color scheme finders using color relationships as keywords. The example in Figure 14.3 shows a **triadic** color scheme using violet as the key color.

Assembling a Color Library

Some designers define the overall color scheme before assigning colors to individual characters, to avoid sorting through millions of color possibilities. Creating a **color library** ensures those decisions are made with the larger color picture in mind, not in a piece-by-piece manner while designing the garments. Dorothy Jeakins, the costume designer for such golden age Hollywood films as *The Ten Commandments* and *The Sound of Music* was admired by fellow designers for her use of color. Her method was to choose a color palette for the entire film inspired by a painting or other sources. She then "laid out the vast color plot on the floor and I pulled from it what became scenes."[6] This method ensured a tight, well-coordinated color scheme that changed appropriately for different

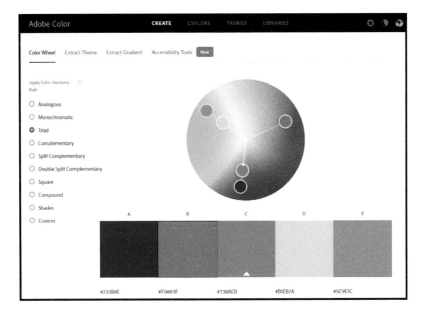

Figure 14.3 Adobe Color provides a color wheel to create schemes. This example shows a triadic color scheme, or three hues placed evenly around the wheel. It also includes shades of two of the chosen hues.

Figure 14.4 Two ways of capturing the colors used in the mural in Figure 14.4. The Photoshop mosaic filter in reduces the image to color swatches (left). The example at right shows painted swatches matched to the colors in the reference mural.

Figure 14.5 Screen capture of Adobe Color Wheel Extract Theme using an uploaded photo. Adobe provides video tutorials to explain using this web or smart phone application.

moments in the story. Adding color swatches to the scene chart or creating a new color chart allows experimentation while choosing the scheme. The Photoshop *mosaic filter* can be adapted to divide any image into color swatches. It reduces the colors in an artwork to square blocks for easy identification. Many color reductions taken from nature lack a contrast or focal point; analyze what added colors may enliven the scheme for stage. (See Figure 4.5.) Photoshop provides color swatch tools and color libraries with Pantone numbers to coordinate with

Pantone books for easier and consistent communication. For tutorials on these tools, see the Extra Resources section.

Digital color apps can make short work of sorting chosen colors into a chart or library. One such tool is Adobe Color's Extract Theme function, available for free on its website. It reduces any uploaded image to four or five dominant colors. These colors may be too limited for many costume schemes, but they provide a start for decision making. ProCreate also offers a color palette tool that will capture the main colors of a live camera image or a stored image.

Once the overall color scheme is decided, step back to analyze how it can be used in the story. Divide the colors into groupings that apply to your project – focal points or foreground, receding colors or background, middle ground, warm or cool colors. One scheme uses the most dynamic or visible colors for leading or dynamic characters, assigning less vibrant colors to the other characters. Middle value colors may be spread among all the characters to unify them all. Another scheme may use only the middling colors for all characters, using the dynamic colors as smaller accents. Sometimes designers begin with a strong color impression for a character, constructing the scheme around that origin point. There are many ways a designer may create a color scheme:

- **Power in numbers.** A larger number of characters or a chorus occupies more physical real estate on the stage, setting a dominant color scheme for that scene. What emotional impact would that bring? How might other characters contrast with the dominant color?
- **Identification.** Colors are a crucial method to signify characters. One example is Shakespeare's *Henry IV* series with armies fighting a civil war. It can be very difficult for the audience to keep track of the many earls and lords. Assigning each political cohort a signature color adds easy markers. An excitable group of characters may wear vibrant colors, and serious characters wear somber colors.
- **Genre.** Some types of stories are well served with bright colors or pure hues, while others may be best served with neutralized tones.
- **Texture.** Color can never be entirely separated from surface texture. A rough fabric will neutralize a tone slightly by breaking up the light. Colors may be assigned that best feature each texture.
- **Response to environment.** The costume color scheme does not stand alone. There are times when coordinating with the scenery is desirable, and times when contrasting with the scenery is best.

The Color Arc

Some stories benefit from color changes over time, or arcs. Characters may grow or ascend in power while others diminish. Some characters may change sides of a disagreement. Some motivations for a change in colors include:

- Emotional or physical high or low points
- Inciting triggers such as betrayal or murder
- Revealing secrets
- Shifts in the environment
- Emotional scenes
- Shifts in power

Use the costume scene chart to review plot turning points and how they might relate to a color scheme. One example is the play *Collected Stories* by Donald Margulies. The play follows the career arcs of a famous writer and her intern, who in turn becomes a noted author. The costume designer chose to use an X-shaped arc tracking changes in color and body proportions to document one's rise and the other's demise. The middle of the X was one crucial scene where the two characters dressed alike, balanced as equals before the power shifted to the younger writer.

Communicating a Color Scheme

Once the color scheme is chosen, communicate that information to the director and scenic and lighting designers. Try to catch undesirable combinations at this early stage so adjustments can be made cheaply and with less stress. Always communicate costume colors using visual samples; don't expect to have a serious color conversation with verbal cues only. No two people see color the same, and few share the same color vocabulary. Designers may share a well-developed understanding of color possibilities, but directors, actors, and vendors do not always use the same technical terminology. Fabric swatches communicate not only the color but also the effect of texture on each hue. Every designer prefers a given method of communicating color early in the communication process. Some designers use special

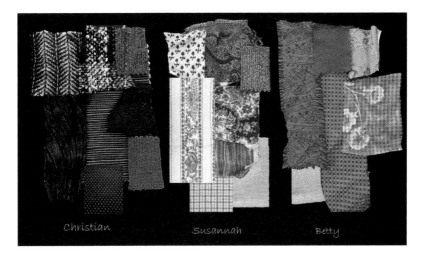

Figure 14.6 Sample swatches from the designer's collection taped to poster board represent texture and pattern for *Jefferson's Garden* by Timberlake Wertenbaker.

methods geared toward each show. One successful communication method is creating a **swatch world** or representation of the entire show palette using swatches from the designer's personal library of fabrics or from the costume shop. The costume designer can talk to the director about color, texture, and the quality before meticulously swatching in fabric stores. Another method is sorting possible fabrics into character collections, using loose-leaf rings. Any fabric the director objects to can be removed, and new fabrics or colors added.

Defining Focus and Clarity

The fourth element of creating a design approach is to harness the principles of focus and clarity. Concentrated focus strongly enhances the importance of whatever the designer chooses. Diffused focus creates a sense of democracy, with every character bearing equal importance. Poor focus provides visual chaos, making it difficult for the audience to process the whole picture or pick a character out of the crowd. This technique is creating **directed seeing**. Chapter 5, Design Principles Create Meaning, explores how designers manipulate the elements of design to direct where viewers look. Understanding the design approach defines the goal or intent for directed seeing. Clarity refers to how easily others understand the visual

rules, and how consistently they are applied. Visual styles may be clean and minimal or complex and lavish. The overall application of these rules, and when to break them, creates a unified look for the entire show.

Style Rules for Focus and Clarity

- **Facial focus.** Unless there is a specific reason to break this rule, effective costumes direct the eye toward the shoulders or face.
- **Comic focus.** Comic characters may benefit from the opposite rule. Featuring another body part may provide an important part of the overall gag. Some examples use exaggeration such as comically short pants putting focus on the feet, or comically tall pants waists putting focus on the legs.
- **Inverse focus.** The more developed the character, the fewer clues need be illustrated in the costume. Undeveloped or one-dimensional characters may rely almost exclusively on the costume to communicate their character.
- **Hierarchy.** Develop a visual arrangement that features importance between characters, between groups.
- **Listen or look.** Human attention cannot be in two places at one time. Plays with wordy, complex dialogue may benefit from easily

recognized costumes so the audience can concentrate. Plays with less dependence on complex conceptual dialogue such as musical reviews may use spectacle to communicate ideas.

- **The rule of three.** Create interest by using odd numbers of elements, shapes, or trims. This is more pleasing to the eye than even-numbered items. For instance, if a costume consists of just two garments such as a t-shirt and jeans, add a third element for interest: a contrast collar at the neck, a second t-shirt visible at top or bottom, a neck scarf.
- **Division.** Dividing the figure into more shapes than the usual thirds adds some camouflage, making the human form more difficult to discern.
- **Shape.** Alter the actor's body through illusion or padding.
- **Repetition.** Apply chosen elements and principles of art consistently across the stage picture. For instance, a character that changes costumes many times will appear more comprehensible if some proportion, silhouette, color, or detail is repeated throughout. Characters that share a common meaning may share an element in common: they think alike.
- **Adaptation.** Some period fashions direct the eyes downward or toward expensive embellishments. Stage designers may have to simplify or adapt historical eras to create an effective stage picture.
- **Be strong.** Indecisive composition appears meek or confusing. Lack of focus, weak contrast, or muddled shapes disappear from view.

Sizing Up the Costume Approach

Creating an overall design approach will focus the next steps of designing, sketching, and assembling the costumes. It ensures a consistent tone, creates a visual style, uses a color scheme and arc, and provides focus and clarity. As the designer proceeds, the approach may shift and evolve, but a starting place contributes confidence and direction. Check with the director to affirm the approach prioritizes and supports their ideas. Also check in with the

Figure 14.7 This ensemble features high contrast on the bodice and in the hat, drawing attention to the face.
Credit: Photo by C.M. Bell, Library of Congress Online Catalog. Gift of the American Genetic Association

scenic designer to pre-visualize how those design approaches work together. In contemporary practice, it is not uncommon to juxtapose an abstract or minimal set design with more complex or historical costumes. But the approaches should be compatible. Some considerations to judge if the scenery and costume approaches are working toward a common tone or attitude include:

- Period and source material shared in common or compatible
- Suitable contrast or harmony between scenery and costumes in design elements
- Harmony or suitable contrast in detail
- Ability of clothed actors to move in the scenic space
- Suitable contrast or harmony in texture

Expecting the Unexpected – The Elevator Speech

The costume designer will be asked many times to summarize the design approach and how those ideas apply to each character. Directors, actors, and makers will all need to grasp the major ideas quickly. Don't be caught off guard – by the time the designer arrives at the production phase, many weeks may have gone by and our original ideas may make sense to us but we can't describe them. As you go through the design process, create and refine a short talk, known as an elevator speech. Imagine that you had just the short time it takes to ride an elevator with someone to explain your idea: it is a brief summary of any complex idea. Be able to explain your design in just a few moments without any visual aids or a deep knowledge of costume design. You can always invite your companion for a longer conversation later. Creating the brief pitch forces the designer to focus on what is important and most descriptive about your ideas. Every designer finds themselves repeating this elevator speech dozens of times to vendors, suppliers, money people, reporters, bloggers, and financial patrons.

Extra Resources

Bridgerton mood boards created by Ellen Mirojnick, shared on Facebook by series author Julia Quinn, July 27, 2019. www.facebook.com/AuthorJuliaQuinn/photos/a.59952827053/10156841108202054/

The Color Arc of the Incredibles https://i.pinimg.com/originals/9f/09/6c/9f096c48980c3ee4915a1f4d4a7413b8.jpg

Photoshop CC Mosaic Filter tutorial www.grosgrainfab.com/2012/05/paint-chip-wall-art-mosaic-how-to.htmlProcreate Color tutorial

Adobe Color Extract Color https://color.adobe.com/create/image

Notes

1 Seth, Radhika. 2020. "Bridgerton's Costume Designer on What it Took to Create Netflix's Regency Romp." *Vogue.com*, December 6, 2020. Accessed February 28, 2021. https://vogue.sg/bridgerton-netflix-period-costume-design-best-looks/

2 Seth, *Vogue.com*.

3 Meah, Asad. 2018. "35 Inspirational Quotes on Style." *Quotes*. Accessed August 15, 2020. https://www.awakenthegreatnesswithin.com/35-inspirational-quotes-on-style/

4 Lubovitch, Lar. 2021. "Global Perspectives and Artistic Practice." *Live Webcast*, April 9, 2021 at University of California, Irvine Department of Dance, Irvine CA.

5 Playbill. n.d. "Designer Paul Tazewell Shares Sketches and Inspiration Behind Hamilton." *Playbill.com*. Accessed April 10, 2021. https://www.playbill.com/gallery/hamilton-costume-designer-paul-tazewell-shares-sketches-and-describes-his-inspiration/?slide=0

6 Farr, Louise. 1986. "Dorothy Jeakins Dressing a Dream." *W Magazine*, July 14–July 21, 1986.

15.
DESIGNING THE CHARACTER COSTUME

Commercial illustrator and *Warby Parker* storefront designer Saskia Keultjes specializes in line drawings. Her schoolmates made fun of her work, however, because she did not draw like everyone else. Taking art classes at school were the last straw "discouraging me from ever drawing again. I thought I couldn't draw." She is now a successful artist who has discovered

> I'm not as excited about technical ability as much as I am about drawings which I can develop an emotional connection with. To me, a "good drawing" is more than a pretty picture. It is *visual thinking*. An exciting drawing is: imperfect, reflective, brimming full of ideas.[1]

Figure 15.1 A Warby Parker store in Brooklyn, New York, featuring line drawings by Saskia Keultjes.
Credit: Photo by Sera Bourgeau

DOI: 10.4324/9781003015284-19

This chapter uses the terms *artistic communication* and *character sketch* to describe any visual delivery system that helps the designer experiment with or talk about ideas. It explores the types of visual communication that aids designing costumes for a production. Some designers work through their first ideas with research collages, as seen in Chapter 13. Some use a rough form of sketching or doodles called **thumbnail** sketches. For costume designers, this stage is the first of an iterative process that results in a character garment design. No matter how undeveloped or elaborate a costume sketch may be, that is not the art we've been hired to create. Sketches represent visual thinking, by whatever means necessary. Some costume designers are very accomplished sketch artists and they are greatly admired for this skill. But some are not. Others hire sketch artists, especially in film. But even accomplished renderers don't always have time to fully paint a show, and they must deliver the stage picture anyway. As Saskia Keultjes' story shows, there is little direct correlation between formal drawing skills and success.

Costume designers do, however, have to be very effective communicators. So what does a character design have to communicate? It must be the basis for action. As we discovered in Chapter 2, arranging elements in a composition is solutions-based thinking. It serves as a model to try ideas, scrap them, alter them. A sketch or collage makes planning the next steps easier. Effective visual communication provides effective leadership; some form of artistic communication frees the designer from having to be in the room for work to continue. And it boosts motivation when everyone working on a project has a road map outlining the objectives. Many designers consider creating the initial costume communication the same as designing the costumes themselves. If they don't know exactly what each costume will be at the start of this phase, they will by the end. This chapter explores the ways costume designers communicate ideas to themselves.

> "Imagination is in control when you begin making an object. . . . But as the piece grows, technique and craft take over, and imagination becomes a less useful tool. A piece grows by becoming specific." —*Art and Fear*[2]

Thinking With the Hand

Sketching creates great frustration for those who are not yet confident in drawing. It is all too easy to fear the sketches do not live up to some imaginary standard. Although no two designers work in the same manner, many do create hasty scribbles or gesture sketches at first with little thought to accepted standards. They give themselves permission to drastically lower expectations – why waste time during the experimentation stage, when the emphasis should be on trying ideas? The benefits of drawing expands well beyond its use in sparking creative ideas; research connects the use of the hand to shaping the development of the brain, language, and human culture.[3] These benefits pertain to any drawing at all using digital or traditional media. Of course, there are other ways to previsualize a design besides drawing. Some designers find 3D modeling more useful, such as putting garments on a dress form to try silhouettes, combinations, and layers. This step may better inform sketching or take the place of it on occasion.

Many worries about creating a design are really concerns about how to begin, or facing the blank page. If the designer created detailed research, the starting point is easier to pinpoint: testing the collected ideas together on the character body. Individual artists create conventions or rituals that will jump start this work, or unlock the process of designing. Reading about other artists' habits reveals some tricks that prime the pump. Painter Joan Miro suffered from bouts of depression, so he raised his serotonin levels with vigorous exercise along the beach or in a gym before working.[4] British-Nigerian punk artist Chris Ofili began his work days tearing a large piece of paper into eight equal squares, making abstract pencil marks on each one as a warm up.[5]

> "I always start by finding visual inspiration in research, and then I have a ghost of an idea. When I started sketching, it was because I couldn't find one visual reference to express the idea or the combination of ideas into one fully fledged character." —Mary Zophres, *La La Land* costume designer[6]

Thumbnail Sketches

Thumbnail sketches are hasty small drawings measuring from 2 to 6 inches tall. They express quick design ideas – basic shapes or gestures drawn rapidly with no corrections. They can be drawn on all kinds of paper. Some designers freeze if they use nice paper, so using the cheapest paper imaginable at this step frees their mind. Although this method appears to be doodling, it is actually an effective first step in the design process, trying ideas before tackling the bigger task of a full sketch. The small size prevents a lot of detail, instead capturing an essence of silhouette and gesture. This system is used extensively in animation and game character design to quickly create multiple possibilities. Remembering the story about the ceramics students in Chapter 1 who did their best work while creating the largest quantity of work, there are real benefits to generating many ideas as first.

Figure 15.2 The costume designer for this show was hired late in the process, leaving only time for thumbnail sketches in pastels and charcoal to meet the deadline for budgeting.

"Whether you use paint or pixels, the end result is the same: to communicate your vision. Although it may seem otherwise, there is room for imperfection so far as sketching goes, and it is important to embrace the 'hand' you have been dealt." —The Costume Designer Magazine[7]

also possible to draw on a glass table with a light source below it or use a glass window in daylight as the light source.

Drawing Over a Croquis

Many fashion designers draw over a **croquis** (krow-kee) to generate ideas quickly without generating a new body each time. Some costume designers elect to use this system for the same reasons, or to alleviate stress for those who don't feel confident with figure drawing. It is now possible to find a range of body styles and poses to use as figure guides using online art community sources such as DeviantArt. For those who draw with digital programs, it is easy to use a photo model as the bottom layer of a document and sketch over it as a guide. Traditional illustrators used a light box and tracing paper to create their first quick sketches using a croquis as a guide. It's

The Nine-Headed Monster

Many classic fashion illustrations laid out the proportions of a figure using the height of nine heads to create the ideal body. This system forced an unnaturally long leg height and torso; a figure precious few people live up to. The nine-heads figure is particularly misleading for costume designs unless the actor is shaped like a supermodel; it creates an incorrect design that does not translate to real human bodies. (See Figure 5.8.) Costume designers work with all body types to create characters. Most humans actually average about seven and a half heads in proportion, but many theatrical sketches use eight heads to approximate the range of proportions, especially if casting is not known at the time of sketching.

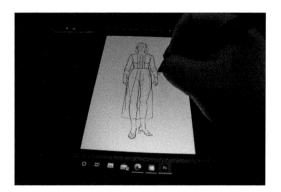

Figure 15.3 Using a croquis layer below (black lines) the drawing layer to create a garment (red lines) with a digital pen.

Credit: Illustration and photo by Sebastian Rock

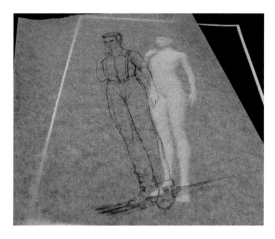

Figure 15.4 Costumed figure created by drawing over a croquis figure with tracing paper.

Credit: Illustration and photo by Sebastian Rock

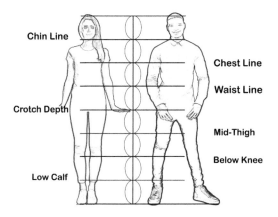

Figure 15.5 These figures are as tall as eight heads, resulting in more realistic proportions to start with.

The eight-head proportion system aligns approximately half of the body as torso, and half as legs. Using more realistic proportions creates accurate designs, especially for people of size or mature performers. The designer can better judge how style lines will fall on the body.

The average size of an American identifying as female is a size 16, with a waist measurement of 38.7 inches. For those identifying as male, the average waist measurement is 40.5 inches.[8] This average includes mature people whose waistlines tend to be larger than youthful ones, but it also includes people of all heritages, whose measurements never matched the outdated "ideal" fashion customers. The typical acting pool for a specific show will vary widely. However, when designing a chorus or ensemble, it is smart to include different body types to be inclusive and accurate. Then the designer will never be caught unprepared by planning too myopically.

The Layered Garment Design

Once the designer is ready to design each garment, using a three-step process will create a framework. Imagine the garment design process as viewing a panoramic vista. The designer starts with the big picture, then zooms in for medium-sized objects and then, finally, smaller objects. This layered system breaks large challenges such as "design that costume" into approachable tasks. It will ensure a cohesive design that considers all the elements of a garment. The layers of design include creating the **structure**, applying **aesthetic** elements, and adding **decorative** details.

Layered Character Design

Create the Structure

1. Figure and Character Stance
2. Silhouette and Scale
3. Manner of Wearing

Apply Aesthetic Elements

4. Fabric, Texture, and Pattern

5. Garment Lines and Proportions
6. Focal Point, Harmony, and Balance
7. Color and Patina

Create Decorative Details

8. Garment Details
9. Accessories and Hair

Creating the Structure

The structure of a design is sometimes called the *bones* of the design. It provides a set of conditions that underlie all the other decisions. In costume design, that structure is literally bones – the body of the actor and how clothing would sit on the body of each character.

Figure, Stance

Stance and posture are powerful keys to the personality and may suggest silhouettes that define each character. Expressive thumbnail sketches are an excellent way to generate these ideas. Powerful or proud characters pose in a way that inhabits more space, perhaps with legs and arms held out. Powerless characters may keep their arms close to the body or crouch slightly to take up less space.

Silhouette and Scale

Establishing a silhouette for characters includes their scale in relation to each other. Before designing details, consider placing all the character thumbnail sketches to note their relative sizes. Who is the largest or smallest? A character's scale may increase by expanding the size of their clothing silhouette or by adding voluminous capes, coats, hats, hair, or beards. The silhouette of any garment identifies its historical era or the occasion it may be worn. Pay particular attention to the placement of the waist, the size of sleeve, and shape of the skirt.

Manner of Wearing

Consider *how* each character would wear their clothing. We all know people that no matter what

Figure 15.6 This costume for a clerk in *Much Ado About Nothing* was inspired by an idea for the character's stance and elongating the silhouette with a top hat. Actor Christian O'Shaugnessy develops the final character in a fitting.

Figure 15.7 These sketches show the difference between characters wearing their clothes carefully or carelessly.

they wear, they resemble a bag of rumpled laundry. Would each character wear clothing neatly, tightly buttoned up, will the shirt tail stick out awkwardly, will over-large clothing form wrinkles around the elbows or ankles? Each character's manner could also be reflected in their facial expressions.

Are their signature features appropriate for each character?

Applying Aesthetic Elements

Aesthetics are the core design and materials that define the costume qualities. This is where many of the elements and principles of design come into play, to create an effective design.

Fabric, Texture, and Pattern

Consider how fabric choices affect silhouettes. Thick fabrics and large textures or patterns will create a powerful image by themselves, eliminating the effectiveness of smaller details. Smoother or finer fabrics will emphasize smaller details. Note which characters benefit from bolder statements, and which benefit from subtle statements.

Garment Lines and Proportions

Chapter 5 explored how interior lines such as seams and darts create proportions or smaller shapes

Figure 15.9 Changing the scale of the print in this hijab makes very different statements.

Credit: Photo by Monstera from Pexels, altered by the author

within the garment. They present the opportunity to define the body and express character elements. Research placement of darts and seam lines that were appropriate for each historical era, and use the design elements to create character statements.

Focal Point, Harmony, and Balance

Consider how to direct the viewer's eye using focal points and movement. Consider the use of contrast, harmony, and variation. Apply the principles of balance, rhythm, and positive and negative space. Which visual elements are the most important for each character? The use of bold contrasting colors may eliminate the need for smaller details. Harmonious colors might require more variety in details or texture. Test the designs as you work by turning the costume sketch upside down or backwards. Where does your eye travel first? Is that what you want the garment to say?

Color and Patina

Color is a strong early motivator for many designs, and it may be added at any point in the design process. Accurately plan skin tones if the actor has been cast, as this will affect the use of color in the garment. A patina is a weathered appearance that applies to clothing that has been aged, distressed, or overdyed. Will some characters wear aged, saggy clothing? Do some wear starchy new clothing?

Figure 15.8 Different fabrics create different silhouettes such as chiffon (left) and lamé (right).

Credit: Illustration by Sebastian Rock

Creating Decorative Details

Many designers feel their work is best exemplified by their attention to detail, and their ability to manipulate them to make a character statement. The decorative elements can move a design from "almost right" to "just right." Details such as construction components, topstitching, closures, and collars add flair and vigor to even the simplest ensemble. Each historical era expressed itself using signature details such as embroidered trim in 18th-century coats or circular ruffles in the skirts of 1930s dresses. Trims should not be an afterthought but used to add emphasis to part of the garment. Including specific choices is an important element of a mature design; unpolished or generic designs look vague and unfinished. Details can be small such as piping in a seam, or large such as a textile pattern. Trim in any era serves three purposes: it creates a **focal point**, trim will **accent edges**, and form **lines** in the composition that add interest. Some uses of trim include:

- **Edgings** – narrow trims following any edge of a garment, ruffles, or flounces
- **Motifs** – trims creating ornament or focal points with embroidery, applique, beading sequins, studs, or other embellishments
- **Necklines** – treatments around the neck or on collars that add a tailored, formal, casual, sporty, youthful, mature air
- **Sleeves** – contrast or match the body, cuff shape and décor add many styles of interest
- **Pockets** – placement on the body, one or pairs
- **Closures** – visible or invisible closures, historic or modern period identification, ease for fast changes, buttons and buttonholes, decorative (frogs, braids)
- **Belts** – contour belts hug and shape the waist, straight belts, buckles, belt loops
- **Dressmaker details** – tucks, smocking, top stitching, shirring and rushing, quilting

Accessories and Hair

Additional items such as hats, hairstyles, glasses, belts, scarves, gloves, jewelry, handbags, and shoes

Figure 15.10 Much of the appeal of a denim jacket is the construction details of pockets, and double top-stitched seams.

Credit: Photo by Olivet Pictures from Pexels

Figure 15.11 The trim incised into this Italian armor is an integral part of the design. It emphasizes the round chest and small waist fashionable for men in the 1500s.

Credit: Metropolitan Museum of Art, New York. Gift of William H. Riggs, 1913

present unlimited opportunity to add panache and specificity to every character. Hairstyles are not only a finishing detail but also an opportunity to create silhouettes. Periodically step back during the design process to evaluate the entire show. Audiences see a large picture, with many characters onstage at the same time. If we lose sight of the stage picture we develop a myopic design. Line up the characters around a room to measure the work in progress against your intended impact. Who stands out of the crowd and who recedes? Does every character demand attention, creating chaos? Do scene groupings make sense? Do costumes make sense with the action and location? Seek feedback from the director and adjust decisions as you progress through the show.

Costume Design Checklist

Overall Aesthetics

- Do these characters look appropriate for the story world? Does any character look like they are visiting from another planet?
- Is this design unified? Do the characters look like they are in the same show?
- Does the design use variation or contrast to add interest?
- Does the style harmonize with the scenery or environment?
- Do the colors work together as intended? Do scene-by-scene groupings work together?
- Is there an emotional or time arc, if needed?
- Do the costumes use interesting textures that will show well under stage light?

Character Apparel

- Does each costume create one clear focus of attention, allowing other visual elements to support that focal point?
- Does each costume display a harmonious intent from the top of the head to the shoes, and front, back, and side?
- Is there a discernible character arc or passage of time, if intended?

- Is each character complete: details, accessories, makeup and hairstyle?
- Will the costumes support or enhance stage movement?
- Will the costumes support fast changes?

Sizing Up Designing the Character Costume

The first set of sketches, whether they be scribbled thumbnails or more detailed sketches, serves as a system designers use to try ideas while designing each costume. They combine ideas from their research and their own inspiration. Also known as *thinking with the hand*, this step is an important aspect of creativity. There are successful designers who do not draw, and those that do; but every designer must be able to communicate their ideas ahead of time. This chapter explored the strategy of using a layered design to create character costumes. The next chapter discusses how designers use sketches and other means as formal communication with their collaborators.

Expecting the Unexpected

Plan ahead for the body types in your cast. It is easy to forget real people are not well represented in fashion images now or certainly in the last century. Fashion for mature women was a very real part of fashion marketing in the past, as matrons were an economic force. Look for terms such as *Mrs. Fashions*, *Gracious Lady*, or even a headline noting *Slimming Styles* or *Comfort*. These were all code words for figures that did not match the current fashion ideal. Some fashion advertisers included a mature or larger-figured person in a grouping. Include these sources in your research. It can be misleading to the design and the performers to draw only one size of body, especially for group costumes such as a chorus. Costume designer Meredith Magoun suggests exploring what different bodies look like with *My Body Model* app or *Tracing Models* (see Extra Resources section). She advises

> If you're designing for a group of people or a chorus, try designing for the largest body

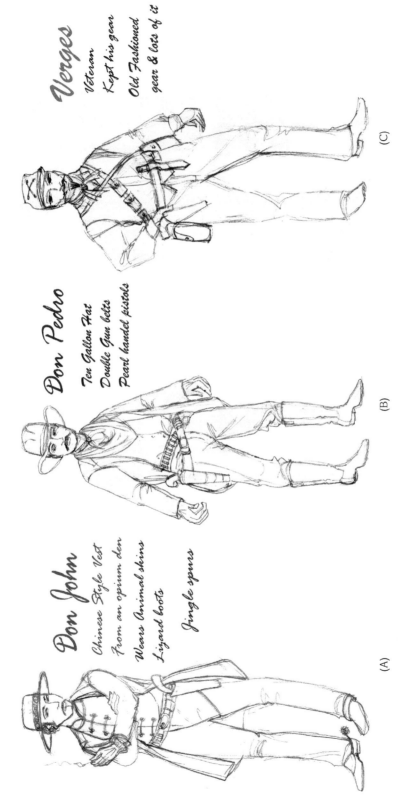

Don John

Chinese Style Vest
From an opium den
Wears Animal skins
Lizard boots

Jingle spurs

(A)

Don Pedro

Ten Gallon Hat
Double Gun belts
Pearl handel pistols

(B)

Verges

Veteran
Kept his gear
Old Fashioned

gear & lots of it

(C)

Figure 15.12 These three characters for *Much Ado About Nothing* were defined by how they would wear the typical accessories of the wild west. Don John's waistcoat suggested the opium den (left). Don Pedro is the highest ranking character and so he wears the largest hat and two gun belts (center). Verges was imagined as a war veteran who kept his gear, now old fashioned for the time period of the story (right).

you have. Then make the rest of the chorus go with that design, not the other way around. So often we will see a chorus on stage with a bunch of thin-bodied people, and then one larger-bodied person and their costume so obviously stands out.[9]

Extra Resources

Basic Human Anatomy: An Essential Visual Guide for Artists, Roberto Osti.

Daily Rituals: How Artists Work, Mason Currey, Knopf, 2013.

Fashion Illustration & Design, Manuela Brambatti, Promopress. This author was Versace's chief illustrator. Particularly useful for drawing fabrics and textile patterns.

Fashion Sketchbook, Bina Abling. Fairchild Publications. Now available in seven editions, contains an encyclopedic collection of dressmaker details and how to draw them.

Using Croquis and Photo Models

My Body Model www.mybodymodel.com/

Tracing Models https://tracingmodels.wordpress.com/

Deviant Art www.deviantart.com/

Notes

1 Keultjes, Saskia. 2013. "Lose the Fear of Drawing, Start Now." *Medium.com*, September 26, 2013. https:// medium.com/@saskiakeultjes/lose-the-fear-of-drawing-25f1f009bfee

2 Bayles, David and Orland, Ted. 1993. *Art and Fear*. Santa Cruz, CA: The Image Continuum, p. 15.

3 Wilson, Frank R. 1998. *The Hand: How its Use Shapes the Brain, Language and Human Culture*. New York: Vintage Books.

4 Cain, Abigail. 2018. "The Morning Routines of Famous Artists." *Artsy.net*, August 15, 2018. https://www.artsy. net/article/artsy-editorial-morning-routines-famous-artists-andy-warhol-louise-bourgeois

5 Phillips, Renée. n.d. "The Rituals and Routines of Famous Artists." *Renee-Phillips.com*. https://renee-phillips.com/the-rituals-and-routines-of-artists/

6 Staff. 2017. "The Working Sketch." *The Costume Designer Magazine*, Fall 2017, p. 22.

7 Ibid.

8 Centers for Disease Control and Prevention. 2021. "Body Measurements. National Center for Health Statistics." *Vital and Health Statistics*, Series 3, Number 46, January 2021. The report notes that "those aged 80 and over, Hispanic persons, black persons, Asian persons and those with low income were oversampled to improve the precision of the statistical estimates for these groups." p. 1. https://www.cdc.gov/nchs/fastats/body-measurements.htm

9 Magoun, Meredith. 2021. "All Shapes and Sizes." *United States Institute for Theater Technology*, Annual Conference, April 2021.

16.
COMMUNICATING THE COSTUME DESIGN

An early career costume maker was at last given her big break to drape a garment for a famous designer. The costume was a biblical shepherd, part of an opera chorus. The rendering showed strips of brown leather braided into a tunic resolving into uneven long hanging tabs at the hem. The rendering specifically featured one tab that curled up in a curious way, pointing back to the hip. There was no time for a mock-up, so the maker worked directly in the final leather. After several trials she opted to heavily wire both edges of the tab, and she was so proud when it looked exactly right! When the designer flew into town to review the costume, he asked why one tab curled up so oddly. The maker showed him the rendering, pointing to that spot. "Oh, my dear," he laughed, "that is a stain from my coffee cup. I must have set it there when I was painting."[1]

Communicating a Design to Others

That story features one thing that went wrong building a costume only from a sketch. But it also depicts what was right – that young maker interpreted almost all of the costume correctly using just the sketch as a guide. It was not a realistic sketch, or even that detailed. In fact, it was so expressionistic that a coffee ring looked just like the other brush strokes on the page. But that sketch communicated the intent of the costume. It contained energy that transferred from the designer to the maker, who combined that with a brief verbal description from the designer and her own research for a final result. Costume renderings are not the final product, the finished costume within context of the show is the final product. Costume sketches continue the *modeling* phase of the creative process. Recall in Chapter 1, one of the most important things costume designers bring to a project is visualizing an approach ahead of time. This chapter explores using sketches and several other styles of communication to translate the character design to others. Learning to draw and paint – whether using traditional or digital media – is a part of many designers' preparation. That topic is too large to include in this book, so for additional information on drawing techniques, consult the Extra Resources section.

We've all been told the "ideal" artistic communication is a perfectly matched set of costume plates rendered in beautiful color. But actual practice does not always support this ideal. There are many reasons designers may opt to use alternative communication either in addition to drawing or in place of it:

- Lack of lead time can force a designer to choose between drawing the show or doing the show.
- Some designers prefer the feel or clarity of working sketches or line drawings.
- Costumes may be added late in the process during rewrites or other new developments.
- The director can't read sketches, preferring to look at real garments or research.
- The designer prefers using a closet of style possibilities before deciding the final approach with the director or performer.

DOI: 10.4324/9781003015284-20

While formal renderings may be ideal for some situations and not attainable in others, what *is* ideal is that everyone on the project has a good idea of the tone and appearance of the costumes. The designs must be represented *in some manner* adequately enough for preproduction assessments such as budgeting, labor allocations, visual approval, and character development. Costume designers themselves need a reference image to answer the many questions once a show is in the shop. Once the hundreds of questions begin, it is easy to make hasty decisions or lose track of prior answers, creating havoc and frustration. The reference image serves as a reminder of their own intent. If the designer has solved a problem on paper, it is easier to translate the solution to a real-life garment. For instance, a color achieved by paint glazes might lead a designer to create that same effect on stage by layering several translucent fabrics.

A Sketch by Any Other Name: Costume Drawings

Sketches that move beyond the scribble or thumbnail stage have many names, all expressing a slightly different state or use. The terms **rough sketch**, **pencil sketch**, and **line drawing** may be interchangeable. The term *line drawing* originated with art school exercises used to train artists in line quality, such as contour drawings or gesture drawings that de-emphasize modeling and color. *Rough sketches* often embrace underdrawing lines used to map out the figure or do-over lines. Roughs embrace those unwanted lines to add depth and patina for a hand-crafted, artistic feel. The intent of these drawings is to communicate ideas in progress. Many designers think the unfinished appearance encourages changes or communications. Costume designer Mary Zophres (*La La Land*) notes, "Sometimes I've found that if I do them [sketches] in pencil and not necessarily attach a color, it is a springboard for conversation. It's part of my prep."[2] Some designers enlarge and refine their thumbnails into rough sketches, especially easy to do with digital drawing. Others skip the thumbnails, progressing directly to larger rough sketches they are comfortable throwing away

during experimentation. Any pencil sketch may be easily refined or painted to produce more finished costume renderings.

The terms **working sketch** and **working drawing** may include more information. That may be a rough sketch with some color indications to impart style, silhouette, mood, and fabric. In other cases, the working sketch may forgo color to emphasize technical information such as seams and dressmaker details for a patternmaker. Working sketches may also be partial sketches placed alongside a color rendering to showcase the back or specific details. Designers who paint atmospheric renderings may use a copy of their pencil sketches to give to costume makers as a working sketch. There are many times when the rough sketch may be the only sketch for a project. When is the best time to use rough sketches as final communication?

- Time is limited and you must choose between painting renderings or doing the show
- Built items contain details such as seams or dressmaker techniques best seen without a color layer
- The producer expects drawn sketches
- Sketching sparks ideas or allows the designer to model several solutions for a design
- It is right for the project or the designer's portfolio

"I had a director ask me to sketch a costume on the spot," recalls costume designer Marcy Froehlich, who was meeting a director who couldn't understand the idea behind her research images. She created thumbnail sketches while he took some phone calls.[3] It is important for the costume designer to determine if their ideas are truly understood. It might be more effective to bring other items to meetings: sample garments, fabric, or video of a performer in movement. When in doubt, ask your directors how they best process information. In contemporary practice with so much imagery available, the first pass at communication is often research boards and perhaps some quick thumbnail sketches. Lay out the materials in **act** and **scene** order. Afterwards you can reassemble the sketches to look at a particular character's arc.

Figure 16.1 Pencil sketches may serve different purposes. The rough sketches at left were quickly drawn to test ideas. The rough sketch at right contains more technical information expressing construction details.

Using the progression of the script communicates a larger understanding of the storytelling and stage pictures. Decisions about the costumes are best made in context of what all the characters in a scene are wearing.

Final Color Renderings

There are many situations where full color renderings are desired, particularly if the show provides adequate preparation time. Designers usually add paint and final details to their rough sketches to create formal renderings. The formal rendering contains pertinent information such as show title, character name, and act/scene information. Some designers scan their roughs to digitally enlarge them for coloring, add backgrounds, to aid printing onto better art paper or to add title blocks. The degree of detail in a rendering is a matter of personal taste and artistic process. Some costume designers use very detailed finished renderings, but

Mary Vogt (*Crazy Rich Asians*) uses the opposite technique.

> My drawings don't look finished, so the director will say "Well, why don't we do this? Why don't we do that?" It's more open to interpretation. . . . I use different kinds of sketches for different purposes. . . . Finished illustrations are impressive and sometimes you need to impress people.[4]

When is the best time to use full color costume renderings?

- It is the correct approach for a specific project
- The designer prefers drawing and painting as part of their artistic process
- The garments are so unique they cannot be communicated using other means
- The garments will be made-to-order
- There are so many parts or pieces it is difficult to imagine the combination adequately

Figure 16.2 Costume rendering for *The Cunning Little Vixen.*

Figure 16.3 Renderings can be very detailed or interpretive.

- A design contract stipulates it or the producer expects it
- To establish credibility as an artist
- To impress the director or producer for future employment
- To work with stars or performers with a strong say in the final approach
- It is a unique project for the designer's portfolio

Alternative Styles of Artistic Communication

There are situations where a drawn sketch is not the practical or appropriate means of communicating an idea. One all-too-common scenario is the costume designer was hired late in the process or the production schedule will move too quickly to accommodate levels of pre-approval. There may be only enough time to sketch a few costumes for leading characters, or those made-to-order. Other scenarios include if research is the correct artistic approach for a project, or if the budget or design fee are so low the costume designer negotiated with the producer to forgo sketches.

Research as Final Communication

Converting the character tear sheet into final communication is an effective means of communication. Take a few hours to polish the character collage by adding the show title and perhaps a subtle back ground image to unify them. These touches combined with a well-arranged composition can communicate some shows extremely well, provided they represent your work with authority and portray an artistic sensibility. Be sure that every character is well represented with the correct intent and tone. Some designers combine their rough sketch with its research. Each project dictates its own best approach, and deciding the best form of communication is also a part of design.

Photo-Collage or Photobashing

With the popularity of Photoshop and similar programs, a new form of digital sketching emerged. Photo-collage, or **photobashing**, derives from

Clarence Darrow

SCOPES TRIAL

The Great Tennessee Monkey Trial
LA Theatre Works National Tour

Figure 16.4 A costume sketch used for a national tour with very little preparation time. A rough sketch combined with research served as the final communication.

a practice used by concept developers to create character images. Existing imagery captured online or from other research combines with painting or manipulation. At its most finished form, it involves expertly merging photos with painting techniques. While still time-consuming, it is significantly less laborious than the same sketch painted completely by hand. Some television shows use this technique for absentee stars, using a photo of their bodies to digitally dress with costume options to gain approval. Some designers use it because it results in a much more refined sketch than they could ever create by hand. Artists who use this technique become extremely adept, downloading textures and assets from many commercial sourcing sites. A less-finished form of

photobashing is used as a pre-visualization tool for brainstorming. It is an easy way to combine different ideas, stacking found images as a model for further discussion. This brainstorming version pays less attention to correct human proportions or to the overall ambiance, since the collected images derive from many sources. (See Extra Resources section. (See Figure 16.5))

Show and Tell

At times costume designers work with directors who are not very visual or who cannot interpret sketches or do not understand much about garments. In such cases, it may be instructive to show the director costumes using different forms of show and tell. Options include dressing full costumes on dress forms to photograph or to show the director in person, and draping a rough approximation of a garment in the final fabric without cutting the fabric. Costumes pulled from a theater's stock provides ample opportunity for a show-and-tell approach. Costume designer Meg Murray notes "For a modern dress show . . . I use a collage of ready-to-wear looks to establish a character's direction, as opposed to the hand-drawn designs I would make for a vintage or fantasy design."[5]

Some shows may afford short-term rentals of costumes or vintage garments for fittings with stand-in fit models or the actors themselves. This technique is used widely for short turn-around projects such as TV pilots or commercials. Some costume designers use vintage or contemporary garments as a character-discovery fitting with an actor before settling on a final design. Ann Roth, the Oscar-winning costume designer for *Ma Rainey's Black Bottom* uses discovery fittings to pitch and build characters.[6] This process also works well if the designer would like to copy vintage clothing into contemporary sizes or different colors. The garment itself serves as design, mock-up, and research. The show-and-tell approach is widely used once a show is underway and new or substitute costumes are added late in the process. Rather than return to the drawing phase, designers will use a stock, rental, or purchased garment as design shorthand.

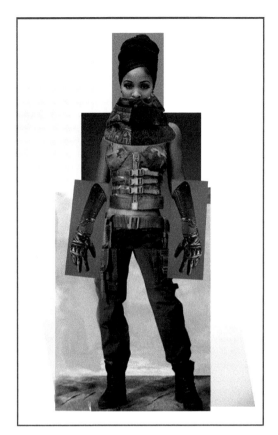

Figure 16.5 Two samples of photobashing for the same character. The figure at left is a brainstorming version placed roughly in human proportions to test ideas. The figure at right used more image manipulation and painting to create a finished look.

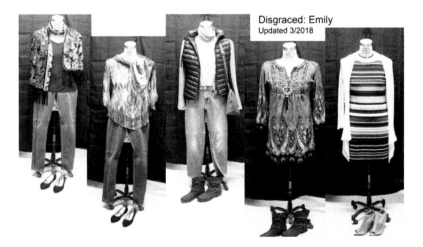

Figure 16.6 This photo show and tell communicates very detailed ideas about each character.

Credit: Photos and costume design for *Disgraced* by Meg Murray, Virginia Stage Company

The Design Workflow

It is the costume designer's responsibility to adequately communicate what the final costumes will look like to those who need to know, and they use many resourceful methods to accomplish that mission. The success of the communication will partly depend on the workflow required to complete it. It's important to develop a sense of your personal productivity and practices when creating sketches or communication for an entire show. Consider where you can streamline the process as you become more practiced. For some, that may be using an assembly line system to create sketches. Instead of fully concentrating on one costume at a time, it may be more efficient to perform the same step to all the sketches in a row. For instance, preparing unique poses for all the characters first, then adding garments across all sketches, then adding facial features. Or this system may be appropriate only for painting. For example, mixing one large container of skin tones to paint all the faces at once, or mixing a large container of black to paint all the tuxedos at once. At the end of each step, any assembly line system presents a snapshot of the entire show in progress so the designer may compare each character or costume in relation to the others. This method has another add value – if you are ever caught short on a deadline, you can present a complete work-in-progress for the whole show instead of for a few characters.

Some designers would be horrified with an assembly line system, as considering each character is an important part of their creative process. They may use the assembly line approach only for repetitive tasks such as scanning and resizing thumbnails into a digital painting program, arranging them on the page or adding them to a template. Other designers can't work fully on a design until they decide what medium or drawing style to use for that project. They will draw a few sample sketches first to test the approach. Decisions about media also support the larger concept by lending a texture or tone to the costumes. Taking time at the beginning of a show to experiment with workflow and media ultimately liberates the designer to concentrate on their ideas. Deciding whether to draw, paint, collage or use research is a big step that can significantly add to preparation time or streamline it. Carefully consider the total number of images required for each project. Creating an elaborate sketch or collage system may be artistically satisfying for seven sketches, but will create a large workflow for 30 sketches, or may require an assistant to complete in time. Tony Award–winning costume designer Gregg Barnes (*Legally Blonde*) notes that over time he learned to streamline his work. At first

> I did everything from scratch. I didn't use any croquis – I'd do a hundred sketches and then only like four. Over time, you develop figures you like and use them over and over. I always work in the same size. I always gauge the work. There's no way timing-wise that I can still draw [everything from scratch] right on the paper.[7]

If time is a concern, consider streamlining the work in creative ways. It may be possible to draw just three sketches to illustrate options for an entire chorus, creating three versions of the design to assign to alternating characters, or used in different color ways. It may be possible to use research for some characters and sketches for others. Or, consider using the show-and-tell method for the majority of the show and drawing only a few sketches. Barnes notes that during his tenure as resident costume designer for the Paper Mill Playhouse, there wasn't time for many sketches.

> I also ran the shop, not that there was a full shop. I was young and it was back-breaking, so I've been on both sides of the aisle. We'd only have the budget in a New York shop to build maybe 20 costumes. The rest were rented or built on kitchen tables or in Canada. It's a miracle I ever did a single sketch – there was no time.

He notes he possess very few sketches that were made during his ten years there.[8]

Using a digital sketch **template** will save time and unify the sketches for any production. If the designer has time, designing the template to complement each show adds an artistic touch. But if time is short, using a universal template will save time across the workflow cycle. Scanned thumbnails may be inserted into the template and correctly sized for consistency. No matter what communication style is chosen, each image must present the essential information consistently across the show. Each image should follow these parameters:

- Use consistent paper size, quality, and color to unify the production
- Use a consistent height and scale for all figures
- Place the title of show in the same location
- Add the character name
- Note the act/scene as needed
- Add your designer signature or logo – always own your work

Creating a digital template saves time and provides a consistent layout for the entire show, even if the final imagery will be hand-drawn or painted. The template can be printed onto many qualities of paper. Large, thick, or stiff papers require the use of a large-format printer or a flat-bed printer that

will not roll the paper around a drum. Practice good compositional layout, remembering the goal is to focus on the show and each character. Ensure any background imagery does compete with the costume for focus. For more information about creating digital sketches, see the Extra Resources section.

Organizing a Workspace

As with any workflow efficiency, it's crucial to have everything within reach to support concentration. Nothing kills being in the zone like rummaging around to find something, or waiting for someone else to get off the computer. Any system is workable if it allows the designer to work without distraction at a moment's notice and avoids elaborate setup or take-down each time. Extended cleanup so family members can use the dining room table may waste 20 minutes each day, adding up to hours across the time it takes to design and draw a show. Designers who live in small spaces have created ingenious solutions. One method is using a dresser drawer or an under-bed storage box as a

Figure 16.7 A rendering template using Photoshop (left). Each character's sketch was placed in the template (right).

studio-in-a-box that can be quickly transported to a workspace and whisked away. One designer built a sleeping platform as his bed, using the floorspace beneath it for a drawing table and supply drawers. Another sacrificed a coat closet, adding boards with hinged legs that operated like a fold-out desk across her hallway. She inserted pantry-style shelving on the sides of the closet to hold supplies. She folded it all away at night, allowing her to "leave" the office mentally and physically. An art director newly arrived in Los Angeles used the walk-in basement of an elderly neighbor's house in exchange for running regular errands.

Costume designers must also balance the amount of time they spend on a project and the design fee they earn. To learn your own work habits and methods, document your process of research, collaging, drawing, painting, and finishing sketches over several projects. Each designer works uniquely and values their time in different ways. One example timetable follows:

Designer's Task – Ten Costumes	Total Time
Create thumbnails for a small-medium show	5 to 15 hours
Create rough sketches/line drawings @ 1.5 hours per costume	15 hours
Draw adjustments per director feedback	0 to 3 hours
Digitally paint in Procreate @ 1 hour per costume	10 hours
Create digital template in Photoshop, insert each sketch	4 hours
Printing and fiddly printer adjustments	3 hours
Total sketch and paint time	**37–50 hours**
Average total time per costume	**3.7–5 hours**

This designer requires 37 to 50 hours to design, draw, and paint a relatively straightforward show with ten costumes. With all the steps considered,

that means an average of 3.7 hours or 5 hours per costume. If the designer can work an uninterrupted week, this task takes about one work week of labor or a little more. If the designer works other jobs, these tasks may spread out across two weeks to accomplish. Every designer will work differently, but understanding the required timetable empowers the designer to use their time well.

Sizing Up Design Communication

Costume renderings are not the final product. The finished costume in context of the show is the final product. Designers sketch costumes to work out the design, continuing the *modeling* phase of the creative process. The designs must be represented adequately enough for the preproduction process, such as design approval, budgeting, labor allocations, and character development. Costume communication takes several forms, all of which may be appropriate as the final "sketch" such as a rough sketch, a research collage, photobashing, show and tell, or a finished color costume rendering. It is essential the designer creates an organized work space and predictable workflow to manage design projects.

Expecting the Unexpected

Costume designers quickly discover not every director can read costume sketches. Broadway producer and master director Martin Platt agrees. "I don't think designers always know how little some of their partners know about costumes: the process, how to read sketches. There are directors and certainly a lot of producers who don't know how to do that." Platt notes poor communication in the beginning might result in a crisis when "everyone approves sketches and then the costume appears, and no one understood it would really look like *that*." He suggests a drawing may not always be the best communication tool. "Their collaborators don't know what questions to ask – such as – is this costume heavy? Then the actor puts it on, and now the actor can't move in it and everyone is surprised," even though there had been a swatch attached to the sketch, and everyone dutifully felt the swatch. He suggests designers spend a little more time making that sketch come alive for the rest of the team. He prefers to see good character work in a sketch, but he often sees sketches that feature movement, especially with women's costumes. "That's not what the costume is going to look like when the actor is standing on the stage talking or singing for 45 minutes. That's what it will look like in that twirl they will do just once." The rest of the time, he notes, that costume will hang like a limp rag. "You want to see what the costume will really look like – not exaggerated with sparkles flying off."[9]

Extra Resources

Character Costume Figure Drawing, Huaixiang Tan. Routledge. A delightful and illuminating guide to creating figures for costume sketches. Includes different character types such as elderly or evil countenances.
Digital Costume Design and Collaboration, Rafael Jaen
Digital Costume Design & Renderings, Annie O. Cleveland. Costume & Fashion Press/Quite Specific Media. Aimed specifically toward entertainment design, this book uses comprehensive instruction for Painter software, with additional instructions for Photoshop.
Fashion Sketchbook, Bina Abling, Fairchild Publications. Now available in seven editions, this is the most comprehensive guide to drawing and painting sketches, fabrics and using different media. Any of the editions are suitable, later editions include digital rendering instruction.
Photobashing: Is it Art? Techniques and Examples https://thegraphicassembly.com/photobashing-art-techniques-examples/

What Is Photobashing & How to Use It + Free Beginner Tutorials https://homesthetics.net/what-is-photobashing-how-to-use-it/
ProCreate Courses Available on Udemy.com
Drawing and Painting on the iPad with Procreate (beginner)
ProCreate: Draw, Sketch, Paint and Design on your iPad (beginner)
ProCreate Masterclass: How to Draw and Paint on iPad (all levels)

Notes

1 This event happened to the author while working as a firsthand at the Santa Fe Opera.
2 Voight, John. 2020. "Qi in Chinese Painting." *Qi Encyclopedia*, March 8, 2020. http://qi-encyclopedia.com/?article=Qi%20In%20Chinese%20Painting
3 Staff. 2020. "The Quest for Internal Energy." *The Journal of Traditional Eastern Health & Fitness*, Winter 2020–21 Issue. Accessed April 10, 2021. https://www.qi-journal.com/aboutjournal/about-our-journal
4 Staff. 2017. "The Working Sketch." *The Costume Designer Magazine*, Fall 2017, p. 22.
5 Froehlich, Marcy, personal interview with author, September 18, 2020.
6 Staff. n.d. "Behind the Costumes of Disgraced: An Interview with Meg Murray." *Virginia Stage.org*.
7 Roth, Ann. 2014. Personal interview with author.
8 Barnes, Gregg. 2021. "From the Page to the Stage, Designer and Maker." *Costume Society of America*, Western Region. Streamed April 11, 2021 via Zoom.
9 Platt, Martin. 2014. Personal interview with the author, August 8, 2014.

PART FIVE

FEASIBILITY

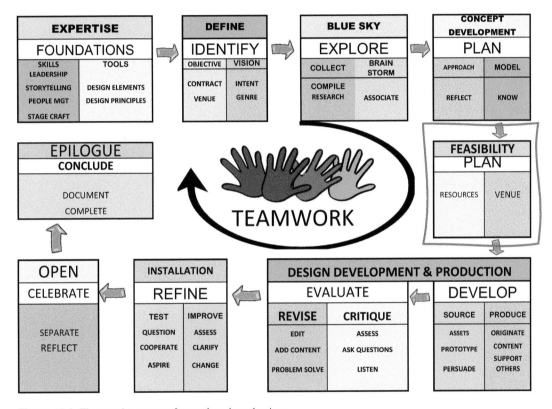

Figure 17.0 The creative process for produced productions.

Credit: Holly Poe Durbin and Ayrika Johnson

17.
DEFINING THE SCOPE OF A SHOW

Accurate estimating of time and resources is essential in the costume profession. You will be asked time after time how long something will take to do or how much something will cost. The costume designer may be the only person in an early planning meeting with enough expertise to provide guidance. In Chapter 7 the costume designer created a guestimate of their own time to design a show, or understand the trade-offs that must be made. This chapter introduces larger show planning. The first step toward feasibility is to **quantify** the number of pieces for each costume and the entire show. The costume rendering may not tell the entire story. For instance, the shape of a period costume comes from hidden underpinnings such as a girdle, corset, petticoat, or compression garments. The designer must decide at this early phase if it is important to use real period styles or substitute modern equivalents. A pregnant character uses a special stomach pad, and specialty characters may use a muscle suit or other enhancements. Characters performing stunts require protective pads, and any actor kneeling on the floor will use knee pads.

The Paper Chase – Creating Effective Lists

Translating the sketch to a finished costume begins with the invisible hero of costume design: paperwork. The foundation of all costume paperwork is the **piece list**: a catalog of what each actor wears. The piece list is later transformed to **pulling lists** and other paperwork used in preproduction. With little effort, the same lists can be adapted during different stages to accumulate information. Organizing well and creating them with adaptability in mind saves hundreds of hours through the span of the show.

The **piece list** translates the visual imagery of rendering and research to words (Table 17.1). Always approach the piece list for each actor in chronological order. Gather the renderings or research collages for each actor. Place them side-by-side in order of appearance onstage. Refer to the **costume scene chart** for fast changes from one costume to another, and note the need for fast rigging now.

- Begin with what the actor wears for the **top of show** (TOS).
- Consider each costume from the skin out and then head to toe.
- Will the blocking require hidden pads for kneeling or stunts?
- Will the same underpinnings work for all the costumes, or will one costume require different underwear? Is a full skin-out change feasible in this situation? If not, how might the design accommodate more than one look?
- Will the character be seen dressing or undressing onstage? Does that require any modesty items for the actor to wear backstage?
- Will there be nudity or special effects that require a bathrobe or slippers backstage?

DOI: 10.4324/9781003015284-22

- Move to the next costume to consider what the actor must add or remove.
- Will some items remain, such as all the underpinnings, or perhaps the trousers?

Using an app such as Google Docs, Word, Excel, or Google sheets provides longevity and adaptability. Excel and Google sheets allow for columns and lines to be hidden or activated on demand. Table 17.1 shows a piece list created for early planning of *Romeo and Juliet*, set in 1920s Los Angeles. The actor playing Paris appears as another character, Gregory, briefly near the end of the play.

The costumes in Table 17.1 are listed in order of appearance, forcing the designer to consider if some items may be repeated to aid fast changes or to streamline the number of items required. This designer used the term *Look* to establish what the character wears in each scene. Paris will repeat two costumes, leading to a total *costume count* of four costumes worn in six looks or appearances onstage. The columns provide space for colors, the source for each item, and notes. The designer made a note for Look 4 that if the first pair of shoes is oxblood color, they can be repeated for this costume, saving money. Working through this list helped the designer plan for streamlining and budget savings. Paris is one of the wealthiest characters in the play; the designer planned to buy two suits new and have them tailored into the 1920s silhouette. The character of Gregory is a ruffian whose clothing would be aged. Sourcing from costume stock would produce garments with a well-worn patina or provide garments that may be dyed. The designer surmises the party costume in Look 2 can be rented, but the sash must be built to be rigged for a fast change. These guesses are based on an understanding of what is available in the theater's stock. If the designer is new to this theater, a preliminary visit to costume stock is essential for planning the piece list.

The Pulling or Shopping List

Small shows with relatively few costumes may require little paperwork past this point. The designer can carry these piece lists to stock or rental sources to assemble options for each costume. For larger shows it may be less efficient to use full piece lists when costume pieces easily number in the hundreds. Work must be divided into manageable units to accomplish large tasks and it may take the aid of several costumers to assemble costumes from multiple sources. In these situations, taking the time to transfer information to a **pulling list** and a **shopping list** will create saved time throughout the show. Table 17.2 shows a pulling list generated from the costume piece list in Table 17.1. The designer prints these lists out to take notes while pulling to record what was found and what still must be located. Do not rely on these lists only in a digital format if dividing the work among several people. Paper lists can be handed off easily. Table 17.2 uses columns to note color, size, and a fuller description. The *Condition* column describes the desired quality of each item – from best to distressed. The *Have/Need* column at the right allows the costumer to check off what has been found or to record options.

It is not unusual to discover while making the list that no matter how carefully we envisioned the costume up to this point, our early ideas may not have included enough detail. Are the trousers styled with a flat front or pleats? Does the shirt include a button-down collar or French cuffs? Do the ladies' shoes have a kitten heel or a chunky stacked heel? This is the step where each character is truly hammered out. It's important to track where each item may come from and what is accounted for so far to avoid double work. These smaller individual lists are much easier to use in rental houses or shopping rather than dragging a full notebook or a single list of hundreds of items.

Anticipating Actors' Sizes

Often the costume designer reaches this phase of planning before the casting is complete or certainly before accurate measurements can be taken. Many resident costume shops maintain a measurement file for actors in past productions. Some theaters tend to cast from the same community pool so it is quite likely prior measurements can be found. If that is not the case for this production, it is useful to turn to the casting office or

Table 17.1 Piece List for the Character of Paris in *Romeo and Juliet* (Note specific decisions the designer made about each item in the Notes column.)

Character / Actor	Paris / Gregory Jermaine Randall	Color	Stock	Buy	Rent	Build	Actor's Own	Notes
Look 1	T-shirt	White		X				Low V-neck for Costume #2
TOS	Underwear						X	
Act 1 Sc 1	Dress socks	Brown		X				
	Blue DB blazer #1	Med Blue		X				Better Quality
	Business shirt point collar	White	X					
	Trousers #1	White		X				Better Quality, small pleat fronts, cuffs
	Straw boater	Natural						
	Shoes #1 slip-on	Brown	X					Dress style, brown to oxblood
	Tie – silk	Yellow	X					Foulard or plain silk
	Pocket square – silk	Yellow	X					Coordinates, does not match tie
	Wrist watch	Gold	?					Rectangular face – 1920s
	Sunglasses	Tortoise	X					Does he wear prescriptions?
Look 2	"The Sheik" film attire							
Party	Burnouse cloak	Red/Gold			X			
Act 1 Sc 4	Romantic shirt #2, open neck	White	X					Full sleeves, open neck – FC IN
	Wide-striped sash	Multi				X		Rig for fast change
	Kaffieyeh – head scarf	Gold		X				
Fast Change Into	**Repeat** Trousers #1	White						
	Repeat Socks #1	Brown						
	Shoes #2 – Balgha	Black			X			Open heel, pointed toe

(Continued)

Table 17.1 (Continued)

Character / Actor	Color	Stock	Buy	Rent	Build	Actor's Own	Notes
Paris / Gregory *Jermaine Randall*							
Look 3	**Return to Look #1**						
Look 4 Wedding Day Act 4 SC 4							
DB Suit Jacket #2	Navy		X				
Suit Trousers #2	Navy		X				Small pleat front, cuffs
Shirt #3	Light Blue	X					French cuffs
Tie	Silver		X				
Tie Tack – jeweled	Diamond	X					Large
Socks #2	Black		X				
Shoes # 3	Black	X					**If Shoes #2 Oxblood, repeat here?**
Boutonniere – flowers	White	X					
Look 5 Gregory Act 5 Sc 1							
Shirt – stripe, aged	Brown	X					Long-sleeve to roll up
Vest – plaid or check	Olive/Navy	X					Vest does not match trousers
Trousers – small stripe	Olive	X					Canvas, rabbit ear back, no cuff
Suspenders	Brown	X					Lively pattern, some contrast
Fedora	Fawn	X					Wide brim to pull over eyes
Shoes # 4 – boots	Brown	X					Heavy Chelsea boot, pull on
Tattoo	Black		X				Coordinate with makeup
Switch blade	PROPS						Must have jacket pocket
Look 6	**Repeat Look #4**						
Mourning	No boutonniere – flowers						
Act 5 Sc 3							

Table 17.2 Pulling Lists for Shirts and Shoes for Four Characters in Romeo and Juliet

Pulling/Rental Item: Shirts

Actor	Character	Color	Size	Notes	Condition	Have/Need
J. Randall	Paris	White	**16–34**	Business, point collar	Best	
		White		Romantic, full sleeves, open front	Better	
		Lt Blue		French cuffs	Best	
	Gregory	Brown		Stripe, aged	Limp, worn	
Pedro Juarez	Capulet	Yellow	**15½–32**	Business, spread collar	Better	
		White		Romantic, full sleeves	Better	
		Lt Gray		French cuffs	Better	
Daniel Jeffs	Montague	Pink	**17–34**	Business, point collar	Better	
		White		Romantic, full sleeves	Better	
		Lt Blue		French cuffs	Better	
	Peter/Servant	White		Business	Good	
Jesus Lopez	Tybalt	Orange	**16½–36**	Extra-long points	Good	

Pulling/Rental Item: Shoes

Actor	Character	Color	Size	Notes	Condition	Have/Need
J. Randall	Paris	Brown or oxblood	**9½**	Slip on style, loafers, dressy	Best	
		Black		Arab shoes, no heels, point toe	Better	
		Black		Dress shoes, captoe		
	Gregory	Brown		Heavy Chelsea boot, pull on		
Pedro Juarez	Capulet	Black	**8**	Oxford	Better	
Daniel Jeffs	Montague	Tan/buff	**12**	Blucher, two tone preferred	Better	
	Peter/Servant	Brown		Heavy Chelsea boot, pull on	Aged	
Jesus Lopez	Tybalt	Black	**10½**	Cuban heel, long point	Good	

company manager for help and permission to contact actors early. Viewing the actor's resume and head shot is somewhat informative – many include basic measurements and lists of where they have worked before, although they may be out of date. Designers may contact the costume shops of theaters where the actors worked recently to see if they have measurements. It is also common to phone or email an actor ahead of time to introduce yourself, ask questions about their general sizes and if there is further information you should know. Most actors are delighted the costume designer is considering their needs in advance. Actors' bodies are the final factor determining where each costume will be sourced, affecting the budget and the distribution of workload. For instance, if your labor situation dictates that you may only build five items, the first instinct for any designer is to assign those builds to the leading characters or most dramatic specialty garments. However, closer inspection of the cast may change that assumption. If an actor is a different size than the available rental costumes, no matter how often that character is onstage or how small the role, that costume may be one of the builds out of necessity, or the costume designer must be prepared to ask for additional budget funds.

Always consider your actors' bodies rationally. Costume designers do not join a production to negatively judge their colleagues. They join to transform the actors they are given into dramatic characters. Trust that each actor brought *something* to the audition the director wanted to include in this performance. The wise costume designer will embrace and celebrate that unique contribution. For instance, if a director has deliberately gone against a casting type, few rental costumes may be available in the correct size or gender assumption for your actor. That choice may bring a dynamic new twist to this show and offer exciting design opportunities. If costume designers grow frustrated or angry over cast sizing, it is usually a sign there is not enough time or money to accommodate this component. They feel trapped by the timeline, labor, or budget allocations. Aim those frustrations in a productive direction: talk to the producer about possible solutions.

Understanding Labor Needs

Most of the designer's planning depends on the labor support available for the show. They must avoid promising costumes they cannot deliver, and they may radically alter their approach to match their resources. The key to success is aligning the design to the available labor and matching tasks to each maker's expertise. The job descriptions for each costume maker will vary widely to match their own local labor pool and resources.

Costume Labor Employment Status

- **Resident** staff works for the producer or theater onsite in a costume shop with a costume manager allocating labor resources to each show, and supervising workflow.
- **Over-hire** workers are employed for a short period of time. They usually expect to work in the theater's costume shop, using resident equipment and supplies.
- **Freelance** makers are contracted to make specific items: one ensemble, a man's suit, three hats. They generally work in their own studios for negotiated rates.
- **Commercial** vendors maintain a business making the product the designer wants, and the designer is a client. Vendors include professional costume, tailoring, or alterations shops, made-to-order fashion suppliers, and online sellers who make vintage or historic reproductions. They estimate a price for the designer's project ahead of time.
- **Interns** are still completing their education or gaining real-world experience. In return, they may be paid a lower wage, work limited hours, or have limited skills. Working with interns requires more supervision, teaching both skills and workplace demeanor.
- **Volunteers** donate their time as part of their patronage to that theater. They may bring years of experience to their tasks, or they may view their shift as a social hour with less responsibility for the final outcome. Like interns, volunteers may require more supervision.

Types of Costume Makers

Costume designers cultivate their own circle of skilled artists and technicians who will reliably work on their projects. The key to success is matching the project carefully to the skills of each maker.

- **Maker** is a catchall phrase that means different things in different areas. It represents a large category of anyone involved in the custom-garment-making fields. While many are skilled stitchers and some are skilled fitters, not all can generate a pattern from scratch, and instead use a historical reproduction pattern or commercial pattern as a starting point.
- **Drapers/tailors/cutters** are skilled full-charge makers who can originate a pattern by draping and drafting. They may specialize in contemporary or period sewing, or both. They understand how to construct garments using advanced fashion fabrics.
- **First hand** is part of a draping or cutting team in larger shops. They adapt and finish a draped muslin or drafted pattern, generating finishing details such as facings. They lay out the pattern and cut it from fabric and supervise stitchers. They often supervise the alterations assigned to a team while the draper/cutter focuses on made-to-order clothing.
- **Stitcher** is a catchall phrase for every level of sewing technician. Some are particularly adept at machine sewing, some at hand finishing. Some are adept at basic fitting and alteration; others sew only as instructed.
- **Knitter/beader/embroiderer, leather** – creates custom applications or embellishments.
- **Specialty** makers have expertise in one or more niche areas such creating soft-sculpture fat suits; walk-around and mascot costumes; sewing with spandex, latex, vinyl, or leather.
- **Millinery, dye, costume crafts** – many crafts technicians are generalists, and others are specialists in dying, millinery, footwear, armor.

The costume supervisor or designer must *ensure* the costumes are altered and completed on time. That is not the same thing as *doing* those tasks. In many cases, the designer can procure very reasonable and fast work using nontheatrical labor such as local drycleaners, dressmakers, and tailors who do alterations. Those businesses are set up for repetitive tasks with industrial machinery that makes short work of the usual tasks like pants hems. They set a price ahead of time and many will negotiate a bulk rate for a repeat customer. An astonishing array of specialists can be contacted through the internet to create custom work from crown making to period eyeglasses.

A common dilemma in theater is the disconnect between expectations of the script or production and the theater's resources. If there is space for negotiation, present likely labor costs to the production manager in a dispassionate way to ascertain if there is additional money to hire labor. Don't automatically assume it is the designer's job to perform every task. Gregg Barnes, the costume designer of *Something Rotten*, recalled that he lost a year of his preparation for that show when the Broadway opening was pushed early. "The shops in New York were too busy. This opened the door to all those makers I'd worked with regionally," such as noted San Diego tailor/draper Ingrid Helton. "When I came to Ingrid, I didn't come with a beautifully organized packet. I came to her with only our friendship."[1] As the costume designer, Barnes was tasked with finding the makers to create his show, and he needed a very good understanding of labor expenses.

Estimating Labor Needs

Costume designers who also lead the operational tasks must generate a labor estimate to ensure the work will stay within budget. The key labor tasks to consider are **fittings**, **alterations**, **crafts**, custom **builds**, and **rebuilds**.

- **Fittings** use a great amount of the designer's time, and it is important to character development with the actor. Basic fittings require approximately **30 minutes**, allowing time for the actor to dress and for conversation. Complex and period garments require at least 15 minutes to dress the actor in a corseted or boned costume and a minimum of 20 minutes to fit each costume. Each fitting usually requires 10 minutes at the end for fitting photos and the actor to re-dress.

- **Alterations** can be controlled somewhat during the fitting. If there is sufficient time and labor, the costume may be fitted with exacting care. A low budget show may make some concessions, fitting some characters more carefully than others. Never skimp on actor comfort and safety.

- **Crafts** is a large term used to categorize anything that is not sewing of garments such as decorating or making hats, shoes, purses, parasols, jewelry, dying and painting fabric, and specialty items.

- **Builds** for made-to-order costumes are unique, requiring a discussion with the maker to estimate their time. This includes patterning and copying costumes in larger sizes or different color fabrics.

- **Rebuilds** occur when a costume is in such a poor state of repair that it requires interventions to be stage-worthy. These are usually surprises, and may eliminate some garments that require too much labor to fix. Examples include weakened fabric, advanced mending, replacing vest backs, relining suit jackets. Surprises like this add 1 to 6 hours to any project.

Estimating Alterations

Many costume makers agree there is no such thing as a job that takes less than 30 minutes in a typical costume shop environment. Yes, it can only take 4 minutes to stitch hems on a pair of trousers. But that is the least of the actual labor. Before those hems can be put under a sewing machine, the prior hem is removed and the press line eliminated. The new length is measured and pinned; the new hem added. A name label must be sewn into the waistband and the trousers are steamed or pressed for final wear. There are also hidden tasks in every job: the thread on the sewing machine had to be changed, the steam iron was empty of water, and the rehearsal hall texted for an answer to a question or an actor stopped in for

measurements. For the purposes of a rough guess, it is useful to imagine simple alterations requiring **20–30 minutes**, and more complex tasks **1 hour**. A typical full costume may require two easy tasks (trouser hems, resetting suspender buttons) and two more complex tasks (taking in a waist and hemming jacket sleeves) for an average of 2 to 3 hours per costume. Of course, some costumes will use only 20 minutes of their allotted time, but others may use 3 hours.

To create a very rough estimate of labor for a show, multiply the number of costumes by 2 hours to determine time for alterations. A contemporary show with ten costumes could then expect alterations time of 15–20 hours. A show with complex period costumes may require 3 hours per costume, with ten costumes using 30–40 hours of alterations. Highly experienced sewers will take less time, inexperienced ones take longer. In some cases, the budget-conscious designer may get more alterations for their money by patronizing commercial establishments such as dry cleaners or dressmakers set up to do repetitive tasks with clear thread and superior machinery that are outside of the chaotic environment of the costume shop.

Estimating Builds

Building a costume for a specific actor is the equivalent of creating a couture fashion design. A legacy house such as Chanel may charge $40,000 for a dress.[2] Most theatrical custom builds use sewing shortcuts, less specialized labor, and more affordable fabrics, but the work of generating a custom design is essentially similar. When estimating the time for builds, keep in mind the experience level of the maker. One who has created the exact style of garment multiple times will be much faster and more efficient than one who must figure it all out for the first time.

There are several variations of made-to-order costumes to consider when estimating time.

Custom design – an original pattern is generated from the designer's sketch to the exact measurements of the performer. This method requires draping and drafting time in addition to making and fitting the garment. This is the most laborious and expensive option. This method may take about 8 hours to generate a drape, and another 8 hours to test with a sample or mock-up.

Copy – a pattern is taken from an existing garment, such as a vintage piece. The patterns are usually graded to a new size. Eliminates much of the estimating and guesswork of custom patterning and gives the designer exactly what they want. But it will not save a significant amount of time over custom patterning.

Pre-made pattern – garments made from commercial patterns or vintage patterns created in systematic sizes. This system drastically reduces the R&D steps of drafting a pattern from scratch. May require some grading and pattern alteration to fit the performer.

Duplicates – using patterns that have been created before. Cutting duplicate costumes in the same sizes is the least laborious method. Add 1.5 hours if pattern must be graded into different sizes. This is the most economical way to create groups of costumes.

Estimating Crafts

Every crafts project is unique and can be much more difficult to estimate. Some designers enjoy

Table 17.3 Estimates to Custom Pattern and Sew Sample Costume Items (Does not include fitting time.)

Women's Wear Garments	Estimate
Tailored Garments	32–45 hours
Formal, Cocktail, Ballgown	50–60 hours
Elaborate Period Gowns	75–100 hours
Corset	25–40 hours
Panier, Crinoline, or Bustle	10–15 hours
Medieval Gowns, Tunics	30 hours
Petticoat or Generic Period Skirt	15 hours
Vests, Trousers, Skirts, Tops	20 hours
Ruffles, Trim, Embellishments	10–20 hours

Menswear Garments	Estimate
Shirt – Period	10–15 hours
Shirt – Contemporary	8–12 hours
Tailored Sack Jacket	40 hours
Tailored Frock Coat	60 hours
Tailcoat	50 hours
Vest	10–25 hours
Trouser	10–20 hours
Cloak, Cape	10–20 hours
Medieval Gown, Long	35–50 hours
Doublet	50–70 hours
Breeches	12–24 hours

Table 17.4 Estimating Build Times for Pre-Patterned Garments

Item – Layout, Cut, and Sew	Time in Hours
Shirt, Blouse	5
Tunic	2.5
Vest, no pockets	5
Pencil Skirt, knee length, zipper	7
Tailored pants, lined, fully stitched	28
Pants, unlined	18
Sundress, simple construction	3–4
Short Dress	6–8
Evening Gown	15–30
Cape, Cloak unlined – full circle, hood	7
Bustle Gown, Commercial Pattern	25
Corset, fully boned	40
Hand finishing – hems	2–7
Fitting Services – each fitting	2
Adjustments from Fitting	1.5

Inspired by *Unit Pricing for Dressmaking*, Karen Howland, Kensinger Press, 1995. Generously contributed by Marjorie Cutting.

this aspect of costumes a great deal and look forward to performing tasks such as decorating hats or creating jewelry. Crafts that must be custom patterned, such as unusual spats, hand bags, grieves (shin protectors), and vambraces (forearm protectors), will use the same amount of time as a smaller garment, although the

Table 17.5 Estimating Crafts Projects

Sample Crafts Task	Estimate
Dye a garment, color matching	2–3 hours
Dye fabric yardage, color matching	3–5 hours
Tech, dip, or knock down men's shirts	1–2 hours
Age, distress physical and painting age	2–4 hours
Build a small accessory – hat, greaves, spats	15–35 hours
Papier Mache items – mask, armor, paint	4–6 hours
Assemble jewelry from found objects	4 hours
Create pattern for any item to rest on the body	1 hour
Adjust, paint or customize footwear	3 hours
Carve a clay mold	4–10 hours
Drape moldable materials over a mold, finish	6–10 hours
Faux-surface painting, gold leafing	3–5 hours
Carve a textile stamp	1–5 hours
Trim hats or other accessories	3 hours
Alterations	30 minutes–1 hour

materials are usually more difficult to sew and require several layers. One aspect of crafts that is often overlooked is drying time for any paints, chemicals, plasters, or other materials. These will vary widely and humid weather may elongate drying times by many hours.

Estimating Fabrics

An important factor of estimating the scope of a show is understanding fabric yardages. Plays that require large-scale costumes use large yardages for built costumes. Even with the cheapest sourcing, it can be a real budget concern if each costume requires 8 yards of fabric. If the budget

absolutely will not support the requirement, the designer then understands early in the process the show must be entirely rented, pulled from stock, or require an incredibly creative alternative to traditional fashion fabrics. Fortunately, commercial pattern companies make their patterns and fabric estimates available online. Each pattern envelope includes estimations useful for defining the scope of a project. Even if a garment will be custom patterned, consulting the fabric estimates for a commercial pattern of similar style will produce a reliable starting point. There are two special considerations to complete an estimate. The first is shrinkage if the fabric will be dyed or washed. That shrinkage can be 10%. Some natural fibers may shrink 20%. The second consideration is the "hidden" fabrics such as linings and interlinings. For yardage and pattern guides, see the Extra Resources section.

Creating the Project Schedule

A **project schedule** is a calendar timetable that sets small and large milestones that ensure each task feeds productively into the next phase of production. Shows are such complex, living organisms that no one should attempt to keep everything in their head. (See Table 17.6.) Plan the schedule *backwards* from the biggest known deadline: the first time the costumes must be on stage. Many tasks are dependent on what goes before it: these are called **task dependencies**. For instance, costumes to be distressed must have alterations and builds completed early, so they can be aged and dry in time for actors to wear them. Note each task dependency in your specific show and set an internal **due date** for each one. Typical task dependencies include:

- Dying or painting fabric yardage before a costume can be built
- Making a muslin sample before cutting in fashion fabric
- Fitting underpinnings or understructures before clothing can be fitted properly
- Constructing and altering garments before distressing or aging

- Rental costumes arrival dates, other garments in that costume may have to wait to be fitted also
- Rental costumes charging by the week must arrive late to save money
- Shoes must be chosen and fitted before hemming skirts and trousers
- Wigs must be chosen or styled before hats can be properly fitted or attached

Once all the due dates are added, the next step is to consider how long each task takes to complete. These tasks include constructing garments, fitting, alterations time, wigs or hairstyling, shoes, accessories. What, then, is the *begin date* for each group of tasks to meet its internal deadline? Set fitting day targets for each character or grouping so you know when all the garments must be in-house. After adding ending and start dates, the designer may find some startling conclusions. There may not be enough time to custom build all that was hoped for, or it may become apparent that the shop must be kept busy with alterations to buy time while rentals arrive or while the designer approves a muslin. Alterations fittings may therefore have to begin right away, possibly changing the order the designer had planned to work. If the designer is working as their own crew, these internal deadlines will dictate when items must be done to stay on schedule. Always plan adequate days off per week to mirror others working for the company. This can be tricky if the designer works a full-time job elsewhere and plans to use weekends for this project. But do not put the show over your long-term mental or physical health. Some other considerations that affect task timelines include:

- Equity rules for fittings – see Extra Resources section.
- Shipping time and purchase arrival dates – when must items can be ordered to fit the work timeline?
- Makers' schedules for garments made out-of-house.
- How many fittings will be practical? If the designer must prepare for one and only one fitting with each actor, then every single item must be present in that fitting.

- Early garments desired for photo calls or early filming to create projections or special effects.

An estimated timeline for any project, no matter how rough at first, is a powerful tool the designer can use to arrange time and tasks and answer questions in production meetings. Share this overview with the stage managers to plan upcoming fitting days. The costume designer often calls the most fittings at about the same time rehearsals begin run-throughs. Any advance planning will ease the way.

Strategies to Trim Money or Time

If the designer's planning reveals it will take five weeks to prepare the show, but the project schedule only allows four or three, what to do? Trimming labor and time requires creative problem solving. In addition to relying on rentals and purchases, there are typical elements to inspect for time or labor savings:

- **Eliminate R&D.** Use commercial patterns for a sample garment instead of custom patterning.
- **Create duplicates**. Make variations to group costumes using limited numbers of patterns. For instance, a designer may outfit a chorus of 18 people using only three styles of patterns. Variety comes from using different colorways. Or, use early down time to pre-build costumes using X-large, large, medium sizes, making small adjustments to individual actors in the fitting.
- **Streamline muslins.** Decide which, if any, characters will be fitted in a muslin sample. All the others will be fitted directly in fashion fabric. Or determine all period skirts will be built directly in fabric, leaving just a bodice to fit in muslin.
- **Outsource to online makers.** Some historical costume makers and online sellers will build their inventory using your fabric or a special fabric. Contact each one to see what can be done.
- **Strategic fitting labor.** The number of hours a maker is standing in a fitting is the number of hours they are not working on the garments. When is it really necessary to have

Table 17.6 Sample Project Schedule

Monday	Tuesday	Wednesday	Thursday	Friday	Saturday	Sunday
May 28 Actor Day Off **Prep Week 1** **Design/Mgt Team** Fabric ordering Online garments ordering	May 29 Pre-Measurements Gathered	May 30 Preliminary Pulling Costume Stock, Rentals	May 31 Pulling, Costume Stock & Rentals	June 1 In-Person Purchasing Fabric, Garments	June 2 In-Person Purchasing Fabric, Garments	June 3 Costumes Day Off
June 4 Actor Day Off **Prep Week 2** Purchase supplies **Fabric Due**	June 5 **Shop Crew Begins**	June 6 Fabric Dye/Pre-treat Purchasing, rentals	June 7 Fabric Dye/Pre-treat	June 8 **Costumes Due for Fittings** **Underpinnings Due**	June 9	June 10 Costumes Day Off
June 11 Actor Day Off **Prep Week 3**	June 12 **First Rehearsal** Fill in last measurements	June 13 **Fittings – 4 actors** **Alterations begin** Pulling & Purchases	June 14 **Fittings – 4 actors**	June 15 **Fittings – 4 actors** **All muslins due**	June 16 **Fittings – 4 actors**	June 17 Costumes Day Off
June 18 Actor Day Off **Prep Week 4 Begin Masks for Party Scene**	June 19	June 20 **Second fittings** Pulling & Purchases	June 21 **Second fittings**	June 22 **Second fittings**	June 23 **Second fittings**	June 24 Costumes Day Off
June 25 Actor Day Off **Prep Week 5**	June 26 **Final fits – Builds** **Final fits – Last Minute Rentals**	June 27 Begin Accessories Hair & Wigs	June 28 Run-thrus, difficult to get actors for fittings	June 29 **Street Characters Done for Aging**	June 30 Age/Distress	July 1 Costumes Day Off
July 2 Actor Day Off **Tech Week 6** **Costume Inventory Dressing Lists** Age/Distress	July 3 **Age/Distress Done** **Wardrobe Begins**	July 4 Company Holiday	July 5 **COSTUME LOAD IN TO THEATER**	July 6 **TECH/DRESS**	July 7 **TECH/DRESS**	July 8 **TECH/DRESS Stitchers Off**
July 9 Actor Day Off **Wardrobe Off** **TECH WEEK 7**	July 10 **TECH/DRESS**	July 11 **PREVIEW**	July 12 **PREVIEW**	July 13 **OPEN**	July 14 **Financial Wrap Due Wed July**	July 15

everyone present? Can other personnel do minor fitting tasks? Is it feasible to hire a fitter who does all the fittings, freeing all the makers to stay at their work?

- **Costumer fittings.** It may be possible in some situations to take a cue from the film industry that costumes hundreds of people for some scenes. Their methods may translate to the theatrical chorus or extras – anyone that does not have a specific character arc. The designer, an assistant, or a costumer assembles the entire ensemble for each actor from head to toe, including socks, suspenders, cufflinks. When actors arrive for the fitting, the costumer dresses the actor and checks for possible alterations, noting each on a work order or tags. There are multiple spare items on a rack in case something does not fit, and the actor keeps trying on items until a suitable ensemble is created. Fitting photos are stored in cloud file sharing. The designer can review the fittings to make suggestions and anyone requiring special attention can be called back for an additional fitting with the designer. This system also allows members of the costume team to practice creativity within boundaries set by the designer.

Figure 17.1 Actor James Michael Cowan posing for a fitting photo with information on a white board.

Theatrical shops pride themselves in their ability to produce high quality work for little money, and can sometimes look askance at time-saving methods. However, it cannot hurt to open our minds toward creative efficiencies. If producers cannot afford personal attention and couture work, it is not reasonable to provide it in every case.

Working With Constraints

When designers identify the parameters or limitations within a project, they are defining the **constraints**. Identifying constraints is part of effective planning, but it need not limit the imagination. There are many ways to solve a challenge. Some constraints are negotiable, some are permanent. Some constraints are **foreseeable** and others will surface only after you've begun the project. Some constraints are **external**: two important examples are deadlines and the budget. Others are **intrinsic**, arising from the nature of the story itself. A common intrinsic constraint is the need for duplicates of the same costume, one in new condition and one in torn condition after a violent event. Two costumes will constrain how the budget must be spent. A third set of constraints arise from **staging** requirements such as actors playing more than one role requiring fast changes. A fourth constraint stems from the **end user** – or the actors wearing the costumes. An actor may be allergic to wool or need special footwear or special sizes. Understanding the restraints we face helps us take charge of the solution. There may be nothing we can do about an end user constraint. But there is a lot we can do about other constraints to turn them into brilliant solutions.

"The largest subsidy for the arts comes not from governments, patrons or the private sector, but from artists themselves in the form of unpaid or underpaid labor." —The United Nations Educational, Scientific and Cultural Organization[3]

Sizing Up the Scope of a Project

This phase of planning produces an educated guess, or **guestimate** about the project. Some projects are focused and manageable. A quick glance at the budget, production calendar, and the availability of costume labor may be enough to reassure the designer there are adequate resources. If a designer has worked with a given theater multiple times, they understand how things proceed. But some projects require additional thought or concessions to fit the project to the resources. If you make adjustments, discuss those compromises with the director to ensure they are acceptable. If it does not look like the project can be completed with the available time or resources, then some negotiation must occur. Always approach the director or producer with possible solutions in mind. They will be grateful and impressed you know how to identify a problem early, presenting it for collaborative discussion. The whole point of doing this early is to move forward in a collegial manner. If the problems become a crisis later, it is very difficult for anyone to remain collegial.

However, we know from studying the creative process that juices start flowing when we start *doing* things. Once the show gets on its feet in rehearsals, the actors and director will have new ideas – well after the planning phases for costumes. Leave some air time in the schedule for allowable growth. One example is a decision to transform the stage crew into "characters" that cross the stage whisking away props as if they were in the scene. If this is an allowable growth, have a contingency plan in the back of your mind. When projects expand in the normal course of events, we call this **scope creep**. It is so common that we will

visit this subject again in Chapter 18, Budgeting Creative Projects.

Expecting the Unexpected

A designer received a cast list for his show to discover that ten additional people had been cast as an ensemble that he had never heard about, effectively doubling the size of the job. He had signed on to design a show of a certain size, and his own schedule could not change to accommodate this surprise decision. He presented the situation to the producer as a post-agreement scope creep, pitching the idea of hiring a costumer who would create, pull, and fit the ensemble using his guidelines. The producers agreed, hiring additional labor for fittings and alterations. He did not create renderings for these characters, instead providing a mood board as a visual guide. The solution was not perfect, but the designer established his ability to be a problem solver, and that scope creep was not his problem to solve alone.

Extra Resources

Reconstructing History, Sewing Patterns for Historical Garments, https://reconstructinghistory.com/
Truly Victorian, Sewing Patterns of the Victorian Era, https://trulyvictorian.info/
The Wardrobe Supervisor's Toolkit, Rebecca Pride. Routledge, 2018
Project Planning for the Stage Rich Dionne, Southern Illinois Press, 2018
*LORT/Actor's Equity Association Rulebook,*www.theproducer sperspective.com/wp-content/uploads/2015/10/LORT-Rulebook-2017.pdf

Notes

1 Barnes, Gregg. 2021. "From the Page to the Stage, Designer and Maker." *Costume Society of America*, Western Region. Streamed April 11, 2021 via Zoom.
2 Sonia Kolesnikov-Jessop, January 2021. Couture Notebook.com. *All You Need to Know About Haute Couture.* https://couturenotebook.com/haute-couture-definition-clients-and-prices
3 Walsh, David. 2022. "UNESCO Report: 10 Million Arts Jobs Lost in 2020 Due to Covid-19." *World Socialist Web Site*, February 23, 2022. https://www.wsws.org/en/articles/2022/02/24/unes-f24.html

18.
BUDGETING CREATIVE PROJECTS

Everyone has heard the phrase *Nobody Calls It Show Art – It's Show Business*. But many creative professionals are ill-prepared to enter the world of show *business*. This situation can be doubly so for designers, whose educations may lack formal budgeting strategies. Many costume designers have learned the hard way that budgets are based on **assumptions**. What we assume to be included in the budget may not be the same assumption the producer held. One young summer stock designer spent her entire budget on the costumes, relieved she'd managed to stay within the goal. She learned differently when an upset production manager called because costumes had gone significantly over budget. It turns out the number she'd been given was meant to cover *all* costume department expenses, including shop supplies, wardrobe costs, and dry-cleaning. The producer had assumed she understood that. Both the designer and producer learned an important lesson about assumptions.

"Never ASSUME. It makes an ASS of U and ME." —Kathy Christiansen, draper[1]

Typical Budgeting Methods

Some shows do not require much financial planning other than accounting for receipts afterwards. But some producers require an estimated budget before "greenlighting" a project. In other cases, costume designers must educate the producer on why a show costs what it does, or make a pitch for a higher budget. If producers rarely see a fully realized costume budget, they do not learn the actual costs. While many administrators do not understand costumes, they *do* understand numbers. They relate to an Excel sheet and it allows them to be part of the planning process. Costume designer Bonnie Kruger recalls the difference it made in her career when she started presenting a full budget proposal at the start of a project. "They took it seriously and I got everything we asked for. It was miraculous."[2]

"Budget: a mathematical confirmation of your suspicions." —A.A. Latimer[3]

What then, is an effective budget? It provides a blueprint where to focus the energies of a production. For instance, if the designer would like a custom-painted set of costumes, that time and supplies must be allocated from the beginning. The designer may decide to offset that expense

DOI: 10.4324/9781003015284-23

elsewhere by using free garments pulled from stock. Discussing costs points everyone's attention to the reality that costumes do not spontaneously appear in the trunk of the costume designer's car. No one understands the power of a good prop like theater people; just by having a clear excel sheet we enhance our credibility and prove that costume design is **quantifiable**. In fact, costumes are more of a numbers game than people realize. There are a known number of actors in the cast and a quantifiable number of costumes. By establishing costs, it is straightforward to discuss options. The key to making effective decisions is translating the artistic desires into products and services. This seems counterproductive in a creative project, but it is an edifying practice. Most of the stress for costume designers stems from the pressure created when the show is larger than its budget, or the time is inadequate. It is liberating to understand an artistic decision is also a business decision.

Designers typically encounter two types of budgets. By far the most common is the **imposed budget**, decided by administrators and handed down. Management makes assumptions, predicting likely expenses for their annual operations. One common prediction tool is *incremental projection*. They use figures from a prior year or a similar project as a guide, adding a given percentage to cover inflation. In such a case, if the base assumptions are incorrect the errors will be handed down year after year.

The other system of creating a budget is building from the bottom up. **Zero-based budgets** cost out the show from scratch using current-market pricing. These budgets still include a ceiling or limit. This system puts more decisions in the hands of the designer and their team to prioritize what they find important for the project. Budgeting a show this way requires a good understanding of the labor market, the build process, and materials suppliers. Although there may be a feeling of freedom in this method, always ensure someone employed by that theater is the responsible party for the budget. If the designers are freelancers, they are not financially responsible for audits and other protocols. Approve expenses with that person, often a production manager or costume director. Report regularly to them,

using their required system for managing receipts or online shopping protocols.

The worst budget method of all is far too common: the budget number is all the theater can afford, so it has to work regardless of actual costs. It may or may not reflect reality in any way.

Formatting a Budget

Producers make other assumptions about a show budget, including the hope that a large percentage of costumes will be available in the theater's own stock. That assumption may or may not turn out to be the case once the show is designed and cast. Many institutions allocate the cost of doing a show through several **budget lines**: the labor may come from an administration budget, the shop supplies and maintenance from an inventory budget, and the cost of costumes from the show budget. Independent projects may use an **all-inclusive** or "all-in" budget expected to cover every costume expense. Talk through the budget very carefully with the production manager to determine their assumptions and methods. A budget may be very simple or complex, but it always benefits from understanding the real sources of expenses. There are ten common categories of expenses to consider:

Fixed expenses are what many people call overhead. For productions, these are the predictable types of expenses that don't really change regardless of the type of show. The producer may categorize their resident labor as fixed, and not include it in the costume budget. Or some costume shops charge each show budget a flat amount, called a **recharge**, for purchasing sewing needs or for using stock fabrics. Some budgets treat dry-cleaning as a fixed expense.

Variable expenses are any costs that depend on the specific production. One show may spend an extraordinary amount on shoes, another on tailored suits. The vast majority of show sourcing expenses fit into this category.

Comfort, safety, and intimacy expenses cover fight pads, knee pads, ankle braces, dance cups and straps, compression shorts, nude body suits or thongs, robes for backstage changes. Shows with violence or nudity require extensive preparations. Mic packs fit in this category if not supplied by the sound department. Separating these into a line item focuses their importance within the budget. Absorbing them into variable expenses or the materials budget renders them invisible and sacrifices the rest of the budget for these nonnegotiable items. Producers should not wish to short change safety and intimacy for the performers.

Expendables are items with a short life span used in the course of the production, such as quarts of stage blood or a daily supply of delicate foam prosthetics, or hairspray. Some costume designers add nylon stockings to this category to remind producers they will need replacements.

Labor is the amount of effort used to produce goods or services for that show. Some theaters budget this expense separately from the show, but there are certainly cases where the budget must also cover labor, especially if there are no full-time employees.

The **cost of doing business** (COB) covers both indirect and direct costs. **Indirect** costs are difficult to allocate to just one project such as equipment upkeep. This is not ordinarily the purview of the designer, but if a sewing machine dies on your show it can wreak havoc. Wear and tear on your personal vehicle is an indirect cost of driving many miles for a production. **Direct** costs are purchases required to make progress on the project itself: transportation, copies of renderings for the rehearsal hall, research, shipping, and other goods or services. Costume designers who lend their own supplies or machinery to a production are incurring indirect or direct costs and should be compensated for that as a **kit fee** or machine rental fee. If the designer bears the brunt of wear and tear to personal machinery and other supplies, she should not be expected to do so for free. Sometimes producers will agree to a trade – the designer can keep all extra supplies

purchased in exchange for use of personal equipment. An important cost to consider is how the costumes will get to the theater. For a small show, this may not be a problem. But transporting a major Shakespeare production with 80 costumes is not so easy a matter. If this is part of the designer's responsibility; it may be necessary to rent a van or truck.

Loss and damage (L&D) sometimes occurs in spite of everyone's best efforts. A pair of trousers is irreparably destroyed during a fight scene and must be replaced. Shows with vigorous movement or violence might well budget for this from the beginning. In other cases management may prefer to hope for the best, facing losses only if they occur. Damage often occurs after a show has opened, and the designer is off contract. It is useful to remind a producer, should damage occur, that calling the designer back in to replace and fit the costume is additional labor beyond the bounds of the contract.

Discounts quantify the designer's *full* contribution to the show and the real costs of costume production. Nothing is free – if you've loaned stock to the show, it has value. Did you call in a professional favor on their behalf? Having that kind of pull makes you valuable, too. Don't allow your extra value to be invisible. Document what those items *would* have cost, then subtract it using a 100% discount. This educates producers to the true value of costume items and services. This also gives the designer some leverage for negotiations, since you are donating goods and services. In Table 18.1 the designer noted a 100% discount for materials donated from his personal fabric stash.

The **contingency** acknowledges circumstances that cannot be predicted. Even the most mundane costs fluctuate with world events. Some shows add new costumes well into rehearsals, or the deeply discounted fabric you swatched is now gone. Some producers require the contingency to be part of the costume budget, others designate a contingency for the whole show and wish to know how much of it may be allocated to costumes.

Table 18.1 Imposed Budget Using Standard Budget Categories

Variable Expenses	*Items*	*Subtotals*	*Totals*
Costume Rentals	Local University Stock	$0.00	
	Tuxedo Rental	$75.00	
	Shipping/Returns	$15.00	
Rentals Total			**$90.00**
Purchases – Garments	Online Supplier	$58.00	
	Specialty Supplier	$28.00	
	Thrift Store	$54.00	
Garments Total			**$140.00**
Underpinnings	T-shirts, undies	$30.00	
	Socks, Stockings	$25.00	
	Spanx, Specialty Items	$70.00	
Underpinnings Total			**$125.00**
Footwear	Shoes	$100.00	
	Repairs	$25.00	
	Insole, Heel Grips, Laces	$15.00	
Footwear Total			**$140.00**
Materials	Online Supplier	$45.00	
	Fabric Store	$15.00	
	Designer's Fabric Stash	$75.00	
	Designer Discount 100%	-$75.00	
Materials Total			**$60.00**
Wigs/Hair/Makeup	Hair Cuts	$80.00	
	Hair Supplies	$25.00	
	Makeup Room Supplies	$35.00	
Hair/Makeup Total			**$140.00**
Comfort, Safety, Intimacy	Knee Pads	$75.00	
	Mic Pacs and Rigging	$5.00	
	Shoe Rubber	$75.00	
Rentals Total			**$155.00**
LABOR			
Alterations	8 hours × $21	$168.00	
	Dress Rehearsal Notes	$75.00	
Alterations Total			**$243.00**
Services	Teching Shirts, etc.	$125.00	
	Designer Discount 100%	-$125.00	
	Build one pair linen trousers	$100.00	

Variable Expenses	Items	Subtotals	Totals
Services Total			**$100.00**
FIXED EXPENSES			
Goods & Services	Fitting Kit	$0.00	
	Safety Pins	$0.00	
	Sewing Machine, Iron	$0.00	
	Rehearsal Costume Cleaning	$0.00	
Goods & Services Total			**$0.00**
Shopping Expenses	Mileage	$40.00	
	Parking	$10.00	
Shopping Total			**$50.00**
EXPENDABLES			
Costume Rentals	Temporary Tattoos	$35.00	
	Scotch Guard – wine stunt	$8.00	
	Oxy Clean – wine stunt	$15.00	
Rentals Total			**$58.00**
COST OF DOING BUSINESS			
Office Supplies	Printer Ink (Fitting Photo Wall)	$85.00	
	Manila Tags – Alters notes	$65.00	
	Garment bags – transpo	$15.00	
Office Supplies Total			**$165.00**
Costume Load-In Dress Rehearsal			
	Use of Car & Gas	$35.00	
	Extra Insurance	$50.00	
Load-In Total			**$85.00**
		BUDGET TOTAL	**$1,551.00**
		Budget as Given	$1,500.00
	Note Designer Discounts	**Over/Under Budget**	**$51.00**
CONTINGENCY 5%			**$75.00**
LOSS & DAMAGE			
Fight Scene	Replace purchased costume	$55.00	
	Day rate for Designer to shop/fit	$175.00	
Fight Scene L&D Total			**$230.00**
		Worst Case Scenario	**$1,856.00**

Working With a Small Budget

The most common type of budget is the *imposed budget*, or a total figure that may not reflect what costumes and labor actually cost. First of all, it is important to realize a truly unrealistic budget may severely cripple what a designer can do. But it is also true some of the most creative ideas have come from limited circumstances that force innovation. Every designer must assess for themselves if the project is viable. Table 18.1 shows a sample imposed budget of $1,500 for a small production end sentence here. How can the designer strategize how to spend this type of budget? This sample budget projects the show may cost $51 more than the budget. As a bargaining tool, the designer notes he is discounting $200 of his own labor and fabric to work within the budget. It would then be reasonable to ask for the additional $51. If the designer is not in a position to give these discounts, the show would be over budget by $251. It is always worth asking if the theater can pay this larger amount. There are several ways a designer may work within a smaller, imposed budget:

Method 1: Determine the Per-Actor or Per-Costume Cost

This method may be most suitable in cases where a theater maintains a usable stock of costumes or has generous reciprocal-lending agreements with other theaters. If the only costs are essentially what will appear onstage, this can be an effective starting method. Assuming a cast of seven actors and 12 costumes, divide the budget by the numbers of actors or costumes. A budget of $1,500 results in $214 *per actor* or $125 *per costume*, head-to-toe. There are many projects where this could be a workable amount. It is reasonable to create your own assumptions, such as new costumes will be purchased for a few characters and all the others are restricted to what can be found in stock or borrowed for free. Figure 18.1 shows one method to estimate costs for specific characters using the **piece list** generated in Chapter 17 (see Figure 17.1). The budget columns, shown in red, will be hidden

later to convert this form into a dressing list. Using a convertible form such as this one saves time by eliminating repetitive paperwork.

Method 2: Subtract Hidden Costs First

Hidden costs are those that are often overlooked, sometimes borne by the designers themselves or accomplished by seat-of-the-pants solutions. One example is the designer will not be doing her own alterations and requires $300 for a colleague's time. What if the theater requires beautiful presentation prints of the costume renderings? Or the designer knows from hard experience that shows shopped in thrift stores actually take *more* shopping time as the inventory is completely serendipitous – will the suitable garments even be there after driving to look? It can take more gas and parking to shop in multiple locations. That designer may wish to have mileage reimbursed so the show is not actually costing them money. Using the sample budget in Figure 18.1, the designer can subtract these hidden costs first:

- $1,500 minus Shopping Expenses of $150 and leaves $1,350
- $1,350 minus the $300 for alterations leaves $1,050
- $1,050 divided by 12 costumes leaves $87.50 per costume head-to-toe

There are many circumstances where $87 per costume is a workable average – an expensive purchase can be offset by a costume found in stock. The per-costume amount will dictate much of your strategy. If the cost per garment is extremely low for that specific show, the majority of costumes must come from no- or low-cost sources such as costume stock and loans. If this budget is workable, make sure the proposed hidden expenses will be approved by the producer. No one likes surprises, and designers are far more likely to make progress through clear conversations.

Advanced Zero-Based Budgeting

In some cases, a project may require advanced budgeting skills. The sample budget in Table 18.2

Show	Romeo and Juliet								
Character	Romeo Nelson Bridges								
Actor		Buy	Rent	Stock	Build	Estimates		Totals	
Look 1	Linen jacket		x			$ 50.00			
	vest			x		$ -			
	Cotton trousers			x		$ -			
	Linen shirt	x				$ 35.00			
	A-shirt	x				$ 15.00			
	untied tie			x		$ -			
	straw driving cap	x				$ 35.00			
	socks			x		$ -			
	two tone shoes			x		$ -			
	belt			x		$ -		$ 135.00	
Look 2	Repeat #1 Shirt, trousers					$ -			
Party	Open kaftan	x				$ 35.00			
Look	Sheik boots			x		$ -			
	Igal- head scarf			x		$ -			
	Wide sash				x	$ 15.00		$ 50.00	
Look 3	Repeat Look #1 no vest, add jacket							$0.00	
Look 4	Suit #2 Light Blue	x				$ 125.00			
Wedding	Duplicate shirt-fight rigged			x		$ -			
	Tie			x		$ -			
	Fedora			x		$ -			
	Wedding ring			x		$ -			
	Two tone shoes- repeat					$ -			
	Dark glasses			x		$ -			
	socks			x		$ -			
	belt			x		$ -		$125.00	
Look 4B	Look #4 Repeat No jacket, tie undone					$ -			
Fight	Repeat rigged shirt			x		$ -		$0.00	
Look 5	Period boxers			x		$ -		$0.00	
Night									
Look 6	Dark suit #3			x		$ -			
Death	Shirt			x		$ -			
suit	dark socks			x		$ -			
	shoes #2 solid, dark			x		$ -			
	belt			x		$ -		$0.00	
								$310.00	

Figure 18.1 Costume piece list with columns (shown in red) to estimate costs.

for *Romeo and Juliet* was created for an independent producer who used a *greenlight* approval process. The cost of costumes was partly determined by the going rate for rental costumes, as indicated in the top section. The designer began with researching sources available for the show, and identifying online items available for purchase. The designer made an educated guess as to which items were likely to be purchased, rentals or loans, stock item, or custom builds. It may be necessary to schedule a scouting trip of stock and other sources for more accuracy. If your vendors will allow you to set aside possible costumes at this stage, reserve anything that might work. Make sure to prioritize items – what is most important for the correct look, or most important for fit? Shows that are pieced from many sources take longer to budget. It is possible to streamline the estimate process by identifying a major supplier such as a suit broker, using those prices for every appropriate character. This unit price gives the designer a cost-reference while shopping. Consider your performer's bodies, if known to you. If you know a particular performer is athletic with larger thighs, it may be difficult to buy trousers except from higher priced brands.

Budgeting line-by-line is time-consuming and not necessary for every circumstance. Shows that use costumes from just a few suppliers are easier to estimate using *categories*. For instance, the cast of an opera may be a combination of rental costumes, a few custom builds, and stock items. To streamline

budgeting, create categories with an automatic price attached to them. For instance, a rental rate might be $250 per costume head-to-toe. Allocate a guesstimated number of costumes to this category. A second category of costumes may be purchased from a historical recreation site for $300 each. A third category could be the cost to build period costumes. Multiply the number of costumes in each category by its rate. This style of budgeting provides a solid guestimate. It is important to include a category that accounts for hidden costs, such as shipping or duplicating costume pieces that don't fit. This method provides an early framework for more detailed planning later.

If the designer is in charge of advanced budgeting or financial strategy for a theater, this, too, is part of the expertise brought to the project. After all, a disorganized and fiscally irresponsible costume area wreaks havoc on everyone. All this calculation is labor that you may or may not be compensated for. Take this into consideration when you estimate the hours of your job. If you work at a theater multiple times that requires you to do the budgeting, point this out to them and ask for a higher fee. Asking might benefit you directly will definitely educate a producer about the job.

Presenting an Estimated Budget

Designers present estimated budgets to their producers for two major reasons: some require an estimated budget for a design before they will *greenlight* a project or authorize spending to begin. The other reason is if the designer wishes to ask for additional money. In this case, the budget is a **persuasive** tool, documenting *why* a show will cost what it will. While many people on the project have an interest in the money, few will read any detailed line-by-line budget generated from piece lists or other methods. Present a **cover sheet** (see Table 18.2) that arranges the budget picture as the designer wishes. For instance, some special requirements may take more budget than anyone realized. Putting those elements on one line to feature them creates talking points for a meeting. By pulling those figures out from the total costume costs, the designer highlights that rental as a large

Category 1: Package Rental from Light Opera Co	$250	30 costumes	$7,500
Category 2: Purchases from Etsy Recreation	$300	10 costumes	$3,000
Category 3: Rent boots, hats for Cat 2 costumes	$150	10 costumes	$1,500
Category 4: Hidden costs – travel to vendor			$1,000
Total Estimate			**$10,700**

Table 18.2 Zero-Based Budget Reflects an Independent Project With No Resident Costume Shop It is a *cover sheet* summarizing categories of expenses, not individual costume costs. This type of template reminds the designer what kinds of items to discuss with a producer.)

VARIABLE EXPENSES			
Costume Rentals	Western Costume × 10	$2,000.00	
$200 EACH	**WCC Restocking**	$200.00	
	Universal Studios – hats, accessories	$500.00	
	Uni Restocking	$150.00	
	Old Globe – Dresses	$0.00	
	Old Globe Pulling Fee	$25.00	
	Shipping/Fitting Returns	$21.88	
Rentals Total			**$2,896.88**
Prep/Fittings	Fitting Room Rental	$500.00	
	Fitting Room Discount – 100%	$500.00	
Fittings Total			**$1,000.00**
Purchases – Garments	Men's Suits (Men's USA)	$1,469.00	
	Women's Wear	$1,954.00	
	General Items	$1,415.00	
	Menswear – Casual, Big/Tall	$462.99	
	Accessories	$175.38	
	Hats	$262.34	
	Jewelry	$11.92	
	Glasses/Lenses – All	$36.29	
Purchases Total			**$5,786.92**
Footwear	Shoes	$1,144.89	
	Taps/Heel Brace	$0.00	
	Insole, Heel Grips, Stretch, Laces, etc.	$34.71	
	Dye/Color/Décor	$56.84	
	Repair/Remakes	$150.00	
	Rentals to Actors	$0.00	
Footwear Total			**$1,386.44**
Fabrics/Materials	Fabric & Trims	$465.82	
	Vendors – Sand Wash	$150.00	
	Accessories Items	$51.78	

(*Continued*)

Table 18.2 (Continued)

VARIABLE EXPENSES			
	Supplies, Notions, Dyes	$27.25	
Fabric Total			**$694.85**
Wigs/Makeup	Wigs & Makeup Supplies	$600.00	
	Wig/Makeup Fee	$1,000.00	
$40/man $60/woman	Hair Cuts	$240.00	
	Hair Cut Discount – 100%	-$240.00	
Wigs/Makeup Total			**$1,600.00**
LABOR			
Shoppers/Day Labor	Fitting Assistants	$1,300.00	
	Additional Shoppers	$800.00	
Day Labor Total			**$2,100.00**
Vendor Labor	Alterations	$1,250.00	
	WCC Tailoring	$85.00	
	Made to Order	$0.00	
	Crafts Build	$0.00	
	Paint/Dye	$0.00	
	Distress/Age	$0.00	
Vendor Labor Total			**$1,335.00**
Other Labor	3 days @ $25	$600.00	
Alterations by Designer	2 days @ $25	$400.00	
Dress Rehearsal notes by Designer	**Designer Discount 100%**	-$1,000.00	
Other Labor Total			**$0.00**
Shopping Expenses	Mileage/Gas	$300.00	
Research	Parking	$150.00	
	Research Expenses (samples)	$35.00	
	Misc.	$15.00	
Shopping Total			**$500.00**
Services	Fabric Treatments – Flame	$35.00	
	Pleaters, Jobbers	$0.00	
	Button/trim making	$0.00	

VARIABLE EXPENSES			
Services Total			**$35.00**
Comfort, Safety, Intimacy	Robes	$0.00	
and Backstage Reqs	Boots/slippers/backstage	$0.00	
Rigging, etc.	Knee, Elbow, Fight pads	$200.00	
	Mic Pac rigging	$0.00	Sound Dept
	Shoe Rubber – outdoor stage	$275.00	
	Nude covers	$50.00	
Comfort, Safety, Intimacy Total			**$525.00**
FIXED EXPENSES			
Goods & Services	Shop/Fitting Room Supply	$70.00	
	Wig/Makeup Replenish	$35.00	
	Rehearsal Costumes Cleaning	$150.00	
Goods & Services Total			**$255.00**
EXPENDABLES			
Makeup and FX	Temporary Tattoos – Tybalt	$175.00	
	Latex Scars – Padre	$50.00	
	Blood, edible	$75.00	
FX Total			**$300.00**
COST OF DOING BUSINESS			
Office Supplies	Printer Ink	$85.00	
	Copy Services	$65.00	
	Manila Tags – Alters notes	$75.00	
	Garment bags – transpo	$75.00	
Office Supplies Total			**$300.00**
Designer Kit Rental	Sewing Machine	$30.00	
	Fitting Kit – exchange for purchases	$0.00	
Kit Rental Total			**$30.00**
Costume Load-In Dress Rehearsal	Van rental – pickups and delivery	$200.00	
	Extra Insurance	$50.00	

(Continued)

Table 18.2 (Continued)

VARIABLE EXPENSES			
	Mileage/gas	$35.00	
Load-In Total			**$285.00**
LOSS & DAMAGE			
Romeo/Tybalt Fight	DUP Romeo Shoes – Fight	$75.21	
	Dup Romeo Suit – Fight	$204.00	
L&D Total			**$279.21**
		BUDGET TOTAL	**$19,309.30**
		Budget as Given	**$18,750.00**
	Note Designer Discounts	**Over/Under Budget**	**$559.30**
	CONTINGENCY – 5%		**$900.00**
		Worst Case Scenario	**$20,209.30**

percentage of the budget. Some examples include military uniforms, stage crew costumes, a dream-ballet, or an added ensemble. Always highlight extra performers added beyond the script requirements. Producers that value offering acting opportunities will want to fund that important element of the show. It's vital they see how much such decisions add to the overall cost.

Negotiating a Budget

Table 18.2 illustrates a projected budget slightly higher than the desired target of $18,750. Now the designer must negotiate how to approach this difference with the producers. Always initiate this discussion in a positive manner: it is a fact-finding meeting to brainstorm solutions. Use the goal of *abundance* to establish tone – everyone wants what is best for this amazing project. Go over each category of items on the budget cover sheet. You will gain trust and credibility by presenting a complete picture of creating costumes. Print special items in color to feature designer discounts for providing services or goods. Always ask if there are items missing from this budget.

Point out this total already includes several compromises, such as your discounted items or using borrowed items instead of purchased. Ask if there are other ways to achieve the desired budget – perhaps the theater has someone on staff who could do all the printing, or a patron that supplies haircuts for free? If the budget overage is very close to the desired ceiling, it's worth asking if the producer is in a position to pay the extra money. But perhaps the producers are on a very tight budget and as much as they would love to help, they cannot find additional money. They will likely ask you to recommend what should be cut from the show, or ask for a justification for how you arrived at some figures. Suggest some solutions, but ultimately let the director and the producers make that decision. Return to the director to solve the problem together. What has to change to meet expectations? Every director has faced the tyranny of a show budget, and they are willing to brainstorm early in the process.

Additional Considerations

Some small theaters expect the designer to not only prepare the show, but run it, design makeup and hair, and return for strike. This is also worth additional negotiation. Ask if that is the theater's policy across the board – are the scenic or lighting designers expected to perform multiple jobs and return to strike their designs, as well? If they are not, then it is important to ask why the costume designer has been singled out. It may be more affordable to hire a PA or wardrobe crew member to manage strike and returns. Of course, the designer's good name is on the line if costume returns are handled badly, so some designers prefer to participate in some way to protect their reputations in a small artistic community. Remind the producer your good vendor relationships are part of your worth to the organization, and ask about a fair day rate to return. Again, you may not receive it, but you are educating a producer. Costume designer Kristin Sauter notes that in community theater, "Sometimes it's not the mission to teach what theater is, and what the correct jobs are, and the boundaries. The basic support structure is missing and they don't even know it's missing."[4]

Scope Creep and Allowable Growth

Creative projects change during rehearsals as a normal course of events. With everyone collected in one space juices start flowing. For many, this is the joy of working in theater. Some of the new ideas may require extra costumes or technical expertise. The wise designer will tuck this possibility into the back of their minds when evaluating the scope of the show or its budget. Designate in your mind what can be **allowable growth**. Pull extra costumes along the way, note where the perfect stash of peasant shirts can be borrowed if need be. There are times, however, that the new requirements are complete surprises or cannot be easily accommodated.

The Power of Yes – and . . .

If the costume designer has submitted a design and budget that was approved, radically changing the scope of the project later must also change the budget. This is a common understanding in business practice. It is not a reasonable expectation that more costumes can be rented, purchased, or built for absolutely no additional cost. When these new parameters occur, it is easy to react emotionally because those changes usually mean making more, scrounging more, calling in more favors, or an abuse of the designer's time. Do not automatically assume you *must* accommodate scope creep without more support. Designers *are* part of the creative team to generate solutions – it is our job to have ideas. Always ask for a little time for research and brainstorming with your team. Strive to thoughtfully offer a realistic solution you can deliver. "*Yes*, we can do that, *and* it will cost $300 dollars *and* take us one extra day *if* we get the fittings when we ask for them." Bargaining for what you justifiably need is a normal expectation. It is the producer's job to evaluate those options and agree to extra requirements or pull the plug on the idea. But at least you took the journey with them as a supportive collaborator.

The Power of No – and . . .

Just saying *No* to requests outright signals an unwillingness to be collaborative and leaves the impression you are not a flexible thinker. Of course, there will be times that *No* is the only answer. The budget or labor situation just will not allow it, or the request presents a moral quandary the designer cannot support or asks more than you are willing to achieve. Always avail yourself of that option if it is correct, and fully explain why there are no workable substitutions. Costume Designer Kristin Sauter explained it is important to set boundaries. When she first started as a freelance designer for community theater

> I wasn't prepared for setting my boundaries and knowing my worth. They want you to work a 50–60 hour week, which is really asking a lot, especially if they are paying just $200 to design a show and the costume budget is Zero.

She learned to say no to some things like doing costume renderings in some cases. She recalls one theater "wanted me to render every costume, and that takes a lot of time. Or the director has a very specific vision, but it's going to be impossible to deliver that with a budget of $50." She will provide character boards instead, noting that on the community theater level that is a better use of her time. Although even that can backfire. At one dress rehearsal, a director turned to her to ask "Where is that red dress?" It turns out the director had fastened on a specific piece of research in a mood board and expected to see that exact dress instead of the affordable substitute the budget could allow.

Educating Our Producers

Many producers have very little training in costumes. It is a very specialized field of expertise and unless someone has worked directly in a costume shop it is difficult to see the work involved. Costume budgets rarely reflect the actual labor involved; after all, we can buy $3 t-shirts made overseas. Many producers have come to expect costumes can be cheated, begged, borrowed, or used out of personal closets. Consider that for many years the actual cost of doing costumes may have been hidden from producers. It is a feather in some costume designers caps to deliver far more bang than the theater's buck allows. Or we are so eager to make a good impression for the sake of our careers that we hide the real cost of doing things. The first step toward educating our producers is **never mixing** the design fee and the show budget. Inexperienced producers have sometimes said "We have this amount to spend on costumes. Whatever you don't spend is your fee." It is the producer's job to decide how much they will pay a designer and how much they can afford as a budget. Don't let them off the hook so easily. If you must, make that decision for them in your budget process and ask for two separate checks.

Managing Money

Part of our credibility as a costume designer is responsibility with other people's money. Whether you are working with a costume supervisor, production manager, or producer, the ability to manage money is important. Designers will be asked to spend money using several methods. Discuss each option with the theater and make sure you understand their reporting requirements.

Petty cash. Producers may hand out part or all of the costume budget in cash, taking little interest in whether the designer uses that to reimburse their credit card expenses from ordering online, or uses it to buy items at garage sales. Some producers have limitations on what kind of receipts they will accept, so check carefully with the accounting person for restrictions. Don't be short-changed because the theater does not like a specific vendor or the way the receipt was issued. Ask for enough petty cash to buy extra items for fittings – it saves much time to buy extra garments with the intent to return those that don't fit. Some theaters use receipt apps available for smart phones using a photo for receipt submission.

Purchasing cards. Producers distribute gift cards to use for purchases, or issue a temporary debit card to the designer. Some require an immediate submission of the receipt if using a debit card, making returns more difficult to negotiate.

Company cards. Producers may require purchases over a certain amount or with specific vendors to be handled by someone on staff with the company credit card. The designer may fill an online shopping cart to forward to the company accountant to process. Or the designer may find himself standing at vendor's check-out desk trying to reach that person on the phone. Alert the company contact when you will be purchasing to coordinate schedules. Many companies require the receipt to be submitted immediately, making returns a tricky negotiation to manage.

Vendor accounts. Local suppliers and national chain stores allow businesses to open direct charge accounts. If the theater has not used this account in a while, it may be dormant. Submit a list of vendors to the theater accountant asking to activate the accounts well before you shop. The designer may be required to carry an ID card authorizing purchasing power for a specific time period. Some designers maintain their own vendor or wholesale accounts, allowing the producer to use them to obtain an advantageous discount.

Tax-exempt certificates. Some states issue a tax exemption for theaters, but not all will do that. Theaters may require you to carry paperwork and a store may require you to fill out paperwork each time you make a purchase. Department stores may require the designer to take the receipt to Customer Service for a special discount process after the initial purchase. This process significantly adds to shopping time. Carefully discuss this process if you have not worked in a tax-exempt state before. Ask what happens if you shop in a home state that does not allow tax exemption. One designer discovered the theater refused to cover sales tax paid in California because their home state used a tax-exempt system that California does not. It is possible to avoid sales tax by asking the store to ship it out of state directly to the theater. While that often costs the same or more than the sales tax, at least the designer will not be asked to refund the value of the tax to the theater.

Figure 18.2 Taping receipts to paper makes it easy to scan or copy for record keeping. This designer grouped receipts in similar categories for easy recording.

Sizing Up Budgeting Creative Projects

Every designer must be able to quickly assess a budget to understand the scope of the project and any limitations. The costume budget is more than predicting or reporting expenses. It provides a blueprint where to focus the designer's energies and the theater's resources. The most commonly used theater budget is the **imposed budget** that may or may not take into account actual market prices. Understanding how theaters create their budgets and how to present a budget can aid negotiations with the producer, if required. Always check the assumptions behind the budget number so there are no misunderstandings before spending money.

Expecting the Unexpected

Most of our collaborators woefully underestimate the amount of labor and expertise required to create costumes. One regional theater booked a show with a major Hollywood star as the lead whose contract stipulated her costumes could only be built by a certain costume shop. That shop specialized in film clients and they were so swamped with upcoming projects they neglected to begin this theater's project. Two weeks before dress rehearsals, the theater's producers decided to pull their job from that costume shop and find a new one. It fell to the Assistant Costume Designer to find a new shop and physically pull the fabrics and supplies from the old shop, driving them to the new shop that day to get started on the builds. The general manager for the theater stopped the harried design assistant in the parking lot to ask how much the new builds were going to cost the budget. She replied "I will have an estimate by tomorrow, but we will pay rush charges at the last minute like this. There are times where you just have to get out the money hose. This might be one of those times."

Extra Resources

Excel Quick Start Tutorial: 36 Minutes to Learn the Basics, Udemy www.udemy.com/course/excel_quickstart/
Basic Budgeting Strategies with Google Sheets, Udemy www.udemy.com/course/basic-budgeting-strategies-with-google-sheets/

Notes

1 Christiansen, Kathy. *Draper at Center Theater Group*, as told to the author in conversations 1991–93.

2 Kruger, Bonnie. In conversation with the author, September 10, 2021.

3 Rose, Jeff. 2020. "The Top 95 Most Hilarious Quotes about Money." *Good Financial Cents.com*, July 7, 2020. https://www.goodfinancialcents.com/funny-money-quotes-and-inspirational-sayings/

4 Sauter, Kristin 2021. Personal interview with the author, September 8, 2021.

19.
LEADING TEAMWORK

Many people are familiar with the childhood game of "telephone" where a sentence is whispered in the ears of a line of participants. By the time the sentence reaches the end, it has changed dramatically from the original. It's easy to see when information is whispered it will be misheard. But even major institutions with giant budgets miscommunicate, such as the first time Coca Cola® was translated into phonetically similar Chinese. The result was a phrase that meant "bite the wax tadpole." Pepsi® also stumbled, translating their slogan "Come Alive with the Pepsi Generation" into Taiwanese as "Pepsi brings your ancestors back from the dead."[1] If major corporations with entire communications divisions can falter, imagine how easy it is to miscommunicate on a theater project with dozens of teams that must interact on a tight schedule.

The costume designer does not work alone on a creative project. It takes large teams to create a show. If even one team member does not perform their part in the complex machinery of a show, it may start veering off the rails. Costume designers quickly figure out that being an artistic leader actually translates to serving as the main communicator between all team members. The key to effective communication is assuming good will for all interchanges. Emotions can be unnecessarily activated if we automatically assume that someone is interfering or trying to derail our progress. Always give due consideration to why a colleague or team member may be asking questions or acting certain ways. Watch how lighting designers handle themselves on headsets during very long hours with crew members. They must solve situations quickly and under the watchful gaze of the entire company. They must undo and redo cues, or track mistakes to correct them and yet keep the team willing and motivated. Most are unfailingly polite, using even formal manners to greet, thank, and jolly the crew along. Costume designers must also work publicly, while nurturing two seemingly contradictory abilities. The first is that we must be self-motivated, able to work alone toward goals. At the same time we must also work in teams to realize our projects. Those who work well alone don't always operate naturally as team members, and those who excel in groups may have difficulty with self-motivation. As artists or idea people, we often tolerate some amount of uncertainty and flexibility – or even chaos – to discover creative solutions. But these qualities can sometimes jeopardize team work, which thrives on certainty and clear goals. The costume designer stands at the vortex of these contrasts.

"It is better to lead from behind and to put others in front, especially when you celebrate victory when nice things occur. You take the front line when there is danger. Then people will appreciate your leadership." —Nelson Mandela

DOI: 10.4324/9781003015284-24

Figure 19.1 Magnolia flowers symbolize dignity, perseverance and healing.

Table 19.1 The Way of the Steel Magnolia

1. **It's not about me**. If others behave aggressively, they reveal their own fears – disguised as criticism of you. Ironically, you will appear stronger by controlling your emotions.

2. **Keep the ball in the air**. Communication is a badminton game – all you have to do is hit the birdie back. Don't panic with an answer because you were caught off guard. Create a bag of replies to buy time – "*I hear you say XYZ, is that what you meant?*" "*How did you solve this problem in the past?*" "*I don't have an answer right now, can I think about it?*"

3. **Win the war. Not every battle.** Fighting *every* battle will exhaust you and no one will want to work with you. Step back and strategize – choose which battles are important. You are allowed ONE major battle per project. BUT don't fail to fight the important battles – you are not a doormat!

4. **Use solutions-based thinking.** Pursue answers instead of dwelling on the problem. "We burned the irreplaceable vintage rayon with the iron" can quickly devolve to blame-game hysterics. Acknowledge the problem and move right to brainstorming solutions.

5. **Use Wonder Woman bracelets.** Some difficult people belittle or intimidate others so they will look powerful. Sidestep and deflect. If you are ambushed, acknowledge they are upset – "*I can see this is very important for you*" – or thank them for bringing a problem to your attention. Keep power over your area, do not give it to a bully.

6. **Dry the wet blankets.** Some people are mired in negativity, making every problem seem too large. Have stock phrases at hand to steer back to solutions-based thinking. Asking wet blankets to envision a possible solution is useful "*What could it look like if we try this?*"

(Continued)

Table 19.2 (Continued)

7. Learn what others know. It's easy to confuse leadership with knowing everything. Listen and learn from what other people know. They may provide new information, or they just want someone to tell their knowledge to – a great way to bond. Others want to contribute to the project, too.	**9. Protect your team.** Never throw a team member under the bus. If the costume area did not deliver something as planned, a leader steps forward to take responsibility and focus on solutions.
	10. Be the expert, not the victim. If you need help – more time, money, or resources, you will gain credibility by addressing the problem early, instead of waiting until a crisis. All storytellers know the value of a good prop – have a spreadsheet or other analysis to show you've thought this through. Then others will solve the problem for you – it's truly miraculous!
8. Use the toddler rule. Sometimes we are asked to do the impossible. Let others help you set priorities or a solution. But you set the parameters, much like a toddler who wants a snack. "*Would you like cheddar fish or a granola bar?*" Most won't notice you omitted alternatives like "*Snickers.*" When they help with outcomes, others buy into the solution, and you offered workable possibilities you could truly deliver.	
	11. Cry in the car on the way home. There is no crying in costumes, but that *is* what your car is for. If you *must* cry, stroll to the parking lot for a dignity-saving break.

Leading From Behind

Creative teams can be particularly tricky to lead. They do not respond to authoritarian techniques. Many creatives have traded away the opportunity to make more money with less creative jobs. Instead they look for a purposeful meaning for their work. As corporations are just now discovering, this means being mindful of employee engagement. An engaged team member is one who believes in the goal and can bring their own contribution to the final result. Artisans cannot do their jobs adequately if constantly undermined or admonished to do as they are told; they must make thousands of decisions in their part of the work using an artistic vision to inform their judgment. Nelson Mandela describes the kind of leadership that works well with creative teams. He calls it *leading from behind*. He calls those leaders *shepherds* that look far down the road, nudging a flock out of danger or toward more desirable destinations.[2] The irony of this style of leadership is being willing to give up the appearance of traditional power. There will be plenty of opportunities to step forward during difficulties to make those wrenching decisions or to be the one to take responsibility.

Recognizing Team Dynamics

Human behavior is unpredictable, and can be more so when we work in a group. Contrasting personalities or too many similar personalities can affect the way work gets done. Leading and participating in teams is difficult work, and not every person is temperamentally suited to it. The so-called soft skills of people management and leading collaborations are highly prized leadership skills. We progress more rapidly in those skills when we develop an awareness of team dynamics. Awareness begins

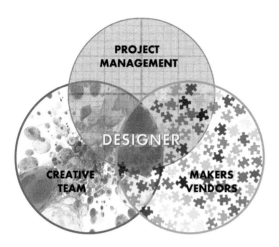

Figure 19.2 Costume designers participate in three interconnected teams.

MULTIPLE INTELLIGENCES

Figure 19.3 Multiple intelligences.

with a system identifying typical interactions between team members.

Design projects ask costume designers to participate with three interconnected webs of teams:

- The creative team of director, co-designers, and actors
- The project management team of production and stage managers, department heads, and upper management
- The costume makers, costume shop, vendors, and wardrobe staff

There are two major sources of research that established a theory of team dynamics. The first is the theory of *multiple intelligences* developed in 1983 by Dr. Howard Gardner at Harvard. He theorized the one-dimensional IQ tests commonly used at that time that did not quantify how people actually interact with the world. The diagram in Figure 19.3 illustrates eight ways people can be smart. For instance, a dancer can be Bodily-Kinesthetic smart, learning nuanced physical moves more rapidly than others. They express themselves in physical or embodied creativity. Many people excel in more than one intelligence. While Dr. Gardner envisioned this information as a way to identify different learning styles, this information works very well as advice for communicating with a team member. One example may be a team member such as a draper who understands things best by

hearing you describe an idea. Another may need visual representation to process the same information. A third may have to try solutions with their hands before understanding the concept. Knowing how to communicate with team members will improve information flow and allow everyone to buy into the success of the project. This approach embraces that everyone brings different skills and experience to a project and may approach tasks differently.

The second source of team dynamics comes from the research of Dr. Meredith Belbin who studied team behaviors at the Henley Business School in the UK. Dr. Belbin eventually formed his own company that consults with institutions about the teams they form, and the role of each individual collaborator in the team. Individuals may also be analyzed by Belbin for their **team role** types. Belbin notes that teams are made of individuals with a diverse mix of talents and behaviors. He defines these as nine major clusters of behaviors, each with strengths.[3]

- **Resource investigator** – Inquisitive, resourceful, finds ideas to bring back to the team
- **Team worker** – Helps the team work well, versatile and group oriented

- **Co-Ordinator** – Focuses on goals, delegates work, and draws out team members
- **Plant** – Highly creative and solves problems in unconventional ways
- **Monitor evaluator** – Uses logic and impartiality to assess situations
- **Specialist** – Brings deep knowledge of specific skills and knowledge
- **Shaper** – Provides momentum and focus, thrives on pressure
- **Implementer** – Creates workable strategy, practical, reliable, efficient
- **Completer finisher** – Detail oriented, quality control, polishes the work

Each role contributes obvious strengths to the team. But each role will also have what Belbin terms *allowable weaknesses* defining qualities that may ultimately prove unproductive within a team. When we are very good at something there is often an accompanying blind spot in our abilities. Teams will work more gracefully if they understand their weakness is the flip side of their strength, not a personality flaw. Team leaders can lead more gracefully by acknowledging strengths and finding ways to offset allowable weaknesses. This can begin with our own work – if the designer is a Plant, he many need an Implementer to translate ideas to reality. And certainly the designer may need Specialists to make costume pieces, paint them or create hats. An individual's traits may sometimes change when working with a different team. Smart people, says Ed Catmull, a co-founder of Pixar Animation Studios, almost certainly will buck up to do things we aren't naturally good at doing or don't enjoy doing when a team needs that skill.[4] Belbin calls this a *team role sacrifice* where individuals take on work that is normally uncomfortable to advance the goals of the team. We often say we are "taking one for the team" when we agree to an unpleasant task.

Using the preceding categories defined by Belbin, it is possible that a team formed with all Plants would be highly creative but might ignore details or need help finishing tasks. Understanding each role lends a productive vocabulary to discuss progress and monitor a team without falling into the trap of blame and resentment. It can be difficult to critique the work or progress by team members because we are afraid if we upset them, they will slow down or do poor work. This is especially stressful when we work with peers, friends, underpaid staff, or volunteers that might lose morale. Thinking of a team through its roles and dynamics allows the creative leader to ask for help and frame upcoming tasks using specific expectations.

> "Collaboration means building on the capability to find new solutions, combine components, and continuously adapt. In this sense, communication demands the same creative attitude as designing a costume or composing a song – since there is no one solution for every situation, a broad repertoire of experiences supports flexibility and exploring the unknown."[5]

Collaborative Leadership

Everyone on a creative project wants to feel some ownership of the final result, and most projects benefit from brainstorming with others. Yet a design-by-consensus will soon wobble from its vision or grind to a halt while everyone discusses all options. The *Harvard Business Review* identified four skills that top leaders possess.[6]

- **Form connections.** Create or maintain ties to many points of view that link people and ideas. In costumes this includes being an efficient connector from the director and rehearsal hall to the costume shop and visiting the scene and prop shops to keep up with the entire creative picture. Report to the costume shop what the project is doing on a large scale. Connections can also mean sharing the larger world of professional events and resources with others, empowering others to share as well.
- **Foster diversity.** Attract the best talent and create teams that represent many points of view whether cultural, linguistic, generational, or through differing disciplines. Empower people with different experiences to contribute, and resist homogenizing everyone into imaginary ideals.

- **Model collaboration.** Set the tone by actively collaborating with colleagues and peers, avoiding the sabotage of turf battles in an organization.
- **Maintain vision.** It is possible to overdo collaboration. Groups cannot always act quickly or may grind into a bureaucracy. Effective collaborative leaders still maintain the ultimate responsibility for the group and its outcome, knowing when to make a final decision. In costumes, the designers must ultimately ensure their costumes gel with the director's vision and the other designers' work.

Solutions-Based Thinking

Solutions-based thinking is a large component of design thinking. It encourages practical and innovative solutions in the face of ambiguity or chaos by trying iterations of ideas. If the first solution does not work, creative thinkers learn from that attempt and create the next version. This style of thinking avoids blame for mistakes made in the pursuit of knowledge, and it lends itself well to leading teams. Every project presents times when the designer may have to express disappointment if things are not going as planned, if work is not progressing or it is lower quality than desired. The typical employment arrangements in theater add to the difficulties: costume designers often lead teams that do not work directly for them. In many cases the costume shop staff works for the theater or a vendor, and the costume designer is hired for just one show. If the designer is not the actual boss, all they can do is lead by persuasion. Each situation requires real-time assessment, but there are some rules of thumb to help navigate correcting work in a positive manner.

- **Lead with the positive.** Begin a conversation with praise first. Is this person a fast worker, a careful worker, innovative? "This looks beautiful, and you've put so much work into it!"
- **Use "I" sentences.** Express your own feelings and expectations, do not blame the person working. "I thought it would look more like this" keeps the conversation rolling, where "You didn't listen to me" is confrontational.

- **Avoid blaming.** Don't make negative generalizations. "Why can't this shop do straight hems!" demoralizes a work force or causes them to stop listening to you. If a glaring mistake occurs, first focus on a solution. Circle back to discuss the situation when everyone is calmer.
- **Use questions.** First try to draw the person into the solution rather than associate them with the problem. "Will you take a look at this with me? Now that I see it, I can tell the hem is bubbling. How can we fix that?" The conversation steers directly to solutions and avoids how it might have gone wrong in the first place. If they don't know how to fix it, offer your solution. "Let's start with cutting every third stitch right here to see if we can pull it looser."
- **Take responsibility.** It is all too easy to miscommunicate in our business, and sometimes we just change our minds. "I realize on the rendering it looked like that, but it doesn't look like I imagined." Using this tactic even if you did *not* cause confusion is a good way to remind everyone there is a final vision and it may take several tries to get there.
- **Become a detective.** Many situations that went wrong are reported by third parties who may not have all the facts. If faced with a volatile situation, suspend all judgment. Seek everyone's side of the issue. "The crew wasn't able to do that fast change, the costume has to change" is an assumption if it is uttered by anyone other than the wardrobe crew. Find out what happened before making any decisions.
- **Use stories.** Provide insight into why something may not work or lessons learned. Share from your experience and listen to others' tales of hard-earned knowledge. "A draper I worked with when I was an apprentice taught me *this* method. Let me tell you, I was scared to death of her!"
- **Protect your team.** When things go wrong, never throw a costume team member under the bus if your area made a mistake or the director or producer is unhappy. No matter how hard it may be, acknowledge the costume is incorrect and focus on a solution. Remember

Nelson Mandela's words that leaders take the front line when there is danger.

All of these techniques provide elegant ways to approach mistakes, offer critique, and motivate a team member. Another approach to effective critique is to determine *who* you should express concerns with. When do you speak directly to the person doing the work, and when do you talk with their supervisor? Speak with the supervisor if the issue has to do with timetables or overall quality of work, not just a specific task. Some shops don't want the designer giving any directions to workers – they prefer only supervisors discuss changes as it may affect the final cost or employee time cards. Adding a large dose of humor to any situation is a guaranteed booster in difficult situations.

Unleash Your Inner Weasel

Ultimately, every designer has to bear the responsibility for the show alone. No one loves your show as much as you do; the costume designer is the fairy godmother for their own production. As loyal or as dedicated as others may be, they may be working on several projects. They will take their rightful days off, they will keep their medical appointments or pick up their children from day care. Every designer needs a healthy dose of charisma or, lacking that, the ability to wheedle or even shamelessly huckster like a used car dealer. If the costumes encounter obstacles, the designer may be the only one motivated to find a solution. Every designer must have an inner weasel that can persuade, cajole, and scheme to get the work done. That inner weasel may have to go into stock and not come out until an old suit has been completely reimagined. That inner weasel may have to charm someone into sewing beads onto a dress they weren't planning to do. The inner weasel may have to wrack its brain for new ideas when everyone else has given up. And that inner weasel often has to smooth over difficult requests from the director that affects the workload of the costume shop – all while delivering well-timed cupcakes.

One young designer worked a day job early in her career researching land deeds for a retail company. She drove around target neighborhoods

Figure 19.4 Every designer needs an inner weasel.
Credit: Unknown, *Nursery Nonsense* ca. 1865 via Old Book Illustrations.com

looking for dilapidated properties. Then she would go to City Hall to research the official survey maps and tax records to see if the property was in arrears. The staff at City Hall was used to her showing up with lists of requests for records they'd have to pull from an inconvenient storage room. While it was their job to accommodate citizen requests, it was yet another thing they had to do on top of all their other tasks. They could be a bit crusty on occasion. Working with scenic and costume shops had taught this designer the effectiveness of a charming inner weasel who brought donuts on occasion; proving that theater training is excellent preparation for life.

Dealing With Difficult People

Try as we might, the costume designer is not going to charm everyone. Some people are just not going to like us. We walk into different environments with individual work cultures. We adapt to each situation and figure out how to get our vision within that environment. Some theaters may employ individuals who are cranky or entrenched in their ways. There may have been years of power plays or turf wars the designer cannot get involved with. One stage manager at a new regional theater started his first conversation with a costume designer by saying "I don't like costume fittings and you won't get any of your fittings during rehearsal hours." At times like this, it is wise to have a few tricks up our sleeves to work with difficult personalities. The good part of show business is that every show *does* end, and that difficult work relationship does not have to be forever. The most important factor is to never lose your temper or allow people to push your emotional triggers. The longer you can stay in the conversation the more chance you have to engage that person productively. Look for the hidden need – what does this person *really* want? It usually boils down to a basic human need such as to be respected or taken seriously. Another important strategy is to imagine that negativity is like quick sand – if you stand too close too long, it will pull you down, too. Don't play into a negative conversation. There are many strategies to guard your own psyche, as well as work productively.

Expecting the Unexpected

People who work in theater are passionate about their work. They pour their hearts and lives into a project. Add the pressure cooker of stress, limited time, or limited budgets and it is almost a guarantee that emotions will run high at times. For every wonderful experience there might be an awful situation or embarrassing failure. For every time a collaborator improved your work, your vision will be trampled by those who don't understand what you're trying to do. The budget just wasn't enough to accomplish your usual style or quality, or you loved the work but received harsh notices from the critics. No one faces as much rejection and public critique as theater people. There will be times you are so angry or frustrated or mad that you want to break something or burst into tears. Learn what

helps you relieve stress so that you can return to the job with an open heart. Theater is a very small community where everyone is connected by just two or three degrees of separation. Don't burn any bridges. You *will* need them in the future.

Sizing Up Leadership

Creative teams do not respond to traditional authoritarian leadership. Costume designers find themselves leading creative teams they don't actually employ, instead relying on tools such as persuasion, people skills, and an understanding of team dynamics. Collaborative leaders focus on solutions-based thinking to focus and motivate team members. But every costume designer must be willing to deploy their inner weasel if necessary.

Extra Resources

Belbin® Team Roles www.belbin.com/
Working with Difficult People: Handling the Ten Types of Problem People Without Losing Your Mind. Amy Cooper Hakim, Muriel Solomon, Penguin, 2016
Managing Difficult People: A Survival Guide for Handling Any Employee. Marilyn Pincus, Adams Media Corporation 2004

Notes

1 Terri Morrison. "Bite the Wax Tadpole." *Industry Week*, December 21, 2004. https://www.industryweek.com/the-economy/trade/article/21949510/bite-the-wax-tadpole
2 Lizza, Ryan. 2011. "Leading from Behind." *The New Yorker*, April 26, 2011. https://www.newyorker.com/news/news-desk/leading-from-behind
3 Belbin. n.d. "Belbin Team Roles." Accessed February 4, 2020. https://www.belbin.com/about/belbin-team-roles
4 Catmull, Ed. 2008. "How Pixar Fosters Collective Creativity." *Harvard Business Review*, September. https://hbr.org/2008/09/how-pixar-fosters-collective-creativity
5 Niermann, Timo. 2019. *Collaborating Backstage*. New York: Methuen Drama, p. 19.
6 Ibarra, Herminia, and Hansen, Morten T. 2011. "Are You a Collaborative Leader?" *Harvard Business Review*, July–August. https://hbr.org/2011/07/are-you-a-collaborative-leader

PART SIX

PRODUCTION

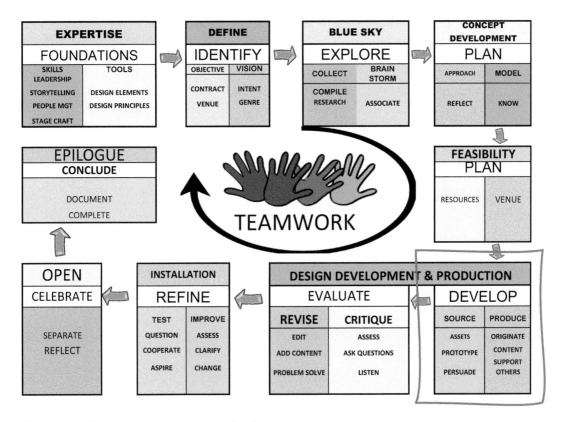

Figure 20.0 The creative process for produced projects.

Credit: Holly Poe Durbin and Ayrika Johnson

20.
PULL IT TOGETHER

Sourcing and Organizing Costumes

A young designer was negotiating for a higher fee with a producer who didn't believe that pulling costumes for a show was worth more money than the fee offered. "The set has to be built from scratch," he explained. "Won't you *just* go to a rental house where the costumes already exist?" The particular house in question was Western Costumes in Los Angeles: a warehouse that covers nearly six football fields. She explained that it took special expertise to pull from a rental house. Many racks were double or triple hung with clothing, requiring hundreds of steps up and down ladders while carrying clothing, not to mention dragging heavy ladders from one aisle to the next. Besides the physical labor, it required a flawless organizational system to accomplish the task in a timely manner. She used advanced expertise for garment styling and sizing systems to choose the *right* shirt from a rack of 300 shirts. Ever since that conversation, that designer kept a photo of those warehouse racks on her phone to show future producers. While not every costume storage is as vast as this one, each presents its own challenges: driving to sketchy neighborhoods, negotiating ancient freight elevators, climbing ladders, lugging heavy costumes up or down racks or staircases, hauling heavy boxes up and down metal shelving, tearing your clothing on protruding bolts, decoding unique storage systems, dim light, accumulated dust, unheated rooms, overheated rooms or rooms with no air flow, and hunting far and wide for something that was returned to the wrong spot. Pushing heavy clothing to one side of a rack to get a view of the garments strains shoulder joints and muscles resulting in repetitive injuries. And all during this physical labor, the costume designer must rely on judgment honed from specialized character analysis, styling expertise, and aesthetic vision to make hundreds of decisions.

Pulling costumes together can be rigorous mental work and hard physical labor. But it is also the exciting moment when ideas on the page take physical form. The most important skills a costume designer needs in this phase of the design process is the ability to see the *potential* in finished garments, and making efficient decisions. Some garments look incorrect at first glance, but may show clues they can be restyled for this show. Every decision must honor the artistic intent, so designers may make more decisions about what *doesn't* work than what does. This phase creates a third modeling step of the creative process: the first two were the research collage and design sketch. Assembling items from stock, purchases, and rentals is an efficient way to explore a design. Some costume designers consider this phase to be the place where they actually create the design.

DOI: 10.4324/9781003015284-26

Figure 20.1 The warehouse of Western Costumes covers about eight acres in North Hollywood, California.
Credit: Photos by Michael Millar

Figure 20.2 Creating character ideas using garments in costume stock for ideas.

Costume Measurements

Accurate measurements are absolutely critical to sourcing costumes. Nothing results in a misuse of

time and bruised egos more than fitting an actor in the wrong sizes. Even though accurate measurements are so important, methods of measuring may vary from one shop to the next. Some measurers insert a finger between the measuring tape and the body, thus ensuring **ease** or breathing room. Others measure with the tape directly against the performer's body, knowing they will add their own ease. The exact method to measure diagonal angles such as bust points vary from one place to another – some measure from the shoulder, some measure down the princess seam, and others measure from the side waist up. Every costume shop asks performers for their retail sizes for purchased clothing such as underwear, shirts, shoes, suits, and trousers, but how useful are those sizes? Chapter 17 explored some strategies for accumulating rough measurements or estimating sizes ahead of time for planning. This chapter explains using accurate measurements to assemble the show.

Every costume designer and assistant must know how to measure an actor should they find themselves doing this task early. A resident shop will take measurements ahead of the production period or, at the latest, on the days around first rehearsal. If the designer must act alone, and the actor and designer are in the same location, it is worth asking the theater if the acting contract allows an early measurement session. In extreme cases, it may be necessary to hire a costumer in the actor's location for a few hours to take measurements and photos. See Table 20.1 for a sample full measurement sheet.

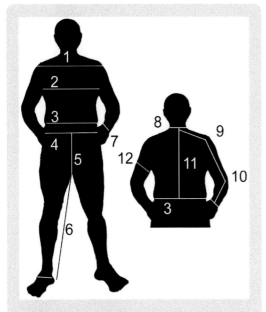

Figure 20.3 Silhouette for measures.

These measurements represent the basic information to pull or purchase costumes. Measurement for made-to-order costumes require more extensive measurements, see Table 20.1.

1 – Across shoulders front, back. Feel for the bony edge of the clavicle.

2 – Chest circumference. At fullest point, keeping tape measure parallel to floor.

3 – Natural waist. Tie a string or elastic around their waist and ask the actor to raise, lower arms.

4 – Trouser waist. Check where the actor currently wears their trousers.

5 – Crotch depth or rise. Ask the actor to sit on a chair, measure from side waist to chair seat top.

6 – Inseam. Ask the actor to hold the tape measure at a comfortable spot, measure to top of foot.

7 – Wrist circumference around the wrist bones.

8 – Neck at the join of shoulders, low neck.

9 – Center back to shoulder.

10 – Shoulder to wrist, with arm bent. For full shirt sleeve, measure from CB to wrist.

11 – Torso length, nape of neck to waist, front and back.

12 – Bicep circumference at largest spot.

Taking measurements is an invasive action; we are asking to touch another person's body. All actors feel some vulnerability during this process, and not all understand what the measurements are. It is natural to worry about being judged. Costume designers may alleviate some of this anxiety using an inclusive measurement etiquette.

• Use common sense to set up a measurement session. Find a discrete location out of sight of others. Never be alone in a closed room with a performer; keep a door open or ask an assistant or family member for child performers to attend.

• When setting the appointment, ask the actor to wear specific styles of underwear that may affect their body shape. For instance, if the costumes will be 1950s styles, ask if the actor might wear a bra with shaped cups, if possible, not a sports bra.

• Do not announce numbers so that others may hear. Moderate your voice or, if an actor is visibly nervous, write the numbers silently using signals between you and an assistant to read the measuring tape.

• Intimacy protocols notes we ask permission before touching a colleague every time – consent given once is not implied forever.

• Ask permission to tie a contrast color elastic or string around the actors waist. Take the time to carefully set it at the smallest circumference in the torso, or the natural waist.

• Always **explain & ask** throughout, dividing the body into zones. As you reach each zone, explain what measurements you will take and ask to touch that zone. Usable zones are (1) head and neck, (2) torso, (3) arms, (4) hips and

Table 20.1 Measurement Form. This form contains the measurements a costume shop needs to draft patterns, and a costume designer could use this form to extrapolate purchasing sizes. It uses a nonbinary approach to measuring the human body.

Costume Shop Measurement Form		
First Name		Last Name
Date:		Pronouns (optional):
Cell #:		Height:
Role/Show:		Weight:
Ready-to-Wear		
Undershirt (S/M/L):	Shirt (16x32/6):	Bra (if applicable):
Pant:	Dress/Suit:	Tights/Socks:
Street Shoe:	Preferred hand:	Contacts/Glasses:
Allergies:		Visible tattoos/piercings?
Head & Neck		
Ear to ear (overhead):		Neckline:
Hatband – crown:		Front hairline to nape:
Torso		
Overbust:	CF neck to waist:	Armseye to armseye (front):
Bust/Chest:	Armseye to waist:	CB Neck to waist:
Chest Expansion:	Shoulder to bust:	Shoulder to shoulder (back):
Ribcage/Underbust:	Shoulder to shoulder (front):	Armseye to armseye (back):
Waist:		Half girth:
High hip: @	Low hip: @	Full girth:
Arm		
CB to wrist (sleeve length):	Shoulder seam:	Forearm:
Shoulder to wrist bone:	Armseye:	Wrist:
Shoulder to elbow:	Bicep:	Hand Circumference (glove size):
Elbow to wrist bone:	Elbow:	Ring size:
Leg		
Rise (seated):	Ankle:	Waist to floor (outseam):
Thigh:	Waist to below knee:	Inseam:
Knee:	Waist to ankle (outseam):	CB to floor:
Calf:		
Notes:		

Credit: Courtesy of Ayrika Johnson, D. Larsson, Cassie Defile, Julie Keen

legs. For instance, explain that you will take three measurements on the arm – a bicep, an arm length, and a shirt sleeve length from the center back. If possible, show the performer on your own body what those are.

- Be understanding if a performer is not comfortable with certain questions or measurements on that day; it is possible to deduce some measurements with partial information or call them back another day.
- For inseam measures, always use a **tailor's inseam tape** with a frame attached to the top of the tape. Ask the performer to place the tape where their torso joins their leg, asking them to judge a comfortable crotch depth. If the actor is wearing trousers similar to the style you want, measure the waist and inseam of the trousers themselves in addition to the body. If the actor is uncomfortable with trouser measurements, ask them to bring in a pair of trousers later that fit well and measure those instead.

Some costume shops use nonbinary measurement sheets to reframe the conversation about gender and clothing assumptions. Some retain the tradition of binary measurements reflecting a division of labor between dressmakers and tailors. Freelance costume designers will work with other people's systems routinely as they work in different shops and it is important to ask questions with patience and humor about how key measurements are taken.

There are two measurements that consistently cause confusion: the **shirt sleeve** and the **trouser waist**. The trouser waist fluctuates with fashion; in some eras it is the same as the natural waist, and in many contemporary fashions it is below the natural waist. We measure the height of the trouser waist using a measurement from crotch seam to waist band, called the **rise**. As you measure the actor, take note of how far below their natural waistline (marked with contrast string) the trouser waistline sits. If you are aware ahead of time of the desired pants waist placement for this show, measure the waist *at that spot*. The second confusing measurement is the **dress shirt sleeve**, which is different from the arm length. The arm length measures from shoulder bone to wrist bone and is most often used in drafting patterns, or measuring women's sleeve

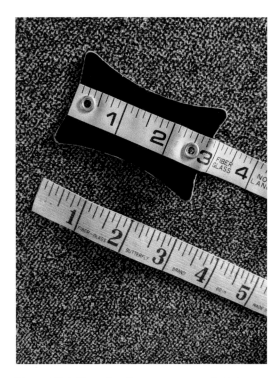

Figure 20.4 The tailors inseam tape at top includes a hard frame called a crotch piece.

lengths. The dress shirt sleeve measures from the center back (CB) between the shoulder blades to the finished shirt sleeve length – the intersection where the hand joins wrist.

Finished Garment Measurements – Lost in Translation

Most costume designers spend more time assessing existing garments than building made-to-order garments. They assess costume stock, vintage items, and retail purchases that are compatible with their design. Costumers experienced with pulling and shopping develop an understanding of the typical fit for each decade, and the fit expected in different retail brands. They have a clear understanding of the finished garment. All manufactured garments are made using specific formula for sizing – as each size goes up, the garment is correspondingly longer and wider, and the placement of neckline and **armseye** (the seam around the armpit) shifts. The US government created standard sizing for consumer clothing in 1941 but eased those definitions in the 1970s. By 1983 manufacturers abandoned them altogether, returning to the pre–World War II practice of

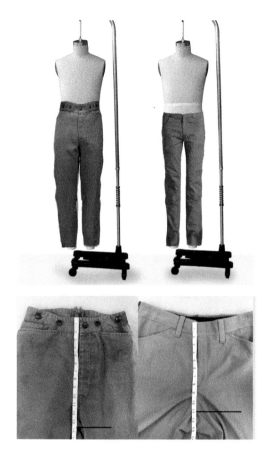

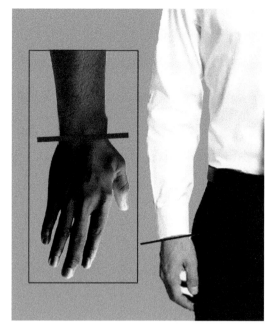

Figure 20.6 The proper length for a dress shirt is the root of the thumb, where the hand meets the wrist.

anything goes. Menswear still retains standard sizing, although that is rapidly declining as casual clothing floods the market. Costumers quickly master the art of judging whether a costume drooping awkwardly on the hanger will be a suitable style and fit on the actor's body.

Figure 20.5 Trouser waists fluctuate according to fashion. The tan trousers at left use a rise of 13 5/8 inches with zipper length 10 inches. The gray trousers at right show a rise of 11 and zipper length 8½ inches.

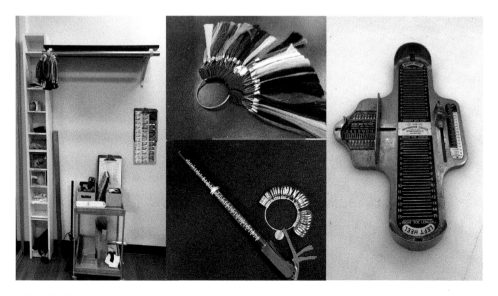

Figure 20.7 Designers may use extra items in a measuring or fitting kit. This fitting room shows extra items on shelves such as t-shirts, bust pads, and shoulder pads. Other extras include a Braddock shoe size device, ring sizers, hair color swatches, and a skin tone guide printed from NARS® Cosmetics online.

Finished garments reflect that **ease** and other considerations are added. **Wearing ease** is a small amount of additional room to allow movement and eliminate chafing or sticking. **Style ease** is any extra amount added by designers to achieve a specific silhouette. Every garment includes one if not both forms of ease, so the measurement of a garment on the hanger is not the same as the measurement of the body that will fit into it. For instance, a blouse made of tightly woven fabric with a chest measure of 36 inches will best fit a body with a chest measurement of approximately 34 to 35 inches to allow movement and breathing. Table 20.2 provides the average amount of ease in different styles of clothing. Although designers ask actors about their retail sizes, always use judgment – while the sizes may be correct, it is just as likely they may not be. If a size appears to be wrong given the larger picture, use manufacturer's size guides available online to try to make sense of the information.

In a Pinch: Working Without Adequate Measurements

When lead times are short, the costume designer may have to pull the majority of costumes before adequate measurements are available. It is possible to parlay partial information into an educated guess, particularly if photos of the actors are available for comparison. Any size information provided may be translated using that final remains of the standard sizing system used by the *Wolf Form Company*, and sizing systems provided by *SizeGuide.net*. These systems provide very basic measurements only. One complete standard measurements system was compiled by blogger Lauren Dahl. She collected information over several years, adjusting them to contemporary shopping using large brands such as Madewell, J Crew, and Banana Republic. She

has provided a free chart for download (see Extra Resources) that includes over 40 pattern drafting measurements for each standard US size. Keeping in mind how well people do or do not fit into standard sizing, it is still an outstanding starting point.

Organizing to Pull Costumes

Most costume storage systems are divided into sections or separate rooms, sometimes even separate buildings. Yet every show uses hundreds of items. Breaking the costumes into manageable units and cutting down on zigging back and forth between locations will save time, heavy labor, and stress. For instance, one costumer with a shoe list can pull all shoes at the same time, while another goes to a main warehouse to pull tailored suits or shirts. Chapter 17 discussed creating the **costume list**, a form that provides information of what's needed, but also allows the designer to track what options were or were not found in each source. There is another form that many use when pulling or purchasing costumes; the measurement **cheat sheet** (Table 20.3). The cheat sheet arranges only the information required in a consistent format on one page, preventing shuffling through sheaves of paper, bulky notebooks or multiple digital files when pulling. Many a costumer accidentally lost their list somewhere under a rack and spent precious time retrieving it. The cheat sheet can be kept on a smart phone to retrieve as needed, or printed so more than one person can use it.

There are several methods used to pull costumes. The first is the designer pulling one character at a time, stopping to match items and making decisions. This system works well for smaller shows and when there is adequate lead time. The second method is **bulk** pulling, useful for large shows,

Table 20.2 Typical Wearing Ease in Finished Garments

	Tight Fit	Fitted	Semi-Fitted	Loose Fit or Boxy
Chest Shirts, Dresses, Tops	1½–2 inches	2–2½ inches	3 inches	4 inches or more
Tailored Jacket Chest	1½ inches	2 inches	3–4 inches	4 inches or more
Waist	1 inch	1½ inches	2–3 inches	4 inches or more
Hip Area Pants, Skirts, Tunics, Dresses	2 inches	2–3 inches	3–4 inches	4–6 inches

Table 20.3 Measurement Cheat Sheet Organizes Information to Speed the Task of Pulling Costumes

ACTOR	CHARACTER	HEIGHT	WEIGHT	SHIRT	PANT	CHEST	WAIST	HIP	SHOE	BRA	SUIT COAT/DRESS
Michael CHOO	Levinson	5' 9"	175	16.5/33	34/30	42	38	41.5	10		40–42R
Jesus DEVARGAS	Stokely C										
Mark MILLER	Strom Thurmond	5' 11"	158	15/33	32/32	37.5	33	38	10.5		40R
Jeff THOMAS	Wallace, Corman	5' 10.5"	150	15.5/33	32/32	40	33	39	9		40R
Max FREEMAN	Abernathy, Butler	6' 2"	230	17/37	36/34	42.5	37.5	45	12		44L
Bill SPIVEY	Deloach	5' 10"	160	15.5/33	32/31	42	34	39	9		40R
John MAYOR	R. Russell										
Darren LOPEZ	Walter Jenkins	6' 0"	170	17/35	31/31	39	32	41	10.5 11		40R
Hallie EARNEST	Lady Bird	5' 5"	105	2–4	2–4	33	26	36.5	7	34B	2–4
Tony CHRISTIE	Coretta King	5' 6"	134	6		37	29	42.25	8	34B	6
Mary ERICS	Muriel Humphrey	5' 8"	150	10	12	38	30	40	7.5	36DD	12

shows with multiples such as uniforms, or when in a hurry. Dividing the costumes into categories also allows the designer to delegate tasks to others. It is possible to combine the methods using a two-step process. The first pull uses the bulk method, sweeping everything out of the warehouse that might work, reserving everything on racks as ***character closets*** or anything that character might wear. It will also become a reservoir of backup garments if first choice garments don't work. The designer schedules a second sorting through the character closet with more care later to create ensembles and note what is missing. Pulling costumes from any storage requires planning and adequate time. Table 20.4 shows that organizing, pulling, and transporting costumes can take anywhere from 9 to 20 hours for one person for every ten costumes; that time may be reduced by using more people to pull.

It's important to review and re-verbalize the design decisions before assembling the costumes. After so many planning steps it can be easy to forget the artistic intent. Other elements that will ease decision making while pulling costumes include:

- **Period cut**. Are you going for an accurate or suggested approach? Where does this garment fall on that spectrum?
- **Styling details.** Does it fit your vision, color scheme, and tone?
- **Fit.** Does the garment fit the actor in the way that right for the character?
- **Alterability.** Is there enough seam allowance or hem to alter the fit as needed? It is easier to alter the width of a garment and nearly impossible to alter torso length.
- **Adaptability.** Can certain style elements change to fit your design, such as eliminating or adding trim, changing dye color, adding new sleeves?
- **Durability**. Will it hold up to stage wear and tear? Are there hidden holes or stains? The best costume in the world will not be so if it dies in dress rehearsals.

Table 20.4 Table of Sample Costume Pulling Times

Task in Costume Storage	Estimated Time
Organize the pulling charts and measurements	2–5 hours
Learn the system and hunting around warehouse	30 minutes
Choosing and measuring costumes – per ten costumes	2–4 hours
Adding/matching accessories, undergarments, socks, belts – per ten costumes	2–4 hours
Sorting, sizing shoes – per ten costumes	1 hour
In Stock: Organizing the rack by character and options while pulling	30 minutes
In Costume Shop: Organize the rack by character and blend with items from other sources	1–3 hours
Total, approximate	**9:00 to 17:00**
Does not include commuting time to the rental source	
Opening an account and financial paperwork	30 minutes
Organize for checkout, obtain a checkout time (May return the next day to pick up rental order)	15 minutes
Copy and clear paperwork, check for correctness	30 minutes
Load into the car	20 minutes
Drive to new location – costume shop	30 minutes–2 hours
Unload in new location (inconvenient loading area or negotiating stairs/elevators add more time)	30 minutes–1 hour
Total in hours: minutes, approximate	**2:35 to 4:45**

Figure 20.8 Seams should include some additional allowance to prevent tearing. The trousers at right have been taken in so much the pockets almost touch, an effect called "kissing pockets." This choice may result in fuller leg widths, an effect that can be desirable for period looks.

Blending Built Costumes With Purchases and Stock

Ensuring a common look across the show is essential when blending a show from many sources and adding made-to-order costumes. We unify the stage picture using the art elements such as color and texture, silhouette, contrast, and reaction to light. How does this translate to unifying garments from different sources?

- Repeat **styling details** on pulled or built costumes on other garments.
- Consistent **intent** and style. Are the garments consistently formal, elegant, dressy, casual, or distressed and aged?
- **Color tone** used across the stage picture. Are any colors too desaturated, too saturated?
- **Undertones** used consistently. For instance, are all the browns from the same family such as red-brown or yellow-brown?
- Consistent **quality** of fabric. Do all fabrics share the desired distinction?
- Consistent style of **trim** – an easy way to unify the show.
- Consistent **scale** of dressmaker details.

Sourcing costumes asks the designer to weigh the role of the *perfect* and *good enough*. Few rental or purchased garments will match the design

Figure 20.9 These two costumes display a consistent color tone, but differ greatly in scale of details. The two costumes express very different intents.

exactly. The designer must decide how much to sacrifice, and how much to stick with the exact design. Making too many compromises will water down the design, and may even result in a confused final result. How much potential a designer sees in each garment will partly be driven by imagination and partly by logistics such as budget and labor to remake costumes extensively. Each designer must establish a hierarchy of potential to base decisions upon. It may be helpful to label each garment under consideration with a few categories in mind. If it is not an exact match, is it intriguing, promising, flawed, or tragic?

Vendor Relations

Sourcing requires cultivating excellent relationships with vendors and suppliers. The designer will often need a favor, such as the ability to pull on a day that is inconvenient for the vendor or to pull much more than will be used. The key to gaining and maintaining these relationships is to always act responsibly with the vendor's property. Handle their costumes gently and professionally. Do not stab tags or pins through the garment fabric – always use a seam to pin through for the least damage. Hang the costumes on racks to roll out to the car, if possible. Load and stack costumes gently, do not heave them into lumps in the back of the car. Mind their rules about garment alterations. Return the garments promptly with all paperwork in order. Arrange the garments on a return rack in the same order they are listed on the check-out sheet so they can check it in quickly. Use their recommended dry cleaner and return all items steamed or pressed. Confess to any damage or missing items, prepared to fix that with a substitution or financial payment. Make sure the vendor is paid on time, turn in your end of the paperwork promptly and act on their behalf by following up with the producer if payment is delayed. Costume designers who mishandle, destroy, lose, or fail to return costumes will develop a reputation for carelessness. Maintaining an excellent reputation with every vendor will ensure that you will be treated with respect in return.

Sizing Up Sourcing Costumes

Pulling costumes together can be rigorous mental work and hard physical labor. But many designers see this as the exciting moment when their ideas come to life. The most important skills a costume designer needs in this phase of the design process is the ability to see the *potential* in finished garments,

and making efficient decisions. Designers assemble costumes from many sources such as stock, vintage items and retail purchases. Experience with pulling and shopping develops an understanding of the typical fit for each decade, and the fit expected in different retail brands. Designers must unify these widely sourced costumes to create a stage picture using art elements and principles such as color, texture, silhouette, contrast, trim, and reaction to light.

Expecting the Unexpected – When Costume Storage Sizes Are Wrong

Many costume stocks measure and neatly tag every garment with a size. Unless you know that rental house's exact system well, never trust the numbers on the tags. Are you sure the person who measured that garment understands there is ease included in a finished piece? Has the same tag been returned to a garment after it was altered? It is not uncommon to encounter incorrect size and measurement information. Even though it adds considerable time to the pulling process, measure every costume at the chest, waist, and inseam to double check. American bodies have changed significantly over the past decades, and many costumes from earlier eras will be too small across the **back** or too short in the **torso** even if the chest and waist match.

Additional Resources

Printable Brannock Shoe Size Measurer, Samuel Hubbard Shoes www.samuelhubbard.com/blog/determining-your-shoe-size/

Standard Body Measurements & How to Create Your Own Size Chart, Lauren Dahl https://web.archive.org/web/201404 18133706/http://laurendahl.com:80/standard-body-measurements-create-size-chart/#navigation November 26, 2013

Wolf Form Company Measurements www.wolfforms.com/measurements/

*SizeGuide.Net*www.sizeguide.net/

A Quantification of the Preferred Ease Allowance for the Men's Formal Jacket Patterns, Hwa Kim, Yun Ja Nam & Hyunsook Han. Fashion and Textiles International Journal of Interdisciplinary Research. https://fashion andtextiles.springeropen.com/articles/10.1186/s40691-018-0165-x

21.
STYLING MENSWEAR

Until the influence of the Bechdel-Wallace test focused on the need for improvement, most scripts were written about men.[1] Male characters outnumber females and binary characters and they do the majority of the speaking.[2] Yet many fashion and costume educations emphasize women's wear only, leaving menswear to specialists or the vagaries of rental stock. The fact is a designer will most likely costume many more male actors than female. It is important to note that not every person wearing "menswear" identifies as male. This book uses the term *tailored garments* and *menswear* to describe clothing historically associated with men made with or influenced by tailor-made techniques. By understanding the traditions and goals of tailored garments it is possible to fit them on anybody. The tailored wardrobe is a fine art on its own, and every costume designer must own several thorough reference books on the subject (see Extra Resources).

Following Suit

Suits originated as clothing of the upper classes to project a confident authority. The predominance of large wars during the 19th century led to the invention of mass-produced military uniforms requiring systems to codify men's sizes. This important development led to the concept of ready-to-wear suits available to the public by the last half of the 19th century. The gold standard remained the custom-tailored suit carefully fitted to each customer, made with fine fabrics and handmade techniques. Those with a discerning eye could distinguish a better-quality suit from mass market suits, and that distinction is still true today. The ready-to-wear industry has gotten more sophisticated with its options over the years, but there remains the skill of sophisticated judgment to match the correct suit style to the body. If that step is ignored or miscalculated the result is an awkward appearance that advertises the wearer is not "in the club" of proper suit knowledge. At its most basic level, a suit is made of two or three matching parts: a jacket, trousers and

sometimes a waistcoat. There are distinctions in the jacket style that dictate when and why each is worn. Jackets fall into one of three categories, but all are called a jacket or coat for tailoring purposes:

- **Suit coat.** The dressiest of business attire made from wool or worsted, although summer versions may be made in cotton or linen. Accompanied by matching trousers. Suit jackets – even if sold as separates – are not properly worn without matching trousers as the subtle fabrics are usually a clue it was part of suit. It will look haphazard if not worn with its match. A suit is available as a single-breasted or double-breasted style.
- **Sport coat.** This least formal version of tailored jacket evolved from tweed hunting coats or "sporting" attire in the 19th century. Not intended to be worn with matching trousers, it retains a slight feel of sportiness by using casual fabrics, colors, and sometimes more eye-catching patterns. Buttons can be

DOI: 10.4324/9781003015284-27

SINGLE BREASTED
NOTCH LAPEL
OPEN QUARTERS

DOUBLE BREASTED
SHAWL LAPEL
CLOSED QUARTERS

SINGLE BREASTED
PEAK LAPEL
OPEN QUARTERS

Figure 21.1 The parts of a suit. For additional terminology, see Chapter 22.

domed, woven leather or traditional horn. Traditionally single-breasted styling.

- **Blazer.** A dressier version of the sports coat, considered a more formal version of sports attire. Derived from yachting coats, they were traditionally blue worn with gray, cream, or white trousers. In classic tailoring, the buttons are *only* domed, typically of gold, silver, or featuring crests. Available in both single- and double-breasted options. In contemporary practice blazer rules have relaxed somewhat.

The Parts of a Suit

Tailored suits are made of traditional styling elements that have evolved over two centuries. Designers mix and match these elements to create character statements. There are rules that dictate some styling choices.

Button style. The most obvious feature of any suit coat is how it buttons: **single breasted** features one row of buttons and the lapels meet at the center. **Double-breasted** features two vertical or V-shaped rows of buttons. The coat closes asymmetrically with one lapel lapped over the other.

Lapels. The second most visible element of suit styling, lapels fold away from the centerline to frame the shirt front, tie, and face. The three major contemporary styles are **peak**, **notch**, and **shawl** lapels. Lapel width and shape differ with each era of fashion

history. Current practice considers a lapel width of 3½ inches at the notch workable for most men, or 4 inches for a peak lapel. Wider lapels make the chest look larger, but may minimize the shoulders. Smaller lapels make the shoulders appear wider. Curved lapels are considered more relaxed, straight lapels more serious or traditional. The curve of the lapel can be called lapel **belly** (see Figure 21.1).

Notch lapels are considered the standard style, most often paired with single-breasted styling.

Peak lapels are more formal that notch lapels. They lend more authority or boldness. Although it is possible to combine peak lapels with single breasted styling, it is most often paired with double breasted styles.

Shawl lapels have no notch, tapering roundly from neck to the top button. Used mostly in tuxedos or dinner jackets.

Collar. A strap of fabric around the back of the neck sewn to the lapels. The collar stands in a fold to circle the neck and fit the jacket closely to the body. The height of the stand is a detail that changes from one era to the next and can be an important distinguisher of period tailoring. The collar is often finished on the bottom with melton wool that looks like flannel or felt.

Gorge. The triangle shape gap created where lapels and collar meet. The standard placement is for the gorge to align with the sternum. Contemporary suits place the gorge higher at the collar bone. Gorge placement rises and falls with each era of menswear, with earlier suits using a lower gorge. A high gorge can add visual width to the chest or height.

Shoulders. The area where the sleeve joins the body of the suit. The shoulder angle is created with padding. An **extended** shoulder is slightly wider than the wearers own body, such as styles popular in the 1980s and 1940s. A **roped** shoulder features sleeves set in with a standing ridge, creating a round peak or ropelike appearance. The **soft** shoulder features smaller pads that create a natural slope from neck to shoulder.

Waist suppression. The technical term for where a jacket cinches in to contrast with the shoulders. The classic suit creates a V-shape from the shoulders to waist.

Drop. The difference in inches between the chest or jacket size and the waist size on the suit trousers. Tailors use this to formulate drafting the parts of a suit. The standard drop is 6 inches or the difference between a 42-inch chest and a 36-inch waist.

Quarters. The two jacket fronts, right and left, below the waist button. The entire circumference below the waist button, front and back, is the **skirt**. There are two major styling features in contemporary tailoring.

Closed quarters meet in the center so that no leg is visible. Most obvious in a double-breasted suit or frock coat.

Open quarters slope or cutaway creating a gap with visible leg. In contemporary tailoring the quarters are shaped with a gentle curve. Suits are styled with more or less opening.

Vent. Vertical slits in the bottom hem of the jacket or skirt to allow a walking stride or ease of sitting. Traditional jackets offer the option of a single vent in the center back, double vents one on each side and no vent. Double vents are associated with British styling and ventless suits with Italian styling.

Rise. The distance in inches from the crotch seam to the waistband. The front rise is used to determine how long the zipper is, and if the pants are high or low waisted.

Suit Silhouette Guidelines

In the course of fashion history, three major schools of tailoring developed, each originating in a country that refined its own attitude toward fashion. Much of the difference in these styles depends on how the jacket shoulder is shaped: a result of padding or the angle of the cut. These schools offer variations in styling and details.[3]

English School

The original tailors of Saville Row influenced how the entire world wears jackets and trousers. The overall effect is conservative sobriety with careful attention to detail.

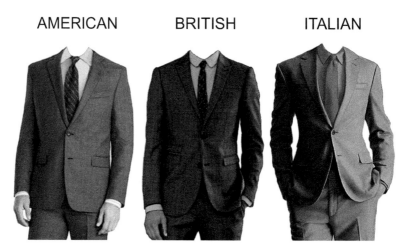

AMERICAN   BRITISH   ITALIAN

Figure 21.2 American, British, and Italian suits.

- *Structured* shoulder: padded shoulders that slope slightly
- *Roped* shoulder option on bespoke suits, sleeve stands slightly higher than shoulder
- Shoulder at sleeve seam appears sharp
- Heavy interior canvas constructions
- Slender fit
- Pronounced fit in a high waist silhouette
- High cut armholes that ease movement
- Three or even four sleeve buttons common
- Trouser pockets sewn into the side seam
- Double vents in jacket common, cut high into the back
- Extra drape across the back shoulder (blade) to ease movement
- Lower gorge (where lapel meets the collar)
- Surgeon's sleeves – sleeve buttons actually unbutton

American School

Brooks Brothers invented the first American-made style that was not just a copy of British tailoring: the 1920s *sack suit*. The sack featured a baggy cut in the torso and wider-legged trousers. Brooks hit on a formula for successful mass manufacture: a baggy style not only fit a broader range of people, but it appealed to the larger American body type. The sack was affordable and was soon seen everywhere, especially on young men. It established the foundation for the Ivy League style.[4] In its first form, American styling was shapeless, but in subsequent decades the suit became shapelier. It eventually gained world fame through Hollywood movies.

- Slightly padded, wider shoulder with natural slope

- Shoulder at sleeve seam appears flat
- Roomy fit, more emphasis on comfort
- Lower waist in jacket and trousers
- Larger armholes that create a larger top sleeve
- Two or three sleeve buttons common
- Fondness for flap pockets on jacket
- Diagonal pockets on trouser front
- Single vent in jacket most common
- Breaks some standard rules of tailoring styles

Italian School

Tailors from Naples and Rome created a silhouette that became a global influence in the 1960s, called the Continental style. Giorgio Armani was one of the first to bring a looser fit and softer shoulder to the Italian school of tailoring in the 1990s. The Italian style is more flamboyant than any other cut. Famous for their light suiting fabrics, some Italian materials have reset the standards for suits around the world.

- *Versatile* shoulders, featuring a *higher*, padded shoulder, OR
- *Soft* shoulder style from Naples, shoulder appears slightly rounded with small vertical wrinkles
- *Roped* shoulder for high end suits
- Body conscious fit
- Higher price suits include a special lapel that rolls over the top button when the jacket is not buttoned, reducing a three-button suit to a two-button (called a 3-roll-2 lapel)
- Higher waist in jacket, lower waist in trousers
- Narrow armholes
- Three sleeve buttons common
- Inset, flapless pockets (besom) in jacket common

A   B   C   D

Figure 21.3 Shoulder styles. A: British structured shoulder, also with roped shoulder detail. The lapel notch is placed high, near the collar bone. B: American natural shoulder. The classic notch lies near the sternum. C: Italian shoulder with a peak lapel. D: Extended shoulder from the 1940s is padded to be wider than the actual shoulder beneath it. Note the extended peak lapel.

- Ventless jacket back
- Light weight fabrics

Other schools of tailoring such as the French, German and Japanese methods derive from one or more of these foundational styles. The American customer also has choices between other variations of the **fit** to the body:

- **Classic cut.** The traditional American style with a noticeable but loosely fitting waist, traditional armholes and sleeves. Trousers are cut moderately wide to form a straight shape down the leg. Uses a traditional 6-inch *drop* (the difference between chest and waist measure). Cut with a standard 3–4 inches of *fitting ease* in the chest.
- **Executive cut.** This style accommodates the figure with a rounder belly. During the 19th century, when a large figured man stood for wealth and respectability, this cut was referred to as *portly* in tailoring manuals. The style includes a roomier jacket with a 4-inch *drop* (difference between chest and waist measure) but smaller drops are also available to a 0 drop, indicating the chest and waist measure the same. Generally uses classic fitting ease of 3–4 inches in the chest.
- **Athletic cut.** Features a wider chest, smaller waist, and roomier biceps and thighs or the V-shaped body. Features an extreme *drop* of 8 inches. Athletic cut suits are difficult to find in a wide range of styles and usually require additional alterations. Generally uses classic fitting ease of 3–4 inches in the chest.
- **Modern cut.** Updates the classic cut with a slightly trimmer fit in the shoulder, closer fit to chest, and slightly higher armholes. The trousers are slimmer in the seat and thigh. Waist band sits just below the classic trouser waist. Cut with a fitting ease of about 2 inches in the chest. Suitable for youthful or slender bodies.
- **Slim cut.** Contemporary fashion markets slim cuts and extreme slim cuts for fashion-forward customers. These cuts fit snugly at the chest, shoulders and waist with higher armholes and slimmer fitted sleeve. The gorge is placed very high on the shoulder line. Trousers are slim through the seat and thigh featuring a low rise and narrow leg opening at the hem. Most often styled with small lapels. Customers may wear a size larger in the slim and extreme cuts than they normally wear. Fitting ease is 1½ to 2 inches.

The Eye of the Beholder – Styling Details

The style and fit of the suit, shirt, and trousers are powerful choices to define each character. A traditional English style suit makes a conservative or posh statement, while the Italian style can look rakish and fashionable. In keeping with the spirit of tailoring, there are other details that will craft a character. Once a designer is aware of the dizzying array of details and decisions for every suit, how best to create the look that best works for each character? Each era of fashion develops its own rules. Most of these rules are based on reshaping the natural body to look more in line with fashion. There are eras that suppress the shoulders and those that enhance them, eras where the waist is small or nonexistent. Many suit styling details create *figure flattery*: elongating the figure to appear taller, as one uninterrupted column. Costume designers know how to use those rules for some characters, and how to break them to create other characters. For instance, the designer may wish to style a character to appear awkward and less proportionate. The generally accepted rules for contemporary tailored garments are as follows.

Styling Tall Bodies

The person 6 feet 2 inches or more is considered Tall, Long, and 6 feet 5 inches or over is X-Long for suit styling. Wearing a third piece such as a vest adds bulk. Avoid soft shoulders that make the suit look like it is slipping off the frame. Avoid pinstripes, which will make the body look even more slender, but checks and bolder patterns are possible. Judicious straight volume and skinny fit trousers are flattering. Balance the top and bottom proportions. Weighty fabrics such as flannel or tweed add bulk and shape. This body wears double breasted suits well. Tall legs can wear trouser cuffs well.

- **Tall, slender bodies.** Jackets with a narrow lapel make the chest appear broader; jackets with structured shoulders make the body appear squarer. Two-button suits fall well; three buttons make the chest look too long. Roped shoulders add definition. Style icons include RuPaul, James Harden, Lebron James, Conan O'Brien, Sacha Baron Cohen.
- **Tall, V-shaped bodies.** Jackets with structured shoulders enhance the shoulder line. Wear trousers with straight volume to balance the torso or fill small hips. Style icons: Dwayne Johnson, Jason Momoa, Chris Pratt, Hugh Jackman.
- **Tall, wider bodies.** Wear two-button jackets to elongate the upper body, the deeper neckline pulls focus upward to the face. A three-button jacket may work if the gorge is not too low. Padded shoulders may balance the bulk, along with wider lapels. Avoid checks and stripes in the suit, but consider them in the shirt to balance bulk. Style icons: Tyler Perry, Will Ferrell, Jimmy Smits.

Styling Regular Bodies

The person 5 feet 8 inches to 6 feet 1 inch is considered a Regular for suit styling. Most classic tailoring styles and fabrics were created for bodies in this category.

- **Regular, slender.** Slender bodies are in the enviable position of wearing just about anything, as well as adding layers and plaids for visual bulk. Style icons: Eddie Murphy, Trevor Noah, Kit Harrington, Hasan Minhaj, Johnny Depp, Anthony Mackie.
- **Regular, wider or V-shaped.** Fitting the shoulder is the key to a good-looking suit. Purchased shirts, jacket sleeves, and trousers may be too long. Every item should be custom hemmed to the correct length. If the shoulders are very wide, consider wearing athletic cut suits. Avoid horizonal stripes or large bulky jackets that compound the wider appearance. Wear slim but not skinny-fit trousers that will

look out of proportion. Wear tops close in color to trousers to avoid cutting the body in half. Style icons: Mike Tyson, Jamie Foxx, Mario Casas Sierra, Mario Cimarro.

- **Longer torso, short legs.** Wear similar colored shoes, socks, and trousers to elongate the leg. Wear a short rise in trousers – a dropped or sagging crotch cuts the legs in half. Wear suit jackets a little shorter to elongate the leg. Match belt to trousers to draw the eye away from the waist. Wear as high a waist trouser as fashion will allow to balance torso and legs. Avoid cuffs or turn ups. Avoid wide or pleated trousers. Tuck in shirts to avoid cutting off the legs, unless they are specifically hemmed to fall just below the belt. Style icons: Sylvester Stallone, Bruce Willis, Seth Rogan.

Styling Short Bodies

The person 5 feet 3 inches to 5 feet 7 inches is considered a Short for suit styling. The fitting requirements are more precise for shorter bodies, and even half an inch can make a difference to create the correct proportion. Make sure that low jacket pockets sit at or just above the hips and the front handkerchief pocket does not approach the arm pit. The jacket hem may need to be taken up a small amount to elongate the leg. One of the suit buttons should fall directly at the waist: with a two-button jacket that is the top button, for a three-button jacket the middle button should fall at the waist. Wear vertical patterns such as stripes, corduroy, herringbone, tweeds. Avoid plaids and large checks. Double-breasted suits add an elongating diagonal, but must fit the body extremely well to avoid adding puddles of fabric.

- **Short, slender.** Slender cuts that hug the body look best, with classic or slender lapels and narrow trousers. Monochromatic colors, such as a sport coat or shirt that is close in color to the trousers, or a full matched suit elongates the body. Use a short trouser rise to elongate the legs. Wear trousers with a slight break over the shoe, but not too much or the trousers will look too big. Uncuffed hems elongate the leg. Style icons: Diego Tinoco, Ken Jeong, Josh Hutcherson, Tom Cruise, Elijah Wood, Daniel Radcliff, Jet Li.

- **Short, wider, or V-shape.** Take great care to feature the face and shoulder, drawing the eye upward from the legs. A structured shoulder is a strong look, but be careful not to go to extremes, this will shorten the entire body. Lapels may be a bit wider. Style icons: Jonah Hill, Bruno Mars, Jack Black, Kevin Hart, Emilio Estevez.

Creating a Style Guide and Priorities

Tailors draft suits and trousers using geometric proportions. Each fashion era made subtle changes to tailored garments such as the rise, the width of the lapel, the circumference of the trouser leg at hip and ankle and other details. It can be extremely challenging to research these exacting details for a period show – even tailors find themselves collecting old tailoring manuals and measuring extant suits in museum collections. It is important for the costume designer to articulate the specific styles when pulling or purchasing tailored garments for a specific era. Otherwise, the characters may end up wearing a grab-bag of styles that do not create a clear picture. Apart from color and fabric, a few additional key components will create stronger consistency:

- **The rise** or height of trouser waist (or zipper length)
- **Pleats** or **flat front** trousers
- **Width of leg** at thigh or ankle
- **Shoulder padding**
- **Style and width of lapel** on suit jacket
- **Height of vest** closure
- **Suit buttons –** height of button placement or cross over to button
- **Shirt collar style**

The designer must also establish priorities. Which of these is the most important? If everything about a suit is correct except the leg width, is that an acceptable allowance? Will there be variances

allowed for each character? Understanding these requirements will make shorter work of sorting through many items in stock or storage. A style guide directs how to fit items on the actor. Figure 21.4 shows a menswear style guide created for a production set in the 1960s.

The last few decades have benefited from a renaissance in tailoring styles, with grooming and style advice readily available for those choosing to wear menswear. Many more resources are available online to guide the well-dressed gentleman or anyone who wishes to look like one. The same kind of advice is more plentiful in some eras than others. Costume designers must be good researchers, and one of the best skills needed is to accurately assess the advice, advertisements and photographs we find. How does a designer assess visual evidence to distinguish menswear styling? Using the seven elements just listed, the designer articulates the styling details he wishes to duplicate.

Piecing a Suit Together

The costume designer with a basic knowledge of tailoring styles and fit can go to a suit seller for advice about suits appropriate to each character. It is always advisable to fully measure the suit, just to check it meets expectations about desired drop and ease. Suits in rental houses or costume stock, however, have been altered in every way imaginable. Even though they may be labeled a 40 Regular and appear to be of Italian styling, the suit may have been changed to fit a specific situation. It is essential to fully measure the entire suit. If the garment is unmarked, use Table 21.1 to size it by measuring the finished garment itself. Every company uses slightly different patterning measurements. Nonetheless, these measurements serve as a general guide.

The shirt and tie are important elements of styling any character. Shirt collars take many shapes to flatter specific face shapes, a marker of formality or casualness or as an accompaniment to suit styles. See Extra Resources for a guide to shirt collar styles. Ties also vary in width and patterns to reflect fashionable trends. A general

All The Way

Menswear Styling for 1963-1964

This was a transitional year from late 1950s clothing to youthful mid- sixties cuts. Conservative dressers such as US Senators and Representatives did not embrace the new cut right away.

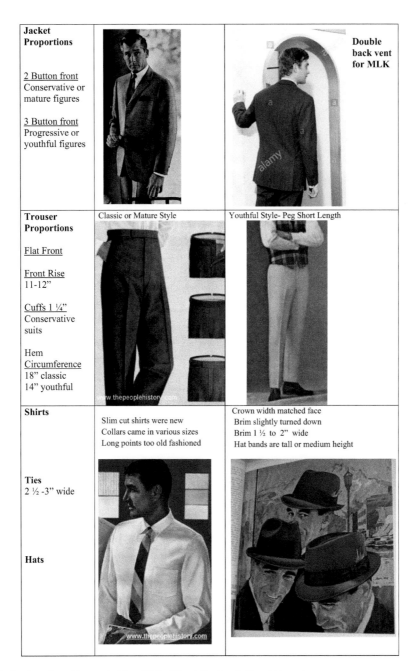

Jacket Proportions 2 Button front Conservative or mature figures 3 Button front Progressive or youthful figures		**Double back vent for MLK**
Trouser Proportions Flat Front Front Rise 11-12" Cuffs 1 ¼" Conservative suits Hem Circumference 18" classic 14" youthful	Classic or Mature Style	Youthful Style- Peg Short Length
Shirts **Ties** 2 ½ -3" wide **Hats**	Slim cut shirts were new Collars came in various sizes Long points too old fashioned	Crown width matched face Brim slightly turned down Brim 1 ½ to 2" wide Hat bands are tall or medium height

Figure 21.4 A suit style guide created for *All the Way* at the South Coast Repertory.

Period Suit Styling Details									
JACKET	**1907**	**1910**	**1924**	**1929**	**1930**	**1935**	**1936**	**1946**	**1945/6**
Chest	41	40	40	40	39	41	40	40	40
SB/DB	SB	SB	SB	SB	SB	DB	SB	DB	SB
Lapel Width	3	3 1/2	3 3/4	3 3/4	3 1/2	4	4 1/4	5 1/4	3 1/4
Button Number	4	3	3	2	3	4	3	4	3
VEST									
Lapels	yes	no	no	no	no	no	no	no	no
Body Length	23 1/8	22 1/4	24 3/4	22 3/8	22	21	24 5/8	22	21 3/8
Button Number	5	6	6	5	6	6	6	5	5
PANTS									
Waist	34	34.25	37	35	33	30	34	31.25	33
Rise	12 3/8	11 1/4	11 1/4	8. 3/4	10 1/4	11 5/8	9 1/2	10 1/2	9 3/4
Width at Ankle	9	8 3/4	8.75	10 1/8	9 1/2	8 3/4	8 1/4	9 1/4	10
Cuff	no	no	no	2 3/8	1 1/2	no	no	1 1/2	1 3/4
Button Fly	yes	yes	yes	yes	yes	yes	yes	yes	yes
Pleats	no	no	no	no	yes	yes	no	yes	yes

Figure 21.5 Sample menswear details from 1900 to 1945. Measurements compiled by Marcy Froehlich from research measuring extant garments by Graham Cottenden.[5]

guide for matching tie width to a suit is to follow the width of lapel at the gorge. A standard 3½-inch lapel partners well with a tie about the same width.

Sizing Up Styling Menswear

The costume designer can shape characters using a clear understanding of the parts of a suit and the styling options for each. The silhouette or school of tailoring makes a strong statement about how characters present themselves to the world. American Ready-to-Wear manufacturers supply suits in several cuts to fit different bodies. The key to a consistent design approach is to articulate a style guide that sums up the menswear of the time period in the play.

Expecting the Unexpected – A Suit for Every Body

The fashion world is making strides to address the notion that traditional suits are made for gender-normative male bodies. Enough brands are blurring the gender lines so that in February 2018 a category for unisex/nonbinary brands debuted at New York Fashion Week.[6] The foundation of the original tailoring formula is that men's bodies are widest at the shoulders. Other bodies are built on different proportions, with chest or hips the widest area. The key to fitting suits is to understand what is alterable and what is not. Fit the suit to the shoulders, first, because those are difficult to alter. Once that fabric is cut to shape, it can rarely be redone. Always consult with a fitter or tailor before assuming some alterations

Table 21.1 Typical Suit and Sportscoat Finished Measurements

SHORT 5 feet 3 inches to 5 feet 7 inches

The Jacket Measures (in inches):	36S	38S	40S	42S	44S	46S	48S	50S
Body Chest Measure	35–36	37–38	39–40	41–42	43–44	45–46	47–48	49–50
Garment Chest *with fitting ease*	38–39	40–41	42–43	44–45	46–47	48–49	50–51	52–53
Shoulder	17	18	18.5	19	19.5	20	20.25	20.50
Jacket Length below collar	29	29.25	29.5	29.75	30	30.25	30.5	30.75
Sleeve from Shoulder	23.5	23.75	23.75	24.25	24.5	24.75	24.75	25.75
Matching Trousers Measure:								
Waist Size	30	32	34	36	38–39	40–41	42–43	44–45
Inseam	34	34	34.5	34.5	35	35	35.5	35.5
REGULAR 5 feet 8 inches to 5 feet 11 inches								
The Jacket Measures (in inches):	**36R**	**38R**	**40R**	**42R**	**44R**	**46R**	**48R**	**50R**
Body Chest Measure	35–36	37–38	39–40	41–42	43–44	45–46	47–48	49–50
Garment Chest with *fitting ease*	38–39	40–41	42–43	44–45	46–47	48–49	50–51	52–53
Shoulder	17	18	18.5	19	19.5	20	20.25	20.50
Jacket Length below collar	30–30.5	30.5	31	31	31	31.5	31.5	31.75
Sleeve from Shoulder	25	24.5	25	25	25.25	25.25	25.25	25.50
Matching Trousers Measure:								
Waist Size	27–30	32	34	36	38–39	40–41	42–43	44–45
Inseam (unhemmed)	35	36	36.5	36.5	37	37	37.5	37.5
LONG 6 feet to 6 feet 3 inches								
The Jacket Measures (in inches):	**36L**	**38L**	**40L**	**42L**	**44L**	**46L**	**48L**	**50L**
Body Chest Measure	35–36	37–38	38–40	41–42	43–44	45–46	47–48	49–50
Garment Chest *with fitting ease*	38–39	40–42	43–44	46	48	50	52	54
Shoulder	18	19	19.5	20	20.5	21	21.5	22
Jacket Length below collar	30–31	32	32.25	32.5	32.75	33	33.25	33.5
Sleeve from Shoulder	26	26.3	26.6	26.8	27	27.3	27.5	27.8
Matching Trousers Measure:								
Waist Size	27–30	32	34	36	38–39	40–41	42–43	44–45
Inseam (unhemmed)	37	37	37.5	37.5	38	38	38.5	38.5

Figure 21.6 Tailored suits can be worn well by any body.

Credit: Photo by Anastasia Shuraeva from Pexels

may be made. It is worth scheduling a fitting with an experienced tailor if the budget allows.

Additional Resources

The Elegant Man, Riccardo Villarosa & Giuliano Angeli, Random House, 1990

Gentleman's Gazette www.gentlemansgazette.com/

Gentleman: The Ultimate Companion to the Elegant Man, Bernhardt Roetzel

Dressing the Man, Alan Flusser

Men's Tailoring, Bespoke, Theatrical and Historical Tailoring 1830–1950, Graham Cottenden, Focal Press Book Routledge, 2019

5 Brands Making Sharp Suits for Gender-Nonconforming People. them. Magazine www.them.us/story/lgbtq-custom-suiting-brands

Permanent Style, The Guide to Shirt Collars, Aug 31, 2020 www.permanentstyle.com/2020/08/the-guide-to-shirt-collars-and-what-suits-you.html

Notes

1 Hickey, Walt. 2014. "The Dollar-And-Cents Case Against Hollywood's Exclusion of Women." *FiveThirtyEight.com*, April 1, 2014. https://fivethirtyeight.com/features/the-dollar-and-cents-case-against-hollywoods-exclusion-of-women/

2 Langston, Jennifer. 2017. "New Tool Quantifies Power Imbalance between Female and Male Characters in Hollywood Movie Scripts." *University of Washington News*, November 13, 2017. https://www.washington.edu/news/2017/11/13/new-tool-quantifies-power-imbalance-between-female-and-male-characters-in-hollywood-movie-scripts/

3 Villarosa, Riccardo and Angeli, Guiliano. 2019. *The Elegant Man, How to Construct the Ideal Wardrobe.* New York: Random House, p. 50.

4 Lee, Christopher. 2019. "British VS Italian VS American Suit Fashions and Silhouettes." *Gentleman's Gazette*, August 30, 2019. https://www.gentlemansgazette.com/british-italian-american-suits/

5 Froehlich, Marcy. n.d. "Research Compiled from Cottendon, Graham." *Men's Tailoring: Bespoke, Theatrical and Historical Tailoring 1830–1950.* New York: Routledge.

6 Lubitz, Rachel. 2018. "New York Fashion Week Calendar Adds Category for Unisex and Non-Binary Fashion." *Mic Magazine*, February 8, 2018. https://www.mic.com/articles/187849/new-york-fashion-week-calendar-adds-category-for-unisex-and-nonbinary-fashion#.Xz6YKf5qX

22.
MEET YOUR MAKER

Made-to-Order Costumes

A young American designer was commissioned to design a show on London's West End for a period costume production. She visited a well-known British theatrical tailor to discuss building period suits. This was the first time she would have custom suits built to her specifications. The tailor asked such detailed questions that she realized even after some years of fitting purchased suits, she had never really internalized the fine details – exactly how long was the dart in the front of the suit jacket? Exactly how many inches above the jacket hem were the pockets placed? How would she translate her sketch into specifics, such as the exact width of the lapel or the width of the trouser at the ankle for the year 1888? After that initial visit she learned to carefully study suit details for every period she designed. She started collecting tailors' manuals from different eras and until she gained more confidence, she brought a sample suit to the tailor – even if she had to rent one for the day.

The Made-to-Order Process

Taking a design from an idea to a physical garment requires the designer to personally interact with a production team. This can involve several phases of communicating as the work moves from one kind of shop or task group to another. For example, fabric may be sent to one artisan to dye or to a printer for a custom pattern. The finished fabric then travels to a sewing shop for patterning and stitching. Similar fabrics and trims may be sent to a milliner for a matching hat, while the shoes go to a cobbler for repairs or enhancements. The costume pieces may all converge with yet another specialist for further painting or aging. Resident shops can produce many of these specialties under one roof, but costume designers for organizations without a resident shop rely on a network of specialty makers. The costume designer may be the single point of communication ensuring common vision, consistency, the quality of work required, and the timetable. Good organization and communication habits are a premiere element of the designer's responsibility during the production phase. If all items are made in a single shop, communication between makers is greatly simplified.

The custom garment process often requires making a **prototype** or **samples**. Creating a thorough prototype is the best way to finalize ideas before using expensive fashion fabrics. Theater costume shops refer to *building* a costume, while film and independent vendors refer to a custom garment as m*ade-to-order*. Regardless of the terms, the steps of manufacture for each maker are the same.

- **Initial conversation.** The most artistic of makers want to understand the designer's intent, not just the dressmaker details. This will be one of many elevator speeches a designer will deliver: a brief summary of the artistic goals. Bring or upload a packet of information including the sketch or character collage, pertinent research for that piece, the fabric or a swatch. Other makers will trust the designer to

DOI: 10.4324/9781003015284-28

ensure artistic intent, asking only construction questions. Designers provide visual material to aid this discussion: research, a rendering, a *working sketch* or technical sketches, vintage sample garments, old sewing patterns – anything that will aid a thorough discussion.

- **Prototype and samples**. The maker creates a mock-up of the costume in muslin or a suitable substitute. A maker may also create smaller samples to test individual techniques before incorporating them into the finished design. A muslin is usually approved on a dress form or stand-in fitting subject before its sewn together for a fitting. This sample confirms the maker interpreted the designer's ideas correctly, and allows the designer to see proportions and details on the human form. The maker and designer consult on what adjustments to make together.

- **Muslin fitting**. The actor tries on the revised mock-up for further adjustments to the design, placement of details and custom fit to the body. (See Figure 26.1.)

- **Garment fittings.** Using the adjustments from the mock-up fitting, the garment is cut and sewn in the final fashion fabric. Subsequent fittings may be necessary for complex or period costumes.

The wise designer uses their allotted shop time well. Don't let work slow down because makers are waiting for decisions or materials. Time wasted at the beginning can never be made up, and shops may grow frustrated if their process is not valued. Think of this process as *feeding the gods* – the regular supply of communication ensures that everyone is working toward the outcome. There are certain goals that everyone must achieve at the same time: readiness for the next fitting.

Meet Your Maker

The designer must respect the people they work with and trust their abilities and experiences. It is very difficult to put your idea into the hands of someone else, but most of the time it is not

Figure 22.1 This elegantly proportioned costume is the result of a successful collaboration between draper and designer. This costume combines stretch fabrics and woven flocked taffeta. Draper Julie Keen expertly matched the velvet pattern across the back seam.

Credit: Costume design for Gertrude by Kathryn Wilson, draper Julie Keen

physically possible for a designer to be in all places. Most makers have more experience doing their specific tasks than the designer does; they will bring informed options to the table. No one works in theater to feel like a factory worker; they wish to be actively involved in a creative project. Working with fellow creative people teaches a designer that everyone will have an opinion. Feedback, both positive and negative, is valuable information. Shop personnel will have worked with many different designers, and they are trying to understand your methods, too. At the same time the designer must not be afraid to ask for changes or adjustments. Ignoring a desire will not make it go away, in very short order it will be too difficult to backtrack.

The more hands-on experience the designer has, the more efficiently these interchanges will go. Those who worked their way up in costume shops will have a distinct advantage. It is informative to learn how our sketches or research are interpreted by those seeing them for the first time. Over time, a designer learns to adjust their style or express more confidence or anticipate frequently asked questions. This is one great joy of working in multiple costume shops – the designer gains an overview of the different ways makers approach each challenge. Early career designers may not be as confident talking with experienced makers who have created hundreds of garments. It is important to realize when a maker offers an opinion or feedback, they are not challenging the designer's authority but rather starting a conversation to learn more about your desires and preferences. They are trying to gain your trust just as you are trying to gain theirs. Listen to as many opinions as possible, but don't lose track of the final artistic intent. The designer is the only person with the entire stage picture in mind. Designers who feel pressure to please people or who are uncertain in their own abilities may experience more difficulty at first. Remember, the designer does not have to have all the answers or ideas. The designer *curates* all the ideas to ensure they create desired impact. Even so, the designer cannot entirely let go, allowing others to make all the decisions. Strike a balance between trust and Murphy's Law – anything that can go wrong, will go wrong. Check with the makers frequently, every day if possible, and never leave a site for the day without a final check-in.

The Initial Meeting

Each maker requires an introductory meeting with the designer to initiate the project. Engaging an outside vendor may include two separate meetings. The first one may be with a shop supervisor or project manager to work up a bid or communicate the overview. The next may be a **table meeting** with the actual maker who will do the work. This is the opportunity to establish a productive working relationship. There is a formula called the *Five W's*; it's considered a fundamental start for journalism or police work: who, what, when, where, and why. This approach works well for collaboration with makers.

- **Who** will wear the costume? Provide the actors head shot, measurements and any other information about the performer such posture or other physical details. Does this maker require some specialty measurements to proceed?
- **What** is the costume? Provide a sketch and all the relevant research. Makers often find research more informative than the sketch. How many pieces make up the costume, and what pieces will this person make? What is the fabric and dressmaker details? Provide fabric swatches or the purchased fabrics if available. What underpinnings will be worn under it? Do they need access to other items to complete the task?
- **When** is it needed? Share the production schedule, and determine when the maker will request fittings. How might this coordinate with other makers doing other pieces of the costume? Is this costume required for photo calls or early press dates? Clearly state the final delivery.
- **Where** will the fittings and performance take place? The size and type of the venue may affect the maker's decisions, as will an outdoor performance. Are there special considerations that must be built into the costume, such as cooling pads?
- **Why** does the costume look like this? Dust off the elevator speech, and explain how this costume fits into the larger artistic goals.

Once the *W's* are covered, the conversation will turn to a final *H*: **how** will the costume be built? This is a longer brainstorming session to discuss approaches and dressmaker details. Recall that Chapter 1 discusses that a vital aspect of designerly thinking is that we can't fully grasp what an object should be until we start down the path of making

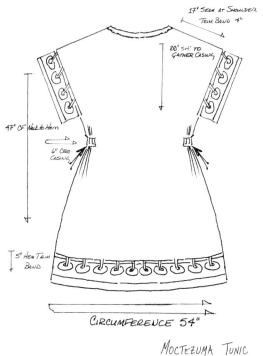

MOCTEZUMA TUNIC

Figure 22.2 (Continued)

Figure 22.2 Three items used to communicate with a shop for construction details: a working sketch (top), a vintage pattern envelope (center), and a technical sketch (bottom).

Credit: Image for downloadable pattern available at Lady Marlowe Studio, ladymarlow.com. Sketches by the author

it. Always arrive prepared with everything needed for creative brainstorming: the sketch, research, line drawings, fabric swatches, actor measurements, and head shot. Be proactive about what *this* specific project requires – bring anything to ease communication.

Synching Terminology

Designers do not have to be expert makers to work with those who are, although designers with some construction experience can communicate quickly using generally accepted terminology. If you are not as confident in garment construction, familiarize yourself with the parts of garments of each era using vintage patterns available online and fashion magazines that describe the garments thoroughly. Plan early trips to rental houses or museums to study how garments are put together or what kind of grain and trims were used. Discuss and agree on terms with your maker – every fashion item bears multiple names depending on the language of its origin or its history. If you believe a *dirndl* or gathered skirt is one thing and the maker thinks it's another, you have the beginnings of misunderstanding. It is a relief to everyone if the

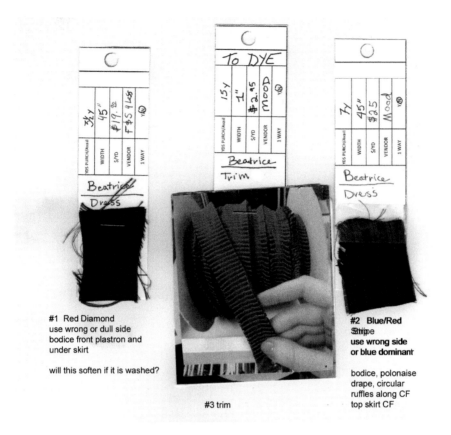

To DYE

15 y / 1" / $2.95 / mood / y

Beatrice Trim

7 y / 45" / $25 / Mood / y

Beatrice Dress

3½ y / 45" / $19.⁰⁰ / F$5 9 Los / y

Beatrice Dress

#1 Red Diamond
use wrong or dull side
bodice front plastron and
under skirt

will this soften if it is washed?

#3 trim

#2 Blue/Red
Stripe
use wrong side
or blue dominant

bodice, polonaise
drape, circular
ruffles along CF
top skirt CF

Figure 22.3 This designer photographed swatches and trim she shipped to a theater in a different city so the draper knew what to expect. The draper created the sample costume in muslin while waiting for the fabric to arrive.

designer initiates a discussion to synch terms. Many fashion textbooks contain useful glossaries for the styles of dress, sleeves, pleats, and other parts of garments. (See the Extra Resources section.)

Working With a Tailor

Traditional tailors make or alter garments incorporating special sewing and pressing techniques to mold the jacket to the body. The work is done in traditional ways handed down for nearly 250 years using methods that can be mysterious to everyone else. It is a specialty that requires years of training. Those with traditional training work their way up the ladder beginning as an apprentice, becoming a trouser maker, vest maker, and possibly a jacket maker. A master tailor is one who can draft and cut the jacket – a feat that requires years of experience. It's important to understand what the costume designer is asking the tailor to do,

and match the job to the correct maker. Suits are categorized by their method of manufacture:

- **Ready-to-wear suits** (RTW). Purchased off the rack in a predetermined style and sizing system created by the manufacturer. This is the most common way of purchasing a suit. In better retailers, the trousers are left unhemmed and the customer may expect one fitting to perform this alteration. Price points range from $200 to $1,000. The price is partly determined by the way the interlinings or inner shaping canvas is connected. The cheapest suits feature glued interlinings that rarely survive multiple dry-cleanings without bubbling. Better manufacturers use a combination of machine and hand techniques.
- **Made-to-measure suits** (MTM). Purchased at better stores and haberdashers. Instead of trying on a pre-made suit the customer may

try on a sample suit or wear a favorite suit to the store. The tailor or sales representative takes measurements, and the customer chooses fabrics and some limited style options. That information is sent to the factory and a suit is made to the customer's measurements. Manufacture takes from one week to several weeks. International tailors that travel to large cities specialize in this custom service, sending the order to China, Singapore, or other countries for affordable making. The customer can expect one fitting when the suit arrives to achieve a refined fit. Prices start at $1,200–$1,500 for a two-piece suit.

- **Bespoke suits**. Created from a pattern to the customer or designer's exact specification. The design begins with a discussion, choosing fabric and all style options. The tailor will take more extensive measures and take into consideration elements such as the customers' posture and habits. The suit may take a month or more to complete using traditional handwork. Expect three or more fittings. Prices start around $3,500 to $5,000 with top-of-the-line suits costing as much as $9,000.

Costume designers will usually work with two kinds of tailors. The first is a theatrical **custom** or bespoke tailor trained in the entertainment industry who understand the sometimes-odd requirements of performing. They will work with nontraditional fabrics and have a thorough understanding of historical styling. They may utilize some theatrical shortcut techniques if required: faster ones for some projects and traditional for other situations. The second type of tailor is the **retail** made-to-measure tailor operating a local business who is willing to take on theatrical work, but may have little experience with stage requirements. They may or may not comply with requests they find illogical or time-consuming. Some will refuse to work with materials they consider difficult. Nonetheless, they can be a reliable and affordable source for fast and accomplished custom work and all manner of alterations. Over time the costume designer builds relationships with different types of makers whose work they value.

Figure 22.4 This traditionally tailored suit uses hand-pad stitching and taped edges to mold the canvas interlining for the chest, lapel, and collar.

Credit: Photo by Tima Miroshnichenko from Pexels

Tailoring Terminology

Tailoring has its own terminology and traditions developed over two centuries. The costume designer must be familiar with the terms to fully communicate with a tailor. If you are not familiar with men's suits, it is helpful to study a suit from stock or visit a menswear store to view details in person. If possible, purchase a thrift store suit to take apart, studying the inside construction. As part of building a custom suit, tailors will ask about many details. If a designer is not confident in their understanding of tailoring details, it is helpful to bring a suit pulled from stock with the correct styling.

Breast pocket. Tailors call this the **outbreast** pocket. A single pocket is normally placed on the left of the wearer's chest. If the pocket is inset, it is finished with a **welt** (defined further down in the list). If the jacket is casual, it may feature a patch pocket with decorative top stitching. Traditional

Figure 22.5 The outbreast pocket angles up toward the shoulder.

Credit: Photo by Tima Miroshnichenko from Pexels

placement angles up slightly toward the shoulder. Placement on the chest varies slightly with styling, but tends to correspond to the chest line.

Buttons. Traditional buttons are made of horn, sustainable corozo, or plastic with prescribed sizes for jacket front and sleeves. Standard button sizes are 5/8 inch for sleeve or trouser, 13/16 inch for a single-breasted coat front, and 7/8 inch for a double-breasted front.

Button point or **stance.** How high up the chest the buttons are placed. A three- or four-button suit will button higher up than a two-button suit. The button stance dictates the length of the lapel. A lower button stance will lengthen the figure, making the wearer look taller and leaner. Italian tailoring features a *2.5* button stance, also called a *3-roll 2.5*-inch stance. The top or third button is hidden by the lapel roll and does not button. This style has become popular in American suits in the last decades.

Canvas or floating canvas. An interlining layer made of special hair canvas fabrics, sewn like a sandwich between the outer fabric and the lining. The weight and manner of attachment vary for the type of fabric and price point of labor. High-quality garment canvases are sewn in by hand; low-quality garments use fusible canvas that can pucker with dry-cleaning.

Blade. The extra fullness at the back of a jacket shoulder blades.

Drop. The difference between the chest size of the jacket and the waist size of the trousers in a suit. Standard sizing uses a 6-inch drop, so that a 40 Regular suit would be drafted to fit a 40-inch chest and 34-inch waist. Slim-cut suits use a slightly larger drop of 7 inches. It may be wise to fit a suit one size up if the actor's body does not adhere to that formula. Athletic-cut suits use an 8-inch drop, to accommodate larger chests or shoulders, arms and legs but a smaller waist. Small drops of 2–3 inches or less used to be termed the portly drop in 19th-century tailoring manuals, but are now termed executive cut.

Gorge. The place on the jacket front where the collar attaches to the lapel. The higher gorge looks more modern, lower gorges look more traditional or vintage. Italian suits use a higher gorge than classic British and American styles. This style shifts with each era; current placement is near the collar bone.

Flap pocket. A pocket with a flap that covers the opening. Some are convertible, meaning the flap may be tucked in to reveal the welt pocket below.

Front dart. A dart sewn from front hem up through the pockets creates a slender fit across the hip and more ease across the chest. Flat front suit jackets such as those worn in the 1960s did not use a dart, lending straighter fit, or sack style. The dart can disrupt the matching of a large plaid and so may substitute with an invisible side dart.

Lapel. Width varies widely from decade to decade. Current practice considers something in the range of 3½ inches wide at the notch standard for a notch lapel, and 4-inch wide for a peaked lapel. Wider lapels make the chest look larger but may minimize the shoulders. Smaller lapels make the shoulders appear wider. Curved lapels such as those worn in the 1930s are considered more relaxed, straight lapels more serious or traditional.

Figure 22.6 This suit uses a high gorge near the collar bone where the collar meets the lapel and a long front dart above the flap pocket. The lower button stance created by a single button closure also creates a long lapel.

Credit: Photo by El Gringo Photos from Pexels

The curve on the edge of the lapel is called the **belly**.

Lapel roll. The lower part of the lapel rolls over at the top button. A strongly set roll creates as much as a finger's width space between the lapel and the chest. This is one of the prized elements of a high-end suit. Not all lapel rolls are the same; some roll past the top button and others stop above it. Cheaply made suits with fused canvas will not roll and are pressed flat.

Lining. Material on the inside of suit jacket and sometimes the upper part of trousers. Sleeve linings are often a different color, using stripes in high quality suits. The best linings are made of cupro, a type of rayon. Bemberg lining is the high-end choice.

Pockets. When tailors draft patterns, they place pocket lines parallel to the hem of the jacket. Pocket terms are defined by their manner of sitting

on or in the material. Patch pockets sit on top of the fabric and are considered casual or sporty. (See welt and flap pocket definitions.)

Quarters. The bottom front portion of the jacket; the two lower panels that button. The portion below the last button is called *closed* quarters if the front flaps hang down hiding the legs. The quarters are open if they curve away from the bottom button revealing a gap. Double breasted jackets feature closed quarters.

Shoulder. The shoulder angle is created with padding. British tailoring uses a more structured, harder shoulder. An *extended* shoulder is slightly wider than the wearer's own measurement, such as styles worn in the 1980s and 1940s. A *roped* shoulder features sleeves set with a raised profile, creating a round peak or ropelike appearance. The *soft* shoulder features smaller pads that slope naturally from neck to shoulder. (See Figure 21.3.)

Sleeve. Traditional tailoring uses a two-piece sleeve, with vertical seams visible in the side front and side back of the sleeve. This was an early hallmark of Chanel suits for women, incorporating the two-piece tailored sleeve into women's wear.

Vent. Vertical slits in the bottom hem of the jacket or skirt allow a walking stride or ease of sitting. Traditional jackets offer the option of a single vent in the center back, double vents one on each side, and no vent. Double vents are associated with British tailoring, ventless suits with Italian tailoring.

Vented cuff. Traditional suit styling features a button flap on the bottom of the sleeve. The buttons work on higher price jackets and are sewn closed with decorative buttons on lower price points. Opening button plackets are called **surgeons' cuffs** so they could roll up their sleeves to perform examinations.

Welt/jetted pocket. Pocket slit bound with flat slivers of matching fabric, also known as a slit pocket. Commonly found on waistcoats to retain a flat fit, they are also featured on jackets, especially in Italian styling.

"I hope the designer listens to people who have the experience. Theatre is a collaborative art form, from the top all the way down. The designer has to be able to give and take a little within that. I would prefer to hear 'This is how I want it to look' instead of 'I want three layers of chiffon.' I can offer at least two options to make it look how they want. . . . I may have even more options. I don't want to say to anybody 'We can't do that' without offering some options. It's not helpful to anybody, it's not collaborative. And if they are unsure about my suggestions, I will make a sample for them." —Suzanne Schwartz Reed, Costume Shop Manager, Pomona College[1]

Figure 22.7 This suit features welt or jetted pockets.
Credit: Photo by Ayodeji Fatunla from Pexels

Even with all the communication in the world, the maker and designer may not communicate well. A costume may not turn out as expected either due to a maker's decision or something amiss with the original design. Negative results are difficult to handle gracefully, but if managed correctly it can energize everyone to learn from that experience. The most important goal is to remain solutions oriented – what can be done? *Should* something be done or can you live with

it? On occasion the designer or maker is pushed out of their comfort zone to figure out a solution – these last-minute fixes can lead to interesting breakthroughs or ideas.

Sizing Up Made-to-Order Costumes

The collaboration between a designer and maker can be an exciting partnership. Good organization and communication skills are a premiere element of the building and made-to-order phase of creating a design. Preparing for a table meeting with a maker or tailor makes the brainstorming process more productive and enjoyable. Designers learn what to bring to a meeting to aid communication, including sample garments if needed. The steps of the made-to-order process are arranged to allow the designer and maker time to make adjustments.

Expecting the Unexpected – Closures

The costume is only as good as the closure holding it onto the body. Not even the most prepared designer is immune to the torment and stress caused by one of the most common clothing closures: the zipper. While zippers bring dressing speed and aid movement, they are one of the least reliable closures, especially the invisible variety. Zippers break, pull apart while on the body, stick closed, the zipper pull falls off – the nightmares are too numerous to tell. Costume shops spend extra time changing some zippers on ready-made clothing to sturdier versions. Even though it seems like the smallest detail to consider while making a costume, the manner and ease of closure can rapidly become the most important one. Stylist Hellin Kay who dresses Laura Prepon and Taryn Manning for red-carpet events says "Zippers are the worst. . . . It's always the zipper! I don't let things stress me out anymore, but a broken zipper 20 minutes before you're supposed to get into the car? That stresses me out."[2]

Additional Resources

Lady Marlowe Studio. Period Patterns available as PDF downloads https://ladymarlowe.com/

Suit Style 1: The Difference Between Bespoke, Made-to-Measure and Ready-to Wear www.permanentstyle.com/2016/04/whats-the-difference-between-bespoke-made-to-measure-and-ready-to-wear.html

The Anatomy of a Suit Jacket www.gentlemansgazette.com/the-anatomy-suit-jacket/

Fashion Dictionary, Women's Wear Daily https://wwd.com/fashion-dictionary/

Notes

1 Reed, Suzanne Schultz, interview with author June 28, 2021.

2 Cheng, Andrea. 2017. "This is Every Hollywood Stylist's Worst Nightmare Before a Major Red Carpet Event." *InStyle Magazine*. Accessed January 6, 2017. https://www.instyle.com/news/hollywood-stylist-red-carpet-prep-nightmare

23.
ACCESSORIES AND COSTUME PROPS

Kerry Washington, the actor who co-founded the Time's Up organization, describes the importance of accessories playing Olivia Pope on *Scandal*.

> I used to go to rehearsal for *Scandal* in sweatpants and a sweatshirt, but I could not do the scene unless I had the shoes . . . four-inch heels because Olivia Pope had a walk. And she had a posture and she had a stance. So I always say I don't know who a character is until I know what shoes they're wearing, until I figure out the walk, until I figure out how they stand.[1]

Many actors find an accessory acts as their hook into a character. It's difficult to imagine Johnny Depp's Captain Jack Sparrow without the headscarf, beads, multiple sashes, and hat that set his costume apart from the usual pirate fare. Costume designer Penny Rose gathered a number of hats for Depp. He tried them all on, and chose the only one that he felt had the right rock 'n' roll swagger.[2] Garments clothe the majority of the body, but accessories make an outsize impact. In our personal lives, we often repeat an ensemble, changing it with accessories. This chapter cannot hope to address how to build accessories or other costume crafts; there are excellent resources available on these specialties. (See the Extra Resources section.) This chapter will discuss typical accessories and considerations for using them onstage.

> "The less you can afford for your frocks, the more care you must take with your accessories." — Christian Dior

Accessories change radically with every fashion era. Historically, many people kept their expensive outfits for longer periods using accessories to update them. Each fashion era developed rules about what accessory was appropriate for the time of day or the tone of an outfit. At one time dressing appropriately was considered a display of good manners. Some of the best advice can be found in etiquette books from each era. One 1956 guide lamented the passing of traditional standards such as wearing hats and gloves every day. It did celebrate the triumph of costume jewelry in the 1950s, but etiquette maven Frances Benton cautioned "We wear . . . more elaborate jewelry at night than in the daytime; with sports clothes (slacks and shorts) nothing but a wedding ring (or other simple ring) and wrist watch are appropriate."[3] Costume designers benefit from understanding the generally accepted rules of each era so they can create characters who follow rules, those who rebel, and those who are oblivious to them.

DOI: 10.4324/9781003015284-29

Overtones: Types of Accessories

Historians surmise humans have been wearing décor and accessories longer than we've been wearing garments. Fashion media brims with advice about new ways to wear the latest accessories. Costume designers research the accessories for each era and take a special delight in designing or building them. There are several considerations for choosing accessories for a character:

- **Mindset.** Accessories offer opportunities to illustrate a character's personality. For instance, a hat with springy feathers that twitch with every movement may imply a scattered mind
- **Tradition.** How traditional is the character on a scale from hidebound to rebellious?
- **Age.** Accessories reinforce generational dressing, such as smaller items for youthful characters and larger items for mature characters
- **Shape focus.** Create only one focal point at a time for a clear stage picture. Hats are an example of shapes creating focus to surround the face.
- **Color focus.** Traditional rules dictate either the garment is the most colorful or the accessories. Characters break this rule to create individualistic statements.
- **Finish.** Accessories make an outfit look more complete. Harmonizing or contrasting scale and color will add the right touches.
- **Consistency.** Choose the same statement pieces or accessory style for a character across every outfit, establishing a "look" the audience can track.
- **Cultural reference.** Use only one culturally specific accessory, such as a necklace or scarf, unless it matches the character's heritage. Dressing more fully in a culture that is not one's own or using sacred imagery may be problematic. Approach this with care, respect, and thorough research.

Menswear accessories also follow trends, such as a traditional rule of harmonizing all the leathers in an outfit: the belt, shoes, and watch strap. Traditional rules suggest tan leather with brown clothing, black or oxblood leather with gray, navy and dark clothing.

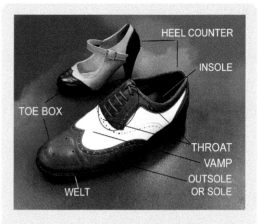

Figure 23.1 The parts of a shoe

Fleet of Foot – Knowing Your Shoes

Fashion has changed the shape of every single part of the shoe to create new looks. Knowing the parts of a shoe helps the designer fit different shoe styles to each actor, and aids conversations with cobblers and crafts artisans. Costume designers encounter every kind of foot imaginable while working with performers. Matching a shoe style to an actor's foot shape ensures better success. Common foot shapes the costumer will accommodate include:

- **Wide toe shape.** Avoid shoe styles with pointed toes or horizontal details across the toe that resist stretching. Horizontal details visually emphasize the width of the foot. A plain toe, diagonal or vertical detailing appears to lengthen the foot and will stretch to fit the actor.
- **High arch**. The center of the foot curves significantly upward. This foot shape can be very difficult to fit in any style that hugs the ankle and slip-on styles.
- **Developed calf.** Take a calf measurement for tall boots. Boots with larger calves may be more challenging to purchase. Elastic gussets may be added to many boot styles to accommodate this situation.
- **Bunions.** Over time, feet develop lumps and bumps adding to the width of shoe or requiring special pads for comfort.
- **Orthotics.** Some actors must wear special inserts in their shoes that affect the style and

shape of shoe they can wear. Study the foot with the orthotic to see what limitations arise.

Shoe styles were relatively nonbinary during much of history, including men wearing high heels in the 17th and 18th centuries. After that, men's shoes changed slowly; the same general styles have been worn since the 1800s with brief eras of post-war flair. Many shoe style names derive from the subtle details of construction. The average person may not even notice some of these distinctions, but they do understand when a shoe gives the wearer a dressy, authoritative, or sporty air. During the 20th century, women adopted many of these 19th-century masculine styles on their own quest for comfortable, serviceable footwear. (See the Extra Resources section.)

Figure 23.2 Shoes with stitching across the toe limit stretch for feet with wide toes. Shoes with vertical or diagonal details, such as the green and black shoes, offer more ease and visually slenderize the foot. The red shoe has no stitching across the vamp or toe and will stretch easily for wider feet.

Figure 23.3 The shoe on left is a *derby*, blucher, or open shoe style with lacing panels sitting above the vamp. This provides a looser fit. The shoe at right is an *oxford*, balmoral, or closed style with the lacing panel sewn into the vamp providing a sleeker look and more formal appearance. The shoe at left has a punched toe design called *broguing*.

Click Your Heels – Wearing Shoes on Stage

After menswear gave up high heel fashions, women's shoes took flight, carrying the torch for fashionable shapes. Many styles derive their names from the style of heel or a distinctive detail. The most classic style, originally worn by wealthy French courtiers, is the **court shoe** or **pump** with a heel from 1½ to 3 inches high. Distinguishing details include the rounded heel shape that curves outward. This style is now considered a formal, conservative style appropriate for day, evening, and business attire.

Performers feel very strongly about the shoes they wear. Not only are they an important character tool, as Kerry Washington described, but they cause great joy or misery when worn. We cannot ask performers to ruin their feet for the sake of a show, and fitting shoes is a thoughtful part of the costume process. In ideal circumstances, the shoes should be fitted early and sent to rehearsal for the performers to work with. This allows time for corrections before the mad days of dress rehearsals. If performers work in their shoes late, it can cause a change in rhythm and style, throwing the actor off their routine. Shoes worn in performance navigate all manner of challenges, such as raked stages or embedded slots for moving scenery. Scenic elements made of industrial grating pose particular challenges. Ask about the dimensions of any breaks in the stage floor, providing shoes with wider heels so the actor does not wedge a shoe or turn an ankle. Raked stages cause particular challenges for heeled shoes. The more severe the incline, the more the actor must lean back to compensate their balance, preventing the use of higher heels. Ask the technical director to build a sample rake platform for the fitting room so actors can stand on the exact angle while choosing shoes. It is imperative to take this into consideration not only for performer safety, but also to prevent repurchasing a large number of shoes late in the timeline.

Most shoes in performance must hug the foot as closely as comfort allows to avoid stumbling. The fit may be slightly adjusted by adding cushioned **insoles** and **moleskin** heel grips. Many mature performers require the use of special **orthotics** inside the shoe. Never fit a pair of shoes without these additions in place. Many shoes

Figure 23.4 The brown shoe uses a stacked heel made of slices of leather to create a sturdy or sporty heel. The white shoe uses a curved court heel. The pink shoe is a kitten heel (a slender heel lower than 2–3 inches), and the navy is a stiletto, or any slender heel over 2–3 inches.

will soften with wear, adding to the comfort level. The average person will tolerate a break-in period, but theater requires an accelerated process. If the actor wears their shoes for the first time during a lengthy dress rehearsal process, it is natural they will find them uncomfortable and want different shoes. Anticipate this issue if shoes feel a bit tight in a fitting. Send them to rehearsal for a break-in period or stretch them with shoe stretcher forms and a spritz of rubbing alcohol or shoe stretch spray.

> "As has been reported a lot in the press, a 'flunky' wears in Her Majesty's shoes to ensure that they are comfortable and that she is always good to go. And yes, I am that flunky."
> —Angela Kelly, LVO, Personal Assistant and Head Dresser to Queen Elizabeth II[4]

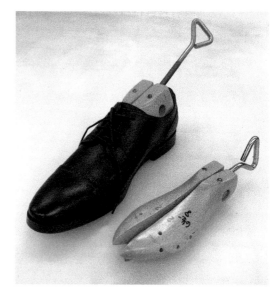

Figure 23.5 Shoes may be stretched with stretching frames and isopropyl alcohol spray.

On occasion a slippery stage requires the sole of the shoe to be roughed up using a micro-plane or gluing rubber sole sheets to the bottom of the shoe. Rubber soling may be applied by a cobbler or in a costume shop equipped with proper ventilation. A word of caution: many shoes are now made of rubber or synthetic soles that prevent attaching additional rubber. Adhesive nonslip pads with a gritty texture are available in retail stores, although in some cases they compound the problem. Outdoor venues pose a particular hazard when dew settles on the stage, causing slipping

hazards. With more shoes made of synthetic materials, the traditional solution of rubbering or roughing all the shoes is no longer the universal solution it once was. Many stage crews use floor treatments mopped into place such as Slip No More® (see Extra Resources) to create the desired resistance.

Spats and Gaiters

Many styles of spatterdashes or *gaiters* were worn through history as protection while riding, hunting, laboring, or during wartime. What began as functional protection became a fashionable way to add color to the foot, with the term *spats* more commonly applied when the intent is decorative. Spats can also play a special role in theatrical costume as an affordable trick for converting contemporary shoes to custom or period boot styles. Since spats do not fit the actual foot, they may be made in relatively few sizes allowing production line assembly in the costume shop with minor adjustments in fittings. Spats can be made of fabrics or leather to add decoration and hardware. There are many video tutorials and other resources for building spats. (See the Extra Resources section.)

The White Glove Test

During the 19th century, all well-dressed people wore fashionable gloves whenever they stepped out in public. Men gave up wearing fashion gloves during the day in the 20th century, but women's fashions required them into the 1950s. Each period developed its own rules for pairing gloves and glove colors with ensembles for day and evening. They may contrast or match one other element of a day wear ensemble such as the purse, belt, hat or fur collar and cuff. During the day, dressy gloves fully cover any skin between the hand and any sleeve worn below the elbow, so that longer gloves are worn with three-quarter sleeves. Summer gloves may be short, to the wrist. One of the last sticklers for proper glove etiquette is Queen Elizabeth II of England; she wears both black and white gloves

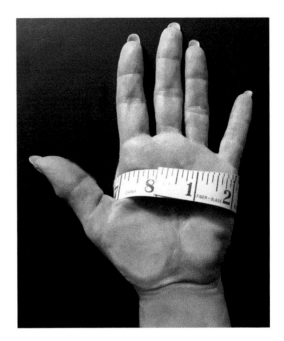

Figure 23.7 Glove measure.

during the day. High-end gloves are available in measured sizes; currently most gloves contain some stretch material making the sizing system of S-M-L-XL serviceable. Glove measurements record a circumference around the dominant hand at the widest area, usually just below the knuckles. (See Figure 23.7.) Trace the hand to document finger length – the same size hand may feature very long or very short fingers. In some cases, gloves must be ordered before accurate measurements can be taken. There is a *very* rough correlation in the general population between hand and foot size, so in a pinch it may be possible to make an educated guess if you know an actor's shoe size.

See and Be Seen – Eyeglasses Onstage

Nothing frames a face so well as a pair of glasses or sunglasses, and they can be a defining feature of creating a character. It's hard to imagine Meryl Streep's character Miranda Priestly in *The Devil Wears Prada* without her habit of peering over those signature reading glasses to strike fear in those around her. Actors love to use personal

Figure 23.6 Spats can add a contrast detail or transform the appearance of a plain shoe with styling details.

Table 23.1 Approximate Correlation Between Shoe and Glove Sizes

Women				Men			
Shoe Size	Glove Size/ Hand Width	Hand Length	Mass Size	Shoe Size	Glove Size/ Hand Width	Hand Length	Mass Size
3–3.5	5–5.5 inches	4.5–5 inches	X-Small	7.5	7–7.5 inches	6.5–7 inches	X-Small
4–4.5	5.5–6 inches	5–5.5 inches	Small	8–8.5	7.5–8 inches	7–7.5 inches	Small
5–6	6–7 inches	5.5–6.5 inches	Medium	9–9.5	8–8.5 inches	7.5–8 inches	Medium
6–7	7–8 inches	6.5–7.5 inches	Large	10–10.5	8.5–9 inches	8–8.5 inches	Large
7–8	8–9 inches	7.5–8.5 inches	X-Large	11–11.5	9–9.5 inches	8.5–9 inches	X-Large
9–12	9+ inches	8.5 + inches	2 X-Large	12–13	9.5 + inches	9–9.5 inches	2X-Large

props to create gestures, and those playing more than one role in a story appreciate the element of disguise glasses bring. Eyeglass styles shift dramatically through historical periods beginning in the late medieval era, so they are an excellent indicator of time period. It is helpful for the costume designer to preselect an assortment of glasses that are suitable for the time period to try with the actor. Eyeglass fitting can be a very personal experience. Some actors require a prescription so the decision must be made to provide clear lenses the actor uses with their own contacts, or switch the glasses to the actor's own prescription. Glasses from vintage stores may have old prescription lenses in them and must be changed for stage use. In some cases, the costume designer may wish to provide anti-glare lenses so stage light does not reflect back into the audience's eyes. A local optometrist is a valuable resource; some provide discounted services as part of their patronage to the theater.

An accurate measurement increases the success of the fit if frames are ordered on the internet. If the actor wears contemporary glasses, their frames will be marked with the correct sizing on the inside of one arm as a long serial number separated by squares. The first number is the **lens width** measured in millimeters, the second is **bridge width** and the third is **temple length**. There may be additional numbers after that indicating style numbers, unique to each manufacturer. For more information on reading glasses measurements, see the Extra Resources section.

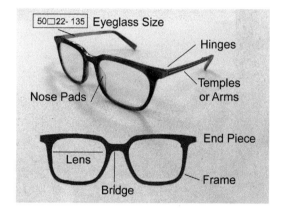

Figure 23.8 Eyeglass size numbers are marked on the temple or bridge, sometimes separated by squares.

The most important measurements for proper fit to the face are **bridge width** and **temple/ arm** length. If possible, fit any style of glasses available in stock on the actor and use those size numbers or measure across the bridge and the arm to the ear.

Sparkle and Shine: Jewelry

Costume jewelry began in the 18th century when the French devised a way to make simulated diamonds, allowing the wealthy to emulate aristocratic jewels. Expensive costume jewelry was still a luxury; cheaply made costume jewelry was scorned by the fashionable set until modernity changed that rule beginning in the early 1900s. Such jewelry no longer emulated fine jewelry styles, setting trends of their own. General rules for choosing jewelry change with each era but general considerations include:

- **Tone.** Jewelry suits different times of day or occasions. Stones cut with facets to sparkle were considered cocktail or evening appropriate and not worn with day wear until the 1980s.
- **Focus.** Choose if the jewelry is the focal point of an ensemble, or the clothing itself. Adding both complex jewelry and garment styling creates a chaotic impression.
- **Scale.** Those with fine features are easily overwhelmed with large jewelry pieces, while fine jewelry will vanish on those with larger features.
- **Complement.** Consider the shape of the neckline when choosing earrings and necklaces to complement or contrast accordingly. Long necklaces can add length to the torso. Strapless garments support larger necklaces and earrings.
- **Mixing.** Older rules maintained that all metal should match, wearing only silver tones or gold tones. These rules were intentionally broken beginning in the 1990s.
- **Sleeves.** The longer the sleeve, the thinner the bracelets. Shorter sleeves support chunky bracelets.
- **Matching.** Matching sets of jewelry were traditionally worn, especially earrings and necklaces, but this fell out of favor after the 1980s.
- **Sport.** Traditional rules dictated wearing leather watch bands and no cut gems with sportswear. Gold, silver, or pearls were acceptable with hunting tweeds or country sports.
- **Character.** Jewelry sends many messages as a key to character development, and every jewelry rule can be broken in the name of creating the correct statement.

Figure 23.9 The matching green turban and earrings provide a focal point using accessories.

Credit: Photo by Jackson David from Pexels

people matched their bag and shoe colors. That rule died when designers marketed signature status bags in the late 1980s. Choose the handbag with logistics in mind – will the actor stash items inside, are there appropriate pockets to hold those props or can pockets be added? Is the clasp easy to work onstage, and the strap sturdy enough to withstand repeated use? Choose these accessories early and send them or an appropriate substitute to rehearsal so the actor can develop character-based movements as they learn their blocking and lines.

Carried Away: Handbags, Walking Sticks, and Parasols

Each era created something for the fashionable to carry in their hands: bags, parasols, canes, or fashion walking sticks. Each of these items is a great boost to character. For a few decades, fashionable

Tie the Knot: Stocks, Cravats, and Jabots

Since the 16th century many items of neckwear were expensive status items on their own, made of precious fabrics. In the 16th century, wealthy people dressing in the Spanish style wore ruffs that required elaborate upkeep. Beginning in the 18th century men tied long cravats around their neck in elaborate signature styles. Neckwear styles are an essential part of researching each era. Common neckwear styles, listed in order of their appearance, include:

- **Cravat.** A long thin scarf tied around the neck originating in the 17th century, named after Croatian soldiers' neckties. Cravat is still used as a term for the modern tie. Gentlemen prided themselves in their unique wrapping and knotting styles.
- **Stock.** Originally a tall stiffened band of fabric worn around the neck as a separate collar, somewhat like a folded bandana today. A cravat could be tied over it, or a small bow tied at the front. Worn as everyday wear in the 18th and 19th centuries, it became a required component of hunting and riding attire. Commonly worn in black or white.
- **Jabot.** Appeared to be an extension of neckwear, but was actually a ruffle sewn to the front opening of a man's shirt in the 17th and 18th centuries. It was accompanied by a stock or cravat tied around the neck. In the 19th and 20th centuries, a flap of ruffles sewn to a neckband evolved into the modern jabot.
- **Stock tie.** The stock and cravat combined in the 19th century to create a wide tie knotted at the collar, with wide ends worn loose or in a long bow.
- **Ascot.** A loose, wide necktie with scarf-like ends. Worn tied under or over the collar to fill in the front of a shirt with a waistcoat.

The ends are tied or laid over each other and pinned into place. First fashionable in the 19th century; 20th-century versions were worn under an open collar to fill in the neckline for casual wear, associated with upper classes.
- **Bow tie.** The cravat and stock tie shrank in width and length during the latter years of the 19th century, becoming a fashionable item in the 20th century.
- **Tie.** The 20th-century version of a cravat, wider at the ends and narrow in the center to pass under a folded collar. Each decade features specific lengths, widths, materials, and patterns
- **Club or regimental tie.** Nineteenth- and 20th-century British ties with sloped stripes indicating membership in a specific club or regiment. Widely adopted for business ties in the 20th century.

Neckwear fashions were extremely expressive; portraits and photographs show many individual styles, or those who clung to styles long after they were out of date. This accessory is another golden opportunity to create a character. Several sources online provide information to research neckwear; see the Extra Resources section.

Talking Through Your Hat

Hats, head dresses, or decorated hairstyles were required wear through much of human history. Anything worn on the head takes on great

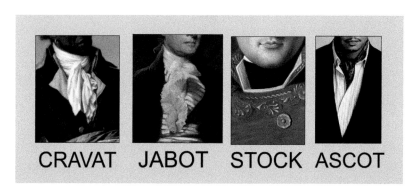

Figure 23.10 Styles of neckwear.

significance, as it is often associated with mindset or status. These accessories provide golden opportunities to create characters using subtle or overt signals. Western fashion required those who considered themselves properly attired to wear hats out of doors into the 1960s, but the prevalence of the automobile killed hats in the American wardrobe. During the 19th century both men's and women's hats were worn in public spaces whether indoors or outdoors. Paintings by Toulouse-Lautrec show men and women inside the Moulin Rouge with hats on, but not wearing hats at dinner. Men removed their hats when entering private spaces such as another person's home or office. Women's hats were considered part of their hairstyles and they were not required to remove them if they visited indoors a short time or when in public venues such as the theater. Women did remove their hats for lengthy visits to private homes. Women did not wear street-style hats inside their own homes, instead choosing to wear at-home soft caps during many eras.

Hats have been made from the same materials throughout much of history, making it possible to remake and restyle hats for stage costumes. The most traditional materials for molded and shaped hats are **leather**, **straw**, and **felt**. Soft caps have been made of cloth such as linen, wool, and cotton with brims stiffened by paste-soaked paper, wires, boning, or wooden slats. A traditional paste-stiffened linen called **buckram** was remade in the 1980s as a more convenient commercial millinery product. Buckram can be used alone to create lightweight hats or be covered with fabric. Many women redecorated their hats to freshen the styles, and there are many video tutorials available on making millinery decorations. Like shoes, traditional men's hats have stayed largely the same since the 19th century, with personal expression reserved for leisure or sport caps. To understand a style, it is important to understand the shape and size of the **crown** and the shape and size of the **brim**. For excellent sources on hat styles and terms, see the Extra Resources section.

Like every accessory, mass market sizing of S/M/L/XL is rapidly superseding traditional hat size methods. Nonetheless, better hats are still sold

Figure 23.11 The parts of a hat.

by size, and vintage hats will be marked by size. Every costume designer should keep a hat size chart handy on their phone or in a show notebook for reference. The use of hats onstage comes and goes as contemporary people no longer wear them and actors become less familiar with handling hats. While many women's hats may be easy to wear off the face, many men's hats with wider brims can block stage lighting and cause the actor to push that hat so far back on the head as to look comical. Ill-fitting hats will fall off at inopportune times. Sometimes the costume designer reaches a compromise – the actors will enter with a hat but take them off immediately, or hat brims will be cheated smaller or at an angle to allow light on the face. Yet many designs and stage pictures benefit greatly from their use. Many costume designers love the sense of character a hat brings to each design and will go out of their way to make them easy for the actors to manage. Hats can be extremely useful for actors playing multiple ensemble roles where some element of disguise is desirable. It is important to show the lighting designer any hats with brims early in the process to avoid surprises at dress rehearsals.

Hats can be an expensive accessory and laborious to create. Many times, the perfect shape or color of hat is not the correct size and the budget cannot afford to purchase a substitute. Fortunately, there is a small amount of leeway fitting hats. Felt hats such as fedoras may be stretched using a hat stretcher and steam. Stretching requires removing and re-adding the inner sweat band. If the hat has no lining, the sweat band may be removed altogether, although it will open that hat up to damage over the long run. Take care not to overstretch the hat. A properly fitting crown is about as wide as the actor's

Table 23.2 Hat Sizes

Head Measure Inches	US Hat Size	Metric Size	Mass Market Hat Size
20 5/8	6 1/2	52.5	X-SMALL
20 7/8	6 5/8	53	SMALL
21 1/8	6 3/4	54	
21 1/2	6 7/8	55	
21 7/8	7	56	MEDIUM
22 1/4	7 1/8	57	
22 5/8	7 1/4	58	LARGE
23	7 3/8	59	
23 1/2	7 1/2	60	X-LARGE
23 7/8	7 5/8	61	
24 1/4	7 3/4	62	2X-LARGE
24 5/8	7 7/8	63	
25	8	64	3X-LARGE

face. An overstretched hat will place a tiny crown on top of a wide band, creating a comical effect. Hats may also be sized smaller by using self-adhesive weather-seal foam tape sold in hardware stores to block drafts on doors and windows. Stick this underneath the sweat band in front and back, or all the way around the hat. Keep in mind the relationship of crown to the actor's face. An overly large hat will make the actor look like a child playing dress up.

Behind the Mask

Masks have been an integral part of religious and theatrical performances since the dawn of history.

Figure 23.12 The hat on the left is being stretched with wooden stretcher beams. The hat on the right was made smaller using weather-seal foam tape tucked under the interior band.

Masks are used in some actor training programs but more often than not, a performer has little experience with them. The costume designer may have to lay extra groundwork on a project using masks. Actors must relearn communication through a physical presence, therefore need access to their masks or a substitute early in the rehearsal process. Comfortable masks require a custom fit that must accommodate movement around the mouth, or embedded microphones. Many designers leave the mouth area clear if the performer has a number of lines to deliver. Designing masks is also an art form, and the designer quickly learns it is an ongoing process that may not be completed until opening day. Masks are an outstanding opportunity for creativity, and there are hundreds of resources available on cultural mask collections and mask making. It helps to focus the design with a specific goal in mind – what purpose does the mask serve in this story; is it one of these common types?

- **Emotive.** A particular expression is frozen into the mask, such as the iconic comedy and tragedy masks of Greek theater. This mask dictates only one style of performance or one character.
- **Representational.** The mask resembles a face ranging from realistic to stylized, such as

animal masks or masks that resemble celebrities, politicians, or an invented character. Many Halloween masks fall into this category, as do the masks made for disfigured British soldiers in World War I to reconstruct facial elements.[5]

- **Disguise.** The characters are hiding their identity to partake in social events where their identity should not be known, or perhaps for criminal purposes. One example is the 18th-century domino mask where escaping one's identity is part of the fun.
- **Metaphor.** While the identity of the wearer is disguised, the choice of mask may reveal inner qualities of that character. One example is choosing an animal that embodies inner traits of the character such as a snake, lion, or owl.
- **Fantasy.** Changing one's identity to assume a fantasy character, such as carnival masks that exude a general feeling of celebration.
- **Ritual.** Masks used around the world for sacred dances, festivals or other celebrations; these usually represent spirits, animals, fertility, death, ancestors, gods, or demons.
- **Contextual.** The audience must possess outside information to understand what each type of mask represents, such as the wide array of masks used in Commedia del'Arte or Noh theater.
- **Neutral.** A blank mask devoid of distinctive expressions often painted a tan, brown, black, or white color. May use realistic or conceptual features.
- **Convertible.** Feature two expressions or characters such as innocent and wicked, or lamb and wolf. The mask may be turned around, upside down or panels may hinge open to employ a reveal.

Act of Violence: Gun Belts, Sword Belts, and Stunt Pads

Handling weapons requires close collaboration between the fight director, props, and costumes. Although every theater may divide these responsibilities differently, the fight director decides what weapons will be used, oversees actor training and safety protocols. Props departments supply the

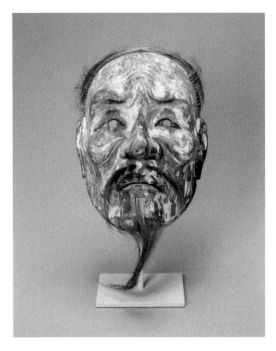

Figure 23.13 This 16th-century Japanese Noh mask is contextual. The audience must know it represents older working-class male characters such as fishermen, foresters, or sailors.

Credit: Unknown Artist, Old Man Asakura Noh Mask, 1501–1599. Frederick W. Gookin Collection, The Art Institute of Chicago.

weapons themselves. Costumes supplies the means to hold the weapons to the body such as sword and gun belts. Sheaths or scabbards that protect the blade are usually supplied with the weapon, but costumes may provide sheaths on occasion. Sheaths are soft, usually made of leather or Kevlar. Scabbards are made of harder materials such as steel or plastic. Most swords are kept in scabbards, most knives use sheaths. Any costume designer about to work on a play with battle scenes would benefit from some quick tutorials on weaponry so he can collaborate with actors and fight director. One excellent overall source of information and rental weapons is *Weapons of Choice*. (See the Extra Resources section.)

Weapon belts change fashion with each era. Holding a weapon to the body requires two separate pieces: the **waist belt** and a **frog** for swords or **holster** for guns. The waist belt can be as fashionable as one would like, as long as it provides a snug fit. Some frogs and holsters use ties to wrap around the leg. Frogs and holsters vary widely depending on the type of weapon used. Once the fight director identifies the weapon it is often necessary to measure the blade width at the hilt. Thanks to medieval reenactors, there are a number of online sources to purchase frogs of many designs. Older hand guns have long been separated from their holsters and may require a custom commission. Gun shops can provide names of leather workers who specialize in all manner of recreations.

Any staged violence requires protective pads for the actors. They must be sturdy to protect from body blows, flexible to allow free movement and low profile to be less visible beneath a costume. Fight or stunt pads are available in a wide variety of styles and materials. Common pads include leather, neoprene or thin high-density foam sewn into compression shirts to guard chest and back, along with elbow and knee pads. Many Hollywood stunt people prefer gel-filled pads that absorb repeated impact while maintaining a low profile under clothing. (See the Extra Resources section.) All weaponry, belts, pads, and any relevant armor pieces must be available in rehearsals from the first days of fight rehearsals. Work out a schedule with stage management and the fight director. Like masks, weaponry requires constant tinkering and repairs as actors work in rehearsals. These notes must often be fixed by the next rehearsal. Actors will discover certain pads don't work for them, or that the angle of the frog is wrong for their arm, or any number of adjustments. It is wise to build into the budget extra frogs, belts and pads for adjustments and emergencies. A larger show with extended battles would do well to hire a crafts person to look after those needs. Make this case to the producers as part of maintaining an orderly rehearsal and safety protocol.

Sizing Up Accessories

Accessories can make or break a costume, making it look complete and reinforcing character types. Early career designers sometimes concentrate more on the garments, thinking of accessories later in the timeline. But many accessories are powerful character identifiers and affect movement in rehearsals,

Figure 23.14 This saber is housed in a scabbard that attaches to the belt with a red leather frog.
Credit: Photo by Mikhail Nilov from Pexels

so it is wiser to think of them early. Many costume designers create an accessories closet for actors to choose during fittings, just as Penny Rose did for Johnny Depp to try hats as Captain Sparrow. Set up an array of hats, ties, shoes in proper colors and shapes during the fitting so the actor can try various combinations. Be willing to live with anything in the group, unless you both agree it does not work. This is also a good way to discover which accessory accentuates the performer's features or brings out the correct attitude for the character. Actors feel they have some input into the character and this builds trust. As Kerry Washington noted with Olivia Pope's walk, many actors cannot find who their character is until something feels correct – the shoe, the hat, the eyeglasses. That's why it can be vital to introduce accessories early in the fitting process. The more the actor can rehearse and explore with a signature piece, the more successful the costume. In stage plays where actors play more than one character, radically different accessories can help the actor fasten on a character.

Expecting the Unexpected

In general, items carried in the hand are considered props, but each theater designates that according to their own rules. Many costume areas tend to assume responsibility for handbags but not wallets, briefcases, or luggage; they may do parasols but not umbrellas. Be sure to discuss any items with potential department cross-over at production meetings to ensure coordination. Even though the props department may supply some of the accessories, the costume designer will wish to weigh in on the appearance of any prop associated with a character's ensemble. Props departments may consult the costume designer on other items that require judgment about a character, such as the luggage they would travel with, the style of briefcase or backpack they would choose. If the designer notices a prop does not jive with the character in dress rehearsal, talk with the scenic designer to see if she is open to suggestion for a better match.

Extra Resources

Anatomy of a Shoe www.oliversweeney.com/pages/anatomy-of-a-shoe

Costume Craftwork on a Budget, Tan Huaixiang Focal Press, 2007

From the Neck Up, An Illustrated Guide to Hatmaking, Denise Dreyer, Madhatter Press, 1981

Gentleman, A Timeless Fashion Bernhard Roetzel, Könemann Verlagsgesellschaft mbH, Cologne, Germany 1999. Provides an excellent section on classic styles of men's hats.

Hats Design and Construction, Stella Ramirez Hat Tree Studio, 1986

*Headcovers Unlimited*www.headcovers.com/resources/hats-scarves/types-of-hats-for-men/Provides a thorough list of contemporary hat styles

Men's Classic Shoe Style Names Man of Many.com https://manofmany.com/fashion/a-definitive-guide-to-dress-shoes

Women's Classic Shoe Style Names Encyclopedia of Women's Shoes Alldaychic.com https://alldaychic.com/encyclopedia-of-womens-shoes-visual-shoe-dictionary/

*How to Read Eyeglass Sizes*www.wikihow.com/Read-Eyeglasses-Size

Collars, Stocks, Cravats: A History and Costume Dating Guide to Civilian Men's Neckpieces 1655–1900. Doriece Colle, Rodale Press, 1972

Making Felt Hats. A Beginner's Guide, Bobbi Heath, Search Press, 2021

*Weapons of Choice.com*https://weaponsofchoice.com/

The Textbook of Theatrical Combat, Richard Pallaziol

How to Make Leather Shoe Spats YouTube https://youtu.be/Xsamac5pfEo

Spats Pattern McCall's Fashion Accessories

Action Factory Pro Store, Santa Clarita, CA. Comprehensive guide to stunt pads https://store.afstunts.com/

Slip No More! StageStep Flooring Solutions www.stagestep.com/faq/slip-no-more/

The Complete Book of Jewelry Making, Carles Codina, Lark Books 2006

Notes

1 Gross, Terry. 2020. "'She Wrote Her Own Rules': Kerry Washington's 'Little Fires' Role Reminds Her of Mom." *National Public Radio*, Aired September 3, 2020. https://www.npr.org/2020/09/03/909171748/she-wrote-her-own-rules-kerry-washington-s-little-fires-role-reminds-her-of-mom

2 Sneak, Elizabeth. 2012. "The Lone Ranger: Johnny Depp Works with 'Pirates' Designer Penny Rose for Tonto Costume." *The Hollywood Reporter*, March 18, 2012. https://www.hollywoodreporter.com/news/general-news/lone-ranger-johnny-depp-works-pirates-designer-penny-rose-tonto-costume-297794/

3 Benton, Elizabeth. 1956. *Complete Etiquette*, 5th ed. New York: Random House, p. 49.

4 Kelly, Angela LVO. 2019. *The Other Side of the Coin. The Queen, the Dresser and the Wardrobe*. London: Harper Collins.

5 Alexander, Caroline. 2007. "Faces of War." *Smithsonian Magazine*, February 2007. https://www.smithsonianmag.com/arts-culture/faces-of-war-145799854/

24.
HAIR AND MAKEUP DESIGN

Hair and makeup is the crowning glory of every costume – it is a crucial aspect of character design. Janet Jackson's box braids in the 1993 film *Poetic Justice* sparked a resurgence of that traditional style for mainstream fashion. The wigs worn in *The Lord of the Rings* film series transformed human proportions, such as Orlando Bloom's Legolas wig that created a lift on the crown elongating his face to a signature elven oval. Appropriate hair and makeup will greatly enhance each character, and shoddy goods will cheapen the entire production. The effect of seeing a different person in the mirror is usually a large "aha" moment for actors. When makeup combines with costume, the performer can completely subsume themselves into a new person. This aspect of character building is so important that every designer should understand how to design hair and makeup as part of the overall character concept.

With this much importance, some shows dedicate significant resources employing specialists to create hair and makeup. Television, film, Broadway, and some large regional theaters maintain professional makeup departments who create the look, head the department, and may apply makeup or style wigs with a crew. But many more venues cannot afford this expertise. Solutions vary widely, with the makeup design sometimes the responsibility of the costume designer or each actor. The majority of theatrical venues expect the performer to apply their own makeup even if it is designed by someone else. Most will expect actors to understand the basics of routine straight makeup, glamour and some aging for their own faces. Even venues requiring complex makeup, such as *Cirque du Soleil*, may provide training and staff to oversee the department, but each performer applies and removes their own makeup. Opera companies and large musical theaters may combine methods, asking the actors to apply their own makeup but providing staff for prosthetics and wig applications.

Some actors take great delight in devising their own makeup, even going so far as to experiment with new prosthetic techniques. Others have little personal interest and will gladly apply whatever they are told. The same is true for costume designers. Some have great interest in hair and makeup design and others are content to leave the details to experts. Low budget or volunteer theaters may expect the costume designer to design and style wigs. Make sure you understand this expectation while negotiating the contract. If you have little makeup and hair experience and are not personally interested in learning, you may consider partnering with a specialist for your projects or using part of the budget to hire one. As with all theatrical specialties, makeup, hairstyling, and wig creation are skills that take years to master. The costume designer who wishes to be a full charge wig, hair and makeup person must consult more advanced sources. (See the Extra Resources section.) All aspects of the hair and makeup industries have been proactive creating online content demonstrating many aspects of wig management, hairstyling, and makeup application. It is possible for costume designers who find themselves in charge of hair and makeup to learn enough from video tutorials to do a passable job.

DOI: 10.4324/9781003015284-30

Assessing the Face to Create Makeup

The head and face are a smaller canvas than garments. In many cases it is effective to choose one feature of a character's temperament as the focal point. Hairstyles contribute the design elements of **shape**, **texture**, and **color** to the characterization. Hair can enlarge the head or frame the face. Makeup contributes **focus** and **shape** using light, shadow and color. We emphasize or negate features using darker colors that recede and lighter ones that protrude to create an illusion of sculpture. Makeup experts identify five important planes and features of the face as an important assessment tool:

1. Forehead
2. Eyes and temples
3. Cheekbones and nose
4. Upper lip, mouth, and chin
5. Jowl and neck

The most expressive facial features are the **eyebrows** and **mouth** with hundreds of muscles

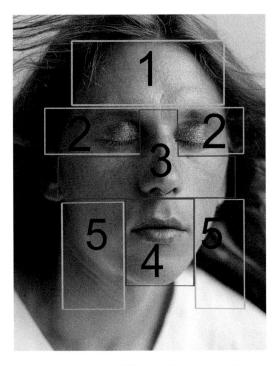

Figure 24.1 The face divides into five major sections to assess the structure and how to apply makeup.

Credit: Original photo by Anna Shvets from Pexels

to animate them. Over time the muscles of the human face can morph into an exaggeration of that person's most common expressions. People who have worried all their lives or scowled may develop downturned brows or mouths.

It is vital to consider the role of hair and makeup in fast changes during the preproduction phase of any show. When performers change costumes they may change hair or makeup as well. Ensemble actors may play more than one role, changing hair or signature makeup features as well. Determine if the actor has adequate time or the venue has adequate support crew to change both garments and hair or makeup backstage. If they cannot, the overall design must be modified to meet these practical operations. The designer can ease these changes for the actor by devising a progression of quickly added items instead of full changes.

Researching Hair and Makeup

The inspiration for every character comes from the costume designer's rendering or research. To avoid going back to the drawing board later in the production process, include hairstyles and facial characteristics in the research phase. Some designers keep ***facial morgues*** as a permanent collection in their image files. We often find the most compelling images when we aren't looking for them. Many designers use Pinterest boards, and makeup designer Kathleen Price recommends using Padlet, an image storage app that stores visual research in convenient columns. (See the Extra Resources section.)

Costume designer and wig/makeup designer Beau Hamilton has worked with both small theaters and large companies such as *Cirque du Soleil*. He notes

> As a designer, I find it helpful for myself to invest time in getting to know what my actors look like and getting to know a few details about them, if time permits. Sometimes we don't have access to their headshots right away, so I tend to utilize their social media/personal websites during the design process. This allows me to get an idea of all the different face shapes, skin tones,

hair textures, and body types that I will be working with. I then take the actors photo and mentally combine their personality, features, and traits I see in their headshot and turn them into the character I'm trying to design. Doing this gives me inspiration for my renderings and allows me to turn it into a final costume/hair rendering. Usually during fittings, I take time to have the actor talk me through their character and their discoveries during the rehearsal process. I find that this can often spark some amazing ideas or lets me know if I need to re-think my design. I know I won't be able to please everyone in this business but when I put some effort into making sure the actors feel heard and are able to build trust with me while designing, more times than not, I have amazing working conditions and it helps set the production up for success.[1]

Collaborating With All Performers

Always present hair and makeup research to your performers that reflects their heritage, especially performers of color. Jerrilyn Lanier is an expert in teaching theater designers and technicians how to work with African American hair and makeup. She notes that

> Research is so important. I hear so many times that performers receive research that doesn't look like them at all. If you don't know something, that is OK. Depending on the time period you can look up noted figures and movement to see what people looked like during the times.[2]

The beauty industry is racing to overcome its Eurocentric view as social media influencers have been calling out the industry and promoting Black-owned companies. Music star Rihanna set a new standard by creating 50 different foundation colors for Fenty Beauty. Many performers of color have taken long, frustrating journeys to find makeup brands and hair products that work for them. They often must pay more for products, so asking them to buy a lot of specialty products can be much more of a financial burden. If the makeup or hair budget is part of the costume designer's task on a show, familiarize yourself with the cost of beauty products for actors of all backgrounds. If the design calls for

styling their own hair consider booking a consultation with the performer for advice on techniques and products. The best way to approach designing for a performer of color is to ask questions. Broadway wig designer Cookie Jordan (*Fela!*) notes that wigs are an important part of black women's lives. "People think that if a black woman is wearing a wig, you can't mention it or that there's a shame involved. That's not it. It's just fashion."[3]

It's alright not to know about textured hair, but not addressing it will make an actor of color feel invisible and unvalued. Be willing to learn more and collaborate with them. One place to begin asking questions is if your performer has **natural**, **relaxed**, or **permed** hair. This will determine the type of products and techniques best suited to the hair. Relaxed and permed hair will hold many styles easily, but may also require products and techniques that add extra moisture. The next step is to ask what **hair type** each performer has, using the **Andre Walker** guide to identify as accurately as possible. During the 1990s, Emmy Award–winning hairstylist Andre Walker created a hair typing system that divided hair into four basic types, with subcategories for texture styles.[4] (See Figure 24.2) Many performers with textured hair will often know their type. Jerrilyn Lanier's website, *Bridging the Gap*, offers information to learn more about this important topic. Contact her for a consultation and specific information on how to match foundation colors for actors of color and suggested products for every styling need. Her Facebook page is updated weekly with research and topics about hair and makeup. (See the Extra Resources section.)

Communicating With Specialists

Regardless of who designs the final makeup and hairstyles, the intent of the character design will most often stem from the costume designer's rendering or character research. And if no one else is available to assess the hair and makeup during dress rehearsals, the costume designer will be expected to offer suggestions on how to improve the final effect under stage light. Designers communicate their vision to a wide array of collaborators, from volunteers to dedicated experts. Many theaters use an arrangement with local salons for haircuts. While

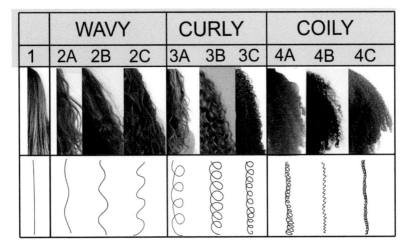

	WAVY			CURLY			COILY		
1	2A	2B	2C	3A	3B	3C	4A	4B	4C

Figure 24.2 The hair typing system created by Andre Walker describes ten types of hair texture.

retail makeup artists or hairdressers understand styling techniques well, they may not grasp character choices or period intentions. Always discuss the desired style ahead of time so everyone involved can do research on their own. Provide headshots of the actor and design research. Establish a common vocabulary using visual research. In many cases the costume designer will consult with the head of the Hair and Makeup Department for a theater who is responsible for carrying out the costume designer's vision. First discuss the artistic goals and world-building rules for the project. Review the research and renderings. Theatrical makeup and hair artists will understand both the need to establish character and the rigorous activity of stage performances. They will ask to see the costumes worn with this hairstyle, and they will also undertake extensive research into period products and techniques.

Advice From Kathleen Price, Makeup Designer, Monster Maker for Knott's Scary Farm, *Cirque du Soleil*

"Color Theory is a game changer. Learn it. Any time spent with brushes in hand is time well spent. There is a French expression 'When you are learning something new, just keep doing it and one day you will discover that your hands have become intelligent.' Start every project as if anything is possible and discover your way to communicate effectively as early as you can."[5]

Working With Makeup Styles

Makeup application styles evolved through history to impart social significance or achieve a ritualistic effect. Contemporary theatrical traditions draw on this long history, using several generally understood styles of makeup. Matching one of these styles to the intent of a character forms an excellent foundation to embellish a design or communicate intent:

Straight/street. Enhances natural features using fashionable techniques such shaping eyebrows or lips and using popular colors. This look is routine for dramas and smaller venues. It may be adjusted slightly by adding aspects of glamour makeup to enhance eyes in large venues.

Glamour. A heavier makeup application that exaggerates eyes and/or and lips using highlight, shadow, and eyeliners. Often includes false eyelashes. This look is routine in musical theater. This application may be extreme for large venues.

Period. Recreates the fashions of historical eras. Some periods were extremely elaborate and others valued a more natural facial quality. By the 20th century, makeup styles changed with each decade to correspond to fashion.

Corrective. Advanced use of highlight and shadow to reduce or enhance features, or create the illusion of specific proportions and reduce bulk. Extreme versions use tapes to pull the skin upward. These techniques can also be used to create a resemblance to an historical character.

Drag glamour. A specialized combination of glamour and corrective makeup to create often exaggerated female signifiers.

Aging. Uses highlight, shadow, and lines to create the illusion of the same face in advanced years. This look strives to look natural, requiring practice to achieve realistically. Exaggerated for large venues.

Character/FX. A large category that changes some configuration of the performer's appearance to create a new appearance. Subtle techniques include changing eyebrow shapes or adding prosthetics. More extreme versions add wounds, bruises, or other effects. All specialty and creature makeup is technically a subset of character makeup. However, those categories have now gotten so specialized it

Figure 24.4 Straight or street makeup enhances the features using fashionable colors and techniques.

Credit: Photo by RF Studio from Pexels

is possible to become an expert in just one application.

Fantasy and animal. A wide range of effects for extravaganzas and social costume events. Includes cosplay applications as well as stage techniques to create animals such as those used in *Cats* or *The Lion King*.

Makeup Sketches and Charts

Designers may find the character rendering, sketches, or research collages contain enough information to instruct an actor how to achieve the desired effect. But in some cases a specific makeup sketch may be required. Using digital tools, it is possible to work over photographs of an actor's face using a photo taken in a fitting. The designer himself may not understand the exact products to use, but digitally painting the

Figure 24.3 Fantasy makeup depicts a concept or character that is evocative or sensational.

Credit: Photo by Marcelo Moreira from Pexels

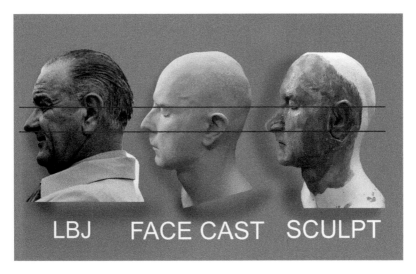

Figure 24.5 Makeup artist Kevin Haney created character makeup using a prosthetic nose, chin, and ears for Hugo Armstrong as Lyndon Baines Johnson (LBJ). Photos of work in progress were lined up with reference photos to synchronize the actor's features to LBJ. South Coast Repertory production of *All the Way*.

final intent serves as a starting point for discussion and experimentation (Figure 24.6). Note areas in the makeup sketch that were highlighted and darkened, and any colors used for eyeshadow or lipstick. With this information in hand the designer and actor can suggest suitable products. For those with enough training to create a makeup design with exact product notes, the formal makeup chart will document the application areas and products to use (Figure 24.7).

Theatrical Makeup Versus Street Makeup

Some performers will ask if they must wear makeup. That answer is usually *yes*. Carrie Meyer, a dancer and dance photographer notes that "make-up is part of your costume." Without it, eyes will frequently fade away and the face will look drab.[6] There is some disagreement about whether it is appropriate to use street makeup for stage purposes. Some performers with sensitive skin balk at wearing stage products, preferring to use specific retail brands. Performers working in intimate venues may avoid theatrical cream foundation products, preferring to use powder. Performers of color might be better served by retail manufacturers who specialize in a wider variety of skin tones. Lower-income students or community performers may be better

served with more affordable products. And some dancers avoid ruining their costumes with makeup smears if they come into contact with others. As with any product, quality varies widely and some performers may have formed their aversion to theatrical makeup during their student days, if they used poor-quality kits.

Makeup artists agree that *foundation* products made especially for film, television, or stage provide better coverage under the glare of lights and protection against perspiration damage. It contains more pigment than retail makeup. Fantasy makeup such as that used at *Cirque du Soleil* requires those heavily pigmented products to completely cover the skin. Street makeup is more sheer with less pigment suspended in the base. Those products are meant to be seen very close up and should blend into the wearer's features. It is certainly possible to wear street makeup in performances. A large majority of any stage makeup kit is made of common retail products such as pencils, eyeliners, shadows, lipsticks, and eyelashes. Retail companies have spent millions of dollars on a wide array of ingredients and staying power. The ultimate decision is between the actor and the costume designer. If the effect looks correct onstage and lasts through the performance without skin rashes or abrasion, then the makeup is successful.

MAKEUP WORKSHEET

BASE: *match skin tone*

MA- 5 Coffee Bean

LOWLIGHT: *temples, under chin*

Contour Wheel Olive—blend well

ROUGE: Cheek

POWDER: Dark Cocoa

EYE SHADOW(S): *Smokey eye, above and below*

EYELINER: Ulta Gel Pencil Black

MASCARA: Glossier Lash Slick Black

HAIR/FACIAL HAIR: Beard, Eyebrows, Wig

Kryolan Medical Adhesive

Figure 24.6 Sample of a makeup worksheet created by painting and collaging over an actor's face. The designer and actor can discuss colors and products to compile produce information together.

Credit: Original photo by David Kuko from Pexels

Advice From Beau Hamilton, *Cirque du Soleil*, Houston Ballet

"A lot of times we are not provided with big budgets or at least when you are first starting out in the industry. I think it's important to set aside a decent amount of money for hair and makeup. There's nothing more distracting on stage than a bad makeup job or that awful, fake sheen from cheap looking synthetic hair under those stage lights. Today, we have numerous options when it comes to wigs and hair. With all the popular technology, cosplay, and drag, it's much easier to find inexpensive synthetic hair options that look amazing on stage and won't kill your budget. I suggest spending the time researching and exploring great wig and makeup supply stores, it will be worth your time in the long run."[7]

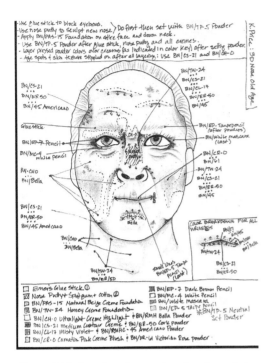

Figure 24.7 Samples of two styles of makeup design communication created by Kathleen Price. The image at left includes detailed product and application information. The image at right created the design using a NYX face template suitable for multiracial performers. (See the Extra Resources section.)

Analyzing a Hairstyle

Communicating about wig and hair needs can be daunting for the novice designer. While many are familiar with makeup applications from daily or performance use of their own, wigs and hairstyling can be more mysterious. Familiarity with the options can help a designer assess the character's hairstyle needs. Costume designers for period shows may spend more of their time devising hairstyles for their characters as elaborate or at the very least well-coifed hair was a sign of respectability and status. The designer can gain confidence with hair designs by learning how to analyze the basic components of each style. Cosmetology schools use a system of sectioning the hair for precise cutting or styling. Designers can modify this approach to evaluate and express their desired intent. This method establishes a foundation for clear communication with others, and aids the designer styling hair or a wig themselves.

1. Hairline, including details such as bangs, baby hairs, edges, or spiral curls
2. Top of the head front
3. Top of the head back
4. The rim or sides of the head
5. The lower back head and nape area

Begin with visual research of the desired style to evaluate each section. Determine what shape or desired effect is required in each section: extra volume, trailing curls, a close crop. These answers offer clues to what kind of wig or hairpiece might be most effective. Always look at all four sides of a hairstyle when analyzing it. Think ahead about sightlines in a hairstyle – does any part fall into the face or hide the eyes? Watch for shadows that may cast across the face. It is common to modify a period or complex hairstyle to accommodate visibility and choreography. Fortunately there are tutorials available on just about every kind of hair technique as a starting point to experiment.

Types of Wigs and Hair Pieces

Wigs are available in **human hair** or a variety of **synthetic hair** options. Human hair wigs are a more expensive investment, but they last longer

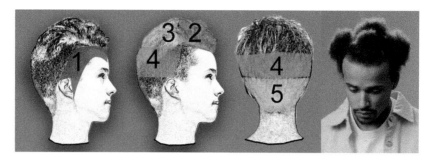

Figure 24.8 Dividing the head into sections for assessment and styling.

Credit: Photo at right by cottonbro from Pexels

Figure 24.9 This Greco-Roman hairstyle can be evaluated using sections of the head. Colors correspond to the sections in Figure 24.8.

Credit: Marble portrait of a young woman ca. AD 98–117. Fletcher Fund, 1927. Metropolitan Museum of Art, New York

and more durable for styling than synthetic wigs. Synthetics have the advantage of affordability, they are available in a large variety of cuts and styles, and they hold a style well. Both types of wigs can be successfully dyed to different colors, cut or enhanced. Just as with makeup, humans have been augmenting their hair since the ancient era, and many types of wigs and hair pieces have evolved for specific uses.

Cascade. Hair sewn onto a rounded or squared fabric base sewn to create a waterfall of curls.

Clip-on. Small hair pieces such as buns or ponytails added to enhance natural hair. Requires a good color match, especially under stage light.

Fall. Generic term for long hair pieces sewn onto a round or square base added to enhance natural hair. Requires a good color match especially under stage light.

French drawn. Top of the line commercial wigs with the most natural look. Hand tied with three layered cap construction. The bottom layer is silk to protect the scalp, the middle layer is mesh to tie individual hairs, and a top layer of fine silk to hide the knots.

Fronted (see Lace Front). A shorthand term for a wig with a small strip of fine mesh added around the hairline. A common construction method in theater.

Hair pieces. A broad category of partial pieces that clip or tie to augment the wearer's hair. Common forms are buns, curls, and ponytails.

Half or ¾ wig. Wigs worn set back from the wearer's hairline. The wearer's front hair is styled with the wig creating a natural transition.

Hand tied. A handmade wig with a full lace cap and hair strands ventilated or hooked into the lace. Considered the finest wigs available, they are lightweight, breathable, and natural looking on stage or film. These are correspondingly expensive.

Hard front. The wig is bound on the edge with a braid or a skin toned rubber edge. The hairstyle begins very abruptly at the hairline, creating a "hard" front line.

Human hair. Wigs made of 100% human hair can be styled and maintained just like other natural hair. More expensive than synthetic wigs. The price varies according to the quality of the hair itself. The advantages to human hair include superior textures, longevity, style-ability, and the best imitation of real hair for shoulder length or longer hair.

Lace front. Wigs with a small panel of sheer lace along the front hairline, sometimes reaching as low as the sideburn area. Small groups of hair are individually tied into the lace for a more natural look that blends into the wearers own hairline. Ordering commercial lace front wigs sometimes requires trimming the lace to fit the wearer.

Monofilament. Uses extremely fine polyester or nylon micro-mesh with individual strands of hair added, creating a realistic scalp appearance. Good flexibility for styling, expensive. **Mono-top** wigs use this technique on top, combined with other wig-making methods.

Puff, pad, or bump. Hair or foam shapes worn under parts of the hair to create fuller volume. Used to shape and support buns, chignons, or crown height.

Pull-through. Intended for those with thinning hair, may also be used to add volume for sculptured styles onstage such as extreme pompadours. Constructed on a honeycomb cap with spaces wide enough to pull the wearer's hair through to blend in.

Remy human hair. The highest quality hair cut from its source from root to tip in the direction it grew. Other types of human hair are gathered in clumps, then combed into a single direction so the cuticles may matte or tangle.

Skin-top or **skin-part.** Includes an area of latex, rubber, or fabric that imitates the look of scalp visible at the edge of the wig or at the part.

Switch. Ponytail pieces or long additions to a hairstyle.

Synthetic wigs. Much less expensive than human hair wigs, available in a vast range of qualities from very realistic to Cosplay artificiality. Not as long lasting, but they maintain a style well. Cannot use heated styling tools.

Toupee. A term used to mean a partial wig for men to cover a bald spot. The hair is long at the sides to brush into the man's own hair below to blend.

Weft/extensions. Hair sewn onto ribbon-like strips, used to sew into wig caps or as extensions to add volume, length, or contrast color to the wearers own hair. Attached with clips, sewing, braiding or glue depending on desired effect. Used to make all manner of special needs, including 1776-style ponytail additions to men's hairstyles.

Wiglet/hair toppers. Hair added to the wearer's own for styles requiring volume, usually added to the top of the head. Some versions are pull-through, and others are pre-styled add-ons.

Styling Wigs

Wigs and false hair have been essential parts of the stage illusion for centuries. Audience expectations have soared in the last decades as higher quality wigs became more readily available and lower-cost fronted wigs were imported cheaply. Broadway shows started spending lavishly on hair and makeup, setting the bar even higher. The wigs used in *Wicked* cost between $1,200 and $2,400 each, and a very good quality wig can cost $5,000.[8] Actors can be understandably more reluctant to chemically process their own hair for a role, as

over the years some of them experienced permanent damage. Wigs solve this problem and provide the opportunity for more elaborate hairstyles. Human hair wigs may be styled using hot irons, curlers, blow driers, or any other device. Most wig professionals advise using curlers and a steamer to style *synthetics* instead of the hot irons and rollers used on regular hair. Synthetics will melt or break with heat and quickly look patchy or fuzzy. Although there are special wig steamers available, any hand-held steamer sold for clothing will work as long as the nozzle can be aimed correctly. The best method requires styling while the wig is on a sized canvas head block instead of the cheap foam heads that are one-sized and fall over easily. When budget is a factor, invest in wig clamps to hold foam heads to a counter.

Figure 24.10 This fall or cascade is set on a circular base. It adds curls and volume to the back of the head.

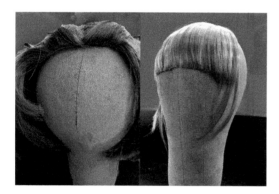

Figure 24.11 The wig at left is a hard front wig. At right a hair piece that adds bangs to a hairstyle.

Figure 24.12 The wig at left is a full lace cap wig, at center a capless or open cap, at right a partial cap wig.

The Parts of a Wig

Extended neck. A new section sewn to the bottom of a wig cap base to allow more coverage for those with long nape hairlines.

Full lace cap. The mesh base that hugs the skull made of a mesh fabric that does not stretch. The hair wefts are sewn to the base, or individual hairs are locked into the mesh. This construction method provides the most sturdiness and longevity. Provides flexibility in styling and parting. More expensive than standard wigs, but realistic looking.

Lace. Fine mesh around the forehead to smooth the transition from hair to skin. Some wigs benefit from gluing the lace in front of the ears to hold the lace taut. The lace can be blended with makeup.

Open cap/capless. Lace ribbons sewn to create the pattern of hair, one is able to stick your fingers through an open base. This style is lightweight, providing more stretch and cooling air flow. Machine made, these are affordable and versatile.

Mesh cap. Hair is sewn to a stretchy mesh or crochet base providing elasticity over the entire wig. These wigs are often hand-made.

Partial cap. A combination of lace cap in front and open cap below the crown.

Skin or silk. A fabric or synthetic covering that looks like skin to create a part or as a forehead edge on some wigs.

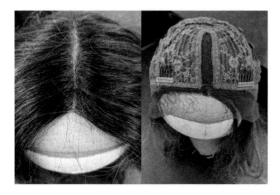

Figure 24.13 This wig is a lace front wig that also incorporates a U-part in the wig cap so the middle part appears more natural.

Measuring for a Wig

The costume designer or costume shop will be the first to see the actors, and if there is no resident wig maker, the costume crew will take wig measurements. Vendors, rental sources, and independent wig makers or stylists will ask for a complete set of measurements. For video instructions, see the Extra Resources section.

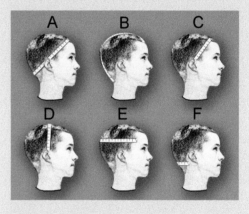

Figure 24.14 Wig measurement photo.

Table 24.1 Wig Measurements

A	Circumference Measure around the head at the hairline
B	Front to Nape Measure from front hairline to low nape
C	Forehead Ear to Ear Measure from top of ear across hairline to top of other ear
D	Ear to Ear Across Top Measure from ear to ear across the top of the head
E	Temple to Temple Front of temple to temple on other side around back of head
F	Nape of Neck Measure across the nape hairline at its lowest point

Creating a Plastic Head Wrap

On occasion the costume designer works with a long-distance wig maker who will make a custom wig or re-front a commercial wig. They may ask for a plastic head wrap of the actor that serves as a mold of their head shape and hairline. The wig maker will use the wrap to create the front of a wig so it seamlessly blends or covers the performer's own hairline. The first step is to prepare the performer's hair so that it is as flat as possible. This is the same prep that would be used to wear the wig itself, so it is important to eliminate strange lumps or bumps. For more instructions on how to prep hair and take a plastic head wrap, see the Extra Resources section. Wig artist Laura Caponera recommends the following technique for preparing a plastic head wrap.[9]

Prepare the hair in pin curls
- Create five pin curls at front of the hairline, about 3/8 inch in from the hairline. These serve as anchor points for the wig.
- Create two pin curls behind the ears as anchor points.
- Forehead wrap: use sticky medical wrap, the kind used to set over fractures and under the plaster cast. Wrap the forehead for a bald cap, receding hairline, or if the actor has extra-thick hair.
- Use hairspray or spray gel to sweep hair off the hairline.
- Use a rattail comb to sweep the hair off the hairline.
- Wig cap: use a wig cap close to the color of the actors hair.
- Use small hair pins to anchor the wig cap.

Create the plastic head wrap
- Use a brand of cling wrap that is wider such as Glad or Smart & Final industrial wrap.
- Stretch the plastic wrap at eyebrow level, wrapping over the ear and down the nape.
- Pull tightly across the back of the head.
- Secure with clear packing tape, the cheap thin type, or scotch tape.

- Tape tightly from center to sides.
- Mark the hairline in *vertical marks* echoing the direction of growth.
- Draw a line from ear to ear over the top of the head, and from center front to center back.
- Measure the actor's head with the pin curls and plastic wrap.

Figure 24.15 Prepping the hair in pin curls.

Figure 24.16 Using a bandage wrap for a bald cap, receding hairline, or extra thick hair.

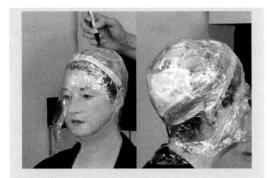

Figure 24.17 Marking the plastic head wrap with vertical marks imitating the direction of hair growth.

Working With Bargain Wigs

Wigs have become an affordable fashion accessory and it is tempting to use them for theatrical productions. And for some budgets, cheap costume wigs are the only solution. The trade-off is the wig will not last beyond a short run. If the show runs for more than a couple of weeks, consider buying two duplicate wigs. The hair on cheaply made wigs may shed unevenly or the texture will change, growing fuzzier. If at all feasible, shop at a beauty supply or specialist wig resource. Employees at brick-and-mortar wig stores are much better informed about the type of hair each wig has, and they are understanding about different budget needs. A costume designer is a potential repeat customer, so form a good relationship with the wig consultant. Investing a little time into a cheap wig will make it look much more expensive.

- **Thin the hair**. Most cheap wigs are made with too much hair so they look fake right out of the box. Turn the wig inside out to discover how the wefts are sewn. Either remove every other weft of hair, or use thinning shears to remove hair.
- **Blend the part.** Many cheap wigs have too-perfect parts with large clumps of hair on either side. Use tweezers to pluck random hairs or use a rattail comb to push some hairs in the opposite direction.
- **Add color depth.** Wigs made with just one color of hair look cartoony or flatten under stage light. Darken the roots two shades darker and add streaks to the body of the hair. Use art markers or hair dye, using a highlighting cap to target specific hairs. If temporary measures are needed, darkening the part with pigmented powder is a removable solution.
- **Blur the shine.** Cheap synthetic wigs have an unnatural high shine that looks even brighter under stage light. Spray the wig with fabric softener, dry shampoo or add a light dusting of hair spray and powder.
- **Add shine.** Light color wigs sold for 18th-century styles or platinum blonde styles may look cottony. Shampoo with olive oil soap or castile soap. Comb a heavy conditioner through the wig and leave for 24 hours before rinsing.
- **Comb gently.** Brushing with a full comb or brush can break the hair of a cheap wig. Use wide-tooth combs and brushes only.
- **Use firm hairsprays.** Strong hold sprays will keep a style in its best form.
- **Soften a hard front.** Some bargain wigs use a hard ribbon or rubber edge that looks unnatural. Carefully remove the sewn in ribbon using a seam ripper, razor blade, or small tailor's points. For more instructions, see the Extra Resources section.
- **Buy duplicates.** Consider buying two wigs for longer runs, so that if one style degrades there is a backup.

Facial Hair

Audiences are very sophisticated observers, and they can spot an obviously fake beard or mustache. Unless the effect is supposed to be comical, the audience is far less likely to overlook its appearance. Cheap versions are overly thick and all one color with unnatural hair growth patterns. These are dead giveaways as cheap costume pieces. While some larger theaters employ hair artists who can ventilate any kind of facial hair on a net backing, many do not. The costume designer may find herself alone trying to solve this problem. Cheaper facial hair can be amended and improved using the same techniques for affordable wigs, described earlier.

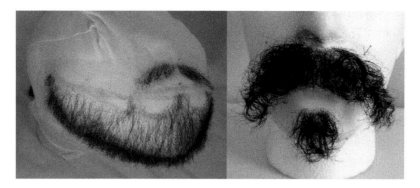

Figure 24.18 This facial hair is an example of fine craftsmanship that looks realistic when applied. The hairs are sparsely and artfully placed in the lace backing.

Credit: Photo and beards by Crystal Stuart-Fawkes, Crystal Faith Creations, Etsy

Fortunately lace-backed ventilated options are available from many professional makeup suppliers. (See the Extra Resources section.)

Working With Student Actors

Hair and makeup require training and practice to accomplish and wear correctly. Student actors may be completely at sea with delicate wigs and makeup requiring a steady hand. Wig, makeup, and costume designer Susan Bussard finds she has to teach her actors how to handle wigs, especially.

> It's important to teach the cast and crew about wigs and their care before the show. . . . You can stand in front of a bunch of students and say 'This is super expensive, don't screw it up' but that's not going to be effective. A lot of my students have a sort of disposable mindset. They think if they mess a wig up, we can just get a new one. So I tell them it's an expensive piece of equipment and they should treat it like they would a lighting instrument or rental costume.

She creates simple tutorials for the crew on the proper way to handle wigs and how to store it on a head block between shows.[10]

Sizing Up Hair and Makeup

Famous film and TV designs thrill us with their complete transformations of actors into characters, such as Naomi Grossman's metamorphosis into Pepper

for *American Horror Story*. However, they spend many hours in hair and makeup to achieve it. For most professional theaters, the Equity half-hour call time limits the show preparation time. Longer calls may require additional salary. That will be necessary for a specialty part, but few producers will allow a longer call as the norm. No matter how elaborate the character looks, actors must be able to apply their makeup and hair within their given call time. When these limitations are imposed, they may drive a designer to use wigs imaginatively, from sewing partial wigs into hats to building adventurous wig helmets from found objects for fantasy characters.

Expecting the Unexpected

Some actors become attached to their own style of makeup, especially when an increasing number of them are social media presences. If you find yourself engaged in a contest of wills over a makeup technique, there are several good ways to navigate the situation. First, talk only to and about the character. Reaffirm your goals for the character and ask if they are still applicable. Ask questions of their character such as "What does Hamlet think about not seeing their eyes – are they trying to avoid eye contact, or maybe fade away?" If "Hamlet" agrees they would like to fade the eyes, then give it a try. Alert the director that the actor is trying that technique. If the director is fine with it, can you live with it? If the director is not fine with losing the face of the leading actor, revisit the discussion with this new information. The second technique asks the actor to solve any problems you discover. After watching a rehearsal, gently alert the actor to the problem, such as their Instagram "signature" melon lipstick glows like a traffic cone under the stage light. Ask them to suggest solutions. Do this out of earshot of the other actors so others don't escalate the situation. If the actor does not know of a solution, be prepared with your desired suggestion. As with any disagreement with a performer, tread lightly. Chances are large you will work with this individual again and it is not worth damaging a professional relationship. Costume designers must be, in the end, masters of persuasion.

Extra Resources

The Ultimate Resource for Makeup

Corson, Richard, and James Glavan, Beverly Gore Norcross. *Stage Makeup 11th Edition.* Routledge, 2019. While many older editions of this classic book are available, the 11th edition discusses inclusivity and diversity with better representations in the photographs and applications.

Staff, "Facial Anatomy & Proportions." *Hair and Makeup Artist.com*, Updated May 31.2021. https://hair-and-makeup-artist.com/facial-anatomy-proportions/

NYX Professional Makeup, *Inclusive Collective of Face Charts.* Templates for designing makeup for diverse performers. www.nyxcosmetics.com/beauty-face-charts.html

The Ultimate Resource for Wig Making, Styling, and Facial Hair

Ruskai, Martha, and Allison Lowery. *Wig Making and Styling: A Complete Guide for Theatre & Film.* Focal Press, 2016.

Hair & Makeup Design for African American Performers

Lanier, Jerrilyn. *Bridging the Gap*, https://bridgingthegap intheatre.com/

Measuring for a Wig Video Instructions

TheHareLife, "How to Properly Measure Your Head for a Wig" *YouTube.* Dec. 21, 2019 https://youtu.be/x5pqptXUVlc

Prepare Hair for Wig Application: Straight Hair

Brewster, Karen with Ryan Fischer. "Hair Preparation & Wig Application" *TD &T Journal* Winter 2012. Available USITT National Office or the Bellman Archives www.

nxtbook.com/nxtbooks/hickmanbrady/tdt_2012winter/index.php?startid=29&qs=wigs#/p/28

Moody, Flora. "Pro-Technique: The Hair Wrap" *You Tube.* Mar. 9, 2014. https://youtu.be/Q06dnqXLrFU

Prepare Hair for Wig Application: Textured or Natural Hair

Teaca, Giulia, "How to Prep Your Natural Hair for a Wig" NAIJ Hair. Aug. 9, 2020. https://naijhair.com/blogs/hair/how-to-prep-natural-hair-for-wigs

The Gloved Natural. "How I Prep My Natural Hair for Wigs" *YouTube.* Apr. 18, 2019. https://youtu.be/hufm6sVMPsw

Prepping and Putting on a Theatrical Wig: Straight Hair

Lyrical Opera Theater. "Putting on a Theatrical Wig Tutorial 2021" *YouTube.* June 9, 2021. https://youtu.be/N-fI3-188D0

Prepping Hair for a Wig With a Sound Mic

Ashford, Georgie. "Musical Theater Hair Tutorial/Wig Prep & Wig Dressing for a Show." *YouTube.* Oct. 16, 2019. https://youtu.be/pDGZdJ0U9XI

Create a Plastic Film Head Wrap

Custom Wig Company https://customwigcompany.com/our-process/

High Quality Facial Hair

Stuart-Fawkes, Crystal Faith. Crystal Faith Creation, Etsy, Manchester UK www.etsy.com/shop/CrystalFaithCreation

Trimming Front Lace on a Lace-Front Wig

Mayvenn. "How to Cut a Lace Front Wig in 4 Steps." Mayvenn.com. May 15, 2020. https://shop.mayvenn.com/blog/hair/how-to-cut-a-lace-front-wig/

NOTE: Theatrical wigs leave more lace over the forehead than streetwear wigs to accommodate wilder stage motion. Makeup and stage light will help blend to the skin.

Hair Textures & Styling

Kenneth. "Hair Type Chart: How to Find Your Curl Pattern with Pictures" *Curlcentric.Com.* Accessed May 15, 2021. www.curlcentric.com/hair-typing-system/

Laying Hair Edges

Luxy. "A Beginner's Guide to Edges" *Luxyhair.com.* Accessed Aug. 20, 2021. www.luxyhair.com/blogs/hair-blog/edges-hair.

Softening a Hard Front Wig

Simons, Jesse M. "How to Make a Hard Front Wig Look Natural" *YouTube*. Sept. 18, 2020. https://youtu.be/rN-3M-EXFyk

Wig Care and Storage

Uslin, Kimberly. "Not a Hair Out of Place, The Care and Upkeep of Wigs" *Educational Theatre Association*. Accessed Aug. 20, 2021. www.schooltheatre.org/about/news/notahairoutofplace

Notes

1 Hamilton, Beau. 2021. Via email with the author September 16, 2021.
2 Lanier, Jerilynn. 2019. "Bridging the Gap, African American Hair & Make Up for the Theater." *United States Institute of Theater Technology Conference*, Louisville, KY, March 2019.
3 Gushue, Jen. 2019. "The Art of Designing Black Hair for the Stage." *TDF*, March 12, 2019. https://www.tdf.org/stages/article/2112/the-art-of-designing-black-hair-for-the-stage
4 Mars, Roman, Day, Leila, and Baba, Hana. "Episode 303 The Hair Chart." *99% Invisible Podcast*. https://99percentinvisible.org/episode/the-hair-chart/
5 Price, Kathleen. 2021 Via email with author, December 1, 2021.
6 Meyer, Carrie. 2016. "A Few Words about Stage & Regular Makeup for Dance." *The Dancers Eye*, April 15, 2016. https://www.thedancerseye.com/blog/a-few-words-about-stage-regular-makeup-for-dance
7 Hamilton, Beau. 2021. Via email with the author, September 16, 2021.
8 Hairloss. n.d. "A Study of the Use of Wigs in Professional Stage and Theater." https://www.hairloss.com/a-study-of-the-use-of-wigs-in-professional-stage-and-theater/
9 Caponera, Laura. 2018. *How to Create a Plastic Headwrap* Workshop, University of California, Irvine, September 20, 2018.
10 Uslin, Kimberly. n.d. "Not a Hair Out of Place." *Educational Theater Association*. https://www.schooltheatre.org/about/news/notahairoutofplace

PART SEVEN

EVALUATE

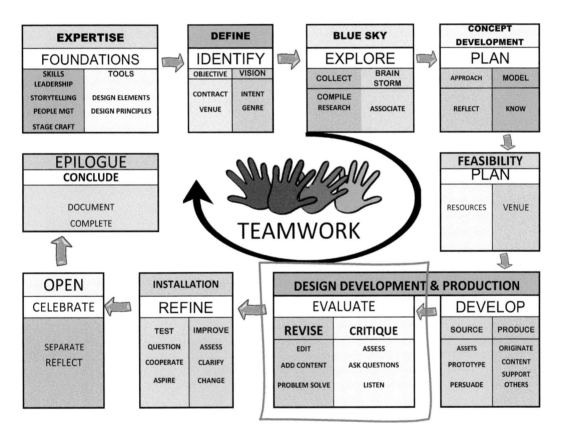

Figure 25.0 The creative process for produced projects

Credit: Holly Poe Durbin and Ayrika Johnson

25.
PREPARING FOR FITTINGS

Ellen Mirojnick, the costume designer of *Bridgerton*, described the process of finding the character of Duke Simon Basset with actor Regé-Jean Page. Discovering his character established the rules for his wardrobe at large.

> First we created a silhouette for him – what he could wear and what he couldn't wear . . . and what we found was #1 [the Duke] would never wear white pants, #2 he would always wear tall boots and #3 his shirts would always be open. . . . He was the only character to wear black. We tried about six different jackets on him until we came to the one that was perfect on him. We raised the depth of his collar, because [he] has a very long neck so it was important for his jaw to be embraced by the collar. Then we took the cravat, turned it into a scarf, and put it inside his shirt.

She also described creating a backstory for the Duke in the fitting room. "Because of the difficulty of [the Duke's] childhood . . . he wanted to take with him everywhere a piece of his mother." They decided "Lady Danbury gave him one of his mother's brooches, and he wears it on his waistcoat, on his lapel the entire time. We created the world of Simon – his spirit, where he came from and where he traveled to."[1]

Fittings are the backbone of the costume designer's job. What is the most important skill a costume designer needs in a fitting? Many people guess an understanding of fit or garment construction. Some guess that an excellent poker face is most essential, and a few guess talking with the actors. These are all essential skills. But the most important skill a costume designer uses in a fitting is **listening**. The designer must have 360-degree listening to the actor, the director, fitting staff, movement needs, the story, the audience, and their own vision.

Torn in Many Directions

What does everyone want when they are in a fitting? The designer wants to arrive at the final modeling of the character, the result of so much preparation. The costume staff wants adequate time to assess items that don't fit, carefully pin alterations or recommend substitutions if needed. The actor wants to meet their performing partner – the costume. They also want to know the costume designer is a trusted collaborator. The director wants to see their vision come to life, and they also want the actors to be satisfied with the costume. The director is often the first person an actor sees after returning to rehearsal from a fitting, and many will ask the actor for a report. The stage manager juggles many balls and wants to keep that day's rehearsal on schedule. The costume designer must be aware of satisfying all these desires, yet still have the backbone to stand up

DOI: 10.4324/9781003015284-32

for their own process. As vital as the fitting is for the costume designer and actor to work together, there are many forces working to restrict the time available for fittings. Actors Equity rules direct the timing and placement of fittings so they may be in direct competition with rehearsal time. Fittings outside of the acceptable work hours require special arrangements and perhaps extra pay. Community and educational schedules must compete with rehearsals, outside employment and classes. And the longer the costume staff spends in fittings, the fewer tasks they can accomplish assembling or altering garments. It is imperative to use fitting time wisely and productively.

Actors and theaters belong to professional associations empowered to negotiate with each other for union contract terms that everyone agrees to work under for a number of years. Actor's Equity maintains code books for every style of theater agreement outlining pay scales, work hours (including fittings and photo calls) and rates for renting actor's personal clothing for the run of a show. One LORT performing venue may operate under several agreements; for instance, the large mainstage theater may operate under a LORT B+ agreement, and their small experimental theater may operate under a LORT D agreement. Costume designers and costume directors must work within these parameters. Ask the producer or stage manager to provide a copy of the current rule books, or call Actor's Equity for information.

Actor's Equity Association	www.actorsequity.org
League of Resident Theater Membership List	www.lort.org
National Dinner Theater Association	www.ndta.us
American Association of Community Theatre	www.aact.org

Planning the Style of Fittings

The fitting is the next-to-last step of *modeling* in the design process. An idea that began as a collection of research, moved to a sketch, and may have been tested on a dress form during the pulling phase now moves onto the actor. Many costume designers talk about the character as the third person emerging during the fitting. Penny Rose (*Pirates of the Caribbean*) describes

> The costume process for a character . . . is that three people come into the room: the costume designer, the actor and the character. At the end of the hour or two hours, whatever, the actor should be able to see the character in the mirror. That's what we try to achieve.[2]

Two essential tasks must take place in the limited time of every fitting. The designer uses **creative time** to build a character and create the final design, and the shop staff requires **fitting time** to plan alterations. It is essential to define the goals of each fitting, and if all tasks cannot be completed, split them into separate fittings, if possible. These are typical kinds of fittings the designer may consider:

- **Character consultation**. The designer and actor meet to try many items and ideas in rapid succession, establishing a dialogue. It may be that no fitting personnel are needed, or this may combine with other fitting tasks.
- **Foundations**. Some costumes require fully fitting underpinnings (corsetry and vintage bras or girdles) or understructures such as padded suits or boned pods to support animal costumes. Fight choreography requires stunt pads. Outer garments cannot be successfully fitted until these items are chosen and fitted first.
- **Rehearsal items**. Period shows, devised pieces, stunt work, and weaponry may require that actors work with items early in rehearsal. Sword belts may have to be fit first over every day rehearsal clothes and then adjusted later to the final costume. Actors wearing hoop skirts must use them in rehearsals. Fewer younger actors are comfortable in leather shoes, having grown up entirely in sneakers.

- **Alterations fitting**. For stock, rented, and purchased costumes, this fitting concentrates on a careful review of all the pieces and how to wear them. Each piece is pinned to fit, or alternative items chosen. Some garments may need extensive work or restyling to satisfy the design.
- **Muslin fitting**. Made-to-order costumes are fit in sample fabric first, or a combination of sample and finished items. More time is required to achieve a refined fit and mark design details such as placement of large trim areas.
- **Fabric fitting**. After made-to-order costumes are sewn, another fitting ensures the costume fits in the fashion fabric. Final adjustments are made.
- **Final fitting**. Occasionally there is time to call actors after everything is complete for a final try. This cements the costume in their heads.
- **Wig/makeup fitting**. Wigs, elaborate hairstyles, and specialty makeup require their own sets of fittings.

There are two additional styles of fitting used in special circumstances, such as spectaculars where many performers wear similar costumes. The first is **group fittings** with several performers scheduled at once in a large dressing room. Each costume is completely assembled with extra choices available. Multiple costumers in the room check the fit, pin alterations and take notes. Another fitting style is **assembly line fittings** with several "feeder" changing rooms and one or two fitting rooms. Performers dress in their changing room and then stand in line for a turn in the fitting room, every 15–20 minutes. Costumers in the changing rooms reassemble the costumes and add tags or other organizational information. Film crews are adept at managing large numbers of **extras** fittings, which can translate to some theater projects. Costumers hand an actor their costume based on prior sizes and direct them to alternatives if items don't fit. Costumers photograph each actor in the finished ensemble using a white board on the wall behind the actor with name, character name, scene number, and costume number. They assemble the fitted costumes and label pieces going out for alterations. These group systems work well for performers

Figure 25.1 A fitting to check alterations on this 1960s' style suit.

that do not require a deep understanding of character. This method can also translate well to stage shows offering performing opportunities to a large number of youth actors, particularly acting camps or children's theater.

Planning the Fitting Schedule

How many fittings will you schedule for your project? It is wisest to schedule fittings that match the timeline for the project. Each show has been given a known quantity of work days, and not every actor will be called every work day. If you are uncertain how to figure out when actors may be called, consult the costume manager or stage manager to create a plan for every week. (Review Chapter 17.) Creating a plan identifies what the designer and shop must prepare each day. Alert the stage manager to types of fittings that take longer so they can suggest best options. If the show is complex, it may be necessary to negotiate extra fitting time with the producer. The logistics of every organization are different and will affect fittings, too. Some considerations are:

- **Proximity.** If the costume shop is located in the same building as the rehearsal hall, fittings may be easily situated with an actor walking down the hall.
- **Distance.** If the costume shop is located in a different building or part of town, how does transportation occur and does that time come out of the time allotted for the fitting?
- **Formal.** The stage manager allots exact times for each fitting, working them around the actor and rehearsal schedules.
- **On-the-fly.** Some organizations run very organic rehearsals with all the actors called. Those not working for the next hour are therefore available for fittings. The costume designer submits a list of needed actors that day and the stage managers send each actor when time allows. This may result in a lot of missed fittings, or fittings ended too soon, but it suits the creative rhythm of some companies.
- **Rehearsal checks.** The designer or an assistant brings small items such as footwear or costume props to rehearsal for the actor to slip on during a predetermined spare moment. This sidesteps the need for more elaborate planning.
- **Outside rehearsal.** Occasionally devised work or a director's working method may preclude *any* fittings during active rehearsals. If this is the case, fittings are usually assigned to slots before and after rehearsal, or scheduled on other days. This method adds gaps to the costume workflow, so plan the schedule carefully with the producer.

The next step is realistically judging the fitting workload. Summer stock shows premiering a new show every week may only allow one fitting per actor, alerting the designer that every item must be accounted for in that one fitting, including accessories. Shows with a longer schedule or complex builds may permit as many as four fittings, although two to three is more the norm. With limited fittings, how should you streamline your time? Some considerations to save time include:

- **Pre-build easy fit items.** Skip the sample phase for items that adjust easily. Build tunics, chemise or sack dresses, petticoats, period skirts, peasant wear directly in fabric leaving the waistband and hem to be adjusted directly on the actor.
- **Use stunt items.** Consider using substitutions for missing items so that no time is lost, such as a stock skirt or one muslin skirt for all the actors to mark individual fit before assembling each individual skirt.
- **Backup options.** Gather many more costume options than you need, reaching for second and third choices to avoid calling a second fitting. This method is efficient in every circumstance to establish the show early.

The Fitting Room Is Your Office

The fitting room is the major setting where the designer will interact with performers, and where the workload for the shop will be determined. It can be a tender time if the actors are nervous, or coming directly from a difficult rehearsal. It is also a satisfying, creative time where the designer pulls everything together to fit their vision, solves problems, and benefits from a creative environment. This time represents your artistry to your colleagues, so keeping a usable space allows everyone to work most efficiently. Take a look around before you begin the onslaught of fittings for a show.

- Does the space represent you and the pride you take in your work? Or does everyone trip over leftover hangers on the floor, or straddle backpacks and piles of clothing? Are there fabric clippings left on the floor?
- Does the setting allow everyone to concentrate in a calm manner, or is it a nightmare to find tags, pins, or a pencil?
- Are garments treated respectfully, properly hung or folded? Or do you dig through a jumble of boxes with crumpled choices?

- Consider how the experience feels to the actor, who will be removing their clothing and revealing intimate secrets to you. Can they feel safe and respected in the space?
- Do you, when working in that space, inspire confidence that everything is under control, or do they see you or the team rushing around?

Resident costume shops arrange the fitting rooms to suit their system. Do you as a designer have particular needs that will help set the tone, respect the costumes and your artistry?

- Is it helpful to your method to have all the bolts of fabric just outside the door to play with on the actor's body?
- Some designers organize preselected accessories by pinning multiple options to canvas covered hangers for each character or costume. This keeps everything in one place, and the designer can hold up the selection of ties, belts, or necklaces to choose during the fitting.
- Give some consideration to your creative method. Are you a magpie, pulling the perfect silk shawl from a bag when inspiration strikes? Are you methodical, doing your best work with laser-like focus?
- Many designers ask that clothing be steamed before fittings so items look their best when talking to the performer. A stained, wrinkled item is hard to imagine at its best, but also presents a worrisome picture that you, the designer, can't see it's a mess.

Discuss *your* preferences with the shop. They will be relieved to know what to expect and many will accommodate your needs as best they can. If no one else is available, be prepared to clean or organize the fittings yourself at the start of each day. Some designers prefer to organize fittings to familiarize themselves with decisions to be made each time. If you are working in a large established shop, the costume manager or resident assistant will organize the fittings. Discuss this ahead of time when working with new people so nothing is left to chance.

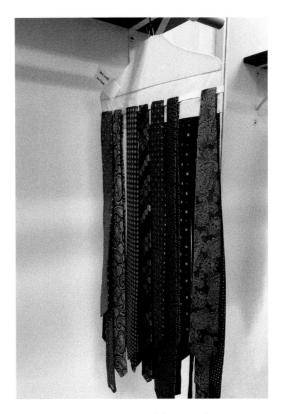

Figure 25.2 Ties hanging in a fitting room for easy access with the performer.

Working Without a Shop

Every costume designer will do some fittings in found spaces and under duress – it's the nature of the job. But consider taking a moment to plan how you might make even the most improvised fitting room work better, such as hanging sheets around a storage room to provide modesty or a neutral space. If the fitting space is unsatisfactory, talk to the production manager or producer about purchasing portable changing rooms, available online. Designers who do a lot of independent shows accumulate their own fitting kits along with the measurement kits, covered in Chapter 20. If you are unsure what to include in a kit review the supplies available at wardrobe suppliers (see the Extra Resources section). There are several unusual items that are useful in fittings. The first is a towel or carpet scrap for the floor to prevent scuffs on shoe soles. Some stores will not take returns if the shoes are marked. Another is spare underwear for the occasional actor

Figure 25.3 A fitting kit with supplies arranged to reach quickly while working. The pins are separated by size and style. They are preset open with points in the cushion for quick handling. For additional fitting room set up, see Figure 20.7.

without their own, and wet wipes and baby powder for those coming directly from a sweaty rehearsal.

Setting Up the Fitting

One of the goals of every fitting is to ask and answer questions while everyone is in the room together. One example is confirming exactly when costume changes occur. Post the renderings, research and costume scene chart for each fitting, and present as complete a picture as possible for the actor and yourself during every fitting. Your extensive preparation work with the costume scene chart (Figures 9.3 and 9.5) answers many of these questions. If you amend it during the course of a fitting, write the change directly on the scene chart so it is always up to date. Early career designers might second-guess themselves once they reach the fitting room. Do not backtrack to remake decisions you already made. Unless the character has radically changed, try the look you envisioned first, then consider adjustments. This is how a designer learns the way garments transfer from idea to reality. And it allows for thoughtful adjustments when ideas don't work.

At the start of each fitting day, make sure all costumes are accounted for and hung on the rack. If many fittings are scheduled back-to-back, set them up ahead of time on racks close to the fitting

room to enable rapid changeovers. Costumes are hung in the order the actor will wear them, so they get used to the sequence as it will be in the show. Each garment of a costume is also hung in wearing order so the performer is decently clothed before fitters enter the room. Make your expectations clear. They will appreciate direction: tell the actor which items to put on first and when to stop, when to call you into the room before proceeding. If you really hope a favorite pair of trousers works, ask the actor to call you into the room after putting them on. If you have no preference which pair of gray trousers they wear, ask them to keep trying until one fits.

Planning Costume Tracking

Fittings serve another function besides finding character and fitting the clothing. This is the best opportunity to track if all the items are accounted for, what items still must be sourced, and plot how the actor changes from one costume to the next in order. Using a **fitting sheet** listing all the pieces

Figure 25.4 This fitting room is set up for a fitting with research collages, fabric, a scene chart taped to the wall, and fitting supplies.

in the costume will remind the entire team what is to be fit and what is missing. It is easy to convert the **piece list** from Chapter 17 (see Table 17.1) to a **fitting sheet**, eliminating the need to spend time creating paperwork. This sheet may be printed for fitting use or stored in file sharing. Some organizations use tablets in fittings to track fitting sheet information using a sharing app such as Google Drive® so that anyone on the team has access. Others prefer written lists and manila tags or some combination of digital and analog tools. Tracking information in the fitting room is vital. Never assume you will remember all the details, especially if fittings are scheduled back-to-back. If the designer holds all the information in their head, it is impossible for other team members to work on items until a major debrief session.

Taking Fitting Photos

The prevalence of smart phones and tablets has changed the way we document costume fittings. Designers use fitting photos as a means to communicate with the director, and remind those doing alterations what the costume looked like on the performer. Preproduction planning has shortened for many shows as rehearsal periods shrink, so photos may take the place of some conversations that used to occur in person. The ability to share same day information brings speed of communication but also promotes possibilities for misunderstanding. Producers and directors now view the fitting photos by themselves, often without the designer to contextualize what they are seeing. Some costume designers manipulate the fitting photo if they know the producers or directors cannot look past the extra folds of fabric pinned for alterations. They may pin extra fabric that will be eliminated in alterations back out of the way just for the photo. Be mindful of distracting backgrounds, or piles of underwear in the corner. Once again be mindful that fitting photos document how you as the costume designer present your work. Many fitting rooms include a folding mirror, plain wall, or curtain to form a background.

If the designer suspects the director cannot read a fitting photo, she may wish to make an appointment to view the photos together. Formatting titles of images to share is an art form in itself so that a director unfamiliar with the lingo and labeling used in the costume shop can understand the order of fitting photos. Discuss the best organization system with the director – would they like to see all the costumes for each *scene* in a single folder to see the stage picture? Would she prefer browsing the costumes arranged by *actor*? Create a mutually agreeable system and use it consistently. Some designers create a *fitting wall* within the costume shop or design office with all fitting photos posted by scene, creating a show-at-a-glance reference. (See Figure 25.5) Place this wall where non-costume personnel won't see it.

Complex projects may employ an intern or production assistant just to take, process and upload the large number of fitting photos. The costume designer must be very aware who the audience for these photos will be. In the age of file sharing, it is paramount to ensure the actor's privacy outside the costume shop. Many theaters maintain extensive shared files so every department can access information on the show. Make sure any folders with fitting photos have limited sharing privileges. One designer was caught entirely unaware of who had access to the folders on a show; one day a member of a completely unrelated department joked with an actor about a funny fitting photo. This situation led to general alarm and discussions of professional propriety.

Fitting Etiquette and Intimacy

Fittings are a bit like going to the doctor's office – we take off our clothes, they poke at our bodies using jargon terms, use odd tools, and do mysterious things to us. This is exactly what a fitting can be like for performers who are new to the process or bring fears or even traumas to the experience. Fitting etiquette must embrace transparency, clear consent, and modesty. In the past, performers may have been told public handling and exposure is part of the job, but that standard is no longer appropriate. The theater should have an Intimacy Policy in place, but if they do not, be ready to use your own. Costume work by its very nature necessitates that costume personnel will touch performers' bodies, hair, and garments; discuss their bodies, hair, or faces; and

Figure 25.5 A costume office with fitting photos on the wall to facilitate planning.

handle garments, including underwear, for alterations and maintenance. Only mutual respect will allow everyone to work in a productive manner. Following these guidelines will enable production conversations:

- Always provide a private location to dress and undress. Always step out of the room unless invited to stay. If staying in the room, provide shirts first to cover underwear while the actor tries on trousers.
- Do not talk about the performer just outside the fitting room door – they can hear you! What seems like a standard clinical discussion to you may create anxiety for the performer.
- Announce the intent to touch the performer and ask permission. Depending on the agreement with the performer, ascertain if you may touch them throughout the fitting, or ask before touching every time.
- If permission is denied, find another creative way to obtain the information, or reschedule

on another day. Do not shame or express frustration with the performer.
- Speak respectfully of the body and all items worn by performers.
- Familiarize yourself with current body-image terminology (see Extra Resources section).
- If working with inexperienced actors, communicate their responsibilities using a pre-recorded video, a handout from the stage manager at rehearsals, an email from the costume shop, or a personal talk about how to prepare for fittings.
- Everyone involved in fitting avoids scented products or vaping/smoking just prior to the fitting, and refrain from engaging with social media during the fitting.
- Never discuss personal information with others. Costume designers are *absolute* secret keepers.

Working With Actors' Body Types

If the designer has the luxury of knowing casting before doing renderings, represent the performer's body accurately, and design the costume for their shape. If you perceive special considerations, initiate a conversation ahead of time. Always discuss nudity and baring skin onstage with actors ahead of time. Performers love to know the costume designer is thinking about them. However, in actual practice many auditions happen after the costumes are designed. If possible, rework the sketch, especially if the performer is a different heritage or race than drawn. This is also an opportunity to rethink the design so it looks as good as you want. Performers seeing themselves in the rendering affirms that you are there to design for them, not force them to wear an inappropriate design.

It is unfortunate that clothing can be difficult to purchase for any body type not represented by fashion industry standards. Actors who wear *real* sizes instead of *aspirational* sizes experience this frustration every time they shop, as do their costume designers. Ask the performer where they shop – they solve this same challenge every day. It's often necessary to purchase higher price brands or order a specialty item, affecting the entire costume budget. It can be very disappointing to give up building a favorite item to afford building a piece that accommodates sizing. But a costume designer cannot ignore this important part of their job – we costume the cast we are given. If these expenditures risk the quality of the design for the entire show, ask for additional funds with the producer. It is not fair to the performer to be cast in a show only to have their needs ignored.

Triggering Language in Fittings

Body shaming is unfortunately a part of everyday American culture. *Fat Activists* work to promote that bodies come in all shapes and have equal value.

Damaging Language	Preferred Language
Obese	Fat (preferred by some activists)
Overweight	Plus size/Person of size
Normal/Typical	Industry standard size

Damaging Language	Preferred Language
Squishy, Top Heavy	Curvy
Stout, Portly	Big & Tall

Costume designers possess a strong superpower: we can make anyone look their best or their worst. Using the Elements and Principles of Design, we can flatter the figure or purposely unflatter it in service of creating a character. Discuss these techniques with the performer before employing them, making your motive clear. While everyone wants to look their best, no one wants to think their bodies require correction. Approach items like shapewear, visually elongating or shortening legs, slenderizing and other tricks through the lens of creating the character. If you are a young designer working with mature actors, research typical figure concerns to ask about in the fitting. Such questions might include "how do you feel about showing your upper arms?" To learn more about patterning and fitting for nonindustry standard bodies, see the Extra Resources section.

Fitting Nonbinary and Transgender Performers

Costume designers do not join a show to judge an actor's DNA, or even know what it is. We are there to transform the body the performer presents into a character. People whose gender identity does not fit binary social definitions use many different terms to describe themselves. Nicky Martinez, a Trans-Advocacy Consultant, advises talking with the director first to understand how the performer's gender identity features in the show. Set aside time to talk directly with the performer before sourcing costumes. They recommend always including the performer in the costume process, but especially when working with smaller companies and limited budgets. It is very difficult to find properly sized clothing in thrift stores and other low-cost sources. Ask the performer for ideas from their own shopping expertise.[3]

Getting Out
Arlie

DEIDRE

GOOD KIDS
BY MEREDITH MAGOUN
CENTRAL THEATER ENSEMBLE

Figure 25.6 Costume designs that embrace real bodies.
Credit: Rendering and costume design by Meredith Magoun

- Volunteer your pronouns to establish an inclusive environment. If the actor volunteers their pronouns use them, and correct yourself when mistakes are made.
- Never snicker or gawk at the performer's body, clothing, or size. Don't complain or suggest the performer change their body. Setting a respectful environment demonstrates a willingness to collaborate.
- Use intimacy protocols explaining what you will do in a fitting and asking permission to touch their body.
- Arrange a time alone to talk and ask questions before others join the fittings.
- Ask if the performer is comfortable with the usual number of staff in the room and provide alternate systems if necessary.
- Always provide privacy to dress and undress, and for measurements. Ask if the performer wears any compression garments that may change the measurement itself.
- Provide a neutral bathrobe in the fitting room in case they wish to talk with you while partially undressed. Alert them the robe is there.

- Some performers may have surgical scars that are sensitive, or they don't wish to reveal. Provide a soft cotton t-shirt for the actor to wear during the fitting and under the costume.
- Redefine underwear. Some performers use compression garments or specially designed articles of clothing. Discuss how they might be incorporated into the costume, or how other garments may be substituted.
- Discuss the body shape goals for the character and ask about their goals.
- If changing the outward appearance of a performer, research proper garments. Familiarize yourself with these garments as you would any form of shapewear.
- If the show is supplying underwear, ask for the brand name and style number and supply that whenever possible.

Martinez suggests that costume designers join a larger community either locally or online to familiarize themselves with resources and experts who can advise.[4] Many of these protocols are common-sense procedures, and they should apply to every performer.

These steps may also apply to performers with religious rules for dress or medical requirements such as biosensors, insulin pumps, or colostomy pouches.

Trans, Nonbinary, and Cross-Dressing Garment Terms to Know

Bodies are our business in costume design. We have worked with every body type to create desired effects. Theater has a long history of cross-dressing costumes for pantomimes, comedies, opera, and Shakespeare, and no one understands better than a costume designer that gender-assigned dress is a fluid construct through time.

Binder. Chest compression gives the appearance of a flat torso. Like so many things humans do to change their shape (high heels come to mind) there can be side effects, so research these thoughtfully. Do not use an ace bandage, plastic or tape. Binders are available in many styles. (See the Extra Resources section.) Binding methods may also include wearing multiple shirts to create a smoother line.

Breast forms. Silicone or foam breast shape pads available as bra-pads or flesh-colored forms attached to a silicone skin that hugs the collar bone. Many styles were originally created as mastectomy forms, now some are made especially for drag shows. Low budget options include sewing rice into nylon stocking material for natural effect, although for extreme sizes, this can be too heavy.

Compression garments. Tight clothing made of strong stretch materials such as Spandex, elastane, and nylon. Made in a variety of styles as shorts or chest garments. Spanx fall into this category, as do bicycle shorts and many others.

Tucking. Hiding external genitals to create a smooth appearance for drag or for daily aesthetic purposes. Performers may need extra support by wearing layers of garments. **Gaffs** are a specific style of compression underwear for this purpose.

Asking for Changes

Early career designers can be shy about asking costume technicians for changes, especially in fittings. They opt to live quietly with outcomes they don't like and resolve to avoid that situation in future. Or if asked how to proceed with a costume they respond with "What's the easiest thing?" Neither of these approaches are satisfactory for a long-term career or mental health. It can also undermine your authority and affect the final outcome. Consider some of these common reasons for hesitations:

- **Concern for others.** We fear asking for changes will hurt someone's feelings or annoy them. Asking for a change *too late* may indeed place them in a bind, when it is very difficult to address. The best way to show respect for anyone and their work is to speak up early. Most costume technicians want to make work they are proud of and many have excellent suggestions.
- **Terminology.** Sometimes we lack the correct vocabulary to ask for change. We know something is not right, but can't express it in technologically correct terms. Sidestep this fear by using solutions-based thinking rather than trying to name the problem. "I wish it looked like this, but it's doing that. How can we fix that?"
- **Experience.** Early career designers find themselves working with people who've been in the business a long time. It's easy to feel like an imposter, or fear others are wondering how we got here. You may think you are the only person who feels that way, but that is not the case. *Everyone* is wondering how they got there.
- **Apology syndrome.** Social engineering teaches many young people, especially women and people of color, to live with unsatisfactory situations. They may sometimes think situations are their fault. No one person could possibly have enough time in their day to be responsible for everything that needs changing, so let go of the thought it is *you*. Do not overuse apologies, or start sentences with "I'm sorry." This is a verbal tick that can be eliminated, and it's very freeing as well.

It is possible to change our mindset for a short period of time, while we work on our inner fears. Research finds that striking a "superhero pose" with legs spread apart and arms on hips before taking on stressful tasks significantly changes your outlook. There are several power poses that not only convey confidence to others, but will also bring confidence to the speaker.[5] We work in an industry that utilizes the entire body as a powerful communication tool. Costume designers are allowed to avail ourselves of those tools, too.

Sizing Up Preparing for Fittings

The skill of 360-degree listening may seem mutually exclusive to creating an artistic vision. As the designer negotiates through fittings, she will listen to the director, the performer, drapers, and tailors and those making the accessories. How does a designer collaborate and still maintain his vision? Every single design that ever happened took place within given parameters and limitations. Successfully negotiating collaboration and an artistic vision requires a sense of humor and an unquenchable curiosity. Others *will* pose good ideas; adopt those with joy and grace – this is how we continue to grow and learn. Other ideas will not be useful *this* time. Working with others and the human body is one of the great joys of being a costume designer, but as with all collaboration it requires specific skills and grace.

Expecting the Unexpected

The costume does not work if it doesn't accommodate the movement. An influential wardrobe malfunction took place in the early 1950s when the still-rising star Elvis Presley split his trousers onstage during his gyrations. He asked his Memphis tailor, Bernard Lansky, for a larger size that was then taken in at the waist, leaving more room in the seat and thighs. This led to Elvis's signature pegged-pants that flopped at the knee during his stage shows.[6] Men all over the world who wanted to look like Elvis adopted the pegged top trouser.

Extra Resources

Fit for Real People: Sew Great Clothes Using Any Pattern (Sewing for Real People Series)

Pants for Real People: Fit and Sew for Any Body (Sewing for Real People Series) Patil Palmer, Palmer-Pletsch Publishing

National Center for Transgender Equality

"Supporting the Transgender People in Your Life: A Guide to Being a Good Ally" https://transequality.org/issues/resources/supporting-the-transgender-people-in-your-life-a-guide-to-being-a-good-ally

*Hudson's FTM Resource Guide*www.ftmguide.org/

National Association to Advance Fat Acceptance https://naafa.org/

Notes

1 Mirojnick, Ellen. 2021. "Design Showcase West/Netflix Costume Design Salon Panel." *You Tube*. Premiered June 12, 2021. https://www.youtube.com/watch?v=4WuB5WKUisg

2 Howell, Peter. 2011. "Fitting Oversized Egos into Small Packages." *Toronto Star*, May 6, 2011. Accessed November 21, 2019. https://www.pressreader.com/canada/toronto-star/20110506/284803577672322

3 Martinez, Nicky. 2021. Personal interview with the author, September 13, 2021.

4 Martinez, Personal interview with the author.

5 Rosenberg, Robin S. 2011. "Why You May Want to Stand Like a Superhero." *Psychology Today*, July 14, 2011. https://www.psychologytoday.com/us/blog/the-superheroes/201107/why-you-may-want-stand-superhero

6 Jones, Mablen. 1987. *Getting it on, The Clothing of Rock 'n' Roll*. New York: Abbeville Press Publishers, p. 49.

26.
FITTING GARMENTS

Learning to fit garments to every body type is one of the hardest things a costume designer will master. Fitting skills take years to hone, and many designers report they did not become truly competent until they had ten years of experience managing the flow, communicating with actors, and solving fitting issues. Many designers learn alteration methods through attending fittings with more experienced fitters, learning proper solutions through repeated observation. For those just starting the fitting journey, there are a few reliable resources for fitting and altering typical ready-to-wear garments. (See the Extra Resources section.) If the designer has worked as an assistant or in a costume shop attending fittings, that experience will accelerate the learning curve and it is well worth taking such jobs to learn this fine art.

A Tangled Web – Garment Sizing

Once you understand fitting, you will become a much more sophisticated judge of garments, able to make fine distinctions while the item is still on the hanger. At the heart of this skill is understanding the difference between **size** and *fit*. The *fit* of clothing has little to do with the *size* purchased. *Size* is the term for industry standards based on averages across a selected population. The ready-to-wear industry established guides for clothing, but in reality, a large number of bodies fall between two sizes. Americans developed the habit of wearing affordable separates available in different sizes, so routinely altering purchased garments or going to a dressmaker/tailor for alterations largely stopped after World War II. When we do buy an all-over garment like a dress or matched suit, many consumers tolerate poorly fitting clothing.

We use the term *fit* to mean how well or poorly the garment sits on an individual body. The first rule for fitting success is choosing garments that *can* be altered successfully. This requires a bit of judgment about how garments are assembled. For instance, it may be wise to buy clothing a bit larger that fits the widest part of the body – usually the shoulders, chest, or hips, and altering the other parts smaller. Or it may be possible to purchase a size intended for a smaller body if there is enough **seam allowance** in the garment to let out. Turn the garment inside out to check all seam allowances. If it has been entirely trimmed away or slashed, that garment can only be altered smaller. And remember that every garment must contain some practical ease of 1–2 inches for movement (see Table 20.2).

A second rule for fitting success is that all the parts of a garment work together. Taking in one part will affect other parts. For instance, taking in the side seams a large amount will affect how the sleeve sits in the armhole. Pulling the center back into a smaller fit pulls the side seams backwards on the body. (See Figure 26.1.) Raising the shoulders will move the bust line upward. Think of a garment as a circular sculpture; it is flat fabric that has been molded to fit round bodies. *How can we*

DOI: 10.4324/9781003015284-33

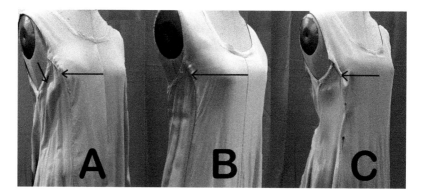

Figure 26.1 This dress is too large and it sags under the arm (A). Pulling all the fullness into the center back or side seam draws the princess line too far to the side, displacing the proportions of the dress (B). Altering the princess seam maintains the proper proportions (C).

Figure 26.2 The dress at left is too large, it sags in vertical folds where it does not fit. The dress at right is too tight, it pulls in horizontal folds that point toward the problem area. In this case the dress is not large enough in the bust.

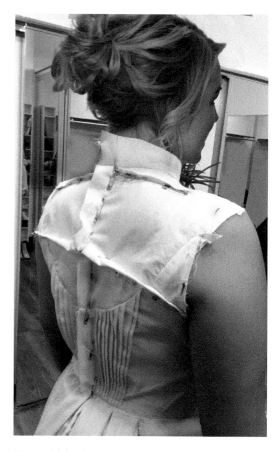

Figure 26.3 This muslin sample has been shortened across the back in two places to correct the fit.
Credit: Fitter Julie Keen, photo by UC Irvine costume staff

tell if something needs adjustment? Figures 26.1 and 26.2 show areas of fabric that sag or pull, creating tension folds that signal a fitting problem.

Creating a Productive Atmosphere

The psychology of a fitting is just as important as determining the character and the alterations. Set a good atmosphere with introductions for everyone in the room, using preferred pronouns to signal a welcoming environment. Start with a quick debrief at the top of the fitting telling the actor what to expect today. Show them the renderings or research of what you will be fitting today and remind everyone the costume is a work in progress. Point to the rack of clothing laid in order and direct them to what

to try. Ask if there are questions, and remind them they can ask for help if needed. Everyone steps out of the fitting room to be called back when the actor is partially or fully dressed. Remember that even though the actor has closed a door, conversations can be clearly heard and never discuss the actor's body while they are in the costume shop. Explain to the actor that ill-fitting clothing does not mean there is anything wrong with them. It is the clothing that needs work.

Give some consideration to how you, as a designer, wish to present ideas to the actor. If you know this actor from prior projects, use what you've learned to create a productive atmosphere. Some designers begin the fitting with their least favorite costume option, working their way up to the favorite, hoping that it will appear even more correct after viewing what is not correct. Some hide a favorite garment as a surprise, or present items beautifully laid out on tables or boxed so they look like gifts. During the early years of your design career, assist or shadow other more experienced designers whenever possible to learn how they approach fittings and actor discussions.

Where Can Fittings Go Wrong?

Fittings may take a wrong turn for many reasons. Some of them may not have anything to do with the costume that day. If the performer seems tense, unhappy or worried, remind them this is the exact right moment to express concerns. If necessary, suspend the business of the fitting and clear the room for a personal discussion. Some other concerns include:

- If difficult conversations must occur with other costume personnel about the fit of a costume, save it for after the fitting. Make notes in the fitting and wait until afterwards to discuss anything the actor may misconstrue as a problem or fault.
- Another sensitive issue may be a discussion about the quality of someone's work. Never call anyone out in front of the actor. Wait until a quiet moment alone.
- Extra comments of any kind during a fitting can sometimes lead to difficulty. Inexperienced team members may blurt out a question or an opinion, not realizing they don't have the authority to make suggestions

to the actor. The fitting room is not an open forum – it is a very delicate situation. Remind any assistants or interns if they spot something they consider a problem, the question or comment should be discussed quietly with the designer or draper on the side, allowing them to decide how to proceed. Develop hand signals if necessary.
- Fittings can get tense if there are too many people in the room. This can be an issue if the director wishes to attend along with the designer, a draper/fitter, a shop manager overseeing the fitting, an assistant designer and a firsthand assisting the draper. If the fitting room is small, consider a different way to manage the crowd.

Through the Looking Glass

Along with 360-degree listening in a fitting, the other valuable skill a costume designer uses frequently is looking carefully at the costume on the body. After dressing the actor in the chosen costume or a muslin, it is time to listen and look often at the same time. Costume Shop Manager Suzanne Schultz Reed recommends looking at the costume in two different steps. The **first look** is to

> Look at the actor in the mirror, rather than head on. The mirror is more removed and that's how you're going to see them onstage, and it gives a full picture. Get an overall sense of how it fits and is it right.

Don't waste time worrying about details if the costume will ultimately be the wrong one. The **second look**, she explains, is to "look more closely, dissect what does or doesn't work. Get into more specifics."[1]

How do we look for those specifics? Use the **cross-check** method to look in a cross shape (see Figure 26.4). After the costume is found generally suitable, it's time to concentrate on details.

- Look at the **vertical** centerline from neck to feet to understand how the garment rests on the body. Does it hang from the shoulders, such as a shift dress or 18th-century cassock

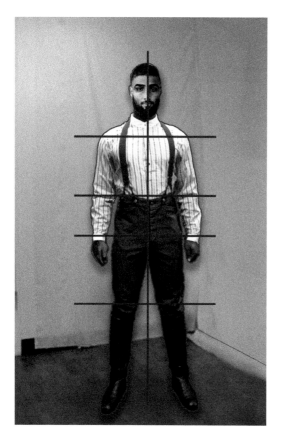

Figure 26.4 Using the cross-check method ensures the designer checks all major body points before deciding if a costume is suitable enough to adjust details.

coat? Does it wrap around the body like a sarong? Is the garment symmetrical or asymmetrical? Does it fit tightly with many cut and tailored panels?

- Look across the body at the major **horizontal** points: shoulders, waist and elbows, low hips and knees. Does everything seem in order? Ask the actor to flex at each joint: can they move their arms and legs in ways that are appropriate for this show? Can they bend at the waist or sit down, bend their knees? Will they sit on the floor?

Assessing the Fit of a Garment

The exact steps used to assess each costume will vary for different styles of garments, but this guide will ensure a thorough fitting.

Sturdiness. Is this costume sturdy enough to withstand the rigors of dress rehearsals, quick changes, repeated cleaning and the full run? If the fabric is shredding or the seams are delicate, part with the garment unless you can afford time and labor to rebuild it.

Body shape. If the actor's body changes to become the character, these decisions must be made first. Fit foundations and padding first.

Outer silhouette. Assess the shape in space. Does it reflect the correct silhouette for the period? If skirts, capes, sleeves are visually too large or too small, can that be fixed? If the costume is not correct for the period or design vision, move onto other choices or note these large changes.

Anchor points. Many fitted garments anchor at the waist. The waist is determined by the fashion of each era. Does the costume waist sit at the correct spot? It can be difficult to lengthen or shorten a torso garment more than an inch or so without re-cutting. If period torso garments such as doublets and bodices are too short or too long, they may not be usable. If trousers do not sit at the fashion waist, they may not be usable.

Hanging points. Most loose-fitting garments or parts hang from a specific spot. Tailored jackets hang from the shoulders, skimming the waist. Most skirts hang from the waist or hips. Do these garments fit those points, hang straight? Is the garment crooked, twisting or tilting forward or back? Determine if it is possible to fix these issues before moving forward.

Interior lines. How does this garment divide the body into proportions? Using the elements and principles of design, determine if the effect provides the focus and composition you wish. Do the proportions define the character correctly? Flatter the figure if required?

Flexion points. How does the costume intersect with the joints? Check for under arm movement to add gussets. Adjust the hip or seat of skirts and trousers for sitting.

Refined fit. What further adjustments will fit the actor's body better, and supply the appropriate ease? Work through remaining adjustments from top to bottom. Remember to consider *ease* for both fit and fashion silhouette.

Edges. Are the hems, neckline, sleeves correct and straight?

Decoration. Check the dressmaker details and trims. If you run out of fitting time, this step can easily be moved to a dress form to finish.

Condition. Examine the entire garment. Are all the buttons there, and in the correct place? Is anything missing or in need of repair? Are there stains or faded spots?

Overall effect. Do all the items work together well: hat, bags, walking sticks, spats? Remember to step well away from the actor before judging. Do a final check standing as far away as the first row of the audience.

> "Gene Kelly was once asked what the hardest thing about dancing on film was. He answered 'Finding pants that fit.'"[2]

Figure 26.5 The sleeve of this bustle dress muslin was fitted more closely but also retained a workable amount of ease. The actor had several large arm movements to consider.

Fitting Tailored Garments

Classic tailored clothing has changed in subtle ways over two centuries of fashionable tradition. Understand the desired fit for each era, such as the location and fit of the waist, width and length of trousers and lapel and shape of the waistcoat. There were times the waistcoat was visible below a short-waisted coat, and times the waistcoat developed long points. These proportions change frequently, and it is impossible to substitute contemporary menswear for period items without compromising the final result. There are however, a few timeless rules about fitting tailored menswear that ring true through most eras.

Assessing the Fit of Tailored Garments

- **Symmetrical fit.** Both sides of the suit should fit the same, and the jacket fronts meet at the same point. Both lapels and shoulders mirror each other across the centerline. If a suit is crooked, adjust it by placing shoulder pads on one side to lift the entire suit. Do not alter the suit to fit an asymmetrical body.

- **Collar gap.** The shirt collar and jacket collar lay smoothly against the back of the neck. Large gaps indicate the jacket shoulders slope more than the body, the chest is too tight or bent posture. This is a tricky alteration to be undertaken only if necessary.

- **Chest fit.** The jacket should button without strain. A too-tight suit will cause wrinkles in an X shape across the front, pointing to the button when closed. A too-large jacket will stand away from the body.

- **Shoulder fit.** The shoulder points of the body are the outer edges of the bony crest formed by the clavicle bones. This is where the sleeve is sewn onto the shoulder of the suit. The shoulder is properly placed if the sleeve hangs naturally with no strain or buckling. If the shoulders are too small, the muscles of the upper arm bulge beyond the shoulder point. Too-large shoulders appear to slide off the body, pushing the sleeve down the arm, causing sagging wrinkles. If you can push down on the

Figure 26.6 A guide to a properly fitting suit

shoulder pad and collapse the shoulder, the jacket is too large.

- **Jacket length.** Shortens or lengthens with fashion. Your research will indicate eras with very short jackets, such as contemporary styles. In general, a classic tailored jacket should cover the entire seat. Use the length of the arm as a guide with the arm held down in a relaxed position. A classic jacket length corresponds roughly to the knuckle area, or one-half of the hand.
- **Sleeves**. The proper shirt length touches the join of hand to wrist, at the root of the thumb. The jacket sleeve shows a "½ inch of linen" according to a tailors tradition, or falls ½ inch shorter than the cuff. That is a guideline only; some wearers prefer slightly longer or shorter jacket sleeves. A bit more shirt sleeve showing makes the arm look longer, but if no shirt shows, it will make the arm look shorter. Many people have different length arms; suit sleeves may be hemmed at slightly different lengths to show the same amount of shirt cuff on both arms to retain the symmetrical look.

- **Kissing pockets.** Trousers that have been taken in too much during a prior alteration will place the back pockets too close together. This will look comical, unless the jacket is never removed – a difficult thing to predict sometimes.
- **Trouser break.** Extra trouser length forms a small fold in the trouser leg. The amount shifts with fashion; check research for the appropriate era. The contemporary rule is *one* subtle horizontal crease above the shoe.
- **Rise.** The length of the zipper and crotch depth fluctuates with fashion. Crotch depth describes the curved seam from the top of the waist band to the point where the seam curves back between the legs. Ensure the length is comfortable to sit within the parameters of the period shape. Trousers with a too long front rise compared to the back rise will drop down in front, collapsing in wrinkles over the thighs. A too-short rise causes bunching and discomfort.
- **Tie width.** The widest part of the tie corresponds to the widest part of the lapel. Fashion eras with skinny lapels also featured skinny ties.

Fitting Tailored Jackets on Curvy Figures

There are special considerations fitting the classic tailored jacket on hourglass figures. Jackets made for men use traditional tailoring methods. Many jackets made for women use dressmaker methods, eliminating the padded fronts and other stiffeners to accommodate more extreme darts or princess seams. Each construction style presents a different set of criteria for alterations. The biggest dilemma comes from the difference between shoulder width and hip circumference. Jackets that fit the widest part of the figure, typically the hips, may be too large in the waist and shoulders. The waist can be altered using vertical darts on both fronts and both sides of the center back seam. If the jacket was made using dressmaker techniques, the shoulder seam is easier to alter. If the jacket was made with menswear techniques, changing the front dart and shoulder are much more difficult alterations. The easiest jacket to fit and alter for hourglass figures is one built along the princess-line shape, creating five total seams to let in or take out over the bust, waist, and hips.

Understanding Corsetry

The past decade has introduced a large number of historical corsets and corset patterns available from online retailers, significantly reducing the laborious patterning process. Experienced shops keep a collection of corset patterns and can build made-to-order corsetry. A corset built for a performer will fit well and even provide comfortable support. But in many cases, we must fit a purchased corset or alter a stock one made for someone else. Fitting corsets requires technical experience, and achieving the desired shape of the body takes imagination and experience. For more than 400 years corsetry shaped bodies to an ideal that straightened the posture, elongated or shortened the torso, flattened the chest, or pushed it forward, upwards or out. It is easy to assume every corset squeezed the body into its smallest size, but that is not the case. Study the desired finished effect on the clothing for corsetry of each period. The corset was just one tool for figure enhancement; many women added more appliances to achieve the final effect, such as hip pads and bust ruffles. When fitting a period dress, it might be necessary to use some of these same enhancers.

To understand the desired effect of a corset study the following elements:

- **Straight or curvy?** Corsets from the 17th and 18th centuries were less concerned with squeezing the waist to its smallest. Their goal

Figure 26.7 This jacket from the 1950s uses additional darts and seams to create an hourglass shape.

Figure 26.8 This ruffled corset cover added more fullness over the bust to enhance the fashionable shape of that era.

Credit: Corset cover, ca. 1902. Isabel Shults Fund, 2002. Metropolitan Museum of New York www.metmuseum.org

was to flatten the back for proper aristocratic bearing. The corseted torso resembled an oval cone, slowly shortening over that era. Corsets from the late 19th century created a curvy hourglass shape.

- **Flat or full?** Tudor bodices suppressed the bustline, while 1880s corsets expanded over the bust to support a fuller shape.

- **Up, down or sideways?** Corsets from the 18th century pushed the bust upwards, the 1900s allowed the bust to drop low and in the 1830s corsets lifted and separated the bustline with a flat space in the center that was considered more natural than its 18th-century predecessors.

- **Plastic, flat, or spiral?** Flat steel bones are used for high stress points such as lacing panels and busks. They cannot bend over curves easily, making them most useful for reproductions of some 17th- and 18th-century corsetry. If a corset is made of these bones, it cannot be made more flexible. Reproductions of curved 19th-century corsets are made using spiral bones that flex, supporting curvature. Corsets made of multiple figure-hugging seams and spiral bones cannot be made stiffer. Many corsets from the 1830s used very soft supports such as cording or quilting to achieve the ideal "natural" shape.

Steel busks and steel boning were not invented until the mid-19th century. Prior to this, reeds and baleen (whale cartilage) created a light springy corset. Historical corsetieres experimenting to find

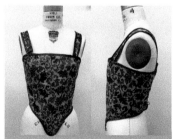

Figure 26.9 The red 16th century-style corset flattens the chest for a straight torso shape. The blue 19th-century-style corset adds curves using compression and added fabric to shape the torso. This theatrical corset includes bust pads to enhance the fashionable curvy bust shape. Blue corset designed by Ashton Montgomery.

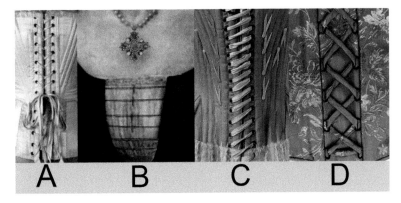

Figure 26.10 Sample lacing styles: double lacing (A), bar lacing (B), spiral lacing (C), and cross lacing (D).

an accurate substitute for baleen use various grades of plastic boning. Theatrical reproductions of early corsets made entirely of steel bones are much heavier than were used in the actual period. Stacking a fully steel-boned corset under a boned costume bodice may actually add unintended bulk and heaviness to the figure. If the designer wishes to create a light approach, consider ways to approach the challenge of recreating historical corsetry. (See the Extra Resources section.)

Fitting Corsets

Always fit a corset over an underlayer such as a camisole or thin tube top for laundering purposes and skin protection. There is some confusion about lacing a corset for fit and correct appearance. Each era used a different technique, and there may well have been many variations because the corset was a personal garment. During eras with visible lacing such as the Medieval, Renaissance and 17th centuries, many portraits document **ladder lacing** that looked like straight bars across the bodice, or **spiral lacing** using one lace that started at one end and ended at the other. Eras with hidden lacing, such as the 18th and 19th centuries, tended to use X-shape lacing similar to the way we lace sports shoes. Many 19th-century corsets use **double lacing**: one lace from top to waist, the second lace from bottom to waist. Some featured tabs that joined the laces so the wearer could pull them tight from the front. Double lacing allowed for a maximum pull and cinching at the waist.

Many theater crews use the double lacing for every corset because it allows for speedy adjustments at the rib or waist without re-lacing the entire corset.

A properly fitting corset will show a lacing gap in the back, with the maximum about 2 inches. If the gap is much larger, the corset it too small and will chafe against the body. A corset that fits edge-to-edge may not support the body properly. The skin should be protected by a flap of fabric called a modesty panel. The center backs of the corset should be relatively parallel to each other once they are laced. For further information on how to fit corset gap, see the Extra Resources section. Once a performer is laced into the corset, fit other items for a few minutes if possible, such as shoes. The corset will warm up and stretch on the body, requiring a re-lace before fitting garments over it. Explain this warm-up to the performer who may be wearing the corset in rehearsal, and the wardrobe crew so they don't try to dress a costume over a cold corset.

Fitting the 16th–18th Century Corset

- **Desired effect.** Some styles feature rounded tabs that splay over the hips to smooth bulges and lift the torso. The bust should thrust forward and upward creating a smooth conical torso and flat back. The performer can bend easily from the hips, although the ability to lift arms above the shoulder may be somewhat restrained.
- **Waist length.** The smallest part of the corset should fit at the desired waist. If the

Figure 26.11 Fitting the 16th–18th century corset.

Credit: Early 18th-century corset, Spanish. Gift of Mr. Clagget Wilson, 1946. Metropolitan Museum of New York. www.metmuseum.org

corset is too long it will rise up from the waist, covering too much of the bust. If it is too short, the corset settles at the waist leaving the bust unsupported.

- **Bust support.** The corset should support the breasts to just about the nipple line. The bustline should be pushed high. Modern bodies may not find this corset very supportive and the breasts may fall below the top of the corset creating a hard ridge. Costume shops stitch crescent shaped pads to the inside under bust for additional support.
- **Back support.** Both sides should lace straight with a small gap.
- **Shoulder straps.** This style of corset used straps over the shoulders. These should fit smoothly over the shoulder area with no gapping.
- **Comfort.** When fitted correctly, this shape should fit snugly, control the bust, and provide good posture. Some actors find it a relief not to hold their backs straight, the corset does the work for them.

Fitting the 19th-Century Corset

- **Desired effect.** The smallest part of the corset should fit snugly at the waist just under the rib cage. Corsets became increasingly complex during this era, with many pattern pieces creating a complex fit. The waist appears smaller than the bust and hip with a full bustline sitting higher or lower, depending on the decade. Wearing a corset over time will force more bulk into the hip and shrink the waist. But that is not the point of theatrical corseting. Consider employing other means such as pads or enhancers to achieve the hourglass shape.
- **Waist length.** These corsets fit over the hip. If it is too long it will interfere with raising the leg or rise up from the waist, covering too much of the bust. If it is too short, the corset settles at the waist leaving the bust unsupported or sits at the bust, creating a too-short waist. If the hip is too small, the center back will splay wide open, causing chafing. The corset should not poke into the hip bones, shoulder blades, or arm pits.
- **Bust support.** These corsets should fit smoothly at the under bust and push the bustline to fill the shaped bust cups. Modern bodies may need the support of crescents or even additional padding to fill the corset, creating the ideal shape. Don't fit the bust area so tightly it flattens the breast. This will create a flat shape and cause discomfort.
- **Upper edge.** Some early photographs show a clear corset edge visible under dresses, and many show a smooth transition over the bustline. It appears that may have been the

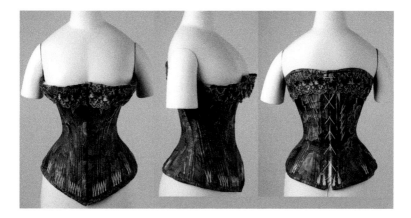

Figure 26.12 Fitting the 19th-century corset.

Credit: Corset ca. 1878, American. Gift of Mrs. E.R. Gerken, 1948. Metropolitan Museum of New York. www/metmuseum.org

vagaries of personal fit and circumstances. In general, the corset should transition smoothly from corset to breast without creating a harsh ridge. With the exception of the early 1900s, the bust should sit high in the corset, supported from below.

- **Back support.** Both sides should lace relatively parallel, with a 2–3 inch gap. The hip area may spread a bit more.
- **Comfort.** If this corset is pinching or causing pain, something is wrong. Less comfortable to wear than earlier corsets, nonetheless women expected a workable amount of comfort when a corset was properly fitted and worn in to shape. The actor can bend fully from the hips.

Assessing Period Costume Shapes

Assessing the fit of period clothing uses the same steps and techniques listed for all other garments with one large exception: some fashion periods change the shape and size of body parts. Many garments in history fall into one or more of these fitting types:

Break at the waist. Garments that break at the waist into a two-piece garment provide more opportunity for close tailoring and more fitting options. A bodice may be shortened or lengthened, trousers or skirt let in or out. Many period garments that break at the waist are then connected again to ensure no gaps form between bodice and skirt. Many European-influenced fashions fall into this category, as do Korean hanbok.

Flow from the shoulder. Garments that flow from the shoulder must provide more ease so the body can move below it, although it may still provide a shapely waist and very full skirts. Until the invention of spandex, looser fitting garments were adjusted to the body with laces or ties. Examples include the medieval bliaut that could be tied to fit smoothly at the waist, 18th-century cassock coats, ancient gowns and tunics, 1960s chemise dresses, and Japanese kimono.

Drape around the body. Garments that drape around the body such as the Ghanaian kente, Indian sari, or Roman toga are created every time the wearer puts it on. These garments require a sense of balance and, for stage purposes, hidden anchors or closures.

The designer's period research should include a study of the desired ideal shape to prepare for fittings. The first decision is how period-correct will this production be, and will some characters be more period-correct than others? If modifications are to be made, what are those and how does that decision translate to the fitting room? For instance, some productions substitute contemporary spandex corsets to allow more movement. Use the **cross-check** method to assess not only the overall fit, but also the ideal desired shape.

Too Close for Comfort

There will be some natural push and pull between the costume designer and performers concerning how comfortable a costume is to wear. Many performers appreciate that costumes force a certain posture or style of movement, especially period shapes. Some opera singers love wearing period corsets because it gives a surface to push against for their style of singing. It is important to closely consider the trade off a costume brings – if it is uncomfortable if the actor slouches or takes special thought to move about, what does that bring to the character? Some actors want every costume to feel as comfy as the loose or stretchy clothing they wear every day. Very early career actors who have never even worn a suit bring very little understanding of clothing to a fitting. Many contemporary directors *do* ask performers to move in ways that period clothing cannot support, such as rolling on the floor, jumping on a bed, or participating in a rowdy fight in a tight period gown. It is important to create an understanding with the director about how much comfort should be accommodated, and how the actor may be asked to adjust to the costume.

Sizing Up Fitting Techniques

There is no such thing as knowing everything about fittings. One of the great joys of theatrical costume is the constant innovation. We wish to do a period differently than before, or mix period garments with contemporary ones. Each set of circumstances will present new challenges fitting the garment to the actor while still allowing appropriate movement. Following the guides in this chapter gives the designer a firm foundation from which to logically assess how the costume should fit the body.

Expecting the Unexpected

Contemporary choreography asks for very large physical movements that never would have been considered by those wearing the actual period garments in history. Before the availability of mass market clothing, people who considered themselves refined were expected to accommodate their clothing's demands. We have diary accounts of women complaining about the weariness of wearing the *robe de cour* with boned bodice in 17th-century France for long periods at court. That bodice straightened the spine and restricted lifting their arms at the shoulder, but those women were wealthy and privileged. Contemporary theater expects to use clothing in the opposite way – refined styles must accommodate dramatically wild gestures or casual posture. One solution includes adding elastic panels into corsets and tightly fitting bodices to accommodate these needs, and we continually invent new solutions.

Extra Resources

Judith Rasband, *Fabulous Fit* Fairchild Publications, 1994 An excellent guide for fitting different figures and corresponding pattern alterations.

Mary A Roehr, *Altering Women's Ready-to-Wear*, 1987

Mary Roehr, *Altering Men's Ready-to-Wear*, 1991

How It Should Fit: The Jacket, AOS https://articlesofstyle. com/blogs/news/how-it-should-fit-the-suit-jacket

How It Should Fit: Trousers AOS https://articlesofstyle. com/blogs/news/how-it-should-fit-the-trouser

Curvy Sewing Collective https://curvysewingcollective. com/

Sew Guide, DIY Alterations https://sewguide.com/alterations/

Evelyn Wood Vintage Sewing School www.vintagesewing school.com

Démodé, 18th C Boning Research & German Plastic Boning Review http://demodecouture.com/18th-c-boning-research-german-plastic-boning-review/

Make No (Whale) Bones About It: Debunking those Corsetry Myths, Stephanie Celiberti, Lancaster History Aug. 21, 2019. www.lancasterhistory.org/debunking corsetrymyths/

Lucy's Corsetry.com. Consult the page titled *The Corset Gap: What does it mean?* https://lucycorsetry.com/2012/ 08/02/the-corset-gap-what-does-it-mean/

Lady of the Wilderness, Troubleshooting Fit in 1780s Stays Dec. 8, 2019 https://ladyofthewilderness.wordpress. com/2019/12/08/troubleshooting-fit-in-1780s-stays/

Notes

1 Suzanne Schultz Reed, Costume Shop Manager Pomona College, interview with author June 28, 2021.
2 Anecdote told by Suzanne Schultz Reed, Costume Shop Manager Pomona College, interview with author June 28, 2021.

27.
THE REHEARSAL PERIOD

The production period officially begins with the first rehearsal. All the collaborators who have been preparing the show come together for the first time. This is when the costume designer must be willing to open their mind for a new phase of creating and modeling. Yes, it may have taken weeks of planning to reach this point, but not all of the early ideas are going to work and new ones will appear. Although the costume designer may spend more production hours in the costume shop preparing costumes, she is part of the director's creative team and will function as the major liaison between rehearsals and the shop. This is where the costume designer develops split loyalties. One of the major contributions the costume designer makes is by attending rehearsals as often as possible. The designer will be asked to solve challenges while keeping the abilities of the shop in mind, and also explaining to the shop why rehearsal developments result in changes. It's important to set a productive and creative tone for exploration from the beginning.

Preparation Week

Many stage managers begin their contracts one week before the show starts rehearsals. This prep week is busy, readying the rehearsal space and contacting creative team members. If stage management does not contact you, initiate a preliminary discussion. Walk them through the costumes, discussing any challenges you may have. For instance, if the show can only afford one corset for each actor, how can you schedule corsets to be worn in some rehearsals, yet returned to the costume shop for use in building the over garments? Give the stage manager a copy of the costume scene chart. Ask if there is a production assistant (PA) or Assistant Stage Manager (ASM) assigned to track costumes in rehearsals. They track entrances and exits, wardrobe change locations, and timings of changes. Try to get an idea of the planned rehearsal workflow from the stage manager. Will that schedule affect some interior

deadlines for costumes? One example is dance rehearsals may require actors to wear their shoes, corsets, and skirts. If you are new to this theater's protocols or union regulations for fittings, ask the stage manager to explain them to you. Determine how fittings in general might work best with the rehearsal plan. It can be a frustrating surprise to ask for many fittings the same day the director schedules a full run-through. Costumes may have to juggle their plans a bit to avoid conflicts, but the process will go much smoother using forethought. If conflicts must occur, warn the stage manager ahead so the two of you can plan together.

The First Rehearsal Meet and Greet

This day is particularly exciting for costume designers, who will meet the actors they've been imagining in their heads for the entire preproduction

DOI: 10.4324/9781003015284-34

planning process. The first rehearsal is filled with the buzz of a new project. It is a noisy reunion for those who have worked together before, with dozens of conversations going on simultaneously. If this is a formal event, the rehearsal room is arranged to accommodate the cast and creative team at a central table. Some theaters hold this event in the theater seats with the creative team seated together. Many resident theaters invite the entire staff to attend the formal start of a project, and some invite special donors to attend as part of a sneak-peek perk. Each theater conducts this first rehearsal or meet and greet differently. Check with the production manager or stage manager well ahead of time. Some theaters expect a formal digital design presentation and others want a low-key conversation. More than one designer has been shocked when someone from the theater pulls up all the files in the design sharing site to show on a big screen without consulting the designer. Formal events follow a pattern somewhat like this:

- **Opening statement.** A representative from the theater such as the artistic director speaks briefly about why the show was placed in the season and why this director is the right person to guide the project.
- **Introductions.** This is probably the only time the entire staff for this show will be in the same room. Everyone introduces themselves. In larger theaters, these introductions can include as many as 50 people. This is the opportunity to attach faces to the names you've been communicating with via email and file sharing.
- **Director statement.** The director presents their vision in a way that sets the tone for the project. One director describes this tone as "*authority* tempered with *humility*, a sense of *preparedness* together with a welcoming *openness*."[1]
- **Design approach.** The director may give a thorough overview of the artistic themes, or may defer to the designers. Generally, the scenic designer or the director presents the set model, then the costume designer speaks,

sharing renderings and research as needed. (See The Costume Design Presentation section that follows.) Lighting, sound, and projection designers may present, along with a music director or composer.
- **Staff representatives.** In some theaters, key members of the staff speak about upcoming ways they will interact with the projects such as press, transportation, or technical expertise. The production manager or technical director may give a short report of work in-progress. The staff may provide everyone a folder of information about that theater, who to contact, where to find lunch nearby, and other details.
- **Meet and greet.** The cast breaks up to nosh at a snack table and mix a little with others in the room. There are several running jokes about food is the only way to make sure people show up to these events, but there is some truth to the gesture. Providing food shows the theater cares about its teams. Many of the actors will have questions for the costume designer, so making yourself available during this break is wise. Some theaters also set this time aside for the costume department to gather very preliminary measurements for those actors new to them.
- **Equity business.** If the show is a union production, all non-Equity personnel leaves the room. The cast will conduct contractual business and elect a cast deputy who will liaison with the stage managers for union protocols.

First impressions are paramount here, and insecurity or undermining your own authority can start the project on shaky ground. Many costume designers feel great anxiety about speaking in front of others, especially those who act professionally. Indeed, this is one situation where costume designers must do a bit of performing themselves. If needed, jot down a few notes, and practice your delivery. Take a page from the ideal director's goals to communicate **authority** and **humility**, **preparedness**, and **openness**.

The Costume Design Presentation

Directors may ask the costume designer to do a full presentation of the design during the first rehearsal or may request a fuller presentation for another time with the actors. Each designer has their own personality and method for communication; the important objective is to communicate your overall artistic goals. The following template may help spark ideas of how to feature your ideas:

- Highlight the one or two elements of the **script** that affected you most, especially those in keeping with the director's goals, or a logical extension of them.
- **Correlate** your artistic decisions, design elements, or principles you chose to those script elements you found significant.
- Feature any special **research** you performed such as live interviews, interesting detective work, and discoveries.
- Offer **background** ideas about situations or groups of characters that demonstrate the theme.
- Present the character **sketches** by act or scene, showing what everyone will look like starting from the top of show.
- Highlight certain **turning points** that made you decide characters would change costumes. Sketches may be passed around the room or projected on a screen.
- Describe major **changes** through the play, such as shifts in color scheme, time shifts that prompt aging and how that will be handled, and other important storytelling devices.
- Reinforce the large **stage picture** that supports the storytelling.
- Resist bogging down in details – this is not the correct audience for that. Present your ideas clearly but as a work-in-progress, stressing that you are just beginning your collaboration with the actors.

The Table Read

The first reading of the script, or table read, is a momentous opportunity for the costume designer, and every attempt should be made to attend. Read along in your script and take notes in the margins with discoveries from the day. This is the first opportunity for the costume designer to hear the characters they've designed, to discover what that actor brings to the role. Listen carefully to vocal qualities – is an actor very precise, do they have a booming or a youthful voice? Does the actor have a natural elegance, a formidable presence or an impish voice that informs the character? This first read is a gold mine of information. Listen for a cadence or pace inherent in the script. No matter how many times a designer has read the script, it cannot match the power of spoken words. The formality or casual tone of the first days are an excellent glimpse into how this director and the theater work. Some theaters give most of the production power to the director, while others closely monitor every aspect of the show.

Rehearsal Costume Plot

Leave as much costume material as possible in the rehearsal room for the actors. Work with stage management to create a costume dramaturgy wall: the costume scene chart and copies of costume renderings, even some research. Actors often ask the stage manager in the middle of blocking, *what am I wearing for this?* Actors and stage managers will study this information in the moments they are not fully engaged in a scene. Many stage management teams will monitor the costume designer's scene chart to update changes. This attention to detail is a valuable gift to the busy designer who is shopping, fitting, and attending rehearsals all at once.

Subsequent Rehearsals

Each theater uses its own approach to rehearsal hours. Fully professional companies rehearse during usual business hours so team members may fulfil family obligations. Showcase, educational and community theaters may rehearse in the evening, so that everyone works around other employment, adding weekend days into the mix. The first read may be followed by several days of discussion to explore the script itself, especially if it is dense or uses mannered language. Plays with very few lead actors may begin with individual scene work first, or the director may start with music, acting, or dance exercises that affect character mindset. Directors may use these common rehearsal approaches:

- **Table work.** Director and actors discuss the script as a literary artwork, sometimes adding in depth discussions about the peculiarities of the language.
- **Devised work.** Some devised pieces use the full rehearsal period to develop the script. Designers find success attending a number of rehearsals as an active part of the process, suggesting items for characters or bringing sample costume items with them for trial-and-error exploration.
- **Scene-by-scene blocking.** Actors create or learn their stage movement while holding their scripts to jot notes. The costume designer may wish to watch rehearsals for key scenes with costume moments. Characters may be moving in ways the designer and director had not particularly anticipated.
- **Stagger-through.** The first time an entire act or the whole show runs with blocking. Actors are generally still "on book" holding their scripts. It is important for the costume designer to pay very close attention to developing blocking, especially fights, scuffles, or unexpected exits and entrances.
- **Run-through/designer run.** Directors aim their workflow to result in a run-through of the entire show in time for the designers to see the work in progress. The run-through is the perfect time to catch major challenges or new changes.
- **Staging rehearsals.** Move into the actual set onstage without costumes, lights, or sound. No matter how carefully a show has been blocked in the rehearsal room, some actions cannot be rehearsed until moving into the playing space. Actions may look completely different once theater sight-lines are taken into consideration.
- **Paper tech.** A meeting with director, stage manager, crew chiefs, and some designers such as lighting and sound to determine all technical

cues and enter them into the stage manager's script. Sometimes the wardrobe crew chief is part of this meeting, so by this point the costume designer must have completed the final costume plot.

- **Dry tech.** A technical rehearsal without actors for scenic, lighting, sound, and projection designs to rehearse complex sequences or parts with overlapping cues.
- **Cue-to-cue.** A rehearsal with or without actors that skips through the script to places with technical cues. Actors eliminate dialogue concentrating on cue lines.
- **Dress parade.** A call for actors in costumes used in some community and academic theaters so actors learn how to dress in their costumes before the stress of a dress rehearsal. Actors appear as a full cast or in scene groups for inspection and director notes. Some directors cannot concentrate on costumes during tech and this step allows the costume shop to receive the bulk of their notes early in the process. Dress parades should be approached with caution: viewing costumes out of the proper context and lighting can lead to misunderstandings and unnecessary notes. Many theaters will not use their salaried actor and crew time this way, preferring to wait until tech.
- **Tech or dress tech.** Rehearsal *with actors* including all technical departments. Some theaters include costumes at this stage, others do not wish the actors to spend such lengthy time in costume. There is a stop-and-start rhythm with many opportunities to reset to the top of a cue sequence.
- **Sitzprobe.** A rehearsal for musical theater and opera where singers sing with the orchestra focusing on timing and synchronization.
- **Dress rehearsals.** Rehearsal with all technical departments. Many theaters invite a photographer during a second dress rehearsal.

Working With Stage Managers

Stage managers work in stressful conditions because they answer to several bosses; the most obvious is the director, whom they will work side-by-side with

Figure 27.1 Some theaters use costumes for tech rehearsals and others wait until full dress rehearsals.

Credit: Photo by Genaro Sevin from Pexels

each day to craft a specific vision. They also report to the theater itself as the point person who will manage the show from first rehearsals to closing night. They must serve everyone on the production: if anyone has a question about the production, they will usually start with the SM. Stage management also serves as the enforcer of Actor's Equity rules. If the actors are union members, the stage manager is also a member of the same union. Stage managers juggle many strong personalities and conflicting desires, expertly negotiating solutions. They work closely with the costume designer to schedule fittings. Your ability to do your job will often depend on collaborating well with the stage manager. Communicate clearly and openly with the stage manager, respecting their time. Ask how and by when they'd like to receive fitting requests. Would they like a full week's requests at once, or several days at a time? What time must requests be submitted to meet union rules about fitting notice or other restrictions? Learn to estimate accurately how long a fitting will last and then stick to it. Habitually returning actors late to rehearsal puts

the stage manager in a terrible spot for interrupting workflow. They may start refusing to send actors during tight scheduling for fear they will not return for a work call. If you cause a delay, communicate with stage management immediately, and stop by rehearsals to explain the situation.

> "I loved stage-managing the world premiere of *Yellowman* by Dael Orlandersmith. . . . This play, starring Dael herself . . . was a stunning exploration of racial equity issues. At the first rehearsal, the show ran about three hours. Each day in rehearsal Dael would come in with new edits and changes. Sometimes things were cut and sometimes things were reinserted in later rehearsals. The designers all needed to be kept apprised of these changes because allusions to design elements were eliminated. The final version ran 81 minutes. The work paid off when the play received a Pulitzer Prize nomination and continues to enjoy productions all over the country." —Paul Michnewicz, Stage Manager of the Kennedy Center, Washington DC[2]

Interacting With Rehearsals

Rehearsals are the lifeblood of every show – it is the room where everything happens and the motivator for everyone's work. In spite of all their preparation, the designer must remain open to the inevitable creative changes. The designer operates as a creative member of the team, keeping a finger on the pulse of work. The stage management team will send a daily rehearsal report so that everyone is aware of developments. They will make note of decisions that affect each area, such as how actors interact with personal props, blocking that may affect the costume. The stage manager may ask questions or seek ideas on behalf of the actors or directors. Many rehearsal reports include requests for items to be sent to rehearsal to incorporate into the action. Common rehearsal items include anything that holds personal props such as handbags or wallets. Items requested include plot points such as rings that must be exchanged between characters, or coats that must be added during a scene. And increasingly, it is important to send clothing items to imitate period fashions. Contemporary actors may never have worn shoes with hard leather soles, or skirts that brush the floor. Some stage managers pro-actively submit long lists of rehearsal items based on the costume sketches and script, or at the director's request. But actors may not always be aware these items have been requested or sent to rehearsal. Before spending a great deal of time fulfilling long lists, talk with each actor in their first fittings. What would they like to have in rehearsal? Do they have something they are already using? Some actors like to use personal items for a sense of familiarity or as part of their process. If the show takes place in a period requiring fitted clothing, rehearsal garments will have to be fitted before or along with other costume items.

Rehearsal notes should be the first thing the costume team attends to at the beginning of the day. Make it a habit to politely respond to the rehearsal notes *each day* so that the stage manager and director understand their notes are being read. Any note coming from the director specifically should receive utmost priority. If you don't have an answer to a question, note that you are thinking or need more information and will swing by rehearsal to discuss it. Interpreting rehearsal notes can take some judgment. In an effort to be helpful, someone on the stage management team may write a solution in the rehearsal notes without explaining what the challenge was. You as the costume designer might solve that challenge a different way, or you might wish to consult the actor or director before making a final decision. Look at each rehearsal note as an opportunity to collaborate: don't hesitate to visit rehearsal routinely or email for more clarification. Think about each request and get more information. Checking in on rehearsals regularly will provide some context for notes, or give the opportunity to solve situations before they become notes.

Some rehearsal notes defy understanding. It's a mystery what interpersonal situations the stage manager or director may be experiencing in the rehearsal room.

Stage manager: The rehearsal watch you sent doesn't work.

Costume designer: That's right. It's a rehearsal watch, so we sent a broken one until we buy the real one.

Stage manager: But we need one that works. It has to tell time.

Costume designer: Oh, but the time is written into the script. I can fix the hands at the same time as the script – or can't the actor just pretend?

Stage manager: *Our* actors don't *pretend*.

Nudity and Intimacy Coordination

Any show including nudity and simulated intimacy follows intimacy protocols and if possible, hires an intimacy coordinator. Costume departments in particular pay attention to intimacy choreography.

Figure 27.2 This fitted corset and petticoat will be sent to rehearsal for the actor to learn new styles of moving in period attire.

We supply the necessary items affecting the choreography and the actors' bodies. Sometimes tear-away garments are required, specifically tailored to match the movement of the scene. Substitute garments and nudity covers may be required, or the costume designer may wish to suggest their use. Rehearsals requiring nudity may also require someone from the costume department to be on hand. Producers often think of nudity as a lack of a costume, but it *is* a costume with many associated costs that can add to the budget. Wardrobe provides comfort items such as a robe and slippers for actors to wear as soon as the actor leaves stage or the lights go down. Different modesty covers may be necessary in rehearsal that will not be worn in the final performance. The costume designer should be aware of what the founders of Intimacy Directors International/Intimacy Directors & Coordinators term the **Five Pillars**: context, communication, consent, choreography, and closure.[3] These pillars provide an opportunity for all parties to define their terms and comfort level every step of the way. For further information, see the Extra Resources section.

Working With a Choreographer

The choreographer brings to life the director's overarching themes using movement. For dance or fight sequences, working with the choreographer is much more informative than the director. The choreographer often serves as the default liaison for dancers. Stage managers may not send specific dance rehearsals notes, so costume designers must stop into dance rehearsals periodically to watch the work in progress. It's imperative to consult the choreographer before completing the design for any dance costume. Color embodies the emotional impact of the piece, and clothing details invoke the theme. How the fabric moves with the body is an essential aspect of the dance itself. The type of shoe defines and supports the dancers' physicality; always ask the choreographer about footwear requirements before purchasing the dance shoes.

Figure 27.3 Consult the choreographer before finalizing a design to ensure costumes accommodate movement.
Credit: Photo by Michael Zittel from Pexels

"Dance shapes the character and [ties] the strings all together in the movement and visual aspects. . . . Some of the most weighted research I've done is around musical theater – dealing with stereotypes, mass incarceration. . . . I'm going to dig in somewhere before every dance, but you dig into yourself, too. . . . You have to allow for difference; otherwise, you're just repeating yourself. After each show I write what I've learned from doing that show." — Camille A. Brown, choreographer *Once on This Island, Netflix, Ma Rainey's Black Bottom*[4]

Working With Actors

Seeing a character come to life is one of the most satisfying parts of working on a production. While it takes a team of people to create the costumes, the final character delivery ultimately rests with the performer. Designers and performers may not always see eye-to-eye on a character or how to best present the visual manifestation of the character. Like it or not, performers are human and they bring their own baggage, hopes, and dreams to the role. Some actors are deep thinkers about the story who wish to subsume their appearance into a character. Others just want to look their best in preconceived ways that have little to do with the story. Most actors, however, are thoughtful storytellers. It is not a sign of weakness to listen to an actor's ideas or concerns. Actors gain more respect for collaborators they can trust, who have enough personal security to concentrate on the story, not their ego. Working with actors often comes down to active listening and controlling the way you present information to them.

Checklist for Active Listening

- Accept that listening is empowering, not a sign of weakness.
- Listen with the goal of learning something new.
- Look at the speaker, avoid wandering eyes.
- Maintain focus, don't let your mind wander to your next reply.
- Ask questions in an encouraging tone using neutral phrases such as "Is this what you mean?"
- Engage body language by nodding. Avoid closed body language like folded arms.
- Know your biases, be tolerant of other speech patterns and habits.
- Listen between the lines; are they repeating the same message in different ways? Not everyone speaks directly.
- Provide feedback that demonstrates you hear what they are saying. This may be a short summary of what you heard.
- Assess what might be opinion and what might be factual.
- Take notes or use memory devices.

There is no shortage of strong personalities in the entertainment business, and costume designers will work with them all as they move between artistic, administrative and production staffs for every show. If a particular project features difficult personalities, there are several excellent books available outlining productive and professional strategies to work with them. (See the Extra Resources section.)

Production Meetings

Production meetings are the chance for all departments to share information and make sure

they are all working toward the same goals and deadlines. They are scheduled on a regular basis in person or as a video conference. The overarching goals are to check if every department is working on schedule and under budget. Anything that may interfere with those goals should take priority. The production manager or stage manager creates the agenda, often recapping that week's rehearsal notes and checking progress in each department. This time is best used to solve challenges that involve more than one department. Costume departments can sometimes feel overlooked in production meetings. Other technical areas will take up so much time over details that costumes may at times be brushed aside, using the excuse that costumes has fitting times to resolve issues. In some cases, costume departments feel reluctant to speak up, as if bringing challenges to the group could be interpreted as not doing their jobs correctly. Don't let yourself or your department be sidelined in these important meetings. Sometimes the costume designer must leave the meeting early to attend a fitting, asking that their questions lead the meeting. Make sure that a spokesperson for the costume area remains.

Costume Production Meeting Agenda Checklist

- Interactions with scenery – floor grooves, surface textures, slippery surfaces, rakes, backstage change areas, width of doors and furniture
- Interactions with props – what is a prop, what is a costume; personal props handled by actors or in pockets, safety or laundry concerns, blood, food, liquids
- Interactions with lights – gel colors and instrument placement, skin tones
- Interactions with sound – size and placement of body mics and packs, interferences with hair, earrings, clothing, who supplies mic packs, matching skin tones as needed
- Interaction with projections or FX – specific colors required for costumes used as projection surfaces

- Interactions with rehearsals – define all rehearsal costume needs, report progress on rehearsal notes
- Interaction with marketing – photo call dates and requirements, use of renderings in programs or lobby
- Interaction with schedule – define all rehearsal expectations and dates, needs, pre-show dressing calls, assigned dressing rooms
- Interaction with stage crew – extra costumes required, fast change rehearsal process

Sizing Up Rehearsals

On occasion, the show may change significantly from its original planning once rehearsals begin. In cases of radical change, the costume designer will have a particularly difficult job keeping up with changes and maintaining a productive schedule to deliver the costumes at dress rehearsals. It is important to keep a level head and accurately appraise the workload and ramifications of changes. Be forthright with the director and producer; suggest ways you can creatively solve problems together. Work the creative juices overtime – it is exactly these kinds of situations that show colleagues that you can problem solve with humor.

Expecting the Unexpected

A costume designer was working on a show starring a well-known television personality. She received a frantic phone call from the producer that the dance ensemble's shoes must be replaced by that night's dress rehearsal to keep the star happy. There had been an early dance rehearsal and the star was very upset. She complained one dancer had stepped hard on her foot, and all the dancers were stomping too loudly on the stage floor. The star blamed the ensemble's shoes, demanding the producer deal with this problem. With new budget approval, the designer barely had enough time to visit three separate dance supply vendors in time to appear at the theater with all new shoes. The designer soon discovered no one had told the dance chorus about the new shoes, and it fell to her to explain the situation, not using any names. One dancer replied "We're tripping because the choreography has changed every single day. Tell them to freeze the dance and we'll stop tripping."

Extra Resources

Intimacy Directors and Choreographers Presents the IDC Resource Guide, First Edition, July 2020, compiled by Marie C. Percy. This document contains further discussions of the Five Pillars. https://static1.squarespace.com/static/5e1c12f49383f8245b857d01/t/5f2470bdc8a09c2a6c405251/1596223729318/IDC+Resource+Guide.pdf

Modesty Covers

BraTenders, New York https://bratenders.com/
Gano Rentals & Expendables, Atlanta https://ganosales.tv/
Western Costume Co. Supply Store, Los Angeles www.wccsupplystore.com/

Notes

1 DeKoven, Lenore. 2006. *Changing Direction, A Practical Approach to Directing Actors in Film and Theater*. New York: Focal Press, p. 102.
2 Siegel, David. 2017. "In the Moment: Interview with Stage Manager Paul D Michnewicz." *DC Metro, Theater Arts*, December 28, 2017. https://dcmetrotheaterarts.com/2017/12/28/moment-interview-stage-manager-paul-d-michnewicz/
3 Purcell, Carey. 2018. "Intimate Exchanges." *American Theater Magazine*, October 23, 2018. https://www.americantheatre.org/2018/10/23/intimate-exchanges/
4 Campbell, Karen. 2021. "Q&A with Camille A. Brown." *Christian Science Monitor*, April 13, 2021. https://www.csmonitor.com/The-Culture/2021/0413/Q-A-with-Camille-A.-Brown-founder-and-artistic-director-of-Camille-A.-Brown-Dancers

PART EIGHT

REFINE THE VISION

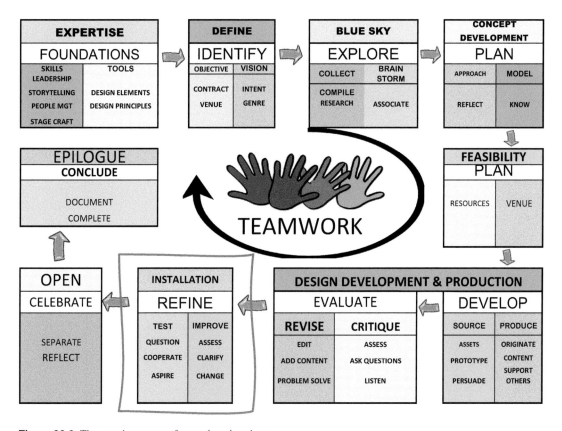

Figure 28.0 The creative process for produced projects.

Credit: Holly Poe Durbin and Ayrika Johnson

28.
DRESS REHEARSALS

There is an old saying that a bad dress rehearsal portends a good opening night. There would be no need to invent this saying if dress rehearsals routinely went smoothly. The odds are actually stacked against that, as director Kent Thompson explains.

> Putting on a costume for the first time is often a thrilling but disorienting moment for the actor. The clothes, the beard, the hat, the boots, and all will affect his physical presence and emotional state. Actors will forget lines, miss entrances, look stunned or worried, as they seek to integrate these most intimate and personal elements into their performance. By the next rehearsal, they will have adjusted to their costume and begun exploring how to use it to best advantage.[1]

Is It Going to Look Like That?

Every costume designer knows how it feels each time an actor encounters a difficulty while wearing a costume for the first time. When a hat falls off or the actor trips, all heads in the theater snap to look at the designer, the director may scurry over to point out the error or multiple people dive into their laptops to record notes about it. The costume designer knows most of these difficulties will sort themselves out with more practice, or a few tweaks in the costume shop will fix the issue. One large part of the designer's job during the first dress rehearsal is to answer questions and soothe everyone's nerves that things will work out. If the theater incorporates full costumes into technical rehearsals, the slow pace and stop/start rhythm gives the actors more time to get comfortable with their costumes. However, if the theater schedules technical rehearsals *without* costumes, all the other areas have had several days to correct their discoveries. By dress rehearsal, everyone is eager to leap into a full run, forgetting that costumes is a major

element for actors to negotiate. Because of this, the costume area often works under more pressure. Any stoppage for costumes can be met with impatience, and the wardrobe crew must be able to work quickly. If the costume designer is lucky, another technical area such as automated scenery will be so demanding it buys extra time to sort out costume discoveries.

There is never enough time to accomplish everything and long hours may lead to an emotional roller coaster. Learn strategies that work for you to keep a calm demeanor and bolster your sense of humor. The artistic pressure, the demands of interacting with dozens of actors and the need to solve problems quickly calls for a costume designer who can manage their emotions. The designer strives for a mix of the four key elements discussed in Chapter 27 "**authority** tempered with **humility**, a sense of **preparedness** together with a welcoming **openness**."[2] Dress rehearsals are the refinement step in the creative process. It is the opportunity to tune your

DOI: 10.4324/9781003015284-36

work, taking all the other design areas into consideration. Even with weeks or months of preparation, the designer cannot consider the design finished at dress rehearsal. This begins a new phase of work answering the question *"Does everything serve the show as we intended?"*

How to Survive Dress Rehearsals

Small routines of self-care have a big impact on the mood. One costume designer wears a crystal tiara to the first dress rehearsal, figuring that everyone will be looking at her for answers anyway, so she might as well *look* magical.

- Enhance your mood with a ritual such as meditation or exercise
- Dress in layers, always bring a sweater to cold theaters
- Wear comfortable shoes, you will walk those 10,000 steps or more
- Bring healthy snacks
- Charge up the laptop, tablet, or notebook
- Remember chargers, cables, earplugs, or other accessories
- Plan a diversion for long stopping periods – other work, emails
- Pack self-care items for the venue: lip balm, hand cream, sunblock
- Walk around the block during breaks

Meeting the Wardrobe Crew

The wardrobe crew joins the project about a week ahead of dress rehearsals to read the script, view a run of the show, study the costume plot, liaise with stage management for presetting garments backstage and fast changes. The head of wardrobe coordinates with stage management and the production manager to identify the number of running crew, based on how many actors change backstage at one time and the number of actors who may need help dressing. Larger theaters employ a separate wig and makeup department head to coordinate all those needs. Smaller theaters may ask an assistant costume designer or shop personnel to perform any of these tasks or act as head of wardrobe to gain a longer employment contract. In general, it is not possible to combine the job of costume designer and wardrobe for the show. The designer must view the entire show from the audience point of view to be an effective part of the director's creative team. The costume designer meets with the wardrobe head to transfer knowledge of the show. Wardrobe creates their own paperwork using the costume designer's **dressing lists** or **costume plot** and **costume scene chart** as a start. They convert this information into check-in sheets to account for every costume piece, tracking sheets to divide up dressing duties and fast changes and maintenance or laundry lists.

Depending on the complexity of the costumes and backstage changes, the designer or wardrobe head may ask stage management to schedule **fast change rehearsals** before a technical or dress run to strategize the choreography. This rehearsal

Figure 28.1 Wardrobe crew member backstage.
Credit: Photo by Ron Lach from Pexels

focuses on alterations to closures if the crew cannot meet the allotted time goal. A quick change rehearsal for special sequences can save time, but it also means using tech time or calling and actor early. Stage managers can be ingenious with scheduling legalities if they know about the situation ahead of time. If time does not permit a separate rehearsal, then each change will be rehearsed in real time during the dress rehearsal. Wardrobe may ask to repeat a fast change to better coordinate the backstage crew. If it appears the crew cannot change the costume in the allotted time, the designer must step in to brainstorm how the costume or blocking might be changed to allow those precious extra seconds.

Preparing the Dressing Lists

Stage management assigns actors to dressing rooms, taking into account the actors' employment contracts and any interpersonal relationships that developed during rehearsals. The costume designer or wardrobe furnishes a **dressing list** for each actor to remind them where to change costumes, and how many pieces there are in each costume. The dressing list is the final version of the **fitting sheet** used to fit each actor. These can be assembled very quickly by converting the same Excel lists used since the planning phases. Hide columns that do not pertain to actors, such as whether a costume was rented or purchased. Ensure the costumes are listed in proper order with

Chris Manikoe		
Carl- Cello		
	Item	**Description**
	Always worn	
	Socks	Black-2 pair for 2 show days
	Undershirt	White crew neck short sleeve- 2 for 2 show days
	Insoles	drugstore insoles in each pair of shoes
	Watch, ring	Watch-green face, gold rim, black band Ring-plain band
	Sc 1	
	Shirt	Tan dress shirt
	Sweater vest	Dark blue
	Suit	Dark gray 2 button 2 piece suit
	Tie	Navy knit tie
	Shoes	Brown Ecco lace ups
	Belt	Black
	Sc 2 -remove jacket(back of chair), tie (pocket)	
	Sc 6 and 7- repeat shoes	
	Shirt	White with green and blue window pane plaid
	Pants	Olive green flat front cordurouy slacks
	Belt	Dark brown
	Sc 8, 9- add sport coat-placed on chair, added as moving into London	
	Sport coat	Brown houndstooth jacket
	Also:	Shirt untucked at start of London, retuck when returning with sandwich

Figure 28.2 An excerpt of a dressing list converted from the fitting sheet. Fitting photos or renderings are included to remind the actors how each costume should look. Note the instructions to add or remove pieces.

instructions to add or remove items to create the next look. Carefully describe the colors so the actor can easily identify each costume. Some theaters add fitting photos to the list to remind actors how to wear their costumes.

Dressing Room Checklist

Equip each dressing room with items for collecting laundry and actor notes should they encounter a problem or need a repair.

- Notes sheet attached to the wall with a pen tied to it
- Individually labeled mesh laundry bags for underpinnings
- Laundry basket to collect mesh bags and larger costume items
- Towels and hand towels
- Comfort robes, if asked to provide one
- Makeup guide if required
- Encouraging signs prompting how to manage laundry or hanging garments

Dress Rehearsal Scheduling

The first time the actors dress in costume they will take much longer than the time allotted, and the sound crew will need additional time wiring each actor for mics. Experienced directors and SMs know this tendency and they schedule other activities to fill the time. The costume designer will be needed in many places at once to answer hundreds of questions and solve last-minute challenges. Once the actors are ready, the director and stage manager gather everyone in the house seats to explain the plan for the day. Many directors understand they are also providing this time for the actors to see everyone else in costume, adjusting to their new world. If the actors are young students or inexperienced, ask the Stage Manager to remind everyone the director and designer are in charge of what each character looks like, and they are to refrain from making comments on anyone else's costume. The SM will explain how to handle difficulties with costumes; when the actor may ask to

hold the rehearsal for a moment and how to communicate with the crew or designer.

Some directors are methodical workers; they cannot advance in their work until each challenge is completely solved. Dress or tech rehearsals may expand over the entire number of days allotted. Some directors wish to prevent actors peaking in their readiness too early, or they like to keep actors on edge. They may use the entire tech/dress time to go through the show once, leaving no room for a run before the preview. This is nerve-wracking for performers, crew and designers, too, who then have no opportunity to see their adjustments before a live audience does. Director Kent Thompson notes that Actors Equity created a rule to prevent this misuse of time: for union shows there must be at least one complete run before an audience performance.[3] But many productions are not governed by union rules. Rehearsals not governed by union protocols may also overlook adequate breaks and meal opportunities for the crew. Remind the SM that the wardrobe crew is usually the last to leave and the first to arrive, often eliminating the break or eating a proper meal. Ask how these breaks might be handled so everyone is treated fairly. The designers themselves often do not get adequate breaks. They may arrive early each day to attend to notes after staying late in the theater. If detrimental scheduling goes past a few days, talk to the director to prioritize notes and adjustments.

LORT Scheduling for Technical Rehearsals

Technical schedules are regulated by agreement between LORT and Actor's Equity. Many non-union organizations use these rules as a template even though they are not required to do so. Understanding the expectations of each work call helps the designer plan work time.

8 out of 10. The span of the workday is 10 hours, but actors only work eight of the hours. Meals and breaks add up to the other two hours. Individual actors may have earlier calls to accommodate costume fittings or publicity. That counts as their work day, and they must take breaks at prescribed times even if they differ from the rest of the cast. A dress rehearsal beginning at 12 noon must end by 10 PM with 2 hours of breaks.

7 out of 9. The span of the workday is 9 hours, actors work seven of those hours. A dress rehearsal beginning at 12 noon must end by 9 PM with breaks. This schedule allows crews the most opportunity to sleep and return for a full morning of adjustments.

10 out of 12. The span of the workday is 12 hours, actors work ten of those hours. A dress rehearsal beginning at 12 noon must end by 12 midnight. This common practice may be falling out of favor as it exhausts everyone, especially the technical crew and designers who remain in the theater after rehearsal for production meetings and work calls.

Costume designers have another important element to organize for dress rehearsals. They must have a good idea of where the budget stands in case changes are needed. The designer may have left a contingency in the budget for this phase. But often there was barely enough money to prepare the costumes to this point. If the designer has worked with a costume director who is responsible for the budget, ask for a general idea of how much money may be available for additional labor and purchases. Understand what labor will be available and at what times are available to work on rehearsal notes. Be prepared to discuss any large changes not only in terms of artistry but also feasibility with the resources you have. Many theaters keep a contingency for tech week changes. The production manager may have to decide which area to throw these resources toward.

Each rehearsal day ends with a production meeting held in the theater seats attended by all designers and department heads. The meeting is run by the production manager or stage manager, according to that theater's custom. The agenda is fairly routine, beginning with the director giving

notes taken during the rehearsal. Each designer and department has an opportunity to ask questions of the director and raise their issues that affect other departments or the production as a whole. Announce visual changes you intend to make that may affect other design areas, such as changing the color of a garment or cutting a costume. The meeting closes with settling the work schedule for the next day. If the costume area has special needs such as fittings or fast change rehearsals, ask about working those into the schedule. Remember the effect of call times on the wardrobe crew and the costume maintenance. Many theaters do not require wearing costumes in afternoon rehearsals on the same day as an evening performance to allow for adequate laundry and crew turnaround.

Working With the Director

Technical and dress rehearsals are at best a stimulus overload for the director. Some love the camaraderie of seeing their world come to life and they lead with humor and excitement. Others feel the heavy weight of others judging their show in this chaotic phase. For a few days, the acting must take a back seat while all the elements come together in the space. Some directors expect their every word to be obeyed without question, while others want to spark extended conversations while the costumes are onstage for reference. Learn the peculiarities of each director you work with, and approach their process sensitively. Learn when to ask questions and when to save them, and learn how to phrase your comments so they will be heard. Always acknowledge hearing or receiving a note from the director, even if you don't agree with it. Then take some time to think about their ideas. Directors are the final judge if all the design elements are intentional and unified. Therefore, they usually don't like surprises. Before dress rehearsal begins, alert them to costumes that are unfinished or a work-in-progress. Unless told otherwise, they will believe what appears onstage is what you intended. Sometimes, in spite of all the designer's communication, the director just did not anticipate the way a costume would look onstage and

Figure 28.3 The designers and crew wait to gather for a production meeting in the house after the end of a tech rehearsal.

Credit: Photo by Efren Delgadillo, Jr., Great Lakes Theatre, Cleveland

asks for major changes. The designer has the right to defend their artistic decision, but has only one chance to make the case. If the director does not agree, switch to problem solving, pitching ideas that may address their objections. Sometimes the designer may be caught between the director's desires and the reality of budget and timeline. Always remain a part of the director's team when brainstorming solutions.

Critiquing the Design

There has been a recent trend to avoid criticism, fearing it may stigmatize people and squelch innovation. This reticence has no place in a finely-tuned creative project, however. Productive critical thinking is imperative to assess whether the hard work everyone has spent months or weeks doing works as intended. Many artists insist the hardest part of the creative project is not the first blush of

creation, but effective revision. Critiquing your own work is a delicate balance between defending your hard work and disappointment because it does not match the perfect idea in your head. In order to refine the work and grow in your art, you must be open to what your own work can teach you. We have been taught to think of our work in terms of strengths and weaknesses. It is more productive to reframe "weaknesses" as those areas you must revise consistently. Add this self-knowledge to your work process. Learn that perhaps you must see certain things on stage before judging the work. Designers learn *most* when we see the result of ideas and risks; some ideas work as planned and some will not. Some elements will not be clear until an audience is present. Imagine putting on a new pair of glasses to see the work from an artistic point of view, regardless of how much work you put into an item. Can it be improved to make the vision better?

Dress Rehearsal Checklist

- Does each costume define the character in context?
- Is the actor wearing the correct costume in each scene?
- Can the actor move appropriately?
- Check for consistency in fit across the show.
- Are there focal points on the costume?
- Check for consistency in historical costumes – time period or interpretation.
- Are the Elements of Design used effectively?
- Are the Principles of Design used effectively?
- Is the emotional tone and manner of presentation correct?
- Are fabrics looking and moving as anticipated?
- Are the costumes complete? Does anyone look partly undressed?
- How do the costumes interact with light – fabric colors, skin tones.
- How do the costumes interact with the set – visually and for movement?
- Does makeup appear too heavy, too light, losing faces, features?
- Are hems correct and straight, do petticoats show under the hems?

On occasion the costume designer may need to critique another designer's work. This situation calls for the utmost diplomacy, and it is valid only if it leads to improving an idea or honing the vision. Phrase any critique in reference to your design area only, such as a wall painted the same color as the actor's faces. Do not volunteer general critique unless directly solicited to do so. Remember how it feels for you as the costume designer to receive critique from everyone who thinks they know something about clothing. Approach the conversation with humility, and ask questions. You will learn only when you understand how the work appears to others. Never act or reply impulsively on criticism, especially if it surprises you. Ultimately it is up to you to filter their observations through your own judgment.

In a perfect world, directors would phrase their critique clearly. But many do not understand the intricacies of clothing well enough to do that. It is the costume designers job to fish for the specific information to act on.

Director: Something is off with the pink suit.
Designer: Do you think it's the color or the way it fits? Do you like that white trim?

Some directors wish to be gentle and supportive with their design team, phrasing their critique as a leading question. Do not take their question too literally, using it to dig a little deeper.

Director: Do you like the way the pink suit looks?
Designer: I noticed it doesn't fit well at the waist yet. What do you think?

Taking Dress Rehearsal Notes

The major task for every designer during dress rehearsals is judging the effectiveness of the design and suggesting changes when items don't live up to that standard yet. Every designer generates long lists of items to accomplish in a short time, and these rehearsal notes are the driving force behind the tech week workload. The designer's success will depend on his ability to prioritize notes, when in fact every note is important to someone. Notes will originate from four equally important sources:

- **Director**. Assign director notes utmost priority. Always show progress on each director note by the next rehearsal or discuss any reasons for delay.
- **Yourself.** Divide notes in your mind as technical adjustments or design adjustments. Much as we wish to work on our artistry, it sometimes takes a back seat to the adjustments that provide comfort, fast change rigging or repairs.
- **Wardrobe.** Dressers generate notes on their own and on behalf of the actors. Prioritize notes that affect fast changes before all others.

- **Actors**. Actors give notes verbally during the day or on the dressing room note board. Prioritize suppling missing items immediately so both actor and wardrobe may track its use. Also prioritize notes that directly affect their ability to wear the costume comfortably. Approach the other notes eventually, but don't forget them.

Be clear if each note is an adjustment to the *design* or an adjustment to the *technical* aspect of the costume, such as construction or closures. If it is a technical difficulty, designers working with a costume staff ask the costume shop to solve the issue. If the problem is a design issue, acknowledge that before asking the shop to make changes. Concede the item does not look as you expected, or the director does not care for a look. Avoid vocal tones or language that may sound like blame, especially when everyone is tired. As always, the ability to temper requests with humor is appreciated. Explain why the decision has been made so the shop has a full picture and can use best judgment completing the notes. Be specific if you are taking notes for technicians who don't attend the dress rehearsals. A vague note like "*Hem the blue trousers*" is not enough information for a technician to use. Take your best guess at the amount, or grab the actor during down time and use a tape measure to determine the exact amount. "*Hem the blue trousers 1 inch shorter*" is an accurate note the technician can work with. Use down time during techs as much as possible for mini-adjustment fittings or to gather more information.

Working With the Lighting Designer

The lighting designer may be asked by both the scenic and the costume designers to adjust their colors onstage. These requests often stem from how colored light interacts with pigment in paint, fabric, and makeup. Look for the following situations to brainstorm solutions.

- **Color shifting.** Every costume will change colors a bit as lighting changes and that is to be expected. But if the change lasts longer or is more extreme than desired, take a note of the exact scene or lines. Also look for a scene where the costume color looked correct. This information can help the lighting designer understand the desired result.
- **Flat textures.** Stage light generally flattens surfaces, unless the venue allows for extensive sidelight. After talking with the lighting designer, be prepared to enhance costume textures in other ways such as painting shadows, airbrushing, and aging.
- **Ashy skin tones.** Lighting designers must accommodate a wide range of skin tones onstage. If you notice a particular skin tone looking ashy, point that out. Many light plots use a warm color on one side of the face and a cool color on the other. Note if one side of the face looks livelier. One tip from TV's *Insecure* cinematographer Ava Berkovsky is to ask performers to heavily moisturize their skin to allow more light to bounce[4] (See the Extra Resources section.)
- **Washed out faces.** Actors faces can be obliterated if they are wearing a color that forms a high contrast with their skin tone. A dark skinned actor wearing a pure white shirt may appear to have a shadow across his face. That shadow is a reaction of our own retinas. A very pale actor wearing all black or in a scene with many people wearing black may wash out with too much light.
- **Lost or shadowed facial features.** If the actor's face is generally visible, but the eyes or lips fade away, ask the actor to correct it with makeup. Likewise, if one color of makeup washes out or turns too bright. Be as specific as you can, since the actor cannot see themselves under light.

There are many other instances where the costume texture or color does not look as you intended from the stage.

Photos at Dress Rehearsals

Many theaters schedule a photocall during dress rehearsals, often before the costumes are well and truly finished. The theater may hire a professional photographer and share those resources with the

Table 28.1 Dress Rehearsal Notes. This designer wrote tech notes using division of labor or task as the guide for easy reading. She used Google Docs so the costume shop in a different building could follow in real time. Any costumes finished early during the tech were retrieved for work. The doc can also be easily downloaded as a physical list.

1st Dress Rehearsal Notes *All the Way*

Director Notes

Tie that LBJ chooses onstage should be rattlesnake colored, not the stripe

Shoes

Landon – Need another pair of shoes – they are cracking, top layer of leather is peeling, he leaves bits all over the stage

Tracey #1 shoes fell into the scenic track and one of her heels twisted – she says it's kind of backwards, please fix and how to make more sturdy?

Dye

Men's shirts tone a small amount – take off the curse of blinding whiteness

Accessories
PULL/Buy

Final LBJ tie that is chosen TOS – we need duplicates. Buy 3. Make 1st one long enough to go over the prosthetics. A dupe should appear in the Manny scene for him to choose

Give Matt another tie after Manny to be Levison

Kathrine Graham – gold chain not visible, did she wear it was there time? let's give her a bigger one that shows over the dress neckline – we're looking straight up

Wallace – tie red with gold shields, make that more narrow, by ¾ inch

Strom Thurmond – pocket square looks like a squid trying to climb out of his pocket – how to tame that?

Prop clothes in MLK's suitcase – place blue dress shirt on top – talk to running crew

LBJ first pocket square slipping, add it to a cardboard card

Singleton – belt is too long, and cant slip into first belt loop at the end, need a smaller size

The silver star ribbon pin spins around – single pin

Designer To Do/Change

Manny – The measuring tape needs to be an inseam measuring tape, he has rigged his own

Did this come from props?

Ladybird – find a different pin for #1 dress this one doesn't read

Garments

MLK – are #1 trousers still basted? Hem stitching is very visible

Strom – Remove/move wardrobe label from his brown coat, he puts it on avista and white label very obvious

Wigs/Makeup

Secretary wig is too big, take the volume down a little

MLK wig – is the back not fit yet? sticking out?

Wardrobe

Check Manny before his entrance, his shirt tail was out in back – what is he doing?

OK to substitute a pair of loafers for Manny fast change if it will help

Bob Moses – looks like a bag of laundry, how can we help him out?

Table 28.2 Costumes and Lighting Interaction

Appearance of Costume	Elements to Consider or How to Design for These Known Conditions	Possible Solutions in Consultation with the Lighting Designer
Costume surfaces appear plain or flat	**Smooth** fabrics don't offer enough interest to overcome the distance between audience and stage	**Use more texture** than normal life; choose fabrics with enhanced textures that still move as desired
		Substitute visual texture for physical texture. Create "solid color" costumes out of small prints that add subtle interest
	Monochromatic colors don't offer enough interest to overcome the distance between audience and stage	**Consider painting** flat looking fabrics with a splatter or sponge technique to add interest
	Color intensity may be too similar throughout the stage picture	**Consider adding depth** by toning down the colors or adding trim or painted shadows and enhancements
		Add depth by adding sheer layers on top of some clothing
Shadows on the actors faces	**Down light** casting shadows from hat, hair, or actor's features	**Embrace the effect** for a short period if it enhances the mood, check with director
	Back light illuminates back of actor throwing shadows across the front	**Consider reshaping** the hat or hairstyle
	Sharp or hard light creating shadows with hard edges	
	Position of lighting instruments – may be limited by venue or budget	**Tilt the brim** to open the face toward the light source
Texture is not reading, surfaces look flat	**Bright illumination** or intensity of light flattens texture	**Alter the costume texture** for higher contrast in depth or larger scale
	Diffuse light does not pick up subtle texture effects, especially in larger venues	
	Low intensity light is dim or moody	
Costume color changes	**Gel colors** combined with pigment colors neutralize the costume hue	**Over dye** the costume to correct for lighting conditions. Note which hues to add back into the mix

Appearance of Costume	Elements to Consider or How to Design for These Known Conditions	Possible Solutions in Consultation with the Lighting Designer
	Diffuse or **Low Intensity light** affects the eye's ability to see color, tipping toward gray *values*, especially in larger venues	**Consult** with lighting designer carefully before changing costume color so both are working toward the same result
		Saturate fabric colors or add higher contrast touches such as light and dark values for emphasis
Shiny elements not visible **such as sequins or beads**	**Diffuse light**, light not strong enough to reflect **Low illumination** or intensity of light	**Consult** lighting designer for possible increase in light or stronger light source **Sequins or beads** may be too small or smooth, add faceted versions to the garment
Painted effects or aging do not show from stage	**Diffuse light** fades the effect **Low illumination** or intensity of light	**Painting** itself is not dark enough or requires higher contrast **Consult** lighting designer for possible increase in light or stronger light source
	High intensity lighting flattens the painted effect	**Consider** painting shadows in an impressionist manner using a triad of colors: purple, rust brown, and dark green to add visual interest
	Gel color and pigment color may neutralize each other	

designers, one of the designers may be a gifted photographer or the designers may be allowed to hire their own photographer. It is important to keep an accurate record of your work under stage light and feature the emotional and physical context of the scene. Ask anyone taking photos for you to make sure to frame a few full-length shots. Most theater photographers work with the theater's marketing department who prefer close up shots. You may wish to take additional photos backstage or on dress forms to record specific details or archive techniques. Some costume departments keep a photography screen on a wall near the dressing rooms, asking the actors to step into that frame for archival photography. No matter what kind of photos you plan to take, approve it ahead of time with the stage manager who will reconcile photography with union protocols.

The First Audience

Many theaters use an invited audience or preview performances to hone the final show with an audience reaction. Directors switch their attention

Figure 28.4 The crew corrects a problem onstage during a break. Designers spend long days in dress rehearsals developing successful strategies to weather stressful days.

Credit: Photo by Vincent Olivieri. *Skintight* at the Geffen Playhouse. Scenic Design Lauren Halpfern, Costume Design China Lee, Lighting Design Pat Collins, Sound Design Vincent Olivieri

back to the acting during final dress rehearsals and preview performances, although they will continue to give design notes. On occasion, a new work may discover it does not land with an audience as expected, leading to rewrites, new blocking, or new design elements. Every show will adjust in some way once the actors and director have seen a preview, so most designer contracts require the designers' presence for some or all previews to make these adjustments. However, not every theater has the budget to support extreme changes by this point. Consult the production manager if required changes will cost extra money or labor. Remain an enthusiastic part of the team by making suggestions and figuring guesstimates for materials and labor for changes. This is where all that time you took to fully understand the script

and story will pay off handsomely. If it looks like the theater cannot afford any options, allow the production manager to make those difficult decisions.

Sizing Up Dress Rehearsals

The costume designer sets a tone during dress rehearsals that reassures everyone problems will be solved. The major task for every designer during this process is judging the effectiveness of the design and suggesting changes when items don't yet meet that standard. Every designer generates long lists of adjustments to accomplish in a short time. Much of the success of this phase depends on the ability to prioritize notes and communicate them effectively. The costume designer collaborates with the scenic and lighting designer to coordinate the overall visual presentation. Dress rehearsals are an exciting time the designer approaches with the willingness to critique their own work.

Expecting the Unexpected

One of the most difficult decisions every designer has to make is cutting a favorite costume from the show. The costume looked great on paper and in the fitting room, but it is obvious once onstage it does not serve the production. The director may ask for a change, or the designer may notice it herself. Designers call this "killing the children" in a nod to *Medea*, the ancient Greek tragedy. Not only is it emotionally wrenching to realize a design decision is wrong, but time, money, and labor to correct the problem are now limited. Making a major change may disrupt the actor's work, as well. The Spanish poet Juan Ramón Jiménez describes the revision process as "This constant struggle between wanting to be finished and wanting to finish well." Every designer must decide for themselves if the problem is one that must be fixed this time, or if it is an opportunity to learn for next time. One designer keeps a design journal for each show using slow moments in dress rehearsals to record lessons learned – both successful and unfortunate choices.

Writing them down purges them from her head and serves as a good reference for the next time she begins a similar project.

Extra Resources

Take a Look Inside a Production Meeting YouTube, harvestraintheatre https://youtu.be/btAmIrnBMwM

Keeping Insecure Lit: HBO cinematographer Ava Berkofsky on properly lighting black faces. Xavier Harding, Mic Magazine, Sept 6, 2017 NOTE: While film and theater lighting are different, this article contains good hints for looking at skin tones.

Why Criticism is Good for Creativity Harvard Business Review, Roberto Verganti and Don Norman. July 16, 2019 https://hbr.org/2019/07/why-criticism-is-good-for-creativity

Notes

1 Thompson, Kent. 2019. *Directing Professionally: A Practical Guide to Developing a Successful Career in Today's Theatre.* New York: Methuen Drama, p. 97.

2 DeKoven, Lenore. 2006. *Changing Direction, A Practical Approach to Directing Actors in Film and Theater.* New York: Focal Press, p. 102.

3 Thompson, *Directing Professionally: A Practical Guide to Developing a Successful Career in Today's Theatre,* p. 101.

4 Latif, Nadia. 2017. "It's Lit! How Film Finally Learned to Light Black Skin." *The Guardian*, September 2017. https://www.theguardian.com/film/2017/sep/21/its-lit-how-film-finally-learned-how-to-light-black-skin

PART NINE

OPENING AND EPILOGUE

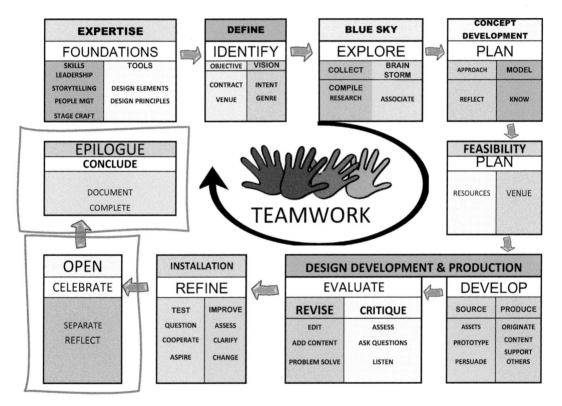

Figure 29.0 The creative process for produced projects

Credit: Holly Poe Durbin and Ayrika Johnson

29.
DESIGN DOCUMENTATION

Opening night – the night we have been working toward so long – is within reach! It is a bitter-sweet moment for many designers. It's a mix of exhilaration and pride mixed with the wistfulness of saying goodbye to something we lived with for weeks or months. Another common feeling is relief and exhaustion. We fueled those last hectic weeks with adrenaline highs and anguished lows, adding the occasional dash of chocolate for good measure. Now all we want to do is celebrate with our colleagues and sleep. But many design contracts end on opening night and there are lingering tasks to accomplish. Every designer must decide for themselves whether it is better to rest now, and extend the work into unpaid time or knuckle down during final dress rehearsals and previews to accomplish every-thing on time. Tasks such as buying opening night gifts for your shop and crew must be accomplished by opening. But there are other tasks that will not wait.

Understudies and Swings

Some regional and commercial theaters include understudies in their cast. Some summer stock companies or educational theaters use swings to rotate the performers. Some contracts stipulate the plan for substitute costumes must be in place by opening night, overseen by the costume designer, assistant designer, or costume director. If this clause is in the contract, ensure those duties are completed on time and in a manner that works with the overall design.

Wrapping Rentals

Many rental sources calculate their fee using the amount of time a costume is worn onstage, and the clock starts ticking with the first public perform-ance. Costumes returned before that performance will avoid extra charges. It is important to stay on top of the rental agreement so the budget works as planned. Costume designers must also protect

their reputations. If we become known for lateness or inconsiderate professional practices, our sources will remember that. They will be less likely to extend us favors next time.

Budget and Final Accounting

Designers whose contracts end must close out their financial dealings with the producer before leaving. Every theater has its own process for receipts and clearing expenses from purchasing cards. Complete this task in an orderly manner, keeping copies of all paperwork for yourself. Review Chapter 18 for budgeting protocols. You may wish to do a **reconciled budget** comparing the estimated budget to the amount you actually spent. A designer learns about their own way of working by doing this. For instance, one designer thinks good quality shoes enhance their designs and may spend more in that category than someone else. A comparison budget may reveal that rentals cost much more or

DOI: 10.4324/9781003015284-38

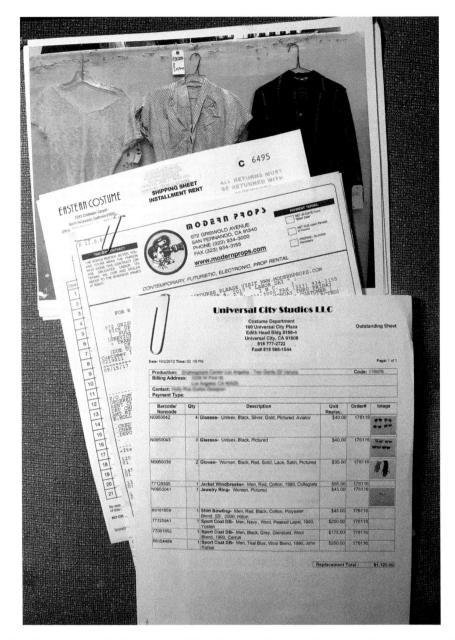

Figure 29.1 Returning rentals before the first public performance. Each rental house uses its own system of organization.

less than anticipated. This knowledge will improve the ability to budget future shows.

The Costume Bible

Costume shops and costume designers generate large amounts of information about each show. Collecting this information together is termed the *costume bible*. In the past it took the form of a large three-ring binder that anyone can refer to for information, but digital versions are now common, along with inventory software such as *Synch on Set*. (See the Extra Resources section.) The costume shop makes its own version of the bible that remains

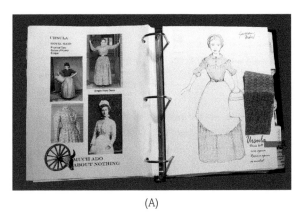

(A)   (B)

Figure 29.2 Retain all show information in a costume bible as a future resource.

with the organization. It is used as resource in case something must be duplicated during the run of the show, or the show may be revived in future seasons. The designer also keeps a bible for their archive. Documenting a show takes discipline, but doing this consistently forms an excellent record of your work and lessons learned from each show. The typical costume bible contains the following elements:

- Costume scene chart breakdown
- Contact information cast, crew, staff, theater
- Budget information and spending logs, record of vendors
- Rental information and record of vendors
- Key notes from production meetings, rehearsal notes
- General organizational information such as cheat sheets, pulling sheets
- A section for each performer with

  - Measurement sheets
  - Copies of costume rendering and research
  - Fabric swatches card completed with swatches, trim and interlinings
  - Working drawings or other technical information
  - Specialty items used and vendor information
  - Makeup and hair information

  - Piece list, dressing list
  - Fitting photos
  - Final or backstage photo (optional)

- Fabric modification or other technique samples
- Dye formula card
- Designer diary or notes for future use
- General wig and hair information, planning, correspondence
- Strike information and copies of all paperwork – returns
- Specialty items or research pertaining to the specific show
- Special maintenance for items during run of show – blood, roller setting patterns
- Costume preset lists from Wardrobe

Expecting the Unexpected

Many designers regret not paying more attention to capturing images for their portfolio websites. Digital photography has made the sharing of photos an easy task, but it is still up to us to contact the photographers, company managers, or our colleagues to gather them. Get in the habit of taking in-process photos of costumes in various stages along the way. One of the most delightful discoveries designers make is that others are actually viewing their online portfolio. Ensure that information is up to date. For advice on creating a digital portfolio, see the Extra Resources section.

ACTOR	Sarah Smiley	COSTUME	Day Dress
ROLE	Gwendolyn	SKETCH #	

SWATCH	FABRIC DETAILS		ITEM
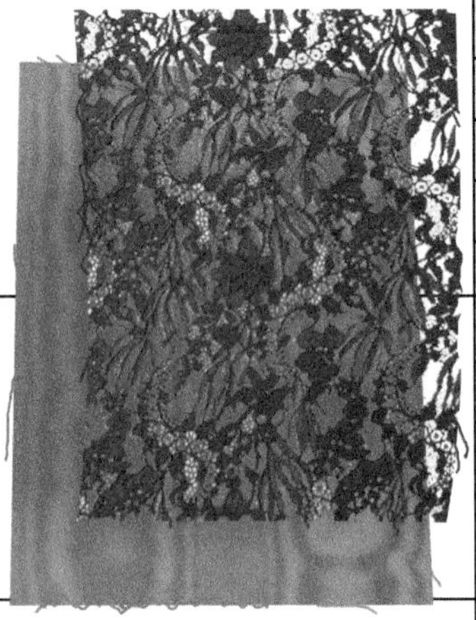	YDS PURCH	10y	Lace Skirt + Bodice
	WIDTH	45"	45 / Rayon 55 % Nylon
	$/YD	$22⁰⁰	
	VENDOR	Mood	
	1 WAY	Y/N	
	YDS PURCH	10y	Coral Skirt + Bodice
	WIDTH	54"	100 % Acetate
	$/YD	$36⁰⁰	Moire
	VENDOR	F&S	
	1 WAY	Y/N	
	YDS PURCH	10y	Green Moire
	WIDTH	54"	100 % Acetate
	$/YD	$36⁰⁰	
	VENDOR	F&S	
	1 WAY	Y/N	
	YDS PURCH		
	WIDTH		
	$/YD		
	VENDOR		
	1 WAY	Y/N	
	YDS PURCH	25 y	Etsy - Shop 99
	WIDTH	1"	
	$/YD	5.34	
	VENDOR	ETSY	
	1 WAY	Y/N	
	YDS PURCH		
	WIDTH		
	$/YD		
	VENDOR		
	1 WAY	Y/N	

Figure 29.3 A swatch page records all the fabrics used to build a costume.

Extra Resources

Developing and Maintaining a Design-Tech Portfolio, Rafael Jaen Focal Press, 2006

10 Tips for Building a Killer Portfolio Website, CreativeBloq. com

Costume Bible for the Original Production of A Doll's Life, Florence Klotz https://digitalcollections.nypl.org/items/878a8e80-2959-0137-ea87-3be930a5955e(A)(B)

30.
GROWING YOUR ART

If you scratch the surface of many professional designers, you will discover they harbor a few fears about imposter syndrome. There is no one authorized way to become a designer, so we don't know how to judge our path. There are scattered apprenticing programs with no real agreement as to what the standards must be. There is little transparency about how to progress in expertise. Comparing ourselves to other designers is an excellent tool for learning and inspiration, but it is not always practical to compare our careers to theirs. Costume designers work in different places, different specialties, lead different lives with different motivations. Regretting that we are not like someone else is similar to a zebra regretting it is not a porpoise. If you are creatively engaged in the performing arts, you have many victories and attributes to celebrate.

Attributes of Successful Costume Designers

Entertainment creators envision works that did not exist before. We work with other creative people; we work within budgets and meet forbidding deadlines. Our efforts are judged publicly by audiences and reviewers. While these parameters are intimidating enough to discourage many people, performing arts creators thrive in this environment. This book is an example of the complex expertise a costume designer must master. It contains 30 chapters and yet it is merely an *introduction* to the knowledge that experienced designers accumulate. This book features many attributes and skills of successful designers:

- **Strong work ethic.** The ability to take initiative and complete tasks using high standards.
- **Collaboration.** Working with creative groups is hard, but we agree to work toward mutual goals each time we take on a new project.
- **Communication.** We express complex ideas to others and keep multiple people updated.

- **Artistry.** Using the elements and principles of design and storytelling knowledge to create effective characters.
- **Punctuality.** The ability to plan complex projects and schedules, meeting deadlines to move work forward in as orderly a pace as possible.
- **Patience.** Creative projects move in fits and starts, ideas may take weeks to gel properly. Approaching as much as possible with humor and grace will make the project much more enjoyable for everyone.
- **Persistence.** The designer will face every kind of obstacle to their desired result, beginning with inadequate budgets, short timelines and labor shortages. Holding onto the final vision in the face of daily tests takes artistic and personal grit.
- **Solutions-based thinking.** When met with constant challenges, costume designers dig down to present creative ideas and new solutions time and again.

DOI: 10.4324/9781003015284-39

- **Flexibility.** Combining active listening with honest critical thinking, being willing to consider new ideas without allowing the project to veer off course.
- **Stamina.** The costume designer will be torn in many directions every day, working with people who don't understand what their job is and how to support that.
- **Designerly thinking.** Understanding how the creative process works and using it to support the work.
- **Curiosity.** See with new eyes every day, learn new things and feed that image bank.
- **Leadership.** Be conscious of your leadership style, never surrender to feelings of negativity or blame and help others along the way.

Growing as an Artist

Designers face uncertain outlets for their self-expression. Unlike playwrights, they do not originate works that will be produced. Unlike producers or artistic directors, designers usually do not decide what shows will be included in a theater's season. We cannot design a show that we have not been offered, so much about our career is out of our control. We sometimes cannot turn down an unwanted show because we need the money or we wish to stay in the good graces of a particular theater. We work on several projects at once in various stages, with our head yanked from one story world to another. As theaters shorten their rehearsal periods, the costume designer's days grow longer. Through all of this it can be very difficult to nurture our own artistry and grow. Every designer builds a network of family and friends to support themselves as a human being. What about supporting the inner artist?

Prepare for the Opportunities to Come

Don't wait for a job offer to try those new ideas. Find your own collaborators or make your own work. Join professional associations to meet people all over the country doing what you do. Design that project you've always wanted to do as a paper project and post it in your portfolio to show what you are capable of doing. Create a 30-day art challenge, join fundraising challenges, enter a design contest or wearable art show. Assemble all the weird stuff you've been saving for "someday" and challenge yourself to make ten pieces of tiny art with it. Make your challenge public on social media to keep motivated. It is all part of your body-of-work as an artist. The work you make now will attract future opportunities. One set designer posted progress on his hobby of making clay miniature worlds, and that turned into a full-time job for animation design.

Feed Your Image Bank

To maintain steady growth, it is vital to stay inspired and exposed to the visual zeitgeist. Regularly make the rounds of galleries, museum exhibitions, and new neighborhoods to get ideas, add to your sketchbook, or photograph inspiring compositions and textures. Do things out of your ordinary routines. Seeing new things will spark ideas for years to come.

Become a Creature of Habit

Remember the advice of choreographer Twyla Tharpe who noted creativity stems from work habits, not lightning strikes of genius. This advice is particularly useful for down times when you are not working on a project or you want to infuse a new spark into your work. Create a habit to make one tiny drawing per day, or work 20 minutes per day on a new skill. Consider that musicians and singers practice every day whether they are performing or not. Why do we think we can improve as artists without that same commitment? Small consistent practice pays off much faster than bursts of excited intensity.

Invest in Quality Supplies

Take your work up a notch nearly overnight by buying good supplies. It can start with just one pencil. When we first begin a new pursuit, we often start with affordable supplies or pre-assembled beginner sets. You will be amazed how much easier it is to sketch with quality pencils, paint with the really good pigments or an expensive fur brush, or using an iPad Pro.

Learn From the Masters

Read books about or by creators you admire in every field of endeavor. Apprentice yourself to a visual master from any point in history by copying their work to figure out how they did it. Copy work has been a standard part of art training for centuries. Copy work also eliminates the stress of creating a composition, freeing the mind to focus on technical competence. Choose an artist whose drawing you admire, or branch out to other media such as expressionist painter Genesis Tramaine, fiber artist Xenobia Bailey, sculptor Nnenna Okore, or installation artist Yayoi Kusama.

Make It Personal

Some costume designers cast about to find their voice because we practice an interpretive art form. We bring to life the vision of others: a playwright and director. Learning how to find our own voice takes patience. One way to discover your path is to explore your capacity for delight or anger. Make note of the things that thrill you and those that outrage you, no matter how small. Turning those subjects into productive expression is key. Keep a written and visual journal to collect your thoughts. Review this journal periodically to find recurring themes or patterns. Can any of those themes be the subject of an art work, a costume approach, a textile design?

Advice From Wendy Partridge, Costume Designer for Netflix *Shadow and Bone*

"Never be afraid to go with your gut. The one thing that steps one designer away from another is who is a bit fearless. Design is not a job that you can add 2 and 2 to get an answer of 4. The answer to designing great costumes is the instinct and the feelings that you get from the character and the script. Obviously, research is a structural base . . . but it's your own instinct and your own gut that will get you moving forward. Push yourself to do whatever is in your heart."[1]

Get Comfortable With Discomfort

There are few correct answers in creative projects. The path to get where we want to be isn't always obvious. This means working diligently over long periods of time toward a goal that you are not always certain will work out. It means making up the steps as you move along, experimenting with new ideas under the stress of a deadline. Navigating constant change can make us feel powerless or directionless. Negotiating uncertainty is an important form of resilience that artists develop to keep the final result in mind, just as ancient mariners steered ships using the North Star. Identify those things that make you most uncomfortable in the costume design process and approach them with curiosity. Explore how you can empower yourself in those moments, whether through self-knowledge or new skills.

Advice From Ellen Mirojnick, Costume Designer for *Bridgerton*

"I use an expression *'Walk in Beauty'* and what that really entails is the art of communication, the art of listening, the art of being truthful to who you are. Being true to your passion and having confidence, and most importantly communication. This is the world we live in as designers, to communicate your idea. But it is equally important to listen to other ideas, to listen really thoroughly, to understand, listen to the director, to the producers. To understand if there is a conflict between both. As the costume designer you are in charge of knitting it together – not to see it as a conflict."[2]

Find a Community

Sometimes if we aren't working on a project we flounder as creatives, losing touch with what inspires us. The idea of growing our art seems bizarre if we're not motivated by a tangible project. We tell ourselves "This isn't real" and lose that edge to complete exploratory work. In fact, knowing you *should* be doing something guarantees the opposite effect. According to researchers Chip and Dan

Figure 30.1 Looking backwards

Credit: Theater figure, Meissen Manufactory, 1750–52. Gift of Irwin Untermyer, 1964. Metropolitan Museum of Art, New York

Heath, the most powerful motivators are not logic, but emotions. (See the Extra Resources section.) They describe the rational brain as a small rider steering a giant elephant. The elephant represents the power of emotions. Motivating with emotions is much more successful, as they give us a sense of progress. One particularly strong emotion that we can leverage is peer pressure. Even if we are solo artists, we often respond better with a group to report to. They provide emotional support, but more importantly, we will feel an obligation to keep up our end of the bargain. If you are not feeling motivated, try starting or joining a physical or virtual artists support group to nurture your creativity.

Look Backwards to See Forwards

Looking at our own body of work will reinforce how far we've come in our trajectory. We may have far surpassed favorite works we thought were such a success years ago. Study your past work to celebrate the areas where you've grown. Then stand back to see what is missing from your portfolio, or what might need more work. Have you always wished you could design fantasy characters or a puppet show, or make French berets from scratch? Identify new ideas to explore.

Extra Resources

The Artists Way: A Spiritual Path to Higher Creativity, Julia Cameron, Tarcher Perigree, 2016

Art & Fear: Observations on the Perils and Rewards of Artmaking. David Bayles, Ted Orland. Image Continuum Press 2001

Steal Like an Artist: 10 Things Nobody Told You About Being Creative. Austin Kleon, Workman Publishing 2012

Steal Like an Artist, Austin Kleon TedxTalks ttps://www.youtube.com/watch?v=oww7oB9rjgw

Switch: How to Change Things When Change Is Hard. Chip Heath, Dan Heath Broadway Books, 2010

Notes

1 Partridge, Wendy. 2021. "Design Showcase West/Netflix Costume Design Salon Panel." *YouTube*. June 12, 2021. https://www.youtube.com/watch?v=4WuB5WKUisg

2 Mirojnick, Ellen. 2021. "Design Showcase West/Netflix Costume Design Salon Panel." *YouTube*, June 12, 2021. https://www.youtube.com/watch?v=4WuB5WKUisg

APPENDIX – SAMPLE RESUME

Rachel Ringtone

Costume Designer

I am a costume designer for theater and independent film. I love all aspects of storytelling.

Contact

☎ 1-234-567-8910

✉ rachel@myserver.com

🌐 rachel@mysite.com

📷 @rachelfabulous

📍 123 Main Street, City Ville

Education

BA 2010 University of Midwest
Major: English Literature
Minor: Spanish

References

Brandon Jimenez, Director
boxingday@gmail.com

Mary Jefferson, Artistic Director
Jeffersonairplane@gmail.org

Martin Chow, Director
eyesonyou@comcast.net

THEATER

The Power of Light	Star Theater, Off Broadway, NY, 2018 Director: Martin Chow
The Codex	Midwest Repertory Theater, 2016 Director: Brandon Jimenez
As You Like It	Shakespeare Festival of Memphis, 2015 Director: Mary Saberson
The Kids Show	Maine Summer Theater, 2014 Director: Martin Chow

FILM/TV/STREAMING

The Candy Jar	Eat My Hat Productions, see Imdb page, 2015 Director: Mark Supter Short Film, international festival screenings
Building the Dream	Vertical Line Productions, 2014 Director: May Powell PBS Documentary with Historical Reenactment sequences Regional Emmy Nomination – Best Documentary
Last Chance	Northstar Entertainment Group, 2013 Director: Bill Regal Netflix Pilot Episode of Turn of the Screw series

RELATED POSITIONS & SKILLS

Crafts Head	Midwest Repertory Theater, 2018–19 Millinery, Fabric Dye & color matching, masks, general crafts
Crafts Artisan	Maine Summer Theater, 2016–2017
Other Skills	Photoshop CC, Procreate, proficient in Excel, basic video recording & editing, fluent in spoken and written Spanish, dremel tool, dye vat

INDEX

Note: Page numbers in **bold** indicate a table. Page numbers in *italics* indicate a figure.

#black AF (TV series) 104, 135

absentee meetings 139
absentee stars 169
abstraction 53, 88
abstraction scale *88*
abundance: goal of 202; texture associated with 29
accessories 260; budget items **199**; considerations in choosing 250; costume props and 249–261; eyeglasses 253–254; hair and 161–162; handbags and parasols 255; hats 256–258; hat sizes **258**; jewelry 254–255; masks 258–259; neckties 255–256, *256*; shoes and accessories for shoes 250–253; shoe and glove sizes **254**; types of 250; weaponry-related 259–260; wild west *163*
Ackerman, Josh 27–28
activation 9
act/scene breakdowns 94–95
actor's sizes 178–182
Afrofuturism 88, 132
alterations *294*; budget item **194**, 196, **200**; collar gap 297; due dates for (estimating time to complete) 186, 187; estimating 184; fitting time for 282, 283; kissing pockets due to 298; pattern 185; pinning fabric for 287; menswear 232, 236, 243, 244; rentals and 77
alterations personnel 74
alterations shops 182
allowable colors onstage 36
allowable expenses 80
allowable growth 203
allowable weakness 211
alter ego 127–128
American Horror Story 276
American menswear 231
analytical reasoning 3
Andre Walker guide 264

apology syndrome 291
Appleton, Eric 85
apprenticeship xii, 212, 243, 338, 340
architecture of performance 114–115
arc *see* character arc; color arc; emotional arc
arcs of change xii, 4, 13
Armani, Giorgio 231
artistic approach 88
artistic characters, costume development for 108
artistic communication 156; alternative styles of 168–170; ideal 165
artistic expertise, development of 10
artistic goals 239; communicating overall 307; discussing 265; importance of sharing 79
artistic intent: forgetting 225; honoring 217; using sketches to communicate 16
artistic leaders, costume designers as 3, 5, 207; *see also* leading teamwork
artistic medium, fabric as 56
artistic opportunity 74, 78, 81
artistic practice by costume designers 7–8
artistic versus practical concerns 82
artistic vision 209, 292
Artist, The 65
Art Nouveau 88, 146
assistant or team: working with 14–15
Astaire, Fred and Adele *88*
attention: discovery 18; orientation 18
Atwood, Margaret 88
authenticity 132–141; authority and 133–134; character collage boards to assist 137–139; costume research storyboard *140*; creative research to enhance 132–133; curating research to tell a story 135–137; emotional aspects research 134–135; factual information research 133–134; using extant garments for research 139
audience 4; characters and 101–110

backstory 4, 95, 102, 114; *Bridgerton* 281; grounding character with 104

balance, principle of 45–46

Bandwagon, The 88

Barris, Kenya 104

Batman (film) 7

Bauhaus 88, 146

behavior clusters, nine major 210–211

Belbin, Meredith 210, 211

Bellantoni, Patti 31

Beller, Genevieve 77–78

Benton, Frances 249

bin Laden, Osama 127

black (color) 32, 35, *37, 38*

black and white film 65

black box theater 115

Black, Jack 234

Black-owned companies 264

Black Panther (film) 69, 102, 132

blue sky process 9

body *see* defining the body with…

body shaming 289

Bogart, Ann 125

bones of a design 159

Bowers, Leighton 134

Braddock shoe size device *222*

brain: anomaly perception 52; approaches to thinking 124; attention 20, 123; contrast perception 43; depth perception 40; emphasis and positive/negative space 44; focal point/end point perception 50; geometry as perceived by 46; groups as perceived by 104; illusion 123; memories 26; realism as perceived by 53; subconscious 123; symmetry perception 45; vision 23; visual weight 50

brainstorming 9, 11, 12, 16; capturing and organizing ideas produced by 128–130; for character traits 105; creative decision loop and *xvi*; for design ideas 125; feedback and 139; goal of *abundance* for 202; photobashing for 169, 170; research and 136, 138, 145, 203

breakdown *see* costume scene breakdown; scene breakdown; script breakdown

breast forms 291

breast pocket 244

breast support 302; *see also* corsets

bridal satin *63*

bridal wear 60

Bridgerton 139, 146, 281

Bridges, Mark 65

Brooks Brothers 231

Brown, Camille A. 311

Brown, Tim 6

budget calculator 100

budgeting methods 191–192

budget lines 192

budgets for costume design 78, 191–205; all-inclusive 192; assumptions regarding 191; educating producers regarding 203; expendables 193; feasibility planning phase and 10; fixed expenses 192; formatting a budget 192; hidden costs 78, 196; imposed 192, **194–195**, 196, 205; loss and damage 193; managing money for 204–205; negotiating 202; power of No 203–204; power of Yes 203; rehearsal costume expectations and 11; *Romeo and Juliet* sample budget **194–195**, *197*; scope creep and allowable growth 203; setting a budget 5; small budget 196; variable expenses 192; zero-based 192, 196, 198, **199–202**

bulk: adding 232; balancing 233; reducing 265; unintended 301

bulk pulling 223–224

bulk rate 183

Burton, Tim 7

Bussard, Susan 276

Campbell, Joseph 105

Caputo, Tony 87

Cardi B 54

Carter, Kollin 54

Carter, Ruth 69

castile soap 275

casting against type 12, 182

casting change 93

casting decisions: costume changes and 96, 190; inclusive 93

casting plan 93

cast shadows 14, 40, 269

casts: community 178; costume budgets and 192, 196; ensemble 102; meet and greet 306; understudies 333; unknown at time of sketching 157; very small 118

cast size 93

Catmull, Ed 211

change arcs xii; *see also* arcs of change; character arc

character arc 14, 86, 162

character archetypes 105, **106–107**, 110

character board 138

character-by-character review 14

character closets 225

character collage *138*, 140

character costume 156–164; accessories and hair 161–162; aesthetic elements 160; color and patina 160; decorative details 161; focal point, harmony, balance 160; garment lines and proportion 160; layered garment design 158–159; manner of wearing 159; nine-headed monster proportion problem 157–158, *158*; posture 159; stance 159; structure 159; thumbnail sketches 156, 157

character psychology and relationships 148

character research 134

characters 4; archetypical 105, **105–107**, 110; audience engaged by 101–110; backstory used to ground 104; comic 87; costumes used to define *169*; leading 103, 151; manner of wearing clothing by 110; types of 103; undeveloped or one-dimensional 151, 152; wealthy versus poor 44; *see also* clothing psychology; individual characters

character sheet 137

character sketch 156

chest binder 291; *see also* corsets

choreographer *see* Lubovich; Tharpe

choreography: costume designing for 304, 313, 318; fast change 318; fight 282; hairstyle modification for 269; intimacy 310, 311

CIA 127

Cirque de Soleil 262, 263, 265, 267, 268

Clapton, Michele 29

clothing psychology 101, 108–110; anachronism in dressing 107; arrested development in 109–110; artistic or exotic dressing 108; complexity and aesthetics in 108; generational divides in 109; nostalgic dressing 108; uniformity in dressing 117; rebellious dressing 107; regional differences in 109; split personalities in 109; symbolic attributes in 109

compression garments 291; *see also* corsets

Cole, Michelle 104

collaboration: communication and 11; costume designer and actors 307; designer and maker 247; draper and designer *240*; feedback and 16; friendship and 78; in-person 91; meaning of 115, 211; negotiating 292; weapons handling 259

collaborative art form: theater as 246: *Reading Frankenstein 115*

collaborative creativity 9–17; sizing up 17

collaborative leadership 211–212, 214

color: acidic 146; additive 40; arcs of change signaled via 4, 99; broken 27, *29*; chemical 147; costume color and stage light 41; defining the body with 39; design element of 19, 25–27, 29–30, 68; emotion created by 31–42; five principle 37; glazing 33, *34*; hue 32; intensity and saturation 32, 33; light color and pigment color, blending *41*; Pantone® color system 38, *39*; patina and 160; plain with smooth, plain with texture 27, *29*; saturated 44; sizing up element of 40; subtractive 32, 36; tint, tone, shade 32; tone and 145; vocabulary of 32–35

color arc 148, 151

color balance 46

color board 148–151

color chips *39*

color day 31

color discrimination 3

color ideas 12, 13

color library 149

color notation system 38

color palettes 31, 33, 147; emotional arc signaled by 99; everyday life and 149; *Incredibles, The* 146, 148; ProCreate tool 150; shaping characters via 86

color plot 14, *148*, 149

color renderings: final 167–168, *168*, 173

color schemes 36–37, 148; Adobe Color and *150*; communicating 151–152; complementary 36; *most, some, least* rule 37

color swatches *150*

color temperature 34–35, 3*4*; cool 34, 35; neutral 34; undertones 34, 35; warm 34, 35

color undertones 34, 35, *35*

color value: human vision and 33

color wheel 36–38, *36*; Adobe Color and *150*; Munsell 37–38, *37*, *38*

concept development 10, 143–174

constraints, working with 189–190; end user 189; external 189; extrinsic 189; foreseeable 189

contrast, principle of 43–44

corsets 300–302, *310*; 16th–18th century *300*, *301*, 301–302; 19th century *300*, 302–303, *303*; bar lacing *301*; busks and bonding 300, *300*; compression *300*; cross lacing *301*; double lacing 301, *301*; historical 300–301; ladder lacings 301; ruffled *300*; spiral lacings *301*, 301

costume bible 334–335, *335*

costume count 99–100

costume design: accessories and hair 161–162; aesthetic elements 160; color and patina 160; decorative details 161; focal point, harmony, balance 160; garment lines and proportion 160; manner of wearing 159; nine principles of 43; posture 159; stance 159; structure 159

costume design as profession: advice regarding 339–341; attributes of successful designers 338–339; conciliatory language, avoiding 83; eight jobs of xii–xvii, **xiii–xiv**; getting paid 73–83; habits and attitudes of successful designers 339–341; negotiating payment 80–82; sample invoice *81*; sample resume *342*; tax benefits 82–83

costume design checklist 162

costume dramaturgy 101–102

costume drawings 166–167

costume lists 99–100

costume looks, planning 98–99

costume makers, types of 182–183

costume plot 9, 307–308, 318

costume props and accessories 249–261

costume scene breakdown 99, 115, 335

costume scene chart 93–94, 177; creating 94; samples and examples of *96–99*; staging and 110

Continental suit style 231

Cottenden, Graham *236*

Counterbalance Theater Company *115*

crafts projects: estimating 185–186, **186**

creative process: for produced products *1*; terms and breakdown of 9–10; *see also* collaborative creativity

creative procrastination 135, 140

creative projects, five assets of 82

creative teams 10–11

crinoline **185**

crinoline cage skirt 23

croquis 157–158, *158*

cross-dressing 291

Cross, Nigel 6, 135

custom designs 184–185

Dahl, Lauren 223

defining body with…: color 39; emphasis 45; fabric 68; line 20; proportion 49; shape 22

defining feature 253

defining focus and clarity 152

defining the color schemes 36–37

defining the design approach 136

defining the scope of show 77, 177–190; costume makers, types of 182–183; costume scene chart 177; due date 186; estimating alterations 184; estimating builds 184–185; estimating crafts 185–186; estimating fabrics 186; estimating labor needs 183–184; guesstimating 190; piece list 177, **179–180**; project schedule 186–187; pulling list 177, 178, **181**; sizing up scope of project 190; task dependencies 186; top of show (TOS) 177; trimming money or time, strategies for 187–189; understanding labor needs 182; working with constraints 189–190

defining the scope of work xvi

defining the challenge 9

defining the problem 6, 128

defining the tone 145–146

defining the visual rules 135

defining visual style 146

Degas, Edgar 19

Depp, Johnny xii, 233, 260

design conference: first 12–13; subsequent 13

design development phase 10

design documentation 333–337; costume bible 334–335, *335*; reconciled budget 333; returning/wrapping up rentals 333–334, *334*; swatch page *336*

design elements 19–30; six (line, shape, form, space, texture, color) 19, *20*; *see also* [elements by name]

designer: conciliatory language 83; getting paid 73–83; negotiating payment 80–82; sample invoice *81*

design ideas, generating 123–131; capturing and organizing 127–130

design journal 130

design principles 19, 42–55; balance 45–46; contrast 43–44; emphasis 44–45; harmony, unity, variation 53–54; movement and direction 50–51; repetition, sequence, rhythm 51–53; scale and proportion 46–50

designerly thinking 6, 132, 242, 339

designers: collaborating with 14

design memory 3

Devil Wears Prada, The (film) 253

devoré 65, *65*; *see also* fabric

digital color apps 150

digital communications xv, 139

digital chart 94

digital design 306

digital drawing or sketching 166, 168

digital dressing 169

digital files 13, 130, 223

digital media 156, 165

digital painting 171, 266

digital pen *158*

digital platforms 14

digital storage 129

digital template 172

digital tools 149, 266, 287

digital tracking applications 83

directed seeing 151

directors: communicating with 11; get-to-know-you meeting with 11–12; first design conference with 12–13; subsequent meetings with 13–14

dramaturgy 101

dramaturgy wall 307

drawing, importance of habit of 8

dressing list 318, *319*, 319–320; fitting sheet 319, *319*

dressing room checklist 320

dress rehearsal 317–329; critiques of costume design 322–323; director 321–322; fast change rehearsal 318; first audience 327–328; lighting designer 324; photos and photocall 324, 327; scheduling 320–321; taking notes 323–324, **325–327**; wardrobe crew *318*, 318–319

due date 186

dyeing or dyed fabrics 64–65; *see also* fabrics

ease (in clothing) 218, 223

Eberle, Bob 127

eight costume jobs xii–xvii; *see also* costume design as a profession

eight-head proportions *158*

eight ways people can be smart 210

eight weaving styles 62–63

Einstein, Albert 53, 128, 132

emotion: keyword collecting and 125; patterns associated with 18, 52–53; musical scripts and 95; using color to create 31–42; using songs to express 117

emotional arc 12, 99, 100, 102, 135, 162

emotional aspects research 133, 134–135, 140

emotional impact 11, 13, 146, **147**; of color 311; of color schemes 36, 151

emotional intelligence 79

emotional framework: tone and 89

emotional responses: to evocative images 126; to pattern 52; to shape 20; to color 35

emotional stakes, raising 86

emotional triggers 214

emphasis, principle of 44–45

Estevez, Emilio 234

estimating alterations 184

estimating builds 184–185

estimating crafts 185–186

estimating fabrics 186

estimating labor needs 183–184

experience bank 125

eyeglasses 253–254

fabric formula: #1 *58*; #2 *59*; #3 *60*; #4 *64*; #5 *65*

fabric layering 33, *34*

fabrics 26–27, 56–69; anatomy of 56; back 56; body 56; brocade and damask 64, *64*; burn tests 58; chemical finishes 66; colorfastness 64; construction 60–61; crocking 64; dyeing or coloring 64–65; face 56; fibers 59, *59*; filaments 59, *59*, 60; finishing 65–66; formula 57–59; grain 56–57, *58*; hand 56; knitted 61–62; massed or felted 61; matching fabrics to designs 67–68; nap 57; natural or synthetic 58; Pantone® colors *39*; pile weaves 64, *64*; rib weaves 62, *62*; satins 63; selvedge 57; silks 60; tailoring 66–67; twills 62–63; woolens and worsted 60, *60*; woven 62–64; yarn styles 59–60; *see also* swatch

fabric swatch: stored *57*; testing of *41*

facial expressions 159

facial features 171, 263; lost or shadowed 324

facial focus 163

facial hair 20, 275–276, *276*

facial morgues 263

factual information research 133

fast changes, designing for 115–116, 318

fat activists 289

feasibility studies 10

feeding your image bank 8, 125–126, 135, 139, 339

feet and foot shapes/problems 250–251; *see also* shoes

felt (fabric) *61*

film noir 89, 126

final costume 16

final designs 9, 13

final product 173

fit: assessing fit of garment 296–297; assessing fit of tailored garments 297–298; definition of 293; size versus 293

fitting accessories 260

fitting corsets 300–302, *310*; 16th–18th century *300*, *301*, 301–302; 19th century *300*, 302–303, *303*; bar lacing *301*; busks and bonding 300, *300*; compression *300*; cross lacing *301;* double lacing 301, *301*; historical 300–301; ladder lacings 301; ruffled *300;* spiral lacings *301*, 301

fitting days 187

fitting ease 232, **237**

fitting eyeglasses 254

fitting garments 13, 77, 293–304

fitting hats 257

fitting labor, strategic 187, 189

fitting nonbinary and transgender performers 289–291; terms relevant to 291

fitting photos *288*, 320

fitting problems: examples (too tight, too loose) *294*

fitting room 94, *222*, *285*, *286*; as costume designer's office 284–285

fittings: alterations and 185; character development and 159; character discovery through 169; costumer 189; creative time for 282; cross-check method for 295, *296*; estimating labor needs for 183–184; first look 295; importance of listening 281, 292; mini-adjustment 324; modeling in 283; petty cash for 204; preparing for 281–292; revising design during 10; second look 295; setting it up 286–287; triggering language in 289; wrong turns in 295

fitting schedule: planning 283–284

fitting sheet 286, 287, 319

fitting shoes 251–253

fitting skills 293

fitting styles 282–283

fitting subject (stand-in) 240

fitting suits 232, 233, 236, **237**; guide *298*; tailoring/made to order and 239, 240–241, 243–244

fitting tailored garments 297, 299

fitting time 281

Five Pillars 311

five senses, importance of 126–127

Five Whys 6; Juliet Capulet and 6–7

focal points: accessories and 250, 255; accessories around the face and 263; character apparel checklist and 162; color groupings and 151; color reductions from nature and 150; decorative details to create 161; dress rehearsal checklist and 323; fabric and 68; harmony and balance and 159, 160; high contrast to create 44; high value colors as *37*; polychromatic colors as 39; positive space as 23; principle of movement and 50, 54; radial balance to create 46; white collars as 30

foreground 151

foreman xv

foresight 3

four-way knit 61; *see also* fabrics

Fox, Brendon 114

frequency illusion 123

Froelich, Marcy 140

Fuchs, Elinor 84

Game of Thrones 6, 29
Gardner, Howard 210
generating ideas 123
genres 89, 151
gentleman, dressing conventions for 234, 256
Gentleman Jack (TV series) 88
Gestalt principles 104
getting paid 73–83; *see also* costume designer as
     profession
Gillespie, Dizzy *132*
gimmicks 87
glamour line 47
glamour makeup 265; drag 266; *see also* makeup
gloves 161, 249, 357; shoe and glove size **254**
golden age of Hollywood 149
golden mean 47, *48*
Gorey, Edward 7
gray 35; hue mixed with 32, 145
gray scale 34, 38, 40
Grossman, Naomi 276
group dynamics 10, 101, 105, 110
group protagonists 89, 104–105
group rules 105
group settings 68
guesstimating 190
Gypsy (musical) 87

hair 262–278; accessories and 161–162; budget item
     194, **200**, 202; character development using
     accessories and 159, 161–162; felted fabrics made
     with 61; "mad scientist" 53; natural, relaxed, or
     permed 264; sample project schedule **188**; velvets
     made with 64; wigs using human or synthetic hair
     269; wild 19; *see also* facial hair; wigs
hair color 108, *222*
hair pieces, types of 269–272
hairspray 193, 274, 275
hairstyles 256; character and 263, 264, 269; hats as part
     of 257
hair type 264
hair typing system 264, *265*
Hamilton, Beau 263, 268
Hamilton (musical) 90, *116*, 149
Handler, Daniel 7
handbags and parasols 255
Hands on a Hardbody 90
harmony, unity, variation, principle of 53–54
Harry Potter (franchise): characters 104, **106**, **107**; Dobby
     weave and 63; group protagonists 89
hats 256–258; hairstyles and 257
hat sizes **258**
Heath, Chip and Dan 340–341
hijab *160*
Hould-Ward, Ann 125, 148
hue 32; tone and 32; *see also* color
hyperrealism 88, *88*

idea board 135
ideas *see* design ideas
image bank *see* feeding your image bank
image collecting 125
imagery 13; brain's conversion of 18; creative
     procrastination and 135; digital templates to
     prepare 172; gathering and design approach to 145;
     modeling and curation of 140; narrative 100; piece
     list in relationship to 177; research boards to convey
     166, 169; sacred 250; script 149
imposter syndrome 338
Incredibles, The 87, 146
individual characters xii, 5, 104; assigning colors to 149;
     see also characters
individuality in dressing *133*
individual personality traits 104–105
inner weasel: unleashing 213, *213*, 214
installation phase 10
Intimacy Directors International 311
intimacy protocols 310–311; Five Pillars 311
isolation 127
Ives, David *148*

Jeakins, Dorothy 149
jetted pocket *see* welt pocket
jewelry 254–255
Johnson, Steven 124
Jordan, Cookie 264
Jung, Carl 105

Kaufman, Moisés 116
Kay, Helen 247
Keen, Julie *240*
Keultjes, Saskia 155, 156
keywords, collecting 125–126
kit fee 193
kitten heel 178, *252; see also* shoes and shoe accessories
knits 60, 61–62; *see also* fabrics

labor market 192
labor needs: estimating 183–184, 321; understanding
     182–183
Lanier, Jerrilyn 264
Lansky, Bernard 292
Laramie Project (play) 116
Latimer, A. A. 191
leadership: collaborative 211–212, 214; solutions-based
     thinking 212–213
leading from behind 209
leading teamwork *208*, 209–214, *210*; recognizing team
     dynamics 209–211
light and surface: design elements of 19, 25–26; diffuse
     26; luster 26; reflection of 26; translucent 26;
     transparent 27
lighting: back 87; costumes interacting with **326–327**;
     ambient 26; stage 257

lighting designer 14, 40–42, 324–329; hats and 257

light plot 324

light receiver/eye receptors 26, *26*

light waves: hue, pigment and 32; matte surfaces and 27, *29*; refraction of 26; undertones, black color, and 35

line: broken or hatched 19; defining a body with 20, 22; as design element 19–22, 29; garment 20; horizontal 20; qualities of 19–20, **21**; smooth or continuous 19; strong 44; vertical 20

line drawings 16

line of a garment (garment line) 19–20; decorative 20; structural 20

Long, William Ivey 117

Lord of the Rings 262

Lubovitch, Lar 148

Lucas, George 105

Lurie, Alison 105, 109

luster 26; fur *28*; gold 29; pearl *28*; satin 63; worsted wool 66

Mackie, Anthony 249

made to measure (MTM) suits 243–244; retail 244

makeup 265–269; aging 266; character/FX 266, *267*; corrective 265; drag glamour 266; fantasy 266, *266*; glamour 265; period 265; straight or street 265; *266*; theatrical versus straight 267

makeup design communication, two styles of *269*

makeup sketches and charts 266–267

makeup worksheet *268*

Mandela, Nelson 209

Ma Rainey's Black Bottom (film) 169, 311

Margulies, Donald 151

Martinez, Nicky 289, 290

masks 258–259

massed fabric (felt or felted) 60, *61*

Measure for Measure (Shakespeare) *130*

measurement form **220**

measurements: average waist (male) 158; basic 181; calf (leg) 250; costume 218–221; custom design 184–185; drop 232; eyeglasses 254; glove *253*; inclusive etiquette for taking 219; inseam 221; finished garment 221–223; made-to-order 219; preliminary 306; rise 221; shirt sleeve 221; silhouette for *219*; suit 234, **237**; taking 219; trouser waist 221; wig *269*; working without adequate measurements 223

measuring cheat sheet **224**

measuring kit *222*, 285

menswear: bespoke 244; estimating craft time for (breakdown of time) **185**; high gorge *246*; ladies' suits *238*, *247*; made to measure 243–244; piecing together a suit 234–236; style guide 1963–1964 *235*; texture and 27; suits 229–230, **237**; suit silhouette guidelines 230–232; standard sizing for 222; styling 228–238; styling for body types 232–234, 236–238; tailoring terminology 244–247; tailors, consultation with 69; tweed fabrics for 67; wool thickness of 66; *see also* neckwear for men

Michnewicz, Paul 309

mind mapping 127, *128*

Minhaj, Hasan 233

Mirojnick, Ellen 139, 146, 281, 340

Miro, Joan *128*, 156

Mode, Edna (fictional character) 148

modeling (dress design): 3D 156; fitting 282; rough sketch 166

modeling (idea testing): creative process phase 165, 173, 217, 305; image banking in 135; language of 6; research gathering in 132, 140

mood: music and 117, 126; story tone or 89

mood board 13, 135, 136, *137*, 138, 139, 140, 190, 204; *Bridgerton* 146

motifs: alternation as 52; direction and 57; favorite 8; jacquard or damask 63, 64; patterns and meanings attached to 53; repetition and 21; sequence as 51; as story device 90, 91, 99, 126, 136; trims as 161

movement and direction, principle of 50–51

multiple intelligences, theory of 210, *210*

Murphy, Eddie 233

musical number 126

musical review (genre of) 153

musical theater 117, 262, 265; Brown on 311; sitzprobe 308

musicals 9; costume scene chart 94; design approach to 145; *Gypsy* 87, 119; *Hamilton* 90; *Hands on a Hardbody* motifs 90; major moments in 89; *Parade* scene chart *97*; script breakdown 95

neckwear for men 255–256, *256*

nine-headed monster problem 47, *48*, 157–158

nine-layered character design 158–159

nine major clusters of behavior 210–211

nine principles used by costume designers 43

nonbinary and transgender performers 289–291; terms relevant to 291

nudity 177, 193, 289

nudity and intimacy coordinators 310–311

observable character traits *101*

observable information 101, 110

observation 3; audiences and 275; developing skills of 135

Once Upon a Time in…Hollywood (film) 109

opening and epilogue 10, 331–341

opera chorus 165

opera, light opera, operetta 94, 95, 117–118; costume budget 198; cross-dressing in 291; hair and makeup 262; sitzprobe 308

opera singers: period corsets and 304

Opus (play) 114

Orlandersmith, Dael 309

Oscar-winning costume designer 169

O'Shaugnessy, Christian 159

overhead (costs) 83

overhead (measurements) *see* measurement form

Page, Regé-Jean 281
Pallasmaa, Juhani 130
panier **185**
panier dress *47*
Parade (musical): costume scene chart *90*
parallels: story device of 90, 81, 99
Parkinson, Claire 125
Partridge, Wendy 340
Pavlova (ballerina) *27*
peers *107*, 211
peer pressure 341
performance formats 116–118; dance 118; ensemble
    or devised work 118; musical theater 117; opera
    117–118; theater for young audiences 118
period costumes and dress 14; assessing shape of
    303–304; authenticity in 102, 139; cost estimation
    for 198; establishing shape of 177; eyeglass styles
    254; fittings 240, 299; hairstyles 269; labor time
    estimation 184–185; makeup 265; military uniforms
    63; silhouette and 133, 296; spats and shoes
    252–253; underpinnings/undergarments and 177
period cut 225
period looks *226*
period sewing 183
period shows 77, 234; rehearsal items and 282
period suits 239, 297; styling details *236*
period tailoring 229
Peter and the Starcatcher 67; costume scene chart for *96*
petticoat 57, 116, 177, **185**, 284, *310*
Phillips, Arianne 109
photobashing 168–169, *170*, 173
photo-collage *see* photobashing
piece list 177, **179**–**180**
plot 84, 86; casting and characters 102–103; costume
    designer's reflection on 90, 91, 92; formulaic crime
    plot 126; observable information and 101; themes
    and 90; typical structure of 86; turning points in 92,
    99; types of characters in 103; *see also* color plot;
    costume plot; light plot
plot area 98
plot device 89
plot gags and gimmicks 87
plot points xii, xiii, 13, 99, 309
plotting costume looks 98–99
plot twist 12
Politician, The 125
presentationalism 87
Presley, Elvis 292
Price, Kathleen *269*
Pride, Rebecca 79
problem solving 4
production phase 10
procrastination *see* creative procrastination
project schedule 186–187
Pulitzer Prize 105, 309
pulling costumes, measurement cheat sheet for **224**

pulling list 177, 178, **181**
pulling times, sample of **225**

Reed, Suzanne Schultz 295
Regency-era fashion 139, 146
regional distinctions in US clothing 109
rehearsal approaches, types of 308
rehearsal costume plot 307
rehearsal notes 310
rehearsals 305–313; actors 311–312; choreographer 311,
    311; nudity and intimacy coordination 310–311;
    presentation of costume design 307; production
    meetings 312–313; stage managers 308–309; table
    read 307; tech rehearsal *308; see also* dress rehearsal
repetition, sequence, rhythm, principle of 51–53
Richards, Keith xii
Rihanna 264
roles, types of 102–103
Romeo and Juliet: beginning or setup for 86; costume
    design for Juliet and the Five Whys 6–7, *7*; costume
    scene chart *98–99*; five major turning points in 86;
    greenlight approval process for 198; imposed budget
    for **194–195**; piece list for 178, **179–180**; piece list
    with estimated costs *197*; plot analysis of 86; pulling
    list for **181**; sample budget **194–195**, 196, *197*, 198;
    story 'moment' in 89; word banking for *126*
Rose, Penny xii, 249, 260
Roth, Ann 169
rough designs 9, 13
rough sketch *169*, 173
rule of three 16, 45, 153
rule of thumb 37, 212
rule of twos 45

sack suit 231
Savile Row 66
scale and proportion, principle of 46–50
SCAMPER 127
scene breakdown: French 94, *96*; types of 94–95
scene breakdown chart 92
scene chart *113*
scene transitions and fluidity 112–114, 119
scope creep 190, 203
scope of project 190
script analysis 84; plot analysis 86; plot gags and
    gimmicks 87; plot presentation 87
script breakdown 93, 100; *Hamlet 93*
script as blueprint 85–86
script clues 101
script mechanics 92–100
seam allowance 293
selective attention 123
Shadow and Bone 340
Shakespeare LA: production of *Romeo and Juliet* 7
Shakespeare, William: Alabama Shakespeare Festival
    5; contemporary rewritings of plays of 91, *134*;

cross-dressing costumes for plays by 291; *El Henry/Henry IV 134*; evocative elements of plays of 87; *Hamlet* xii, *93*, 276; *Henry IV* 151; *Measure for Measure 130*; minor characters in plays of 104; transportation costs for costumes of 193; *Twelfth Night* 6; *see also Romeo and Juliet*

shape or silhouette 19, 29; altering the body using 153; body shapes 233, 289, 290; defining the body with 22, *23*, *49*; focal points and 44; eyebrow 266; geometric or organic 20; golden mean and 47; hairstyle 263; hat 257, 260; mind mapping 127; off-center 47; onstage 112–116; qualities of 20–22; sample style terms related to **147**; skirt 159; V-shaped bodies 233; V-shaped suit 230

shaped cups (bra) 219

shape focus 250

shape language 20

shaper 211

shapewear 289, 290

Shepard, Sam 92

shoes and accessories for shoes 250–253

shoe and glove sizes **254**

shoulder styles, menswear *231*

show bible 79

silhouette *see* shape or silhouette

size versus fit 293; *see also* actor's sizes; fit; fittings

sizing up: accessories 260–261; authenticity research 139–140; budgets 205; collaborative creativity 17; creative ideas 130; design elements 29–30; designing character costume 162; dress rehearsal 328–329; engaging characters/costumes 110; fabrics 68–69; getting paid 82; hair and makeup 276; ideas 130; leadership 214; preparing for fittings 292; principles of design/design elements 54; rehearsals 313; scope of project 190; script mechanics 100; staged stories 118–119

skin: baring 289; revealed 24; sensitive 267; *see also* nudity

skin-out change 116, 177

skin tone 14, 34, 160, 171, 263

slender cuts 233

slender figures 117

slender fit 231, 245

slenderizing tricks *251*, *252*, 289

slow hunch 124, 135

solutions-based thinking 5, 156, 208, 212–213, 214, 291

Sound of Music (film) 149

space: architecture of 119; backstage 119; design element of 19, 29; performance 112; poetic 114; positive and negative 23, 24, *25*, 44, 160; public and private, wearing of hats in 257; theatre 115

space and mood, shadows and 40

stage crew 202

stage designers 153, 241

stage picture 156, 162, 167; costume designer as creator of xii, 5, 39, 40, 43, 44; fitting photos and 287; focal points and 250; hats and 257; hues and 34; stage designer and 241; storytelling and 307; unifying 226

starbursting technique 127, *128*

Star Wars 105

stiletto *252*

story 3, 84; authenticity of 132, 133; backstory 102, 104, 281; characters and 103, 105; color arcs in 148, 151; costume designer and character's relationship to 79; curating research related to 135; director consult related to 139; emotional responses to 134; importance of allegiance to 5; metaphor 90; motifs 90; parallels 90; presentation 87–89; script, plot and 84–91; staging 112–119; unfolding onstage 112–119; visual imagery in relationship to 18, 26

storyboard: costume research *140*

story devices 110

story genres 9, 88, 89

story "givens" 89

story location 90, 128, 132

story mechanics 4

story moments 89

story style 9

storytellers: actors as 311–312; costumer designers as xv; props valued by 209

storytelling 11, 14; designers as collaborators with 15; emphasis as vital part of 44; stage picture to support 307; tone and 145; using space in 23

story time 89

story tone 89, 145

story world: swatches and *69*; taste (sense of) inside, 126; unity inside 54

Streep, Meryl 358

structural visualization 3

style ease 223

style guide for menswear 234

style terms, sample **147**

styling: regular or average bodies (male) 233; short bodies (male) 233–234; tall bodies (male) 231–232

subgrouping 104, 105

suits *see* menswear

swatch 68; brown fabric *35*; color 31; contingency 193; fabric 151; hair color *222*; painted *150*; photographs of *243*; Photoshop color *150*; sample *152*; storage on rings *57*; testing *41*

swatch books 134

swatch card *69*, 335

swatching for a production 68

swatch page *336*

swatch world 68, *69*, 152

tailoring terminology for suits 244–247

tailors, consultation with 69

tangential thinking 127

task dependencies 186

Tazewell, Paul 116

team leaders 211; *see also* leadership

team role sacrifice 211
team role types 210–211
Ten Commandments (film) 149
texture: broken colors 27, *29*; color and 151; color
    with added 29; design element of 19, 24–25, 29;
    determinate or indeterminate 26, *26*; fabric, pattern,
    and 160; faux 25; five sense and 126; nap (texture)
    57; natural or manufactured 25, *25*; psychology of
    27–29; rough or rigid 28
textured hair 264; ten types of *265*
Tharpe, Twyla 7, 129, 339
thinking, types of *124*, 124
Thompson, David ix
Thompson, Ken 5, 317, 320
thumbnail sketches 156, 157, 159, 162, 166, 171, 172, 173
ties *see* neckwear for men
Time Flies (play) *148*
Toledo, Ruben and Isobel 56
top of show (TOS) 177
Top Secret (film) *138*
trans advocacy 289
trans garment terms 291
trimming money or time, strategies for 187–189
tucking 291
tutu *27*
tweed fabrics 66, 67, 228, 232, 233, 255

understanding labor needs *see* labor needs
unique expertise 5
United Scenic Artists contracts 10

value (lightness or darkness of a color) 29, 32; color
    shifting and 32–34; grey scale 40; low *37*; middle 151;
    most, some, least applied to *37*; Munsell tree and *38*
value judgements 54
visual aids 154
visual approval 166
visual artists 5
visual cues 4
visual harmony 14
visual imagery 139, 145, 177
visual isolation 127
visualization 3, 165, 169
visual mechanics 7
visual research 13, 263, 265, 269
visual rules 18
visual style, defining 146, 153; color and 146–147
visual thinking 155, 156
visual vocabulary 146; six elements of 29–30; *see also*
    color; line; shape or silhouette; space; texture; value
visual zeitgeist 339
Vogler, Christopher 105

Walker, Andre 264, *265*
Walt Disney Imagineering 10

WandaVision (TV show) 89
wardrobe crew 318–319
wardrobe malfunction 292
Washington, Kerry 260
weaponry-related costumes and accessories 259–260
wearing ease in finished garments 223, **223**
Weasley boys (*Harry Potter*, fictional characters) 104,
    106
wedding party *4*
weight or hand (of fabric) 67
Weis, Robert 10
welt 244
welt pocket 245, *247*
Wertenbaker, Timberlake *152*
what-if technique 127–128
wig and makeup departments 318
wig maker 274
wigs 14, 20, 79; bargain 275; *Bridgerton*'s use of 146;
    Black women's use of 264; budget item 118, **194**,
    200, **201**; fittings 283; hairstyles and 269; hats
    and 187; *Lord of the Rings* use of 264; measuring
    for 269, *269*; parts of 273; plastic and other head
    wraps for 274, *274–275*; student actors and 276;
    styling 271–272; types of *268*, 269–272; *see also*
    facial hair; hair
wig stores 275
Wilde, Oscar xvi
Williams, Kiviett and Thomas Dennis *88*
Wilson, Cintra 109
Wolf Form Company 223
wool fabric 59; blends 67; cavalry 63; fashion 67; felted
    61; grams per meter (g/m) weight classifications
    66; herringbone 63; superfine 67; tropical 66; tweed
    66–67; woolens and worsteds 60
wool suits 27, *28*, 228
woolens 56, 66
wool thickness 6
wool weaving 67
word banking 125–126, *126*
working in…: creative teams 10–11
working with…: assistant or team 14–15; constraints
    189–190; costume makers 15–16; fellow designers
    14; performers 15
workspace 172, 173
world building xii, 3, 14, 265
worsted 60, 66, *67*

Yeboah, Ernest Agyemang 5
Yellowman (play) 309

zeitgeist *see* visual zeitgeist
zero-based budget 192, 196, 198, **199–202**
zippers 78; breaking of 247; front rise and 230, 234, 298;
    hidden 116; trouser length and *222*
Zwicky, Arnold 123